BY THE SAME AUTHOR

FORDHAM UNIVERSITY PRESS SERIES

MAKERS OF MODERN MEDICINE
Lives of the men to whom nineteenth century medical science owes most. Second Edition. New York, 1910. $2.00 net.

THE POPES AND SCIENCE
The story of Papal patronage of the sciences and especially medicine. New York, 1908. $2.00 net.

MAKERS OF ELECTRICITY
Lives of the men to whom important advances in electricity are due. In collaboration with Brother Potamian, F.S.C., Sc.D. (London), Professor of Physics at Manhattan College. New York, 1909. $2.00 net.

EDUCATION, HOW OLD THE NEW
Lectures and addresses in the history of education, literary, scientific, medical for 6000 years. New York, 1910. $2.00 net.

IN PREPARATION
MAKERS OF OLD-TIME MEDICINE
MAKERS OF ASTRONOMY

THE DOLPHIN PRESS SERIES

CATHOLIC CHURCHMEN IN SCIENCE
(First Series.) Lives of seven founders in physical science who were churchmen. Reprint. Philadelphia, 1910. $1.00 net.

CATHOLIC CHURCHMEN IN SCIENCE
(Second Series.) Lives of Albertus Magnus, Pope John XXI. the ophthalmologist, Guy de Chauliac and Regiomontanus, besides the Jesuit astronomers and clerical pioneers in electricity. Philadelphia, 1909. $1.00 net.

IN COLLABORATION
ESSAYS IN PASTORAL MEDICINE
O'MALLEY AND WALSH
A manual of information on medical subjects for the clergy, religious superiors, superintendents of hospitals, nurses and charity workers. Longmans, New York, 1906. $2.50 net.

LE BEAU DIEU (AMIENS)

THE THIRTEENTH

Greatest of Centuries

BY

JAMES J. WALSH, K.C.St.G., M.D., Ph.D., LL.D.
Litt.D. (Georgetown)

DEAN AND PROFESSOR OF THE HISTORY OF MEDICINE AND OF NERVOUS
DISEASES AT FORDHAM UNIVERSITY SCHOOL OF MEDICINE;
PROFESSOR OF PHYSIOLOGICAL PSYCHOLOGY AT
CATHEDRAL COLLEGE, NEW YORK

GEORGETOWN UNIVERSITY EDITION
(Fifth Thousand)

CATHOLIC SUMMER SCHOOL PRESS
NEW YORK, 1910

To Right Rev. Monsignor M. J. Lavelle,

Rector of St. Patrick's Cathedral, New York, sometime President of the Catholic Summer School, to whose fatherly patronage this book is largely due, and without whose constant encouragement it would not have been completed, it is respectfully and affectionately dedicated by the author.

PROEM.

(EPIMETHEUS.)

WAKE again, Teutonic Father-ages,
  Speak again, beloved primeval creeds;
Flash ancestral spirit from your pages,
  Wake the greedy age to noble deeds.

. . . . . .

Ye who built the churches where we worship,
  Ye who framed the laws by which we move,
Fathers, long belied, and long forsaken,
  Oh, forgive the children of your love!

(PROMETHEUS.)

There will we find laws which shall interpret,
  Through the simpler past, existing life;
Delving up from mines and fairy caverns
  Charmed blades to cut the age's strife.
        —*Rev. Charles Kingsley.—The Saints' Tragedy.*

PREFACE.

"Why take the style of these heroic times ?
For nature brings not back the mastodon—
Nor we those times ; and why should any man
Remodel models ? "

What Tennyson thus said of his own first essay in the Idyls
of the King, in the introduction to the Morte D'Arthur,
occurs as probably the aptest expression of most men's
immediate thought with regard to such a subject as The
Thirteenth, Greatest of Centuries. Though Tennyson was
confessedly only remodeling the thoughts of the Thirteenth
Century, we would not be willing to concede—

"That nothing new was said, or else,
Something so said, 'twas nothing,"

for the loss of the Idyls would make a large lacuna in the
literature of the Nineteenth Century. "If it is allowed to
compare little things with great," a similar intent to that of
the Laureate has seemed sufficient justification for the paradox the author has tried to set forth in this volume. It may
prove "nothing worth, mere chaff and draff much better
burnt," but many friends have insisted they found it interesting. Authors usually blame friends for their inflictions
upon the public, and I fear that I can find no better excuse,
though the book has been patiently labored at, with the idea
that it should represent some of the serious work that is being
done by the Catholic Summer School on Lake Champlain,

now completing nearly a decade and a half of its existence. This volume is, it is hoped, but the first of a series that will bring to a wider audience some of the thoughts that have been gathered for Summer School friends by many workers, and will put in more permanent form contributions that made summer leisure respond to the Greek term for school.

The object of the book is to interpret, in terms that will be readily intelligible to this generation, the life and concerns of the people of a century who, to the author's mind, have done more for human progress than those of any like period in human history. There are few whose eyes are now holden as they used to be, as to the surpassing place in the history of culture of the last three centuries of the Middle Ages. Personally the author is convinced, however, that only a beginning of proper appreciation has come as yet, and he feels that the solution of many problems that are vexing the modern world, especially in the social order, are to be found in these much misunderstood ages, and above all in that culmination of medieval progress—the period from 1200 to 1300.

The subject was originally taken up as a series of lectures in the extension course of the Catholic Summer School, as given each year in Lent and Advent at the Catholic Club, New York City. Portions of the material were subsequently used in lectures in many cities in this country from Portland, Me., to Portland, Ore., St. Paul, Minn., to New Orleans, La. The subject was treated *in extenso* for the Brooklyn Institute of Arts and Sciences in 1906, after which publication was suggested.

The author does not flatter himself that the book adequately represents the great period which it claims to present. The subject has been the central idea of studies in leisure moments for a dozen years, and during many wanderings in Europe, but there will doubtless prove to be errors in detail, for which the author would crave the indulgence of more serious students of history. The original form in which the material was cast has influenced the style to some extent, and has made the book more wordy than it would otherwise have been, and has been the cause of certain repetitions that appear more striking in print than they seemed in manuscript. There were what seemed good reasons for not delaying publication, however, and leisure for further work at it, instead of growing, was becoming more scant. It is intrusted to the tender mercies of critics, then, and the benevolent reader, if he still may be appealed to, for the sake of the ideas it contains, in spite of their inadequate expression.

PREFACE THIRTEENTH CENTURY.

(SECOND EDITION).

Representing a digest of Summer School lectures, this work was meant for popular reading. For this reason long citations of authorities and the filling up of the bottom of pages with notes was deliberately avoided. It has seemed advisable in the second edition, however, to present in an appendix some authoritative opinions that will enable readers to see that many of the author's ideas which may appear paradoxical are shared by men who have devoted the better part of their lives to the special study of the questions on which their opinions are quoted and who, if any, know whereof they speak. It has not been difficult to quote a wide range of scholarly writers who are in thorough agreement with even the most startling paradoxes of the book, the expressions that have been most questioned by critics and that have caused some hesitation even among benevolent readers. Besides these additions, some corrections and revisions have been made in the body of the text.

NEW YORK, April, 1909.

PREFACE.

(GEORGETOWN UNIVERSITY EDITION).

This third edition is published under the patronage of Georgetown University as a slight token of appreciation for the degree of Doctor of Letters, conferred on the author for this
work at the last Commencement. This issue has been enlarged
by the addition of many illustrations selected to bring out the
fact that all the various parts of Europe shared in the achievements of the time and by an appendix containing in compendium Twenty-Six Chapters that Might Have Been. Each of
these brief sketches could easily have been extended to the
average length of the original chapters. It was impossible to
use all the material that was gathered. These hints of further
sources are now appended so as to afford suggestions for study
to those who may care to follow up the idea of the Thirteenth
as The Greatest of Centuries, that is, of that period in human
existence when men's thoughts on all the important human interests were profoundly valuable for future generations and
their accomplishments models for all the after time.

CONTENTS.

CHAPTER I

INTRODUCTION, THE THIRTEENTH, GREATEST OF CENTURIES.

CHAPTER II

UNIVERSITIES AND PREPARATORY SCHOOLS.

CHAPTER III

WHAT AND HOW THEY STUDIED AT THE UNIVERSITIES.

CHAPTER IV

THE NUMBER OF STUDENTS AND DISCIPLINE.

CHAPTER V

POST-GRADUATE WORK AT THE UNIVERSITIES.

CHAPTER VI

THE BOOK OF THE ARTS AND POPULAR EDUCATION.

CHAPTER X

THE CID, THE HOLY GRAIL, THE NIBELUNGEN.

CHAPTER XI

MEISTERSINGERS, MINNESINGERS, TROUVÈRES, TROUBADOURS.

CHAPTER XII

GREAT LATIN HYMNS.

CHAPTER XIII

THE THREE MOST READ BOOKS.

CHAPTER XIV

SOME THIRTEENTH CENTURY PROSE.

CHAPTER XV

ORIGIN OF DRAMA.

CHAPTER XVI

FRANCIS, THE SAINT—THE FATHER OF THE RENAISSANCE.

CHAPTER XVII

AQUINAS, THE SCHOLAR.

CHAPTER XVIII

LOUIS, THE MONARCH.

CHAPTER XIX

DANTE, THE POET.

CHAPTER XX

THE WOMEN OF THE CENTURY.

CHAPTER XXI

CITY HOSPITALS—ORGANIZED CHARITY.

CHAPTER XXII

GREAT ORIGINS IN LAW.

CHAPTER XXVI

GREAT BEGINNINGS OF MODERN COMMERCE.

APPENDIX I

APPENDIX II

TWENTY-SIX CHAPTERS THAT MIGHT HAVE BEEN.

APPENDIX III

CRITICISMS, COMMENTS, DOCUMENTS.

LIST OF ILLUSTRATIONS.

I
INTRODUCTION

THE THIRTEENTH, THE GREATEST OF
CENTURIES

It cannot but seem a paradox to say that the Thirteenth was the greatest of centuries. To most people the idea will appear at once so preposterous that they may not even care to consider it. A certain number, of course, will have their curiosity piqued by the thought that anyone should evolve so curious a notion. Either of these attitudes of mind will yield at once to a more properly receptive mood if it is recalled that the Thirteenth is the century of the Gothic cathedrals, of the foundation of the university, of the signing of Magna Charta, and of the origin of representative government with something like constitutional guarantees throughout the west of Europe. The cathedrals represent a development in the arts that has probably never been equaled either before or since. The university was a definite creation of these generations that has lived and maintained its usefulness practically in the same form in which it was then cast for the seven centuries ever since. The foundation stones of modern liberties are to be found in the documents which for the first time declared the rights of man during this precious period.

A little consideration of the men who, at this period, lived lives of undying influence on mankind, will still further attract the attention of those who have not usually grouped these great characters together. Just before the century opened, three great rulers died at the height of their influence. They are still and will always be the subject of men's thoughts and of literature. They were Frederick Barbarossa, Saladin, and Richard Cœur De Lion. They formed but a suggestive prelude of what was to come in the following century, when such great monarchs as St. Louis of France, St. Ferdinand of Spain, Alfonso the Wise of Castile, Frederick II of Germany, Edward I, the English Justinian, Rudolph of Hapsburg, whose descendants still rule in Austria, and Robert Bruce, occupied the thrones of Europe. Was it by chance or Providence that the same century saw the rise of and the beginning of the fall of that great Eastern monarchy which had been created by the genius for conquest of Jenghiz Khan, the Tatar warrior, who ruled over all the Eastern world from beyond what are now the western confines of Russia, Poland, and Hungary, into and including what we now call China.

But the thrones of Europe and of Asia did not monopolize the great men of the time. The Thirteenth Century claims such wonderful churchmen as St. Francis and St. Dominic, and while it has only the influence of St. Hugh of Lincoln, who died just as it began, it can be proud of St. Edmund of Canterbury, Stephen Langton, and Robert Grosseteste, all men whose place in history is due to what they did for their people, and such magnificent women as Queen Blanche of Castile, St. Clare of Assisi, and St. Elizabeth of Hungary. The century opened with one of the greatest of the Popes on the throne, Innocent III, and it closed with the most misunderstood of Popes, who is in spite of this one of the worthiest successors of Peter, Boniface VIII. During the century there had been such men as Honorius IV, the Patron of Learning, Gregory IX, to whom Canon Law owes so much, and John XXI, who had been famous as a scientist before becoming Pope. There are such scholars as St. Thomas of Aquin, Albertus Magnus, Roger Bacon, St. Bonaventure, Duns Scotus, Raymond Lully, Vincent of Beauvais, and Alexander of Hales, and such patrons of learning as Robert of Sorbonne, and the founders of nearly twenty universities. There were such artists as Gaddi, Cimabue, and above all Giotto, and such literary men as the authors of the Arthur Legends and the Nibelungen, the Meistersingers, the Minnesingers, the Troubadours, and Trouvères, and above all Dante, who is universally considered now to be one of the greatest literary men of all times, but who was not, as is so often thought and said, a solitary phenomenon in the period, but only the culmination of a great literary movement that had to have some such supreme expression of itself as this in order to properly round out the cycle of its existence.

If in addition it be said that this century saw the birth of the democratic spirit in many different ways in the various countries of Europe, but always in such form that it was never quite to die out again, the reasons for talking of it as possibly the greatest of centuries will be readily appreciated even by those whose reading has not given them any preliminary basis of information with regard to this period, which has unfortunately been shrouded from the eyes of most people by the fact, that its place in the midst of the Middle Ages would seem to preclude all possibility of the idea that it could represent a great phase of the development of the human intellect and its esthetic possibilities.

There would seem to be one more or less insuperable objection to the consideration of the Thirteenth as the greatest of centuries, and that arises from the fact that the idea of evolution has consciously and unconsciously tinged the thoughts of our generation to such a degree, that it seems almost impossible to think of a period so far in the distant past as having produced results comparable with those that naturally flow from the heightened development of a long subsequent epoch. Whatever of truth there may be in the great theory of evolution, however, it must not be forgotten that no added evidence for its acceptance can be obtained from the intellectual history of the human race. We may be "the heirs of all the ages in the foremost files of time," but one thing is certain, that we can scarcely hope to equal, and do not at all think of surpassing, some of the great literary achievements of long past ages.

In the things of the spirit apparently there is very little, if any, evolution. Homer wrote nearly three thousand years ago as supreme an expression of human life in absolute literary values as the world has ever known, or, with all reverence for the future be it said, is ever likely to know. The great dramatic poem Job emanated from a Hebrew poet in those earlier times, and yet, if judged from the standpoint of mere literature, is as surpassing an expression of human intelligence in the presence of the mystery of evil as has ever come from the mind of man. We are no nearer the solution of the problem of evil in life, though thousands of years have passed and man has been much occupied with the thoughts that disturbed the mind of the ruler of Moab. The Code of Hammurrabi, recently discovered, has shown very definitely, that men could make laws nearly five thousand years ago as well calculated to correct human abuses as those our legislators spend so much time over at present, and the olden time laws were probably quite as effective as ours can hope to be, for all our well intentioned purpose and praiseworthy efforts at reform.

It used to be a favorite expression of Virchow, the great German pathologist, who was, besides, however, the greatest of living anthropologists, that from the history of the human race the theory of evolution receives no confirmation of any kind. His favorite subject, the study of skulls, and their conformation in the five thousand years through which such remains could be traced, showed him absolutely no change. For him there had been also no development in the intellectual order in human life during the long period of human history. Of course this is comparatively brief if the long æons of geological times be considered, yet some development might be expected to manifest itself in the more than two hundred generations that have come and gone since the beginning of human memory. Perhaps, then, the prejudice with regard to evolution and its supposed effectiveness in making the men of more recent times superior to those of the past, may be considered to have very little weight as an *a priori* objection to the consideration of the Thirteenth Century as representing the highest stage in human accomplishment. So far as scientific anthropology goes there is utter indifference as to the period that may be selected as representing man at his best.

To most people the greater portion of surprise with regard to the assertion of the Thirteenth as the greatest of centuries will be the fact that the period thus picked out is almost in the heart of the Middle Ages. It would be not so amazing if the fifth century before Christ, which produced such marvelous accomplishments in letters and art and philosophy among the Greeks, was chosen as the greatest of human epochs. There might not even be so much of unpreparedness of mind if that supreme century of Roman History, from fifty years before

VIRGIN WITH THE DIVINE CHILD (MOSAIC,
ST. MARK'S, VENICE)

Christ to fifty years after, were picked out for such signal notice. We have grown accustomed, however, to think of the
Middle Ages as hopelessly backward in the opportunities they
afforded men for the expression of their intellectual and artistic faculties, and above all for any development of that human liberty which means so much for the happiness of the race
and must constitute the basis of any real advance worth while
talking about in human affairs. It is this that would make the
Thirteenth Century seem out of place in any comparative study
for the purpose of determining proportionate epochal greatness. The spirit breathes where it will, however, and there
was a mighty wind of the spirit of human progress abroad in
that Thirteenth Century, whose effects usually miss proper
recognition in history, because people fail to group together in
their minds all the influences in our modern life that come to
us from that precious period. All this present volume pre-
tends to do is to gather these scattered details of influence in
order to make the age in which they all coincided so wonderfully, be properly appreciated.

If we accept the usual historical division which places the
Middle Ages during the thousand years between the fall of the
Roman Empire, in the Fifth Century and the fall of the Grecian
Empire of Constantinople, about the middle of the Fifteenth,
the Thirteenth Century must be considered the culmination of
that middle age. It is three centuries before the Renaissance,
and to most minds that magical word represents the beginning of all that is modern, and therefore all that is best, in the
world. Most people forget entirely how much of progress
had been made before the so-called Renaissance, and how many
great writers and artists had been fostering the taste and developing the intelligence of the people of Italy long before the
fall of Constantinople. The Renaissance, after all, means
only the re-birth of Greek ideas and ideals, of Greek letters
and arts, into the modern world. If this new birth of Greek
esthetics had not found the soil thoroughly prepared by the
fruitful labor of three centuries before, history would not
have seen any such outburst of artistic and literary accomplishments as actually came at the end of the Fifteenth and
during the Sixteenth centuries.

In taking up the thesis, The Thirteenth the Greatest of Centuries, it seems absolutely necessary to define just what is meant by the term great, in its application to a period. An historical epoch, most people would concede at once, is really great just in proportion to the happiness which it provides for the largest possible number of humanity. That period is greatest that has done most to make men happy. Happiness consists in the opportunity to express whatever is best in us, and above all to find utterance for whatever is individual. An essential element in it is the opportunity to develop and apply the intellectual faculties, whether this be of purely artistic or of thoroughly practical character. For such happiness the opportunity to rise above one's original station is one of the necessary requisites. Out of these opportunities there comes such contentment as is possible to man in the imperfect existence that is his under present conditions.

Almost as important a quality in any epoch that is to be considered supremely great, is the difference between the condition of men at the beginning of it and at its conclusion. The period that represents most progress, even though at the end uplift should not have reached a degree equal to subsequent periods, must be considered as having best accomplished its duty to the race. For purposes of comparison it is the amount of ground actually covered in a definite time, rather than the comparative position at the end of it, that deserves to be taken into account. This would seem to be a sort of hedging, as if the terms of the comparison of the Thirteenth with other centuries were to be made more favorable by the establishment of different standards. There is, however, no need of any such makeshift in order to establish the actual supremacy of the Thirteenth Century, since it can well afford to be estimated on its own merits alone, and without any allowances because of the stage of cultural development at which it occurred.

John Ruskin once said that a proper estimation of the accomplishments of a period in human history can only be obtained by careful study of three books—The Book of the Deeds, The Book of the Arts, and the Book of the Words, of the given epoch. The Thirteenth Century may be promptly ready for this judgment of what it accomplished for men, of what it wrote for subsequent generations, and of the artistic qualities to be found in its art remains. In the Book of the Deeds of the century what is especially important is what was accomplished for men, that is, what the period did for the education of the people, not alone the classes but the masses, and what a precious heritage of liberty and of social coordination it left behind. To most people it will appear at once that if the most important chapter of Thirteenth Century accomplishment is to be found in the Book if its Deeds and the deeds are to be judged according to the standard just given of education and liberty, then there will be no need to seek further, since these are words for which it is supposed that there is no actual equivalent in human life and history for at least several centuries after the close of the Thirteenth.

As a matter of fact, however, it is in this very chapter that the Thirteenth Century will be found strongest in its claim to true greatness. The Thirteenth Century saw the foundation of the universities and their gradual development into the institutions of learning which we have at the present time. Those scholars of the Thirteenth Century recognized that, for its own development and for practical purposes, the human intellect can best be trained along certain lines. For its preliminary training, it seemed to them to need what has since come to be called the liberal arts, that is, a knowledge of certain languages and of logic, as well as a thorough consideration of the great problems of the relation of man to his Creator, to his fellowmen, and to the universe around him. Grammar, a much wider subject than we now include under the term, and philosophy constituted the undergraduate studies of the universities of the Thirteenth Century. For the practical purposes of life, a division of post-graduate study had to be made so as to suit the life design of each individual, and accordingly the faculties of theology, for the training of divines; of medicine, for the training of physicians; and of law, for the training of advocates, came into existence.

We shall consider this subject in more detail in a subsequent chapter, but it will be clear at once that the university, as organized by these wise generations of the Thirteenth Century, has come down unchanged to us in the modern time. We

still have practically the same methods of preliminary training and the same division of post-graduate studies. We
specialize to a greater degree than they did, but it must not
be forgotten that specialism was not unknown by any means
in the Thirteenth Century, though there were fewer opportunities for its practical application to the things of life. If this
century had done nothing else but create the instrument by
which the human mind has ever since been trained, it must be
considered as deserving a place of the very highest rank in the
periods of human history.

It is, however, much more for what it accomplished for the
education of the masses than for the institutions it succeeded
in developing for the training of the classes, that the Thirteenth
Century merits a place in the roll of fame. This declaration
will doubtless seem utterly paradoxical to the ordinary reader
of history. We are very prone to consider that it is only in our
time that anything like popular education has come into existence. As a matter of fact, however, the education afforded
to the people in the little towns of the Middle Ages, represents an ideal of educational uplift for the masses such as
has never been even distantly approached in succeeding centuries. The Thirteenth Century developed the greatest set of
technical schools that the world has ever known. The technical
school is supposed to be a creation of the last half century
at the outside. These medieval towns, however, during the
course of the building of their cathedrals, of their public
buildings and various magnificent edifices of royalty and
for the nobility, succeeded in accomplishing such artistic results that the world has ever since held them in admiration,
and that this admiration has increased rather than diminished
with the development of taste in very recent years.

Nearly every one of the most important towns of England
during the Thirteenth Century was erecting a cathedral.
Altogether some twenty cathedrals remain as the subject of
loving veneration and of frequent visitation for the modern
generation. There was intense rivalry between these various towns. Each tried to surpass the other in the grandeur
of its cathedral and auxiliary buildings. Instead of lending
workmen to one another there was a civic pride in accomplish-

PULPIT (PISANO, SIENA)

ing for one's native town whatever was best. Each of these towns, then, none of which had more than twenty thousand inhabitants except London, and even that scarcely more, had to develop its own artist-artisans for itself. That they succeeded in doing so demonstrates a great educational influence at work in arts and crafts in each of these towns. We scarcely succeed in obtaining such trained workmen in proportionately much fewer numbers even with the aid of our technical schools, and while these Thirteenth Century people did not think of such a term, it is evident that they had the reality and that they were able to develop artistic handicraftsmen —the best the world has ever known.

With all this of education abroad in the lands, it is not surprising that great results should have flowed from human efforts and that these should prove enduring even down to our own time. Accomplishments of the highest significance were necessarily bound up with opportunities for self-expression, so tempting and so complete, as those provided for the generations of the Thirteenth Century. The books of the Words as well as of the Arts of the Thirteenth Century will be found eminently interesting, and no period has ever furnished so many examples of wondrous initiative, followed almost immediately by just as marvelous progress and eventual approach to as near perfection as it is perhaps possible to come in things human. Ordinarily literary origins are not known with sufficient certainty as to dates for any but the professional scholar to realize the scope of the century's literature. Only a very little consideration, however, is needed to demonstrate how thoroughly representative of what is most enduring in literary expression in modern times, are the works in every country that had origin in this century.

There was not a single country in civilized Europe which did not contribute its quota and that of great significance to the literary movement of the time. In Spain there came the Cid and certain accompanying products of ballad poetry which form the basis of the national literature and are still read not only by scholars and amateurs, but even by the people generally, because of the supreme human interest in them. In England, the beginning of the Thirteenth Century saw the putting into shape of the Arthur Legends in the form in which they were to appeal most nearly to subsequent generations. Walter Map's work in these was, as we shall see, one of the great literary accomplishments of all time. Subsequent treatments of the same subject are only slight modifications of the theme which he elaborated, and Mallory's and Spenser's and even our own Tennyson's work derive their interest from the humanly sympathetic story, written so close to the heart of nature in the Thirteenth Century that it will always prove attractive.

In Germany, just at the same time, the Nibelungen-Lied was receiving the form in which it was to live as the great National epic. The Meistersingers also were accomplishing their supreme work of Christianizing and modernizing the old German and Christian legends which were to prove such a precious heritage of interest for posterity. In the South of Germany the Minnesingers sang their tuneful strains and showed how possible it was to take the cruder language of the North, and pour forth as melodious hymns of praise to nature and to their beloved ones as in the more fluent Southern tongues. Most of this was done in the old Suabian high German dialect, and the basis of the modern German language was thus laid. The low German was to prove the vehicle for the original form of the animal epic or stories with regard to Reynard, the Fox, which were to prove so popular throughout all of Europe for all time thereafter.

In North France the Trouvères were accomplishing a similar work to that of the Minnesingers in South Germany, but doing it with an original genius, a refinement of style characteristic of their nation, and a finish of form that was to impress itself upon French literature for all subsequent time. Here also Jean de Meun and Guillaume de Lorris wrote the Romance of the Rose, which was to remain the most popular book in Europe down to the age of printing and for some time thereafter. At the South of France the work of the Troubadours, similar to that of the Trouvères and yet with a spirit and character all its own, was creating a type of love songs that the world recurs to with pleasure whenever the lyrical aspect of poetry becomes fashionable. The influence of the Troubadours was to be felt in Italy, and before the end of the

Thirteenth Century there were many writers of short poems that deserve a place in what is best in literature. Men like Sordello, Guido Cavalcanti, Cino da Pistoia, and Dante da Maiano, deserve mention in any historical review of literature, quite apart from the influence which they had on their great successor, the Prince of Italian poets and one of the immortal trio of the world's supreme creative singers—Dante Alighieri. With what must have seemed the limit of conceit he placed himself among the six greatest poets, but posterity breathes his name only with those of Homer and Shakespeare.

Dante, in spite of his giant personality and sublime poetic genius, is not an exception nor a solitary phenomenon in the course of the century, but only a worthy culmination of the literary movement which, beginning in the distant West in Spain and England, gradually worked eastward quite contrary to the usual trend of human development and inspired its greatest work in the musical Tuscan dialect after having helped in the foundation of all the other modern languages. Dante is the supreme type of the Thirteenth Century, the child of his age, but the great master whom medieval influences have made all that he is. That he belongs to the century there can be no doubt, and of himself alone he would be quite sufficient to lift any period out of obscurity and place it among the favorite epochs, in which the human mind found one of those opportune moments for the expression of what is sublimest in human thought.

It is, however, the book of the Arts of the Thirteenth Century that deserves most to be thumbed by the modern reader intent on learning something of this marvelous period of human existence. There is not a single branch of art in which the men of this generation did not accomplish excelling things that have been favorite subjects for study and loving imitation ever since. Perhaps the most marvelous quality of the grand old Gothic cathedrals, erected during the Thirteenth Century, is not their impressiveness as a whole so much as their wonderful finish in detail. It matters not what element of construction or decoration be taken into consideration, always there is an approach to perfection in accomplishment in some one of the cathedrals that shows with what thoroughness the men of the time comprehended what was best in art, and how finally their strivings after perfection were rewarded as bountifully as perhaps it has ever been given to men to realize.

Of the major arts—architecture itself, sculpture and painting—only a word will be said here since they will be treated more fully in subsequent chapters. No more perfect effort at worthy worship of the Most High has ever been accomplished than is to be seen in the Gothic cathedrals in every country in Europe as they exist to the present day. While the movement began in North France, and gradually spread to other countries, there was never any question of mere slavish imitation, but on the contrary in each country Gothic architecture took on a national character and developed into a charming expression of the special characteristics of the people for whom and by whom it was made. English Gothic is, of course, quite different to that of France; Spanish Gothic has a character all its own; the German Gothic cathedrals partake of the heavier characteristics of the Northern people, while Italian Gothic adds certain airy decorative qualities to the French model that give renewed interest and inevitably indicate the origin of the structures.

In painting, Cimabue's work, so wonderfully appreciated by the people of Florence that spontaneously they flocked in procession to do honor to his great picture, was the beginning of modern art. How much was accomplished before the end of the century will be best appreciated when the name of Giotto is mentioned as the culmination of the art movement of the century. As we shall see, the work done by him, especially at Assisi, has been a source of inspiration for artists down even to our own time, and there are certain qualities of his art, especially his faculty for producing the feeling of solidity in his paintings, in which very probably he has never been surpassed. Gothic cathedrals in other countries did not lend themselves so well as subjects of inspiration for decorative art, but in every country the sacred books in use in the cathedral were adorned, at the command of the artistic impulse of the period, in a way that has made the illuminated missals and office books of the Thirteenth Century perhaps the most precious that there are in the history of book-making.

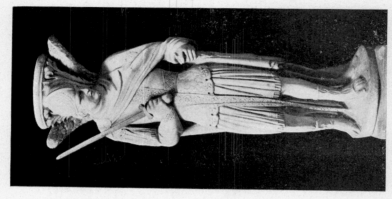

ARCHANGEL MICHAEL
(PISA, GIOV. PISANO)

CHRIST
(FLORENCE ANDREA PISANO)

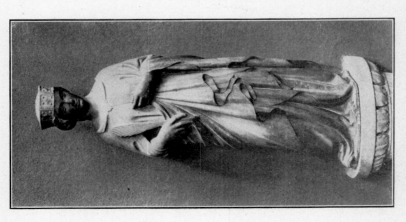

STA REPARATA
(FLOR. ANDR. PIS.)

It might be thought that in sculpture, at least, these Thirteenth-Century generations would prove to be below the level of that perfection and artistic expression which came so assuredly in other lines. It is true that most of the sculptures of the period have defects that make them unworthy of imitation, though it is in the matter of technique that they fail rather than in honest effort to express feelings appropriately within the domain of chiseled work. On the other hand there are some supreme examples of what is best in sculpture to be found among the adornments of the cathedrals of the period. No more simply dignified rendition of the God Man has ever been made in stone than the statue of Christ, which with such charming appropriateness the people of Amiens have called *le Beau Dieu,* their beautiful God, and that visitors to their great cathedral can never admire sufficiently, admirably set off, as it is, in its beautiful situation above the main door of the great cathedral. Other examples are not lacking, as for instance some of the Thirteenth-Century effigies of the French kings and queens at St. Denis, and some of the wonderful sculptures at Rheims. In its place as a subsidiary art to architecture for decorative purposes, sculpture was even more eminently successful. The best example of this is the famous Angel Chair of Lincoln, one of the most beautiful things that ever came from the hand of man and whose designation indicates the belief of the centuries that only the angels could have made it.

In the handicrafts most nearly allied to the arts, the Thirteenth Century reigns supreme with a splendor unapproached by what has been accomplished in any other century. The iron work of their gates and railings, even of their hinges and latches and locks, has been admired and imitated by many generations since. When a piece of it is no longer of use, or loosens from the crumbling woodwork to which it was attached, it is straightway transported to some museum, there to be displayed not alone for its antiquarian interest, but also as a model and a suggestion to the modern designer. This same thing is true of the precious metal work of the times also, at least as regards the utensils and ornaments employed in the sacred services. The chalices and other sacred vessels were made on severely simple lines and according to models which have since become the types of such sacred utensils for all times.

The vestments used in the sacred ceremonials partook of this same character of eminently appropriate handiwork united to the chastest of designs, executed with supreme taste. The famous cope of Ascoli which the recent Pierpont Morgan incident brought into prominence a year or so ago, is a sample of the needlework of the times that illustrates its perfection. It is said by those who are authorities in the matter that Thirteenth-Century needlework represents what is best in this line. It is not the most elaborate, nor the most showy, but it is in accordance with the best taste, supremely suitable to the objects of which it formed a part. It is, after all, only an almost inevitable appendix to the beautiful work done in the illumination of the sacred books, that the sacred vestments should have been quite as supremely artistic and just as much triumphs of art.

As a matter of fact, every minutest detail of cathedral construction and ornamentation shared in this artistic triumph. Even the inscriptions, done in brass upon the gravestones that formed part of the cathedral pavements, are models of their kind, and rubbings from them are frequently taken because of their marvelous effectiveness as designs in Gothic tracery.

Their bells were made with such care and such perfection that, down to the present time, nothing better has been accomplished in this handicraft, and their marvelous retention of tone shows how thorough was the work of these early bellmakers.

The triumph of artistic decoration in the cathedrals, however, and the most marvelous page in the book of the Arts of the century, remains to be spoken of in their magnificent stained-glass windows. Where they learned their secret of glassmaking we know not. Artists of the modern time, who have spent years in trying to perfect their own work in this line, would give anything to have some of the secrets of the glassmakers of the Thirteenth Century. Such windows as the Five Sisters at York, or the wonderful Jesse window of Chartres with some of its companions, are the despair of the modern

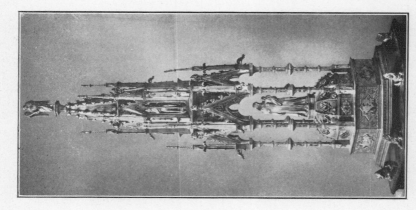

RELIQUARY (VIERI, ORVIETO)

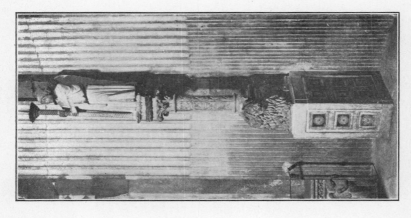

PASCHAL CANDLE-STICK
(FLORENCE)

artists in stained glass. The fact that their glass-making was not done at one, or even a few, common centers, but was apparently executed in each of these small medieval towns that were the site of a cathedral, only adds to the marvel of how the workmen of the time succeeded so well in accomplishing their purpose of solving the difficult problems of stained glasswork.

If, to crown all that has been said about the Thirteenth Century, we now add a brief account of what was accomplished for men in the matter of liberty and the establishment of legal rights, we shall have a reasonably adequate introduction to this great subject. Liberty is thought to be a word whose true significance is of much more recent origin than the end of the Middle Ages. The rights of men are usually supposed to have received serious acknowledgment only in comparatively recent centuries. The recalling of a few facts, however, will dispel this illusion and show how these men of the later middle age laid the foundation of most of the rights and privileges that we are so proud to consider our birthright in this modern time. The first great fact in the history of modern liberty is the signing of Magna Charta which took place only a little after the middle of the first quarter of the Thirteenth Century. The movement that led up to it had arisen amongst the guildsmen as well as the churchmen and the nobles of the preceding century. When the document was signed, however, these men did not consider that their work was finished. They kept themselves ready to take further advantage of the necessities of their rulers and it was not long before they had secured political as well as legal rights.

Shortly after the middle of the Thirteenth Century the first English parliament met, and in the latter part of that half century it became a formal institution with regularly appointed times of meeting and definite duties and privileges. Then began the era of law in its modern sense for the English people. The English common law took form and its great principles were enunciated practically in the terms in which they are stated down to the present day. Bracton made his famous digest of the English common law for the use of judges and lawyers and it became a standard work of reference. Such it has remained down to our own time. At the end of the century, during the reign of Edward I, the English Justinian, the laws of the land were formulated, lacunæ in legislation filled up, rights and privileges fully determined, real-estate laws put on a modern basis, and the most important portions of English law became realities that were to be modified but not essentially changed in all the after time.

This history of liberty and of law-making, so familiar with regard to England, must be repeated almost literally with regard to the continental nations. In France, the foundation of the laws of the kingdom were laid during the reign of Louis IX, and French authorities in the history of law, point with pride, to how deeply and broadly the foundations of French jurisprudence were laid. Under Louis's cousin, Ferdinand III of Castile, who, like the French monarch, has received the title of Saint, because of the uprightness of his character and all that he did for his people, forgetful of himself, the foundations of Spanish law were laid, and it is to that time that Spanish jurists trace the origin of nearly all the rights and privileges of their people. In Germany there is a corresponding story. In Saxony there was the issue of a famous book of laws, which represented all the grants of the sovereigns, and all the claims of subjects that had been admitted by monarchs up to that time. In a word, everywhere there was a codification of laws and a laying of foundations in jurisprudence, upon which the modern superstructure of law was to rise.

This is probably the most surprising part of the Thirteenth Century. When it began men below the rank of nobles were practically slaves. Whatever rights they had were uncertain, liable to frequent violation because of their indefinite character, and any generation might, under the tyranny of some consciousless monarch, have lost even the few privileges they had enjoyed before. At the close of the Thirteenth Century this was no longer possible. The laws had been written down and monarchs were bound by them as well as their subjects. Individual caprice might no longer deprive them arbitrarily of their rights and hard won privileges, though tyranny might still assert itself and a submissive generation might, for a time, allow themselves to be governed by measures beyond the domain of legal justification. Any subsequent generation might, however, begin anew its assertion of its rights from the old-time laws, rather than from the position to which their forbears had been reduced by a tyrant's whim.

Is it any wonder, then, that we should call the generations that gave us the cathedrals, the universities, the great technical schools that were organized by the trades guilds, the great national literatures that lie at the basis of all our modern literature, the beginnings of sculpture and of art carried to such heights that artistic principles were revealed for all time, and, finally, the great men and women of this century—for more than any other it glories in names that were born not to die—is it at all surprising that we should claim for the period which, in addition to all this, saw the foundation of modern law and liberty, the right to be hailed—the greatest of human history?

THE CHURCH [SYMBOLIZED] (PARIS)

II

UNIVERSITIES AND PREPARATORY SCHOOLS.

To see, at once, how well the Thirteenth deserves the name of the greatest of centuries, it is necessary, only, to open the book of her deeds and read therein what was accomplished during this period for the education of the men of the time. It is, after all, what a generation accomplishes for intellectual development and social uplift that must be counted as its greatest triumph. If life is larger in its opportunities, if men appreciate its significance better, if the development of the human mind has been rendered easier, if that precious thing, whose name, education, has been so much abused, is made readier of attainment, then the generation stamps itself as having written down in its book of deeds, things worthy for all subsequent generations to read. Though anything like proper appreciation of it has come only in very recent times, there is absolutely no period of equal length in the history of mankind in which so much was not only attempted, but successfully accomplished for education, in every sense of the word, as during the Thirteenth Century. This included, not only the education of the classes but also the education of the masses.

For the moment, we shall concern ourselves only with the education offered to, and taken advantage of by so many, in the universities of the time. It was just at the beginning of the Thirteenth Century that the great universities came into being as schools, in which all the ordinary forms of learning were taught. During the Twelfth Century, Bologna had had a famous school of law which attracted students from all over Europe. Under Irnerius, canon and civil law secured a popularity as subjects of study such as they never had before. The study of the old Roman Law brought back with it an interest in the Latin classics, and the beginning of the true new birth —the real renaissance—of modern education must be traced from here. At Paris there was a theological school attached to the cathedral which gradually became noted for its devotion to philosophy as the basis of theology, and, about the middle of the Twelfth Century, attracted students from every part of the civilized world. As was the case at Bologna, interest after a time was not limited to philosophy and theology; other branches of study were admitted to the curriculum and a university in the modern sense came into existence.

During the first quarter of the Thirteenth Century both of these schools developed faculties for the teaching of all the known branches of knowledge. At Bologna faculties of arts, of philosophy and theology, and finally of medicine, were gradually added, and students flocked in ever increasing numbers to take advantage of these additional opportunities. At Paris, the school of medicine was established early in the Thirteenth Century, and there were graduates in medicine before the year 1220. Law came later, but was limited to Canon law to a great extent, Orleans having a monopoly of civil law for more than a century. These two universities, Bologna and Paris, were, in every sense of the word, early in the century, real universities, differing in no essential from our modern institutions that bear the same name.

If the Thirteenth Century had done nothing else but put into shape this great instrument for the training of the human mind, which has maintained its effectiveness during seven centuries, it must be accorded a place among the epoch-making periods of history. With all our advances in modern education we have not found it necessary, or even advisable, to change, in any essential way, this mold in which the human intellect has been cast for all these years. If a man wants knowledge for its own sake, or for some practical purpose in life, then here are the faculties which will enable him to make a good beginning on the road he wishes to travel. If he wants knowledge of the liberal arts, or the consideration of man's duties to himself, to his fellow-man and to his Creator, he will find in the faculties of arts and philosophy and theology the great sources of knowledge in these subjects. If, on the other hand, he wishes to apply his mind either to the disputes of men about property, or to their injustices toward one another and the correction of abuses, then the faculty of law will supply his wants, and finally the medical school enables him, if he wishes, to learn all that can be known at a given time with regard to man's ills and their healing. We have admitted the practical-work subjects into university life, though not without protest, but architecture, engineering, bridge-building and the like, in which the men of the Thirteenth Century accomplished such wonders, were relegated to the guilds whose technical schools, though they did not call them by that name, were quite as effective practical educators as even the most vaunted of our modern university mechanical departments.

It is rather interesting to trace the course of the development of schools in our modern sense of the term, because their evolution recapitulates, to some degree at least, the history of the individual's interest in life. The first school which acquired a European reputation was that of Salernum, a little town not far from Naples, which possessed a famous medical school as early as the ninth century, perhaps earlier. This never became a university, though its reputation as a great medical school was maintained for several centuries. This first educational opportunity to attract a large body of students from all over the world concerned mainly the needs of the body. The next set of interests which man, in the course of evolution develops, has to do with the acquisition and retention of property and the maintenance of his rights as an individual. It is not surprising, then, to find that the next school of world-wide reputation was that of law at Bologna which became the nucleus of a great university. It is only after man has looked out for his bodily needs and his property rights, that he comes to think of his duties toward himself, his fellow-men, and his Creator, and so the third of these great medieval schools, in time, was that of philosophy and theology, at Paris.

It is sometimes thought that the word university applied to these institutions after the aggregation of other faculties, was due to the fact that there was a universality of studies, that all branches of knowledge might be followed in them. The word university, however, was not originally applied to the school itself, which, if it had all the faculties of the modern university, was, in the Thirteenth Century, called a *studium generale*. The Latin word universitas had quite a different usage at that time. Whenever letters were formally addressed to the combined faculties of a *studium generale* by reigning sovereigns, or by the Pope, or by other high ecclesiastical authorities, they always began with the designation, Universitas Vestra, implying that the greeting was to all of the faculty, universally and without exception. Gradually, because of this word constantly occurring at the beginning of letters to the faculty, the term universitas came to be applied to the institution. *

While the universities, as is typically exemplified by the histories of Bologna and Paris, and even to a noteworthy degree of Oxford, grew up around the cathedrals, they cannot be considered in any sense the deliberate creation, much less the formal invention, of any particular set of men. The idea of a university was not born into the world in full panoply as Minerva from the brain of Jove. No one set about consciously organizing for the establishment of complete institutions of learning. Like everything destined to mean much in the world the universities were a natural growth from the favoring soil in which living seeds were planted. They sprang from the wonderful inquiring spirit of the time and the marvelous desire for knowledge and for the higher intellectual life that came over the people of Europe during the Thirteenth Century. The school at Paris became famous, and attracted pupils during the Twelfth Century, because of the new-born interest in scholastic philosophy. After the pupils had gathered in large numbers their enthusiasm led to the establishment of further courses of study. The same thing was true at Bologna, where the study of Law first attracted a crowd of earnest students, and then the demand for broader education led to the establishment of other faculties.

* Certain other terms that occur in these letters of greeting to university officials have a more than passing interest. The rector of the university, for instance, was always formally addressed as Amplitudo Vestra, that is, Your Ampleness. Considering the fact that not a few of the rectors of the old time universities, all of whom were necessarily ecclesiastics, must have had the ampleness of girth so characteristic of their order under certain circumstances, there is an appropriateness about this formal designation which perhaps appeals more to the risibilities of the modern mind than to those of medieval time.

Above all, there was no conscious attempt on the part of any supposed better class to stoop down and uplift those presumably below it. As we shall see, the students of the university came mainly from the middle class of the population. They became ardently devoted to their teachers. As in all really educational work, it was the man and not the institution that counted for much. In case of disagreement of one of these with the university authorities, not infrequently there was a sacrifice of personal advantage for the moment on the part of the students in order to follow a favorite teacher. Paris had examples of this several times before the Thirteenth Century, and notably in the case of Abelard had seen thousands of students follow him into the distant desert where he had retired.

Later on, when abuses on the part of the authorities of Paris limited the University's privileges, led to the withdrawal of students and the foundation of Oxford, there was a community of interest on the part of certain members of the faculty and thousands of students. This movement was, however, distinctly of a popular character, in the sense that it was not guided by political or other leaders. Nearly all of the features of university life during the Thirteenth Century, emphasize the democracy of feeling of the students, and make it clear that the blowing of the wind of the spirit of human liberty and intellectual enthusiasm influencing the minds of the generation, rather than any formal attempt on the part of any class of men deliberately to provide educational opportunities, is the underlying feature of university foundation and development.

While the great universities of Paris, Bologna, and Oxford were, by far, the most important, they must not be considered as the only educational institutions deserving the name of universities, even in our modern sense, that took definite form during the Thirteenth Century. In Italy, mainly under the fostering care of ecclesiastics, encouraged by such Popes as Innocent III, Gregory IX, and Honorius IV, nearly a dozen other towns and cities saw the rise of Studia Generalia eventually destined, and that within a few decades after their foundation, to have the complete set of faculties, and such a number of teachers and of students as merited for them the name of University.

ADORATION OF THE MAGI (PULPIT, SIENA, NIC. PISANO)

Very early in the century Vicenza, Reggio, and Arezzo became university towns. Before the first quarter of the century was finished there were universities at Padua, at Naples, and at Vercelli. In spite of the troublous times and the great reduction in the population of Rome there was a university founded in connection with the Roman Curia, that is the Papal Court, before the middle of the century, and Siena and Piacenza had founded rival university institutions. Perugia had a famous school which became a complete university early in the Fourteenth Century.

Nor were other countries much behind Italy in this enthusiastic movement. Montpelier had, for over a century before the beginning of the thirteenth, rejoiced in a medical school which was the most important rival of that at Salernum. At the beginning this reflected largely the Moorish element in educational affairs in Europe at this time. During the course of the Thirteenth Century Montpelier developed into a full-fledged university though the medical school still continued to be the most important faculty. Medical students from all over the world flocked to the salubrious town to which patients from all over were attracted, and its teachers and writers of medicine have been famous in medical history ever since. How thorough was the organization of clinical medical work at Montpelier may perhaps best be appreciated from the fact, noted in the chapter on City Hospitals—Organized Charity, that when Pope Innocent III. wished to establish a model hospital at Rome with the idea that it would form an exemplar for other European cities, he sent down to Montpelier and summoned Guy, the head of the Hospital of the Holy Ghost in that city, to the Papal Capital to establish the Roman Hospital of the Holy Ghost and, in connection with it, a large number of hospitals all over Europe.

A corresponding state of affairs to that of Montpelier is to be noted at Orleans, only here the central school, around which the university gradually grouped itself, was the Faculty of Civil Law. Canon law was taught at Paris in connection with the theological course, but there had always been objection to the admission of civil law as a faculty on a basis of equality with the other faculties. There was indeed at this time some rivalry between the civil and the canon law and so the study of civil law was relegated to other universities. Even early in the Twelfth Century Orleans was famous for its school of civil law in which the exposition of the principles of the old Roman law constituted the basis of the university course. During the Thirteenth Century the remaining departments of the university gradually developed, so that by the close of the century, there seem to be conservative claims for over one thousand students. Besides these three, French universities were also established at Angers, at Toulouse, and the beginnings of institutions to become universities early in the next century are recorded at Avignon and Cahors.

Spain felt the impetus of the university movement early in the Thirteenth Century and a university was founded at Palencia about the end of the first decade. This was founded by Alfonso XII. and was greatly encouraged by him. It is sometimes said that this university was transferred to Salamanca about 1230, but this is denied by Denifle, whose authority in matters of university history is unquestionable. It seems not unlikely that Salamanca drew a number of students from Palencia but that the latter continued still to attract many students. About the middle of the Thirteenth Century the university of Valladolid was founded. Before the end of the century a fourth university, that of Lerida, had been established in the Spanish peninsula. Spain was to see the greatest development of universities during the Fourteenth Century. It was not long after the end of the Thirteenth Century before Coimbra, in Portugal, began to assume importance as an educational institution, though it was not to have sufficient faculty and students to deserve the more ambitious title of university for half a century.

While most people who know anything about the history of education realize the important position occupied by the universities during the Thirteenth Century and appreciate the estimation in which they were held and the numbers that attended them, very few seem to know anything of the preparatory schools of the time, and are prone to think that all the educational effort of these generations was exhausted in connection with the university. It is often said, as we shall see, that one reason for the large number of students reported as in attendance at the universities during the Thirteenth Century is to be found in the fact that these institutions practically combined the preparatory school and the academy of our time with the university. The universities are supposed to have been the only centers of education worthy of mention. There is no doubt that a number of quite young students were in attendance at the universities, that is, boys from 12 to 15 who would in our time be only in the preparatory school. We shall explain, however, in the chapter on the Numbers in Attendance at the Universities that students went to college much younger in the past and graduated much earlier than they do in our day, yet apparently, without any injury to the efficacy of their educational training.

In the universities of Southern Europe it is still the custom for boys to graduate with the degree of A. B. at the age of 15 to 16, which supposes attendance at the university, or its equivalent in under-graduate courses, at the age of 12 or even less. There is no need, however, to appeal to the precociousness of the southern nations in explanation of this, since there are some good examples of it in comparatively recent times here in America. Most of the colleges in this country, in the early part of the nineteenth century and the end of the eighteenth, graduated young men of 16 and 17 and thought that they were accomplishing a good purpose, in allowing them to get at their life work in early manhood. Many of the distinguished divines who made names in educational work are famous for their early graduations. Dr. Benjamin Rush, of Philadelphia, whom the medical profession of this country hails as the Father of American Medicine, graduated at Princeton at 15. He must have begun his college course, therefore, about the age of 12. This may be considered inadvisable in our generation, but, it must be remembered that there are many even in our day, who think that our college men are allowed to get at their life-work somewhat too late for their own good.

It must be emphasized, moreover, that in many of the university towns there were also preparatory schools. Courses

were not regularly organized until well on in the Thirteenth
Century, but younger brothers and friends of students as well
as of professors would not infrequently be placed under their
care and thus be enabled to receive their preparation for university work. At Paris, Robert Sorbonne founded a preparatory school for that institution under the name of the College
of Calvi. Other colleges of this kind also existed in Paris.
This custom of having a preparatory school in association
with the university has not been abandoned even in our own
day, and it has some decided advantages from an educational
standpoint, though perhaps these are not enough to balance
certain ethical disadvantages almost sure to attach to such a
system, disadvantages which ultimately led in the Middle Ages
to the prohibition that young students should be taken at the
universities under any pretext.

The presence of these young students in university towns
probably did add considerably to the numbers reported as in
attendance. It must not be thought, however, that there were
no formal preparatory schools quite apart from university
influence. This thought has been the root of more misunderstanding of the medieval system of education than almost any
other. As a matter of fact there were preliminary and preparatory schools, what we would now call academies and colleges,
in connection with all of the important monasteries and with
every cathedral. Schools of less importance were required by
a decree of a council held at the beginning of the Thirteenth
Century to be maintained in connection with every bishop's
church. During the Thirteenth Century there were some
twenty cathedrals in various parts of England; each one had
its cathedral school. Besides these there were at least as many
important abbeys, nearly a dozen of them immense institutions,
in which there were fine libraries, large writing rooms, in
which copies of books were being constantly made, many
of the members of the communities of which were university
men, and around which, therefore, there clung an atmosphere
of bookishness and educational influence that made them preparatory schools of a high type. The buildings themselves
were of the highest type of architecture; the community life
was well calculated to bring out what was best in the intellect-

uality of members of the community, and, then, there was a rivalry between the various religious orders which made them prepare their men well in order that they might do honor to the order when they had the opportunity later, as most of those who had the ability and the taste actually did have, to go to one or other of the universities.

This system of preparatory schools need not be accepted on the mere assumption that the monasteries and churches must surely have set about such work, because there is abundant evidence of the actual establishment and maintenance of such schools. With regard to the monasteries there can be no doubt, because it was the members of the religious orders who particularly distinguished themselves at the universities, and the histories of Oxford, Cambridge, and Paris are full of their accomplishments. They succeeded in obtaining the right to have their own houses at the universities and to have their own examinations count in university work, in order that they might maintain their influence over the members of the orders during the precious formative period of their intellectual life. With regard to the church schools there is convincing evidence of another kind.

In the chapter on the foundation of City Hospitals we have detailed on the authority of Virchow all that Innocent III. accomplished for the hospital system of Europe. This chapter was published originally in the form of a lecture from the historical department of the Medical School of Fordham University and a reprint of it was sent to a distinguished American educator well known for his condemnation of supposed church intolerance in the matter of education and scientific development. He said that he was glad to have it because it confirmed and even broadened the idea that he had long cherished, that the Church had done more for Charity during the despised Middle Ages than national governments had ever been able to accomplish since, though it was all the more surprising to him that it should not have under the circumstances, done more for education, since this might have prevented some of the ills that charity had afterward to relieve. This expression very probably represents the state of mind of very many scholars with regard to this period. The Church is supposed to have interested herself in charity almost to the exclusion of educational influence Charity is of course admitted to be her special work, yet these scholars cannot help but regret that more was not done in social prophylaxis by the encouragement of education.

In the light of this almost universal expression it is all the more interesting to find that such opinions are founded entirely on a lack of knowledge of what was done in education, since the same Pope, in practically the same way and by the exertion of the same prestige and ecclesiastical authority, did for education just what he did for charity in the matter of the hospitals and the ailing poor. Virchow, as we shall see, declared that to Innocent III. is due the foundation of practically all the city hospitals in Europe. If the effect of certain of the decrees issued in his papacy be carefully followed, it will be found that practically as many schools as hospitals owe their origin to his beneficent wisdom and his paternal desire to spread the advantages of Christianity all over the civilized world. This policy with regard to the hospitals led to the foundation before the end of the century of at least one hospital in every diocese of all the countries which were more closely allied with the Holy See. There is extant a decree issued by the famous council of Lateran, in 1215, a council in which Innocent's authority was dominant, requiring the establishment of a Chair of Grammar in connection with every cathedral in the Christian world. This Chair of Grammar included at least three of the so-called liberal arts and provided for what would now be called the education of a school preparatory to a university.

Before this, Innocent III,* who had himself received the benefit of the best education of the time, having spent some years at Rome and later at Paris and at Bologna, had encouraged the

---

*Most of the details of what was accomplished for education by Pope Innocent III, and all the references needed to supply further information, can be found in the *Hestoire Litterature de la France*, recent volumes of which were issued by the French Institute, though the magnificent work itself was begun by Benedictines of St. Maur, who completed some fifteen volumes. The sixteenth volume, most of which is written by Daufiou, is especially valuable for this period. Du Boulay, in his History of the University of Paris, will furnish additional information with regard to Pope Innocent's relations to education throughout Europe, especially, of course, in what regards the University of Paris.

CATHEDRAL (YORK)

CATHEDRAL (LINCOLN)

sending of students to these universities in every way. Bishops who came to Rome were sure to hear inculcated the advisability of a taste for letters in clergymen, hear it said often enough that such a taste would surely increase the usefulness of all church-men. Schools had been encouraged before the issuance of the decree. This only came as a confirmatory document calculated to perpetuate the policy that had already been so prominently in vogue in the church for over fifteen years of the Pope's reign. It was meant, too, to make clear to hesitant and tardy bishops, who might have thought that the papal interest in education was merely personal, that the policy of the church was concerned in it and recalled them to a sense of duty in the matter, since the ordinary enthusiasm for letters, even with the added encourage-ment of the Pope, did not suffice to make them realize the neces-sity for educational establishments.

The institution of the schools of grammar in connection with cathedrals was well adapted to bring about a definite increase in the opportunities for book learning for those who desired it. In connection with the cathedrals there was always a band of can-ons whose duty it was to take part in the singing of the daily office. Their ceremonial and ritual duties did not, however, oc-cupy them more than a few hours each day. During the rest of the time they were free to devote themselves to any subject in which they might be interested and had ample time for teaching. The requirement that there should be at least a school of gram-mar in connection with every cathedral afforded definite oppor-tunity to such of these ecclesiastics as had intellectual tastes to devote themselves to the spread of knowledge and of culture, and this reacted, as can be readily understood, to make the whole band of canons more interested in the things of the mind, and to make the cathedral even more the intellectual center of the district than might otherwise have been the case.

For the metropolitan churches a more far-reaching regulation was made by this same council of Lateran under the inspiration of the Pope himself. These important Archiepiscopal cathe-drals were required to maintain professors of three chairs. One of these was to teach grammar, a second philosophy, and a third canon law. Under these designations there was practically in-cluded much of what is now studied not only in preparatory

schools but also at the beginning of University courses. The regulation was evidently intended to lead eventually to the formation of many more universities than were then in existence, because already it had become clear that the traveling of students
to long distances and their gathering in such large numbers in towns away from home influences, led to many abuses
that might be obviated if they could stay in their native cities, or
at least did not have to leave their native provinces. This was a
far-seeing regulation that, like so many other decrees of the century, manifests the very practical policy of the Pope in matters
of education as well as charity. As a matter of fact this decree
did lead to the gradual development of about twenty universities during the Thirteenth Century, and to the establishment
of a number of other schools so important in scope and attendance that their evolution into universities during the Fourteenth
Century became comparatively easy. This formal church law,
moreover, imposed upon ecclesiastical authorities the necessity
for providing for even higher education in their dioceses and
made them realize that it was entirely in sympathy with the
church's spirit and in accord with the wish of the Father of
Christendom, that they should make as ample provision for education as they did for charity, though this last was supposed to
be their special task as pastors of the Christian flock.

All this important work for the foundation of preparatory
schools in every diocese and of the preliminary organization
of teaching institutions that might easily develop into universities, as they actually did in a score of cases in metropolitan
cities, was accomplished under the first Pope of the Thirteenth
Century, Innocent III. His successors kept up this good work.
Pope Honorious III., his immediate successor, went so far in
this matter as to depose a bishop who had not read Donatus,
the popular grammarian of the time. The bishop evidently
was considered unfit, as far as his mental training went, to occupy the important post of head of a diocese. Pope Gregory
IX., the nephew of Innocent III., was one of the most important patrons of the study of law in this period (see Legal Origins in Other Countries), and encouraged the collection of the
decrees of former Popes so as to make them available for purposes of study as well as for court use. He is famous for hav-

ing protected the University of Paris during some of the serious trouble with the municipal authorities, when the large increase of the number of students in attendance at the University had unfortunately brought about strained relations between town and gown.

Pope Innocent IV. by several decrees encouraged the development of the University of Paris, increased its rights and conferred new privileges. He also did much to develop the University of Toulouse, and especially to raise its standard and make it equal to that of Paris as far as possible. The patronage of Toulouse on the part of the Pope is all the more striking because the study of civil law was here a special feature and the ecclesiastical authorities were often said to have looked askance at the rising prominence of civil law, since it threatened to diminish the importance of canon law; and the cultivation of it, only too frequently, seemed to give rise to friction between civil and ecclesiastical authorities. While the pontifical court of Innocent IV. was maintained at Lyons it seemed, according to the Literary History of France,* more like an academy of theology and of canon law than the court of a great monarch whose power was acknowledged throughout the world, or a great ecclesiastic who might be expected to be occupied with details of Church government.

Succeeding Popes of the century were not less prominent in their patronage of education. Pope Alexander IV. supported the cause of the Mendicant Friars against the University of Paris, but this was evidently with the best of intentions. The mendicants came to claim the privilege of having houses in association with the university in which they might have lectures for the members of their orders, and asked for due allowance in the matter of degrees for courses thus taken. The faculty of the University did not want to grant this privilege, though it was acknowledged that some of the best professors in the University were members of the Mendicant orders, and we need only mention such names as Albertus Magnus and St. Thomas Aquinas from the Dominicans, and St. Bonaventure, Roger Bacon and Duns Scotus from the Franciscans, to show the truth of this assertion. To give such a privilege

*Histoire Litteratire de la France, Vol. XVI, Introductory Discourse.

seemed a derogation of the faculty rights and the University refused. Then the Holy See interfered to insist that the University must give degrees for work done, rather than merely for regulation attendance. The best possible proof that Pope Alexander cannot be considered as wishing to injure or even diminish the prestige of the University in any way, is to be found in the fact that he afterwards sent two of his nephews to Paris to attend at the University.

All these Popes, so far mentioned, were not Frenchmen and therefore could have no national feeling in the matter of the University of Paris or of the French universities in general. It is not surprising to find that Pope Urban IV., who was a Frenchman and an alumnus of the University of Paris, elevated many French scholars, and especially his fellow alumni of Paris, to Church dignitaries of various kinds. After Urban IV., Nicholas IV. who succeeded him, though once more an Italian, founded chairs in the University of Montpelier, and also a professorship in a school that it was hoped would develop into a university at Gray in Franche Comte. In a word, looked at from every point of view, it must be admitted that the Church and ecclesiastical authorities were quite as much interested in education as in charity during this century, and it is to them that must be traced the foundation of the preparatory schools, as well as the universities, and the origin and development of the great educational movement that stamps this century as the greatest in human history.

JACQUES CŒUR'S HOUSE .
(BOURGES)

LATERAN CLOISTER (ROME)

III

WHAT AND HOW THEY STUDIED AT THE UNIVERSITIES.

It is usually the custom for text books of education to dismiss the teaching at the universities of the Middle Ages with some such expression as: "The teachers were mainly engaged in metaphysical speculations and the students were occupied with exercises in logic and in dialectics, learning in long drawn out disputations how to use the intellectual instruments they possessed but never actually applying them. All knowledge was supposed to be amenable to increase through dialectical discussion and all truth was supposed to be obtainable as the conclusion of a regular syllogism." Great fun especially is made of the long-winded disputations, the time-taking public exercises in dialectics, the fine hair-drawn distinctions presumably with but the scantiest basis of truth behind them and in general the placing of words for realities in the investigation of truth and the conveyance of information. The sublime ignorance of educators who talk thus about the century that saw the rise of the universities in connection with the erection of the great Cathedrals, is only equaled by their assumption of knowledge.

It is very easy to make fun of a past generation and often rather difficult to enter into and appreciate its spirit. Ridicule comes natural to human nature, alas! but sympathy requires serious mental application for understanding's sake. Fortunately there has come in recent years a very different feeling in the minds of many mature and faithful students of this period, as regards the Middle Ages and its education. Dialectics may seem to be a waste of time to those who consider the training of the human mind as of little value in comparison with the stocking of it with information. Dialectical training will probably not often enable men to earn more money than might have otherwise been the case. This will be emi-

nently true if the dialectician is to devote himself to commercial enterprises in his future life. If he is to take up one of the
professions, however, there may be some doubt as to whether
even his practical effectiveness will not be increased by a good
course of logic. There is, however, another point of view
from which this matter of the study of dialectics may be
viewed, and which has been taken very well by Prof. Saintsbury of the University of Edinburgh in a recent volume on the
Thirteenth Century.

He insists in a passage which we quote at length in the
chapter on the Prose of the Century, that if this training in
logic had not been obtained at this time in European development, the results might have been serious for our modern languages and modern education. He says: "If at the outset of the
career of the modern languages, men had thought with the
looseness of modern thought, had indulged in the haphazard
slovenliness of modern logic, had popularized theology and vulgarized rhetoric, as we have seen both popularized and vulgarized since, we should indeed have been in evil case." He
maintains that "the far-reaching educative influence in mere
language, in mere system of arrangement and expression, must
be considered as one of the great benefits of Scholasticism."
This is, after all, only a similar opinion to that evidently entertained by Mr. John Stuart Mill, who, as Prof. Saintsbury says,
was not often a scholastically-minded philosopher, for he quotes
in the preface of his logic two very striking opinions from very
different sources, the Scotch philosopher, Hamilton, and the
French philosophical writer, Condorcet. Hamilton said, "It is to
the schoolmen that the vulgar languages are indebted for what
precision and analytical subtlety they possess." Condorcet
went even further than this, and used expressions that doubtless will be a great source of surprise to those who do not realize how much of admiration is always engendered in those who
really study the schoolmen seriously and do not take opinions
of them from the chance reading of a few scattered passages,
or depend for the data of their judgment on some second-hand
authority, who thought it clever to abuse these old-time
thinkers. Condorcet thought them far in advance of the old
Greek philosophers for, he said, "Logic, ethics, and metaphysics

itself, owe to scholasticism a precision unknown to the ancients themselves."

With regard to the methods and contents of the teaching in the undergraduate department of the university, that is, in what we would now call the arts department, there is naturally no little interest at the present time. Besides the standards set up and the tests required can scarcely fail to attract attention. Professor Turner, in his History of Philosophy, has summed up much of what we know in this matter in a paragraph so full of information that we quote it in order to give our readers the best possible idea in a compendious form of these details of the old-time education.

"By statutes issued at various times during the Thirteenth Century it was provided that the professor should read, that is expound, the text of certain standard authors in philosophy and theology. In a document published by Denifle, (the distinguished authority on medieval universities) and by him referred to the year 1252, we find the following works among those prescribed for the Faculty of Arts: Logica Vetus (the old Boethian text of a portion of the Organon, probably accompanied by Porphyry's Isagoge); Logica Nova (the new translation of the Organon); Gilbert's Liber Sex Principorium; and Donatus's Barbarismus. A few years later (1255), the following works are prescribed: Aristotle's Physics, Metaphysics, De Anima, De Animalibus, De Caelo et Mundo, Meteorica, the minor psychological treatises and some Arabian or Jewish works, such as the Liber de Causis and De Differentia Spirititus et Animae."

"The first degree for which the student of arts presented himself was that of bachelor. The candidate for this degree, after a preliminary test called responsiones (this regulation went into effect not later than 1275), presented himself for the determinatio, which was a public defense of a certain number of theses against opponents chosen from the audience. At the end of the disputation, the defender summed up, or determined, his conclusions. After determining, the bachelor resumed his studies for the licentiate, assuming also the task of cursorily explaining to junior students some portion of the Organon. The test for the degree of licentiate consisted

in a *collatio,* or exposition of several texts, after the manner
of the masters. The student was now a licensed teacher; he did
not, however, become magister, or master of arts, until he had
delivered what was called the *inceptio,* or inaugural lecture,
and was actually installed (*birrettatio*). If he continued to
teach he was called *magister actu regens;* if he departed from
the university or took up other work, he was called *magister
non regens.* It may be said that, as a general rule, the course
of reading was: (1) for the bachelor's degree, grammar, logic,
and psychology; (2) for the licentiate, natural philosophy;
(3) for the master's degree, ethics, and the completion of the
course of natural philosophy."

Quite apart from the value of its methods, however, scholasticism in certain of its features had a value in the material
which it discussed and developed that modern generations only
too frequently fail to realize. With regard to this the same
distinguished authority whom we quoted with regard to
dialectics, Prof. Saintsbury, does not hesitate to use expressions which will seem little short of rankly heretical to those
who swear by modern science, and yet may serve to inject
some eminently suggestive ideas into a sadly misunderstood
subject.

"Yet there has always in generous souls who have some
tincture of philosophy, subsisted a curious kind of sympathy
and yearning over the work of these generations of mainly
disinterested scholars, who, whatever they were, were
thorough, and whatever they could not do, could think. *And
there have even, in these latter days, been some graceless ones
who have asked whether the Science of the nineteenth century,
after an equal interval, will be of any more positive value—
whether it will not have even less comparative interest than
that which appertains to the Scholasticism of the Thirteenth."*

In the light of this it has seemed well to try to show in terms
of present-day science some of the important reflections with
regard to such problems of natural history, as magnetism, the
composition of matter, and the relation of things physical
to one another, which we now include under the name science,
some of the thoughts that these scholars of the Thirteenth Century were thinking and were developing for the benefit of the

enthusiastic students who flocked to the universities. We will find in such a review though it must necessarily be brief many more anticipations of modern science than would be thought possible.

To take the example for the moment of magnetism which is usually considered to be a subject entirely of modern attention, a good idea of the intense interest of this century in things scientific, can be obtained from the following short paragraph in which Brother Potamian in his sketch of Petrus Peregrinus, condenses the references to magnetic phenomena that are found in the literature of the time. Most of the writers he mentions were not scientists in the ordinary sense of the word but were literary men, and the fact that these references occur shows very clearly that there must have been widespread interest in such scientific phenomena, since they had attracted the attention of literary writers, who would not have spoken of them doubtless, but that they knew that in this they would be satisfying as well as exciting public interest.

"Abbot Neckam, the Augustinian (1157-1217), distinguished between the properties of the two ends of the lodestone, and gives in his De Utensilibus, what is perhaps the earliest reference to the mariner's compass that we have. Albertus Magnus, the Dominican (1193-1280), in his treatise De Mineralibus, enumerates different kinds of natural magnets and states some of the properties commonly attributed to them; the minstrel, Guyot de Provins, in a famous satirical poem, written about 1208, refers to the directive quality of the lodestone and its use in navigation, as do also Cardinal de Vitry in his Historia Orientialis (1215-1220), Brunetto Latini, poet, orator and philosopher (the teacher of Dante), in his Tresor des Sciences, a veritable library, written in Paris in 1260; Raymond Lully, the enlightened Doctor, in his treatise, De Contemplatione, begun in 1272, and Guido Guinicelli, the poet-priest of Bologna, who died in 1276." *

The metaphysics of the medieval universities have come in for quite as much animadversion, not to say ridicule, as the

* The letter of Petrus Peregrinus on the Magnet, A. D. 1269, translated by Bro. Arnold, M. Sc., with an Introductory Note by Bro. Potamian, N. Y., 1904.

dialectics. None of its departments is spared in the condemnation, though most fun is made of the gropings of the medieval mind after truth in the physical sciences. The cosmology, the science of matter as it appealed to the medieval mind, is usually considered to have been so entirely speculative as to deserve no further attention. We have presumably, learned so much by experimental demonstration and original observation in the physical sciences, that any thinking of the medieval mind along these lines may, in the opinion of those who know nothing of what they speak, be set aside as preposterous, or at best nugatory. It will surely be a source of surprise, then, to find that in the consideration of the composition of matter and of the problem of the forces connected with it, the minds of the medieval schoolmen were occupied with just the same questions that have been most interesting to the Nineteenth Century and that curiously enough the conclusions they reached, though by very different methods of investigation, were almost exactly the same as those to which modern physical scientists have attained by their refined methods of investigation.

One or two examples will suffice, I think, to show very clearly that the students of the Thirteenth Century had presented to them practically the same problems with regard to matter, its origin and composition, as occupy the students of the present generation. For instance Thomas Aquinas usually known as St. Thomas, in a series of lectures given at the University of Paris toward the end of the third quarter of the Thirteenth Century, stated as the most important conclusion with regard to matter, that *"Nihil omnino in nihilum redigetur,"* "Nothing at all will ever be reduced to nothingness." By this it was very evident from the context that he meant that matter would never be annihilated and could never be destroyed. It might be changed in various ways but it could never go back into the nothingness from which it had been taken by the creative act. Annihilation was pronounced as not being a part of the scheme of things as far as the human mind could hope to fathom its meaning.

In this sentence, then, Thomas of Aquin was proclaiming the

doctrine of the indestructibility of matter. It was not until well on in the nineteenth century that the chemists and physicists of modern times realized the truth of this great principle. The chemists had seen matter change its form in many ways, had seen it disappear apparently in the smoke of fire or evaporate under the influence of heat, but investigation proved that if care were taken in the collection of the gases that came off under these circumstances, of the ashes of combustion and of the residue of evaporation, all the original material that had been contained in the supposedly disappearing substance could be recovered or at least completely accounted for. The physicists on their part had realized this same truth and finally there came the definite enunciation of the absolute indestructibility of matter. St. Thomas' conclusion "Nothing at all will ever be reduced to nothingness" had anticipated this doctrine by nearly seven centuries. What happened in the Nineteenth Century was that there came an experimental demonstration of the truth of the principle. The principle itself, however, had been reached long before by the human mind by speculative processes quite as inerrable in their way as the more modern method of investigation.

When St. Thomas used the aphorism "Nothing at all will ever be reduced to nothingness" there was another signification that he attached to the words quite as clearly as that by which they expressed the indestructibility of matter. For him *Nihil* or nothing meant neither *matter* nor *form,* that is, neither the material substance nor the energy which is contained in it. He meant then, that no energy would ever be destroyed as well as no matter would ever be annihilated. He was teaching the conservation of energy as well as the indestructibility of matter. Here once more the experimental demonstration of the doctrine was delayed for over six centuries and a half. The truth itself, however, had been reached by this medieval master-mind and was the subject of his teaching to the university students in Paris in the Thirteenth Century. These examples should, I think, serve to illustrate that the minds of medieval students were occupied with practically the same questions as those which are now taught to the university students of our day. There are, however, some even more striking anticipations of modern teaching that will serve to demonstrate this community of educational interests in spite of seven centuries of time separation.

In recent years we have come to realize that matter is not the manifold material we were accustomed to think it when we accepted the hypothesis that there were some seventy odd different kinds of atoms, each one absolutely independent of any other and representing an ultimate term in science. The atomic theory from this standpoint has proved to be only a working hypothesis that was useful for a time, but that our physicists are now agreed must not be considered as something absolute. Radium has been observed changing into helium and the relations of atoms to one another as they are now known, make it almost certain that all of them have an underlying sub-stratum the same in all, but differentiated by the dynamic energies with which matter in its different forms is gifted. Sir Oliver Lodge has stated this theory of the constitution of matter very clearly in recent years, and in doing so has only been voicing the practically universal sentiment of those who have been following the latest developments in the physical sciences. Strange as it may appear, this was exactly the teaching of Aquinas and the schoolmen with regard to the constitution of matter. They said that the two constituting principles of matter were prime matter and form. By prime matter they meant the material sub-stratum the same in all material things. By form they meant the special dynamic energy which, entering into prime matter, causes it to act differently from other kinds and gives it all the particular qualities by which we recognize it. This theory was not original with them, having been adopted from Aristotle, but it was very clearly set forth, profoundly discussed, and amply illustrated by the schoolmen. In its development this theory was made to be of the greatest help in the explanation of many other difficulties with regard to living as well as non-living things in their hands. The theory has its difficulties, but they are less than those of any other theory of the constitution of matter, and it has been accepted by more philosophic thinkers since the Thirteenth Century than any other doctrine of similar nature. It may be said that it was reached only by deduction and not by experimental observation. Such an expression, however, instead of being really an objection is rather a demonstration of the fact that great truths may be reached by deduction yet only demonstrated by inductive methods many centuries later.

Of course it may well be said even after all these communities of interest between the medieval and the modern teaching of the general principles of science has been pointed out, that the universities of the Middle Ages did not present the subjects under discussion in a practical way, and their teaching was not likely to lead to directly beneficial results in applied science. It might well be responded to this, that it is not the function of a university to teach applications of science but only the great principles, the broad generalizations that underlie scientific thinking, leaving details to be filled in in whatever form of practical work the man may take up. Very few of those, however, who talk about the purely speculative character of medieval teaching have manifestly ever made it their business to know anything about the actual facts of old-time university teaching by definite knowledge, but have rather allowed themselves to be guided by speculation and by inadequate second-hand authorities, whose dicta they have never taken the trouble to substantiate by a glance at contemporary authorities on medieval matters.

It will be interesting to quote for the information of such men, the opinion of the greatest of medieval scientists with regard to the reason why men do not obtain real knowledge more rapidly than would seem ought to be the case, from the amount of work which they have devoted to obtaining it. Roger Bacon, summing up for Pope Clement the body of doctrine that he was teaching at the University of Oxford in the Thirteenth Century, starts out with the principle that there are four grounds of human ignorance. "These are first, trust in inadequate authority; second, the force of custom which leads men to accept too unquestioningly what has been accepted before their time; third, the placing of confidence in the opinion of the inexperienced; and fourth, the hiding of one's own ignorance with the parade of a superficial wisdom." Surely no one will ever be able to improve on these four grounds for human ignorance, and they continue to be as important in the twentieth century as they were in the Thirteenth. They could only have emanated from an eminently practical mind, accustomed to test by observation and by careful searching of authorities, every proposition that came to him. Professor Henry Morley, Professor of English Literature at University College, London, says of these grounds for ignorance of Roger Bacon, in his English Writers, Volume III, page 321: "No part of that ground has yet been cut away from beneath the feet of students, although six centuries ago the Oxford friar clearly pointed out its character. We still make sheep walks of second, third, and fourth and fiftieth-hand references to authority; still we are the slaves of habit; still we are found following too frequently the untaught crowd; still we flinch from the righteous and wholesome phrase, 'I do not know'; and acquiesce actively in the opinion of others that we know what we appear to know. Substitute honest research, original and independent thought, strict truth in the comparison of only what we really know with what is really known by others, and the strong redoubt of ignorance has fallen."

The number of things which Roger Bacon succeeded in discovering by the application of the principle of testing everything by personal observation, is almost incredible to a modern student of science and of education who has known nothing before of the progress in science made by this wonderful man. He has been sometimes declared to be the discoverer of gunpowder, but this is a mistake since it was known many years before by the Arabs and by them introduced into Europe. He did study explosives very deeply, however, and besides learning many things about them realized how much might be accomplished by their use in the after-time. He declares in his Opus Magnum: "That one may cause to burst forth from bronze, thunderbolts more formidable than those produced by nature. A small quantity of prepared matter occasions a terrible explosion accompanied by a brilliant light. One may multiply this phenomenon so far as to destroy a city or an army." Considering how little was known about gunpowder at this time, this was of itself a marvelous anticipation of what might be accomplished by it.

Bacon prophesied, however, much more than merely de-

RATHHAUS (TANGERMÜNDE)

structive effects from the use of high explosives, and indeed it is almost amusing to see how closely he anticipated some of the most modern usages of high explosives for motor purposes. He seems to have concluded that some time the apparently uncontrollable forces of explosion would come under the control of man and be harnessed by him for his own purposes. He realized that one of the great applications of such a force would be for transportation. Accordingly he said: "Art can construct instruments of navigation such that the largest vessels governed by a single man will traverse rivers and seas more rapidly than if they were filled with oarsmen. One may also make carriages which without the aid of any animal will run with remarkable swiftness."* When we recall that the very latest thing in transportation are motor-boats and automobiles driven by gasoline, a high explosive, Roger Bacon's prophesy becomes one of these weird anticipations of human progress which seem almost more than human.

It was not with regard to explosives alone, however, that Roger Bacon was to make great advances and still more marvelous anticipations in physical science. He was not, as is sometimes claimed for him, either the inventor of the telescope or of the theory of lenses. He did more, however, than perhaps anyone else to make the principles of lenses clear and to establish them on a mathematical basis. His traditional connection with the telescope can probably be traced to the fact that he was very much interested in astronomy and the relations of the heavens to the earth. He pointed out very clearly the errors which had crept into the Julian calendar, calculated exactly how much of a correction was needed in order to restore the year to its proper place, and suggested the method by which future errors of this kind could be avoided. His ideas were too far beyond his century to be applied in a practical way, but they were not to be without their effect and it is said that they formed the basis of the subsequent correction of the calendar in the time of Pope Gregory XIII three centuries later.

* These quotations are taken from Ozanam's Dante and Catholic Philosophy, published by the Cathedral Library Association, New York, 1897.

It is rather surprising to find how much besides the theory of lenses Friar Bacon had succeeded in finding out in the department of optics. He taught, for instance, the principle of the aberration of light, and, still more marvelous to consider, taught that light did not travel instantaneously but had a definite rate of motion, though this was extremely rapid. It is rather difficult to understand how he reached this conclusion since light travels so fast that as far as regards any observation that can be made upon earth, the diffusion is practically instantaneous. It was not for over three centuries later that Römer, the German astronomer, demonstrated the motion of light and its rate, by his observations upon the moons of Jupiter at different phases of the earth's orbit, which showed that the light of these moons took a definite and quite appreciable time to reach the earth after their eclipse by the planet was over.

We are not surprised to find that Bacon should praise those of his contemporaries who devoted themselves to mathematics and to experimental observations in science. Of one of his correspondents who even from distant Italy sent him his observations in order that he might have the great Franciscan's precious comments on them, Bacon has given quite a panegyric. The reasons for his praise, however, are so different from those which are ordinarily proclaimed to have been the sources of laudation in distant medieval scientific circles, that we prefer to quote Bacon's own words from the Opus Tertium. Bacon is talking of Petrus Peregrinus and says: "I know of only one person who deserves praise for his work in experimental philosophy, for he does not care for the discourses of men and their wordy warfare, but quietly and diligently pursues the works of wisdom. Therefore, what others grope after blindly, as bats in the evening twilight, this man contemplates in all their brilliancy because he is a master of experiment. Hence, he knows all natural science whether pertaining to medicine and alchemy, or to matters celestial and terrestrial.

"He has worked diligently in the smelting of ores as also in the working of minerals; he is thoroughly acquainted with all sorts of arms and implements used in military service and in

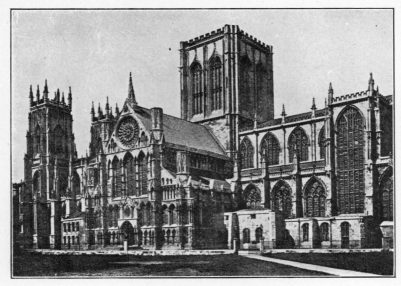

CATHEDRAL (YORK)

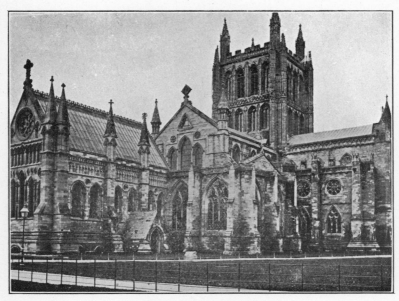

CATHEDRAL (HEREFORD)

hunting, besides which he is skilled in agriculture and in the measurement of lands. It is impossible to write a useful or correct treatise in experimental philosophy without mentioning this man's name. Moreover, he pursues knowledge for its own sake; for if he wished to obtain royal favor, he could easily find sovereigns who would honor and enrich him."

Lest it should be thought that these expressions of laudatory appreciation of the great Thirteenth Century scientist are dictated more by the desire to magnify his work and to bring out the influence in science of the Churchmen of the period, it seems well to quote an expression of opinion from the modern historian of the inductive sciences, whose praise is scarcely if any less outspoken than that of others whom we have quoted and who might be supposed to be somewhat partial in their judgment. This opinion will fortify the doubters who must have authority and at the same time sums up very excellently the position which Roger Bacon occupies in the History of Science.

Dr. Whewell says that Roger Bacon's Opus Majus is "the encyclopedia and Novam Organon of the Thirteenth Century, a work equally wonderful with regard to its general scheme and to the special treatises with which the outlines of the plans are filled up. The professed object of the work is to urge the necessity of a reform in the mode of philosophizing, to set forth the reasons why knowledge had not made a greater progress, to draw back attention to the sources of knowledge which had been unwisely neglected, to discover other sources which were yet almost untouched, and to animate men in the undertaking by a prospect of the vast advantages which it offered. In the development of this plan all the leading portions of science are expanded in the most complete shape which they had at that time assumed; and improvements of a very wide and striking kind are proposed in some of the principal branches of study. Even if the work had no leading purposes it would have been highly valuable as a treasure of the most solid knowledge and soundest speculations of the time; even if it had contained no such details it would have been a work most remarkable for its general views and scope."

It is only what might have been expected, however, from

Roger Bacon's training that he should have made great progress in the physical sciences. At the University of Paris his favorite teacher was Albertus Magnus, who was himself deeply interested in all the physical sciences, though he was more concerned with the study of chemical problems than of the practical questions which were to occupy his greatest pupil. There is no doubt at all that Albertus Magnus accomplished a great amount of experimental work in chemistry and had made a large series of actual observations. He was a theologian as well as a philosopher and a scientist. Some idea of the immense industry of the man can be obtained from the fact that his complete works as published consist of some twenty large folio volumes, each one of which contains on the average at least 500,000 words.

Among these works are many treatises relating to chemistry. The titles of some of them will serve to show how explicit was Albert in his consideration of various chemical subjects. He has treatises concerning Metals and Minerals; concerning Alchemy; A Treatise on the Secret of Chemistry; A Concordance, that is a Collection of observations from many sources with regard to the Philosopher's Stone; A Brief Compend on the Origin of the Metals; A Treatise on Compounds; most of these are to be found in his works under the general heading "Theatrum Chemicum."

It is not surprising for those who know of Albert's work, to find that his pupil Roger Bacon defined the limits of chemistry very accurately and showed that he understood exactly what the subject and methods of investigation must be, in order that advance should be made in it. Of chemistry he speaks in his "Opus Tertium" in the following words: "There is a science which treats of the generation of things from their elements and of all inanimate things, as of the elements and liquids, simple and compound, common stones, gems and marble, gold and other metals, sulphur, salts, pigments, lapis lazuli, minium and other colors, oils, bitumen, and infinite more of which we find nothing in the books of Aristotle; nor are the natural philosophers nor any of the Latins acquainted with these things."

In physics Albertus Magnus was, if possible, more advanced

and progressive even than in chemistry. His knowledge in the physical sciences was not merely speculative, but partook to a great degree of the nature of what we now call applied science. Humboldt, the distinguished German natural philosopher of the beginning of the Nineteenth Century, who was undoubtedly the most important leader in scientific thought in his time and whose own work was great enough to have an enduring influence in spite of the immense progress of the Nineteenth Century, has summed up Albert's work and given the headings under which his scientific research must be considered. He says:

"Albertus Magnus was equally active and influential in promoting the study of natural science and of the Aristotelian philosophy. His works contain some exceedingly acute remarks on the organic structure and physiology of plants. One of his works bearing the title of 'Liber Cosmographicus de Natura Locorum,' is a species of physical geography. I have found in it considerations on the dependence of temperature concurrently on latitude and elevation, and on the effect of different angles of incidence of the sun's rays in heating the ground, *which have excited my surprise.*"

To take up some of Humboldt's headings in their order and illustrate them by quotations from Albert himself and from condensed accounts as they appear in his biographer Sighart and in Christian Schools and Scholars*, will serve to show at once the extent of Albert's knowledge and the presumptuous ignorance of those who make little of the science of the medieval period. When we have catalogued, for instance, the many facts with regard to astronomy and the physics of light that are supposed to have come to human ken much later, yet may be seen to have been clearly within the range of Albert's knowledge, and evidently formed the subject of his teaching at various times at both Paris and Cologne, for they are found in his authentic works, we can scarcely help but be amused at the pretentious misconception that has relegated their author to a place in education so trivial as is that which is represented in many minds by the term scholastic.

"He decides that the Milky Way is nothing but a vast

---

* Christian Schools and Scholars, Drane.

assemblage of stars, but supposes naturally enough that they occupy the orbit which receives the light of the sun.   The figures visible on the moon's disc are not, he says, as hitherto has been supposed, reflections of the seas and mountains of the earth, but configurations of her own surface.   He notices, in order to correct it, the assertion of Aristotle that lunar rainbows appear only twice in fifty years; 'I myself,' he says have observed two in a single year.' He has something to say on the refraction of a solar ray, notices certain crystals which have a power of refraction, and remarks that none of the ancients and few moderns were acquainted with the properties of mirrors."

Albert's great pupil Roger Bacon is rightly looked upon as the true father of inductive science, an honor that history has unfortunately taken from him to confer it undeservedly on his namesake of four centuries later, but the teaching out of which Roger Bacon was to develop the principles of experimental science can be found in many places in his master's writings.   In Albert's tenth book, wherein he catalogues and describes all the trees, plants, and herbs known in his time, he observes : "All that is here set down is the result of our own experience, or has been borrowed from authors whom we know to have written what their personal experience has confirmed : for in these matters experience alone can give certainty" (*experimentum solum certificat in talibus*).   "Such an expression," says his biographer, "which might have proceeded from the pen of (Francis) Bacon, argues in itself a prodigious scientific progress, and shows that the medieval friar was on the track so successfully pursued by modern natural philosophy.   He had fairly shaken off the shackles which had hitherto tied up discovery, and was the slave neither of Pliny nor of Aristotle."

Botany is supposed to be a very modern science and to most people Humboldt's expression that he found in Albertus Magnus's writings some "exceedingly acute remarks on the organic structure and physiology of plants" will come as a supreme surprise. A few details with regard to Albert's botanical knowledge, however, will serve to heighten that surprise and to show, that the foolish tirades of modern sciolists, who have often expressed their wonder that with all the beauties of nature around them, these scholars of the Middle Ages did not devote themselves to nature study, are absurd, because if the critics but knew it there was profound interest in nature and all her manifestations and a series of discoveries that anticipated not a little of what we consider most important in our modern science. The story of Albert's botanical knowledge has been told in a single very full paragraph by his biographer. Sighart also quotes an appreciative opinion from a modern German botanist which will serve to dispel any doubts with regard to Albert's position in botany that modern students might perhaps continue to harbor, unless they had good authority to support their opinion, though of course it will be remembered that the main difference between the medieval and the modern mind is only too often said to be, that the medieval required an authority while the modern makes its opinion for itself. Even the most skeptical of modern minds however, will probably be satisfied by the following paragraph.

"He was acquainted with the sleep of plants, with the periodical opening and closing of blossoms, with the diminution of sap through evaporation from the cuticle of the leaves, and with the influence of the distribution of the bundles of vessels on the folial indentations. His minute observations on the forms and variety of plants intimate an exquisite sense of floral beauty. He distinguished the star from the bell-floral, tells us that a red rose will turn white when submitted to the vapor of sulphur, and makes some very sagacious observations on the subject of germination. . . . The extraordinary erudition and originality of this treatise (his tenth book) has drawn from M. Meyer the following comment: 'No Botanist who lived before Albert can be compared to him, unless Theophrastus, with whom he was not acquainted; and after him none has painted nature in such living colors or studied it so profoundly until the time of Conrad Gesner and Cesalpino.' All honor, then, to the man who made such astonishing progress in the science of nature as to find no one, I will not say to surpass, but even to equal him for the space of three centuries."

We point out in the chapter on Geography and Exploration how much this wonderful Thirteenth Century added to the knowledge of geographical science. Even before the great explorers of this time, however, had accomplished their work, this particular branch of science had made such great progress as would bring it quite within the domain of what we call the science of geography at the present time. When we remember how much has been said about the ignorance of the men of the later Middle Ages as regards the shape of the earth and its inhabitants, and how many foolish notions they are supposed to have accepted with regard to the limitation of possible residents of the world and the queer ideas as to the antipodes, the following passages taken from Albert's biographer will serve better than anything else to show how absurdly the traditional notions with regard to this time and its knowledge, have been permitted by educators to tinge what are supposed to be serious opinions with regard to the subject matters of education in that early university period :

"He treats as fabulous the commonly-received idea, in which Bede had acquiesced, that the region of the earth south of the equator was uninhabitable, and considers, that from the equator to the South Pole, the earth was not only habitable, but in all probability actually inhabited, except directly at the poles, where he imagines the cold to be excessive. If there be any animals there, he says, they must have very thick skins to defend them from the rigor of the climate, and they are probably of a white color. The intensity of cold, is however, tempered by the action of the sea. He describes the antipodes and the countries they comprise, and divides the climate of the earth into seven zones. He smiles with a scholar's freedom at the simplicity of those who suppose that persons living at the opposite region of the earth must fall off, an opinion that can only rise out of the grossest ignorance, 'for when we speak of the lower hemisphere, this must be understood merely as relatively to ourselves.' It is as a geographer that Albert's superiority to the writers of his own time chiefly appears. Bearing in mind the astonishing ignorance which then prevailed on this subject, it is truly admirable to find him correctly tracing the chief mountain chains of Europe, with the rivers which take their source in each; remarking on portions of coast which have in later times been submerged by the ocean, and islands which have been raised by volcanic action above the level of the sea; noticing the modification of climate caused by mountains, seas and forests, and the division of the human race whose differences he ascribes to the effect upon them of the countries they inhabit! In speaking of the British Isles he alludes to the commonly-received idea that another distant island called Tile or Thule, existed far in the Western Ocean, uninhabitable by reason of its frightful climate, but which, he says, has perhaps not yet been visited by man."

Nothing will so seriously disturb the complacency of modern minds as to the wonderful advances that have been made in the last century in all branches of physical science as to read Albertus Magnus' writings. Nothing can be more wholesomely chastening of present day conceit than to get a proper appreciation of the extent of the knowledge of the Schoolmen.

Albertus Magnus' other great pupil besides Roger Bacon was St. Thomas Aquinas. If any suspicion were still left that Thomas did not appreciate just what the significance of his teachings in physics was, when he announced that neither matter nor force could ever be reduced to nothingness, it would surely be removed by the consideration that he had been for many years in intimate relations with Albert and that he had probably also been close to Roger Bacon. After association with such men as these, any knowledge he displays with regard to physical science can scarcely be presumed to have been stumbled upon unawares. St. Thomas himself has left three treatises on chemical subjects and it is said that the first occurrence of the word amalgam can be traced to one of these treatises. Everybody was as much interested then, as we are at the present time, in the transformation of metals and mercury with its silvery sheen, its facility to enter into metallic combinations of all kinds, and its elusive ways, naturally made it the center of scientific interest quite as radium is at the present moment. Further material with regard to St. Thomas and also to the subject of education will be found in the chapter, Aquinas the Scholar.

After this brief review of only a few of the things that they taught in science at the Thirteenth Century universities, most

people will scarcely fail to wonder how such peculiar erroneous impressions with regard to the uselessness of university
teaching and training have come to be so generally accepted.
The fault lies, of course, with those who thought they knew
something about university teaching, and who, because they
found a few things that now look ridiculous, as certain supposed facts of one generation always will to succeeding generations who know more about them, thought they could conclude
from these as to the character of the whole content of medieval
education. It is only another example of what Artemus Ward
pointed out so effectively when he said that "there is nothing
that makes men so ridiculous as the knowing so many things
that aint so." We have been accepting without question ever
so many things that simply are not so with regard to these
wonderful generations, who not only organized the universities but organized the teaching in them on lines not very different from those which occupy people seven centuries later.

What would be the most amusing feature, if it were not unfortunately so serious an arraignment of the literature that has
grown up around these peculiar baseless notions with regard
to scholastic philosophy, is the number of men of science who
have permitted themselves to make fun of certain supposed
lucubrations of the great medieval philosophers. It is not so
very long ago that, as pointed out by Harper in the Metaphysics of the School, Professor Tate in a lecture on Some
Recent Advances in Physical Science repeated the old slander that even Aquinas occupied the attention of his students
with such inane questions as: "How many angels could dance
on the point of a needle?" Modern science very proudly insists that it occupies itself with observations and concerns itself little with authority. Prof. Tate in this unhappy quotation, shows not only that he has made no personal studies in
medieval philosophy but that he has accepted a very inadequate
authority for the statements which he makes with as much confidence as if they had been the result of prolonged research in
this field. Many other modern scientists (?) have fallen into
like blunders. (For Huxley's opinion see Appendix.)

The modern student, as well as the teacher, is prone to
wonder what were the methods of study and the habits of life

of the students of the Thirteenth Century, and fortunately we have a short sketch, written by Robert of Sorbonne, the famous founder of the Sorbonne, in which he gives advice to attendants at that institution as to how they should spend their time, so that at least we are able to get a hint of the ideals that were set before the student. Robert, whose long experience of university life made him thoroughly competent to advise, said:

"The student who wishes to make progress ought to observe six essential rules.

"First: He ought to consecrate a certain hour every day to the study of a determined subject, as St. Bernard counselled his monks in his letter to the Brothers of the Mont Dieu.

"Second: He ought to concentrate his attention upon what he reads and ought not to let it pass lightly. There is between reading and study, as St. Bernard says, the same difference as between a host and a guest, between a passing salutation exchanged in the street and an embrace prompted by an unalterable affection.

"Third: He ought to extract from the daily study one thought, some truth or other, and engrave it deeply upon his memory with special care. Seneca said *'Cum multa percurreris in die, unum tibi elige quod illa die excoquas'*— When you have run over many things in a day select one for yourself which you should digest well on that day.

"Fourth: Write a resume of it, for words which are not confided to writing fly as does the dust before the wind.

"Fifth: Talk the matter over with your fellow-students, either in the regular recitation or in your familiar conversation. This exercise is even more profitable than study for it has as its result the clarifying of all doubts and the removing of all the obscurity that study may have left. Nothing is perfectly known unless it has been tried by the tooth of disputation.

"Sixth: Pray, for this is indeed one of the best ways of learning. St. Bernard teaches that study ought to touch the heart and that one should profit by it always by elevating the heart to God, *without, however, interrupting the study.*"

Sorbonne proceeds in a tone that vividly recalls the modern university professor who has seen generation after generation of students and has learned to realize how many of them waste their time.

"Certain students act like fools; they display great subtility over nonsensical subjects and exhibit themselves devoid of intelligence with regard to their most important studies. So as not to seem to have lost their time they gather together many sheets of parchment, make thick volumes of note books out of them, with many a blank interval, and cover them with elegant binding in red letters. Then they return to the paternal domicile with their little sack filled up with knowledge which can be stolen from them by any thief that comes along, or may be eaten by rats or by worms or destroyed by fire or water.

"In order to acquire instruction the student must abstain from pleasure and not allow himself to be hampered by material cares. There was at Paris not long since two teachers who were great friends. One of them had seen much, had read much and used to remain night and day bent over his books. He scarcely took the time to say an 'Our Father.' Nevertheless he had but four students. His colleague possessed a much less complete library, was less devoted to study and heard mass every morning before delivering his lecture. In spite of this, his classroom was full. 'How do you do it?' asked his friend. 'It is very simple,' said his friend smiling. 'God studies for me. I go to mass and when I come back I know by heart all that I have to teach.' "

"Meditation," so Sorbonne continues, "is suitable not only for the master, but the good student ought also to go and take his promenade along the banks of the Seine, not to play there, but in order to repeat his lesson and meditate upon it."

These instructions for students are not very different from those that would be issued by an interested head of a university department to the freshmen of the present day. His insistence, especially on the difference between reading and study, might very well be taken to heart at the present time, when there seems to be some idea that reading of itself is sufficient to enable one to obtain an education. The lesson of learning one thing a day and learning that well, might have been selected as a motto for students for all succeeding generations with manifest advantage to the success of college study.

In other things Sorbonne departs further from our modern ideas in the matter of education, but still there are many even at the present time who will read with profound sympathy his emphatic advice to the University students that they must educate their hearts as well as their intellects, and make their education subserve the purpose of bringing them closer to God.

A word about certain customs that prevailed more or less generally in the universities at this time, and that after having been much misunderstood will now be looked at more sympathetically in the light of recent educational developments will not be out of place here.

One of the advantages of modern German university education has often been acclaimed to be the fact that students are tempted to make portions of their studies in various cities, since all the courses are equalized in certain ways, so that the time spent at any one of them will be counted properly for their degrees. It has long been recognized that travel makes the best possible complement to a university course, and even when the English universities in the Eighteenth Century sank to be little more than pleasant abiding places where young men of the upper classes "ate their terms," the fact that it was the custom "to make the grand tour" of continental travel, supplied for much that was lacking in the serious side of their education. Little as this might be anticipated as a feature of the ruder times of the Thirteenth Century, when travel was so difficult, it must be counted as one of the great advantages for the inquiring spirits of the time. Dante, besides attending the universities in Italy, and he certainly was at several of them, was also at Paris at one time and probably also at Oxford. Professor Monroe in his text book in the History of Education has stated this custom very distinctly.

"With the founding of the universities and the establishment of the nations in practically every university, it became quite customary for students to travel from university to university, finding in each a home in their appropriate nation. Many, however, willing to accept the privileges of the clergy and the students without undertaking their obligations, adopted this wandering life as a permanent one. Being a privileged order, they readily found a living, or made it by begging. A monk of the early university period writes: 'The scholars are accustomed to wander throughout the whole world and visit all the cities, and their many studies bring them understanding. For in Paris they seek a knowledge of the liberal arts; of the ancient writers at Orleans; of medicine at Salernum; of the black art at Toledo; and in no place decent manners.' "

With regard to the old monk's criticism it must be remembered that old age is always rather depreciative in criticism of the present and over-appreciative of what happened in the past *se pueris.* Abuses always seem to be creeping in that are going to ruin the force of education, yet somehow the next generation succeeds in obtaining its intellectual development in rather good shape. Besides as we must always remember in educational questions, evils are ever exaggerated and the memory of them is prone to live longer and to loom up larger than that of the good with which they were associated and to which indeed, as anyone of reasonable experience in educational circles knows, they may constitute by comparison only a very small amount. Undoubtedly the wanderings of students brought with it many abuses, and if we were to listen to . some of the stories of foreign student life in Paris in our own time, we might think that much of evil and nothing of good was accomplished by such wandering, but inasmuch as we do so we invite serious error of judgment.

Another striking feature of university life which constituted a distinct anticipation of something very modern in our educational system, was the lending of professors of different nationalities among the universities. It is only at the beginning of the Twentieth Century that we have reestablished this custom. In the Thirteenth Century, however, Albertus Magnus taught for a time at Cologne and then later at Paris and apparently also at Rome. St. Thomas of Aquin, after having taught for a time at Paris, lectured in various Italian universities and then finally at the University of Rome to which he was tempted by the Popes. Duns Scotus, besides teaching in Oxford, taught also at Paris. Alexander of Hales before him seems to have done the same thing. Roger Bacon, after studying at the University of Paris, seems to have commenced teaching there, though most of his professional work was accomplished at the University of Oxford. Raymond Lully probably had professional experiences at several Spanish Universities besides at Paris. In a word, if a man were a distinguished genius he was almost sure to be given the opportunity to influence his generation at a number of centers of educational life, and not be confined as has been the case in the centuries since to but one or at most, and that more by accident than intent, to perhaps two. In a word there is not a distinctive feature of modern university life that was not anticipated in the Thirteenth Century.

FLYING BUTTRESS (AMIENS)

IV

THE NUMBER OF STUDENTS AND DISCIPLINE.

For most people the surprise of finding that the subjects with which the students were occupied at the universities of the Thirteenth Century were very much the same as those which claim the attention of modern students, will probably be somewhat mitigated by the thought that after all there were only few in attendance at the universities, and as a consequence only a small proportion of the population shared in that illumination, which has become so universal in the spread of opportunities for the higher education in these later times.   While such an impression is cherished by many even of those who think that they know the history of education, and unfortunately are considered *by others* to be authorities on the subject, it is the falsest possible idea that could be conceived of this medieval time with which we are concerned.   We may say at once that it is a matter of comparatively easy collation of statistics to show, that in proportion to the population of the various countries, there were actually more students taking advantage of the opportunity to acquire university education in the Thirteenth Century, than there were at any time in the Nineteenth Century, or even in the midst of this era of widespread educational opportunities in the Twentieth Century.

Most people know the traditions which declare that there were between twenty and thirty thousand students at the University of Paris toward the end of the Thirteenth Century.   At the same time there were said to have been between fifteen and twenty thousand students at the University of Bologna.   Correspondingly large numbers have been reported for the University of Oxford and many thousands were supposed to be in attendance at the University of Cambridge.   It is usually considered, however, that these figures are gross exaggerations. It is easy to assert this but rather difficult to prove.   As a matter of fact the nearer one comes to the actual times in the

history of education, the more definitely do writers speak
of these large numbers of students in attendance. For instance
Gascoigne, who says that there were thirty thousand students at
the University of Oxford at the end of the Thirteenth Century,
lived himself within a hundred years of the events of which he
talks, and he even goes so far as to declare that he saw the
rolls of the University containing this many names. There is
no doubt at all about his evidence in the matter and there is no
mistake possible with regard to his figures. They were written out in Latin, not expressed in Arabic or Roman numerals,
the copying of which might so easily give opportunities for
error to creep in.

In spite of such evidence it is generally conceded that to accept these large numbers would be almost surely a mistake.
There were without any doubt many thousands of students at
the Thirteenth Century universities. There were certainly
more students at the University of Paris in the last quarter of
the Thirteenth Century than there were at any time during the
Nineteenth Century. This of itself is enough to startle modern
complacency out of most of its ridiculous self-sufficiency.
There can be scarcely a doubt that the University of Bologna
at the time of its largest attendance had more students than any
university of modern times, proud as we may be (and deservedly) of our immense institutions of learning. With regard to
the English universities the presence of very large
numbers is much more doubtful. Making every allowance, however, there can be no hesitation in saying that Oxford had during the last quarter of the
Thirteenth Century a larger number than ever afterwards within her walls and that Cambridge, though never so
numerous as her rival, had a like good fortune. Professor
Laurie of Edinburgh, a very conservative authority and one not
likely to concede too much to the Middle Ages in anything,
would allow, as we shall see, some ten thousand students to
Oxford. Others have claimed more than half that number for
Cambridge as the lowest possible estimate. Even if it be conceded, as has sometimes been urged, that all those in service in
the universities were also counted as students, these numbers
would not be reduced very materially and it must not be forgot-

ten that, in those days of enthusiastic striving after education, young men were perfectly willing to take up even the onerous duties of personal services to others, in order to have the opportunity to be closely in touch with a great educational institution and to receive even a moderate amount of benefit from its educational system. In our own time there are many students who are working their way through the universities, and in the Thirteenth Century when the spirit of independence was much less developed, and when any stigma that attached to personal service was much less felt than it is at the present time, there were many more examples of this earnest striving for intellectual development.

If we discuss the situation in English-speaking countries as regards the comparative attendance at the universities in the Thirteenth Century and in our own time, we shall be able to get a reasonably good idea of what must be thought in this matter. The authorities are neither difficult of consultation nor distant, and comparatively much more is known about the population of England at this time than about most of the continental countries. England was under a single ruler, while the geographical divisions that we now know by the name of France, Spain, Italy and Germany were the seats of several rulers at least and sometimes of many, a circumstance which does not favor our obtaining an adequate idea of the populations.

That but two universities provided all the opportunities for whatever higher education there was in England at this time, would of itself seem to stamp the era as backward in educational matters. A little consideration of the comparative number of students with reference to the population of the country who were thus given the opportunity for higher education—and took advantage of it—at that time and the present, will show the unreasonableness of such an opinion. It is not so easy as might be imagined to determine just what was the population even of England in the Thirteenth Century. During Elizabeth's reign there were, according to the census, an estimate made about the time of the great Armada, altogether some four millions of people. Froude accepts this estimate as representing very well the actual number of the population. Certainly there were not more than five millions at the end of the Sixteenth Century. Lingard, who for this purpose must be considered as a thoroughly conservative authority, estimates that there were not much more than two millions of people in England at the end of the Twelfth Century. This is probably not an underestimate. At the end of the Thirteenth Century there were not many more than two millions and a half of people in the country. At the very outside there were, let us say, three millions. Out of this meagre population, ten thousand students were, on the most conservative estimate, taking advantage of the opportunities for the higher education that were provided for them at the universities.

At the present moment, though we pride ourselves on the numbers in attendance at our universities, and though the world's population is so much more numerous and the means of transportation so much more easy, we have very few universities as large as these of the Thirteenth Century. No American university at the present moment has as large a number of students as had Oxford at the end of the Thirteenth Century, and of course none of them compares at all with Paris or Bologna in this respect. Even the European universities, as we have suggested, fall behind their former glory from this standpoint. In the attendance to the number of population the comparison is even more startling for those who have not thought at all of the Middle Ages as a time of wonderful educational facilities and opportunities. In the greater City of New York as we begin the Twentieth Century there are perhaps fifteen thousand students in attendance at educational institutions which have university privileges. I may say that this is a very liberal allowance. At universities in the ordinary sense of the word there are not more than ten thousand students and the remainder is added in order surely to include all those who may be considered as doing undergraduate work in colleges and schools of various kinds. Of these fifteen thousand at least one-fourth come from outside of the greater city, and there are some who think that even one-third would not be too large a number to calculate as not being drawn directly from our own population. Connecticut and New Jersey furnish large numbers of students and then, besides, the post-graduate schools of the universities have very large numbers in attendance even from distant states and foreign countries.

It will be within the bounds of truth, then, to say, that there are between ten and twelve thousand students, out of our population of more than four millions in Greater New York taking advantage of the opportunities for the higher education provided by our universities and colleges. At the end of the Thirteenth Century in England there were at least ten thousand students out of a population of not more and very probably less than three millions, who were glad to avail themselves of similar opportunities. This seems to be perfectly fair comparison and we have tried to be as conservative as possible in every way in order to bring out the truth in the matter.

It can scarcely fail to be a matter of supreme surprise to find that a century so distant as the Thirteenth, should thus equal our own vaunted Twentieth Century in the matter of opportunities for the higher education afforded and taken advantage of. It has always been presumed that the Middle Ages, while a little better than the Dark Ages, were typical periods in which there was little, if any desire for higher education and even fewer opportunities. It was thought that there was constant repression of the desire for knowledge which springs so eternally in the human heart and that the Church, or at least the ecclesiastical authorities of the time, set themselves firmly against widespread education, because it would set people to thinking for themselves. As a matter of fact, however, every Cathedral and every monastery became a center of educational influence, and even the poorest, who showed special signs of talent, obtained the opportunity to secure knowledge to the degree that they wished. It is beyond doubt or cavil, that at no time in the world's history have so many opportunities for the higher education been open to all classes as during the Thirteenth Century.

In order to show how thoroughly conservative are the numbers in attendance at the universities that I have taken, I shall quote two good recent authorities, one of them Professor Laurie, the Professor of the Institutes and History of Education in the University of Edinburgh, and the other Thomas Davidson, a well-known American authority on educational subjects. Each of their works from which I shall quote has been published or revised within the last few years. Professor Laurie in "The Rise and Early Constitution of the University with a Survey of the Medieval Education," which formed one of the International Educational Series, edited by Commissioner Harris and published by Appleton, said:

"When one hears of the large number of students who attended the earliest universities—ten thousand and even twenty thousand at Bologna, an equal, and at one time a greater, number at Paris, and thirty thousand at Oxford—one cannot help thinking that the numbers have been exaggerated. There is certainly evidence that the Oxford attendance was never so great as has been alleged (see Anstey's 'Mon Acad.'); but when we consider that attendants, servitors, college cooks, etc., were regarded as members of the university community, and that the universities provided for a time the sole recognized training grounds for those wishing to enter the ecclesiastical or legal or teaching professions, I see no reason to doubt the substantial accuracy of the tradition as to attendance—especially when we remember that at Paris and Oxford a large number were mere boys of from twelve to fifteen years of age."

As to the inclusion of servitors, we have already said that many, probably, indeed, most of them, were actual students working their way through the university in these enthusiastic days. Professor Laurie's authority for the assertion that a large number of the students at Paris and Oxford were mere boys, is a regulation known to have existed at one of these universities requiring that students should not be less than twelve years of age. Anyone who has studied medieval university life, however, will have been impressed with the idea, that the students were on the average older at the medieval universities rather than younger than they are at the present time. The rough hazing methods employed, almost equal to those of our own day! would seem to indicate this. Besides, as Professor Laurie confesses in the next paragraph, many of the students were actually much older than at present. Our university courses are arranged for young men between 17 and 22, but that is, to fall back on Herbert Spencer, presumably because the period of infancy is lengthening with the evolution of the race. There are many who consider that at the present time students are too long delayed in the opportunity to get at the professional studies, and that it is partly the consequence of this that the practical branches are so much more taken up under the elective system. As we said in the chapter on Universities and Preparatory Schools, in Italy and in other southern countries, it is not a surprising thing to have a young man graduate at the age of 16 or 17 with his degree of A. B., after a thoroughly creditable scholastic career. This means that he began his university work proper under 13 years of age; so that we must judge the medieval universities to some extent at least with this thought in mind.

Mr. Thomas Davidson in his "History of Education,"* in the chapter on The Medieval University has a paragraph in which he discusses the attendance, especially during the Thirteenth Century, and admits that the numbers, while perhaps not so large as have been reported, were very large in comparison to modern institutions of the same kind, and frankly concedes that education rose during these centuries which are often supposed to have been so unfavorable to educational development, to an amazing height scarcely ever surpassed. He says:

"The number of students reported as having attended some of the universities in those early days almost passes belief; *e. g.,* Oxford is said to have had thirty thousand about the year 1300, and half that number even as early as 1224. The numbers attending the University of Paris were still greater. These numbers become less surprising when we remember with what poor accommodations—a bare room and an armful of straw— the students of those days were content, and what numbers of them even a single teacher like Abelard could, long before, draw into lonely retreats. That in the Twelfth and following centuries there was no lack of enthusiasm for study, notwithstanding the troubled condition of the times, is very clear. The instruction given at the universities, moreover, reacted upon the lower schools, raising their standard and supplying them with competent teachers. Thus, in the Thirteenth and Four-

* A History of Education, by Thomas Davidson, author of Aristotle and Ancient Educational Ideas. New York: Scribners, 1900.

CHRIST DRIVING OUT MONEY
CHANGERS (GIOTTO)

HEAD FROM ANNUNCIATION (GIOTTO)

BRIDE MARRIAGE AT CANA (GIOTTO)

SAINT'S HEAD (MOSAIC,
ST. MARK'S, VENICE)

teenth centuries, education rose in many European states to a height which it had not attained since the days of Seneca and Quintilian."

A very serious objection that would seem to have so much weight as to preclude all possibility of accepting as true the large numbers mentioned, is the fact that it is very hard to understand how such an immense number of students could have been supported in any town of the Middle Ages. This objection has carried so much weight to some minds as to make them give up the thought of large numbers at the medieval universities. Professor Laurie has answered it very effectively, however, and in his plausible explanation gives a number of points which emphasize the intense ardor of these students of the Middle Ages in their search for knowledge, and shows how ready they were to bear serious trials and inconveniences, not to say absolute sufferings and hardships, in order that they might have opportunities for the higher education. The objection then redounds rather to the glory of the medieval universities than lessens their prestige, either as regards numbers or the enthusiasm of their students.

"The chief objection to accepting the tradition (of large numbers at the universities) lies in the difficulty of seeing how in those days, so large a number of the young men of Europe could afford the expense of residence away from their homes. This difficulty, however, is partly removed when we know that many of the students were well to do, that a considerable number were matured men, already monks and canons, and that the endowments of Cathedral schools also were frequently used to enable promising scholars to attend foreign universities. Monasteries also regularly sent boys of thirteen and fourteen to university seats. A papal instruction of 1335 required every Benedictine and Augustinian community to send boys to the universities in the proportion of one in twenty of their residents. Then, state authorities ordered free passages for all who were wending their way through the country to and from the seat of learning. In the houses of country priests—not to speak of the monastery hospitals—traveling scholars were always accommodated gratuitously, and even local subscriptions were frequently made to help them on their way. Poor traveling scholars were, in fact, a medieval institution, and it was considered no disgrace for a student to beg and receive alms for his support."

After reading these authoritative opinions, it would be rather difficult to understand the false impressions which have obtained so commonly for the last three centuries with regard to education in the Middle Ages, if we did not realize that history, especially for English-speaking people, has for several centuries been written from a very narrow standpoint and with a very definite purpose. About a century ago the Comte de Maistre said in his Soirées de St. Petersburg, that history for the three hundred years before his time "had been a conspiracy against the truth." Curiously enough the editors of the Cambridge Modern History in their first volume on the Renaissance, re-echoed this sentiment of the French historical writer and philosopher. They even use the very words "history has been a conspiracy against the truth" and proclaim that if we are to get at truth in this generation, we must go behind all the classical historians, and look up contemporary documents and evidence and authorities once more for ourselves. It is the maintenance of a tradition that nothing good could possibly have come out of the Nazareth of the times before the Reformation, that has led to this serious misapprehension of the true position of those extremely important centuries in modern education—the Thirteenth and the Fourteenth.

To those who know even a little of what was accomplished in these centuries, it is supremely amusing to read the childish treatment accorded them and the trivial remarks that even accredited historians of education make with regard to them. Occasionally, however, the feeling of the reader who knows something of the subject is not one of amusement, but far from it. There are times when one cannot help but feel that it is not ignorance, but a deliberate purpose to minimize the importance of these times in culture and education, that is at the basis of some of the utterly mistaken remarks that are made. We shall take occasion only to give one example of this, but that will afford ample evidence of the intolerant spirit that characterizes the work of some even of the supposedly most enlightened historians of education. The quotation will be from Compayré's

"History of Pedagogy" which is, I understand, in use in nearly every Normal School in this country and is among the books required in many Normal School examinations.

M. Compayré in an infamous paragraph which bears the title "The Intellectual Feebleness of the Middle Age," furnishes an excellent example of how utterly misunderstood, if not deliberately misrepresented, has been the whole spirit and content and the real progressiveness of education in this wonderful period. After some belittling expressions as to the influence of Christianity on education—expressions utterly unjustified by the facts—he has this to say with regard to the Thirteenth Century, which is all the more surprising because it is the only place where he calls any attention to it. He says:

"In 1291, of all the monks in the convent of St. Gall, there was not one who could read and write. It was so difficult to find notaries public, that acts had to be passed verbally. The barons took pride in their ignorance. Even after the efforts of the Twelfth Century, instruction remained a luxury for the common people; it was the privilege of the ecclesiastics and even they did not carry it very far. The Benedictines confess that the mathematics were studied only for the purpose of calculating the date of Easter."

This whole paragraph of M. Compayré (the rest must be read to be appreciated), whose history of education was considered to be of such value that it was deemed worthy of translation by the President of a State Normal School and that it has been adopted as a work of reference, in some cases of required study, in many of the Normal Schools throughout the country, is a most wonderful concoction of ingredients, all of which are meant to dissolve every possible idea that people might have of the existence of any tincture of education during the Middle Ages. There is only one fact which deeply concerns us because it refers to the Thirteenth Century. M. Compayré says that in 1291 of all the monks of the Convent of Saint Gall there was not one who could read and write. This single fact is meant to sum up the education of the century for the reader. Especially it is meant to show the student of pedagogy how deeply sunk in ignorance were the monks and all the ecclesiastics of this period.

Before attempting to say anything further it may be as well to call attention to the fact that in the original French edition the writer did not say that there was not a single monk. He said, "There was but one monk, who could read and write." Possibly it seemed to the translator to make the story more complete to leave out this one poor monk and perhaps one monk more or less, especially a medieval monk, may not count for very much to modern students of education. There are those of us, however, who consider it too bad to obliterate even a single monk in this crude way and we ask that he shall be put back. There *was one* who could read and write and carry on the affairs of the monastery. Let us have him at least, by all means.

In the year 1291 when M. Compayré says that there was but a single monk at the monastery of St. Gall who could read and write, he, a professor himself at a French Normal School, must have known very well that there were over twenty thousand students at the University of Paris, almost as many at the University of Bologna, and over five thousand, some authorities say many more than this (Professor Laurie would admit more than ten thousand), at the University of Oxford, though all Christian Europe at this time did not have a population of more than 15,000,000 people. He must have known, too, or be hopelessly ignorant in educational matters, that many of the students at these universities belonged to the Franciscans and Dominicans, and that indeed many of the greatest teachers at the universities were members of these monastic orders. Of this he says nothing, however. All that he says is "Education was the privilege of the ecclesiastics and they did not carry it very far." This is one way of writing a history of education. It is a very effective way of poisoning the wells of information and securing the persistence of the tradition that there was no education until after the beginning of the Sixteenth Century.

Meantime one can scarcely help but admire the ingenuity of deliberate purpose that uses the condition of the monastery of St. Gall to confirm his statement. St. Gall had been founded by Irish monks probably about the beginning of the Eighth Century. It had been for at least three centuries a center of education, civilization and culture, as well as of religion, for the

barbarians who had settled in the Swiss country after the trans-
migration of nations. The Irish had originally obtained their
culture from Christian Missionaries, and now as Christian Missionaries they brought it back to Europe and accomplished their
work with wonderful effectiveness. St. Gall was for centuries
a lasting monument to their efforts. After the Tenth Century,
however, the monastery began to degenerate. It was almost
directly in the path of armies which so frequently went down to
Italy because of the German interest in the Italian peninsula
and the claims of the German emperor. After a time according
to tradition, the emperor insisted that certain of the veterans
of his army should be received and cared for in their old age at
St. Gall. Gradually this feature of the institution became more
and more prominent until in the Thirteenth Century it had become little more than a home for old soldiers. In order to live
on the benefices of the monastery these men had to submit to
ecclesiastical regulations and wear the habit. They were, it is
true, a sort of monk, that is, they were willing, for the sake of
the peace and ease which it brought, to accept the living thus
provided for them and obey to some degree at least the rules of
the monastery. It is not surprising that among these there
should have been only one who could read and write. The soldiers of the time despised the men of letters and prided themselves on not being able to write. That a historian of pedagogy,
however, should take this one fact in order to give students an
idea of the depth of ignorance of the Middle Ages, is an exhibition of some qualities in our modern educated men, that one
does not like to think of as compatible with the capacity to
read and write. It would indeed be better not to be able to
read and write than thus to read and write one's own prejudices
into history, and above all the history of education.

Compayré's discussion of the "Causes of the Ignorance" of
the Middle Ages in the next paragraph, is one of the most curious bits of special pleading by a man who holds a brief for one
side of the question, that I think has ever been seen in what was
to be considered serious history. He first makes it clear how
much opposed the Christian Church was to education, then he
admits that she did some things which cannot be denied, but
minimizes their significance. Then he concludes that it was not

the fault of the Church, but in this there is a precious bit of damning by faint praise. It would be impossible for any ordinary person who had only Compayré for authority to feel anything after reading the paragraph, but that Christianity was a serious detriment and surely not a help to the cause of progress in education. I quote part of the paragraph:

"What were the permanent causes of that situation which lasted for ten centuries? The Catholic Church has sometimes been held responsible for this. Doubtless the Christian doctors did not always profess a very warm sympathy for intellectual culture. Saint Augustine has said: It is the ignorant who gain possession of heaven (indocti coelum rapiunt.) Saint Gregory the Great, a Pope of the Sixth Century, declared that he would blush to have the holy word conform to the rules of grammar. Too many Christians, in a word, confounded ignorance with holiness. Doubtless, towards the Seventh Century, the darkness still hung thick over the Christian Church. Barbarians invaded the Episcopate, and carried with them their rude manners. Doubtless, also, during the feudal period the priest often became a soldier, and remained ignorant. It would, however, be unjust to bring a constructive charge against the Church of the Middle Age, and to represent it as systematically hostile to instruction. Directly to the contrary, it is the clergy who, in the midst of the general barbarism, preserved some vestiges of the ancient culture. The only schools of that period are the Episcopal and claustral schools, the first annexed to the Bishops' palaces, the second to the monasteries. The religious orders voluntarily associated manual labor with mental labor. As far back as 530, St. Benedict founded the Convent of Monte Cassino, and drew up statutes which made reading and intellectual labor a part of the daily life of the monks." When this damning by faint praise is taken in connection with the paragraph in which only a single monk at the Monastery of St. Gall is declared to have been able to read and write, the utterly false impression that is sure to result, can be readily understood even by those who are not sympathetic students of the Middle Ages. This is how our histories of education have been written as a rule, and as a consequence the most precious period in modern education, its great origin, has been ignored even by

PERTRARCA OMNIUM VIRTUTUM
MONARCA

DANTE THEOLOGUS NULLIUS
DOGMATIS EXPERS

Portraits
Bennozo Gozzoli

GIOTTO, PICTOR EXIMIUS (PORTRAITS
BENOZZO GOZZOLI)

professional scholars, to the great detriment not only of historical knowledge but also of any proper appreciation of the evolution of education.

It will be said by those who do not appreciate the conditions that existed in the Middle Ages, that these numbers at the universities seeking the higher education, mean very little for the culture of the people, since practically all of those in attendance at the universities belonged to the clerical order. There is no doubt that most students were clerics in the Thirteenth Century. This did not mean, however, that they had taken major orders or had in any way bound themselves irrevocably to continue in the clerical vocation. The most surprising thing about the spread of culture and the desire for the higher education during the Thirteenth Century, is that they developed in spite of the fact that the rulers of the time were all during the century, embroiled in war either with their neighbors or with the nobility. Anyone who wanted to live a quiet, intellectual life turned naturally to the clerical state, which enabled him to escape military duties and gave him opportunities for study, as well as protection from many exactions that might otherwise be levied upon him. The church not only encouraged education, but supplied the peaceful asylums in which it might be cultivated to the heart's content of the student.

While this clerical state was a necessity during the whole time of residence at the university, it was not necessarily maintained afterward. Many of the clerics did not even have minor orders—orders which it is well understood carry with them no absolute obligation of continuing in the clerical state. Sextons and their assistants were clerics. When the word canon originally came into use it meant nothing more than that the man was entered on the rolls of a church and received some form of wages therefrom. Students at the universities were by ecclesiastical courtesy then, clerics (from which comes the word clerk, one who can read and write) though not in orders, and it was because of this that the university was able to maintain the rights of students. It was well understood that after graduation men might take up the secular life and indeed most of them did. In succeeding chapters we shall see examples of this and discuss the question further. Professors at the universities had to maintain their clerical condition so that even professors of law and of medicine were not allowed to marry. This law continued long beyond the Thirteenth Century, however. Professors of medicine were the first to be freed from the obligation of celibacy, but not until the middle of the Fifteenth Century at Paris, while other professors were bound thus for a full century later. Certain minor teaching positions at Oxford are still under this law, which evidently has seemed to have some advantage or it would not have been maintained.

It might perhaps be thought that only the wealthier class, the sons of the nobility and of the wealthy merchants of the cities had opportunities at the universities. As a matter of fact, however, the vast majority of the students was drawn from the great middle class. The nobility were nearly always too occupied with their pleasures and their martial duties to have time for the higher education. The tradition that a nobleman should be an educated gentleman had not yet come in. Indeed many of the nobility during the Thirteenth Century rather prided themselves on the fact that they not only had no higher education, but that they did not know even how to read and write. When we reflect, then, on the large numbers who went to the universities, it adds to our surprise to realize that they were drawn from the burgher class. It is evident that many of the sons even of the poor were afforded opportunities in different ways at the universities of the time.

Tradition shows that from the earliest time there were foundations on which poor students could live, and various arrangements were made by which, aside from these, they might make their living while continuing their studies. Working one's way through the university was more common in the Thirteenth Century than it is at the present day, though we are proud of the large numbers who now succeed in the double task of supporting and educating themselves, with excellent success in both enterprises. There are many stories of poor students who found themselves about to be obliged to give up their studies, encountering patrons of various kinds who enabled them to go on with their education.

There is a very pretty set of legends with regard to St. Edmund of Canterbury in this matter. He bears this name because he was afterward the sainted primate of England. For many years he taught at the University of Oxford. The story is told of a clerical friend sending him up a student to Oxford and asking that his bills be sent to him. St. Edmund's answer was that he would not be robbed of an opportunity of doing good like this, and he took upon himself the burden of caring for the student. At the time there were many others dependent on his bounty and his reputation was such that he was enabled to help a great many through the benefactions of friends, who found no higher pleasure in life than being able to come generously to Edmund's assistance in his charities.

Those who know the difficulty of managing very large bodies of students will wonder inevitably, how the medieval universities, with their less formal and less complete organizations, succeeded in maintaining discipline for all these thousands of students. Most people will remember at once all the stories of roughness, of horse play, of drinking and gaming or worse that they have heard of the medieval students and will be apt to conclude that they are not to be wondered at after all, since it must have been practically impossible for the faculties of universities to keep order among such vast numbers. As a matter of fact, however, the story of the origin and maintenance of discipline in these universities is one of the most interesting features of university life. The process of discipline became in itself a very precious part of education, as it should be of course in any well regulated institution of learning. The very fact, moreover, that in spite of these large numbers and other factors that we shall call attention to in a moment, comparatively so few disgraceful stories of university life have come down to us, and the other and still more important fact that the universities could be kept so constantly at the attainment of their great purpose for such numbers, is itself a magnificent tribute to those who succeeded in doing it, and to the system which was gradually evolved, not by the faculty alone but by teachers and students for university government.

With regard to the discipline of the medieval universities not much is known and considerable of what has been written on this obscure subject wears an unfavorable tinge, because it is unfortunately true that "the good men do is oft interred with their bones" while the evil has an immortality all its own. The student escapades of the universities, the quarrels between town and gown, the stories of the evils apparently inevitable, where many young men are congregated—the hazing, the rough horse play, the carousing, the immoralities—have all come down to us, while it is easy to miss the supreme significance of the enthusiasm for learning that in these difficult times gathered so many students together from distant parts of the world, when traveling was so difficult and dangerous, and kept them at the universities for long years in spite of the hardships and inconveniences of the life. With regard to our modern universities the same thing is true, and the outside world knows much more of the escapades of the few, the little scandals of college life, that scarcely make a ripple but are so easily exaggerated, and so frequently repeated and lose nothing by repetition, the waste of time in athletics, in gambling, in social things, than of the earnest work and the successful intellectual progress and interests of the many. This should be quite enough to make the modern university man very slow to accept the supposed pictures of medieval student life, which are founded mainly on the worse side of it. Goodness is proverbially uninteresting, a happy people has no history and the ordinary life of the university student needs a patient sympathetic chronicler; and such the medieval universities have not found as yet. But they do not need many allowances, if it will only be remembered under what discouragements they labored and how much they accomplished.

The reputation of the medieval universities has suffered from this very human tendency to be interested in what is evil and to neglect the good. Even as it is, however, a good deal with regard to the discipline of the universities in the early times is known and does not lose in interest from the fact, that the main factor in it was a committee of the students themselves working in conjunction with the faculty, and thus anticipating what is most modern in the development of the disciplinary regime of our up-to-date universities. At first apparently, in the schools from which the universities originated there was no thought of the necessity for discipline. The desire for education was considered to be sufficient to keep men occupied in such a way that further discipline would not be necessary. It can readily be understood that the crowds that flocked to hear Abelard in Paris, and who were sufficiently interested to follow him out to the Desert of the Paraclete when he was no longer allowed to continue his lectures in connection with the school at Paris, would have quite enough of ruling from the internal forum of their supreme interest, not to need any discipline in the external forum.

In the course of time, however, with the coming of even greater numbers to the University of Paris, and especially when the attendance ran up into many thousands, some form of school discipline became an absolute necessity. This developed of itself and in a very practical way. The masters seem to have had very little to do with it at the beginning since they occupied themselves entirely with their teaching and preparation for lectures. What was to become later one of the principal instruments of discipline was at first scarcely more than a social organization among the students. Those who came from different countries were naturally attracted to one another, and were more ready to help each other. When students first came they were welcomed by their compatriots who took care to keep them from being imposed upon, enabled them to secure suitable quarters and introduced them to university customs generally, so that they might be able to take advantage, as soon as possible, of the educational opportunities.

The friendships thus fostered gradually grew into formal organizations, the so-called "nations." These began to take form just before the beginning of the Thirteenth Century. They made it their duty to find lodgings for their student compatriots, and evidently also to supply food on some cooperative plan for at least the poorer students. Whenever students of a particular nationality were injured in any way, their "nation" as a formal organization took up their cause and maintained their rights, even to the extent of an appeal to formal process of law before the magistrates, if necessary. The nations were organized before the faculties in the universities were formally recognized as independent divisions of the institution, and they acted as intermediaries between the university head and the students, making themselves responsible for discipline to no slight de-

gree. At the beginning of the Thirteenth Century in Paris all
the students belonged to one or other of four nations, the
Picard, the Norman, the French, which embraced Italians,
Spaniards, Greeks and Orientals, and the English which embraced the English, Irish, Germans, Poles (heterogeneous collection we would consider it in these modern days) and in addition all other students from the North of Europe.

Professor Laurie, of the University of Edinburgh, in his Rise
and Early Constitution of Universities in the International
Educational Series* says:

"The subdivisions of the nations were determined by the lo-
calities from which the students and masters came. Each sub-
division elected its own dean, and kept its own matriculation-
book and money-chest. The whole "nation" was represented, it
is true, by the elected procurators; but the deans of the subdivisions were regarded as important officials, and were frequently, if not always, assessors of the procurators. The procurators, four in number, were elected, not by the students as
in Bologna and Padua, but by the students and masters. Each
nation with its procurator and deans was an independent body,
passing its own statutes and rules, and exercising supervision
over the lodging-houses of the students. They had each a seal
as distinguished from the university seal, and each procurator
stood to his "nation" in the same relation as the Rector did to
the whole university. The Rector, again, was elected by the
procurators, who sat as his assessors, and together they constituted the governing body; but this for purposes of discipline,
protection and defense of privileges chiefly, the *consortium
magistrorum* regulating the schools. But so independent were
the nations that the question whether each had power to make
statutes that overrode those of the *universitas,* was still a question so late as the beginning of the Seventeenth Century."

It is typical of the times that the governing system should
thus have grown up of itself and from amongst the students,
rather than that it should have been organized by the teachers

*The Rise and Early Constitution of Universities, with a survey of
Medieval Education, by S. S. Laurie, LL.D., Professor of the Insti-
tutes and History of Education in the University of Edinburgh. New
York, D. Appleton & Company, 1901.

and imposed upon the university. The nations represented the rise of that democratic spirit, which was to make itself felt in the claims for the recognition of rights for all the people in most of the countries during the Thirteenth Century, and undoubtedly the character of the government of the student body at the universities fostered this spirit and is therefore to a noteworthy degree, responsible for the advances in the direction of liberty which are chronicled during this great century. This was a form of unconscious education but none the less significant for that, and eminently practical in its results. At this time in Europe there was no place where the members of the community who flocked in largest numbers to the universities, the sons of the middle classes, could have any opportunities to share in government or learn the precious lessons of such participation, except at the universities. There gradually came an effort on the part of the faculties to lessen many of the rights of the nations of the universities, but the very struggle to maintain these on the part of the student body, was of itself a precious training against the usurpation of privileges that was to be of great service later in the larger arena of national politics, and the effects of which can be noted in every country in Europe, nowhere more than in England, where the development of law and liberty was to give rise to a supreme heritage of democratic jurisprudence for the English speaking peoples of all succeeding generations.

V

POST-GRADUATE WORK AT THE UNIVERSITIES.

In modern times it has often been said that no university can be considered to be doing its proper work unless, besides teaching, it is also adding to the existing body of knowledge by original research. Because of unfortunate educational traditions, probably the last thing in the world that would enter into the minds of most people to conceive as likely to be found in the history of the universities of the Thirteenth Century, would be original research in any form. In spite of this almost universal false impression, original work of the most valuable kind, for much of which workers would be considered as amply deserving of their doctorates in the various faculties of the post-graduate departments of the most up-to-date of modern universities, was constantly being accomplished during this wonderful century. It is, as a matter of fact, with this phase of university activity that the modern educator is sure to have more sympathy than with any other, once the significant details of the work become clear.

All surprise that surpassing original work was accomplished will cease when it is recalled that, besides creating the universities themselves, this century gave us the great Cathedrals— a well-spring of originality, and a literature in every civilized country of Europe that has been an inspiration to many subsequent generations. At last men had the time to devote to the things of the mind. During what are called the Dark Ages, a term that must ever be used with the realization that there are many bright points of light in them, men had been occupied with wars and civic and political dissensions of all kinds, and had been gradually climbing back to the heights of interest in intellectual matters which had been theirs before the invasion of the barbarians and the migration of nations. With the rebirth of intellectual interests there came an intense curiosity to know everything and to investigate every manifestation. Everything that men touched was novel, and the wonderful advances they made can only be realized from actual consultation of their works, while the reader puts himself as far as possible at the same mental point of view from which they surveyed the world and their relations to it.

The modern university prides itself on the number of volumes written by its professors and makes it a special feature of its announcements to call attention to its at least supposed additions to knowledge in this mode. It must have been immensely more difficult to preserve the writings of the professors of the medieval universities for they had to be copied out laboriously by hand, yet we have an enormous number of large volumes of their works, on nearly every intellectual topic, that have been carefully preserved. There are some twenty closely printed large folio volumes of the writings of Albertus Magnus that have come down to us. For two centuries, until the time of printing, ardent students must have been satisfied to spend much time in preserving these. While mainly devoted to theology, they treat of nearly everything else, and at least one of the folio volumes is taken up almost exclusively with physical science. St. Thomas Aquinas has as many volumes to his credit and his work is even of more importance. Duns Scotus died at a very early age, scarcely more than forty, yet his writings are voluminously extensive and have been carefully preserved, for few men had as enthusiastic students as he. Alas! that his name should be preserved for most people only in the familiar satiric appellation 'dunce.' The modern educator will most rejoice at the fact that the students of the time must have indeed been devoted to their masters to set themselves to the task of copying out their work so faithfully for, as Cardinal Newman has pointed out, it is the personal influence of the master, rather than the greatness of the institution, that makes education effective.

First with regard to philosophy, the mistress of all studies, whose throne has been shaken but not shattered in these ultimate times. After all it must not be forgotten that this was the great century of the development of scholastic philosophy. While this scholastic philosophy is supposed by many students of modern philosophy to be a thing of the past, it still continues to be the basis of the philosophical teaching in the Catholic seminaries and universities throughout the world. Catholic philosophers are well known as conservative thinkers and writers, and yet are perfectly free to confess that they consider themselves the nearer to truth the nearer they are to the great scholastic thinkers of the Thirteenth Century. Even in the circle of students of philosophy who are outside the influence of scholasticism, there is no doubt that in recent years an opinion much more favorable to the Schoolmen has gradually arisen. This has been due to a study of scholastic sources. Only those despise and talk slightingly of scholasticism who either do not know it at all or know it only at second hand. With regard to the system of thought, as such, ever is it true, that the more close the acquaintanceship the more respect there is for it.

With regard to theology the case is even stronger than with regard to philosophy. Practically all of the great authorities in theology belong to the Thirteenth Century. It is true that men like Saint Anselm lived before this time and were leaders in the great movement that culminated in our century. Saint Anselm's book, *Cur Deus Homo,* is indeed one of the best examples of the combination of scholastic philosophy and theology that could well be cited. It is a triumph of logical reasoning applied to religious belief. Besides, it is a great classic and any one who can read it unmoved by admiration for the thinker who, so many centuries ago, could so trenchantly lay down his thesis and develop it, must be lacking in some of the qualities of human admiration. The writers of the Thirteenth Century in theology are beyond even Anselm in their marvelous powers of systematizing thought. One need only mention such names as Albertus Magnus, Thomas Aquinas, Bonaventure, Duns Scotus, and Raymond Lully to make those who are at all acquainted with the history of the time realize, that this is not an idle expression of the enthusiasm of a special votary of the Thirteenth Century.

As we shall see in discussing the career of Saint Thomas Aquinas, the Catholic Church still continues to teach scholastic theology on exactly the same lines as were laid down by this great doctor of the church in his teaching at the University of Paris. Amid the crumbling of many Christian systems of thought, as upheld by the various protestant sects, there has been a very general realization that the Catholic Church has built up the only edifice of Christian apologetics, which will stand the storms of time and the development of human knowledge. Confessedly this edifice is founded on Thirteenth Century scholasticism. Pope Leo XIII., than whom, even in the estimation of those who are least sympathetic toward his high office, there was no man of more supremely practical intelligence in our generation, insisted that St. Thomas Aquinas must in general principle at least, be the groundwork of the teaching of philosophy and theology as they are to form the minds of future Catholic apologists.

The scholastic theology and philosophy of the Thirteenth Century have come to us in absolute purity. The huge tomes which represent the indefatigable labors of these ardent scholars were well preserved by the subsequent generation which thought so much of them, and in spite of the absence of printing have come down to us in perfectly clear texts. It is easy to neglect them and to say that a study of them is not worth while. They represent, however, the post-graduate work and the research in the department of philosophy and theology of these days, and any university of modern time would consider itself honored by having their authors among its professors and alumni. Any one who does not think so need only turn to the volumes themselves and read them with understanding and sympathy, and there will be another convert to the ranks of that growing multitude of scholars, who have learned to appreciate the marvelous works of our university colleagues of the Thirteenth Century.

With regard to law, not much need be said here, since it is well understood that the foundations of our modern jurisprudence (see chapters on Legal Origins), as well as the methods of teaching law, were laid in the Thirteenth Century and the universities were the most active factors, direct and indirect, in this work. The University of Bologna developed from a law school. Toward the end of the Twelfth Century Irnerius revived the study of the old Roman law and put the curriculum of modern Civil Law on a firm basis. A little later Gratian made his famous collection of decretals, which are the basis of Canon

Law. Great popes, during the Thirteenth Century, beginning with Innocent III., and continuing through such worthy emulators as Gregory IX. and Boniface VIII., made it the special glory of their pontificates to collect the decrees of their predecessors and arrange and publish them, so that they might be readily available for consultation.

French law assumed its modern form, and the basis of French jurisprudence was laid, under Louis IX., who called to his assistance, in this matter, the Professors of Law at the University of Paris, with many of whom he was on the most intimate terms. His cousin, Ferdinand of Castile, laid the foundation of the Spanish law about the same time under almost similar circumstances, and with corresponding help. The study of law in the English universities helped to the formulation of the principles of the English Common Law in such simple connected form as made them readily accessible for consultation. Just before the beginning of the last quarter of the Thirteenth Century, Bracton, of whose work much more will be said in a subsequent chapter, drew up the digest of the English Common Law, which has been the basis of English jurisprudence ever since. It took just about a century for these countries, previously without proper codification of the principles of their laws, to complete the fundamental work to such a degree, that it is still the firm substructure on which rests all our modern laws. Legal origins, in our modern sense, came not long before the Thirteenth Century; at its end the work was finished, to all intents and purposes. Of the influence of the universities and of the university law departments. in all this there can be no doubt. The incentive, undoubtedly, came from their teachings. The men who did so much for legal origins of such far-reaching importance, were mainly students of the universities of the time, whose enthusiasm for work had not subsided with the obtaining of their degrees.

It is in medicine, however, much more than in law or theology, that the eminently practical character of university teaching during the Thirteenth Century can be seen, at least in the form in which it will appeal to a scientific generation. We are so accustomed to think that anything like real progress in medicine, and especially in surgery, has only come in very recent years, that it is a source of great surprise to find how much these earnest students of a long distant century anticipated the answers to problems, the solutions of which are usually supposed to be among the most modern advances.   Professor Allbutt, the Regius professor of Physic in the University of Cambridge, a position, the occupant of which is always a leader in English medical thought, the present professor being one of the world's best authorities in the history of medicine, recently pointed out some of these marvels of old-time medicine and surgery.   In an address On the Historical Relations of Medicine and Surgery to the end of the Sixteenth Century, delivered at the Congress of Arts and Sciences at the St Louis Exposition in 1904, he (Prof. Allbutt) spoke with regard to one of the great university medical teachers of the Thirteenth Century as follows:

"Both for his own great merits, as an original and independent observer, and as the master of Lanfranc, William Salicet (Guglielmo Salicetti of Piacenza, in Latin G. Placentinus de Saliceto—now Cadeo), was eminent among the great Italian physicians of the latter half of the Thirteenth Century. Now these great Italians were as distinguished in surgery as in medicine, and William was one of the protestants of the period against the division of surgery from inner medicine; a division which he regarded as a separation of medicine from intimate touch with nature.   Like Lanfranc and the other great surgeons of the Italian tradition, and unlike Franco and Ambroise Paré, he had the advantage of the liberal university education of Italy; but, like Paré and Wurtz, he had large practical experience in hospital and on the battlefield.   He practised first at Bologna, afterward in Verona.   William fully recognised that surgery cannot be learned from books only.   His Surgery contains many case histories, for he rightly opined that good notes of cases are the soundest foundation of good practice; and in this opinion and method Lanfranc followed him.   William discovered that dropsy may be due to a *'durities renum';* he substituted the knife for the Arabist abuse of the cautery; he investigated the causes of the failure of healing by first intention; he described the danger of wounds of the neck; he sutured divided nerves; he forwarded the diagnosis of sup-

purative disease of the hip, and he referred chancre and phage-
dæna to their real causes.

This paragraph sets forth some almost incredible anticipations of what are usually considered among the most modern
phases of medicine and surgery.   Perhaps the most surprising
thing is the simple statement that Salicet recognized that surgery cannot be learned from books alone.   His case histories
are instructive even to the modern surgeon who reads them.
His insistence on his students making careful notes of their
cases as the soundest foundation of progress in surgery, is a
direct contradiction of nearly everything that has been said
in recent years about medieval medicine and especially the
teaching of medicine.   (See Appendix.)

William's great pupil, Lanfranc, followed him in this, and
Lanfranc encouraged the practise at the University of Paris.
There is a note-book of a student at the University of Paris,
made toward the end of the Thirteenth Century, carefully preserved in the Museum of the University of Berlin.   This note-
book was kept during Lanfranc's teaching and contains some
sketches of dissections, as well as some illustrations of opera-
tive procedures, as studied with that celebrated surgeon.   The
tradition of case histories continued at the University of Paris
down to the beginning of modern surgery.

Some of the doctrines in medicine that William of Salicet
stated so clearly, sound surprisingly modern.   The connection, for instance, between dropsy and *durities renum* (hardening of the kidneys) shows how wonderfully observant the old
master was.   At the present time we know very little more
about the dropsical condition associated with chronic Bright's
disease than the fact that it constantly occurs where there is a
sclerosis or contraction of the kidney.   Bright in his study of
albuminuria and contracted kidney practically taught us no
more than this, except that he added the further symptom of the
presence of albumin in the urine.   It must have been only as the
result of many carefully studied cases, followed by autopsies,
that any such doctrine could have come into existence.   There
is a dropsy that occurs with heart disease; there is also a dropsy
in connection with certain affections of the liver, and yet the
most frequent cause is just this hardening of the kidneys

spoken of by this middle-of-the-Thirteenth Century Italian professor of medicine, who, if we would believe so many of the historians of medicine, was not supposed to occupy himself at all with ante and post-mortem studies of patients, but with the old-time medical authorities.

Almost more surprising than the question of dropsy is the investigation as to the causes of the failure of healing by first intention. The modern surgeon is very apt to think that he is the only one who ever occupied himself with the thought, that wounds might be made to heal by first intention and without the occurrence of suppuration or granulation. Certainly no one would suspect any interest in the matter as far back as the Thirteenth Century. William of Salicet, however, and Lanfranc, both of them occupied themselves much with this question and evidently looked at it from a very practical standpoint. Many careful observations must have been made and many sources of observational error eliminated to enable these men to realize the possibilities of primary union, especially, knowing as they did, nothing at all about the external causes of suppuration and considering, as did surgeons for nearly seven centuries afterward, that it was because of something within the patient's tissues that the cases of suppuration had their rise.

Unfortunately, the pioneer work done by William and his great disciple did not have that effect upon succeeding generations which it should have had. There was a question in men's minds as to whether nature worked better by primary union or by means of the suppurative process. In the next century surgeons took the wrong horn of the dilemma and even so distinguished a surgeon as Guy de Chauliac, who has been called, not without good cause, the father of surgery, came to the conclusion that suppuration was practically a necessary process in the healing of large wounds at least, and that it must be encouraged rather than discouraged. This doctrine did not have its first set-back until the famous incident in Ambroise Paré's career, when one morning after a battle, coming to his patients expecting to find many of them very severely ill, he found them on the contrary in better condition than the others for whom he had no forebodings. In accord with old custom he poured boiling oil into the wounds of all patients, but the great surgeon's supply of oil had failed the day before and he used plain water to cleanse the wounds of a number, fearing the worst for them, however, because of the poison that must necessarily stay in their wounds and then had the agreeable disappointment of finding these patients in much better condition than those whom he had treated with all the rules of his art, as they then were. Even this incident, however, did not serve to correct entirely the old idea as to the value of suppuration and down to Lister's time, that is almost the last quarter of the Nineteenth Century, there is still question of the value of suppuration in expediting the healing of wounds, and we hear of laudable pus and of the proper inflammatory reaction that is expected to bring about wound repair.

The danger of wounds of the neck is, of course, not a modern doctrine, and yet very few people would think for a moment that it could be traced back to the middle of the Thirteenth Century and to a practical teacher of surgery in a medieval Italian university. Here once more there is evidence of the work of a careful observer who has seen patients expire in a few minutes as the result of some serious incident during the course of operations upon the neck. He did not realize that the danger was due, in many cases, to the sucking in of air into the large veins, but even at the present time this question is not wholly settled and the problem as to the danger of the presence of air is still the subject of investigation.

As to the suture of divided nerves, it would ordinarily and as a matter of course be claimed by most modern historians of surgery and by practically all surgeons, as an affair entirely of the last half century. William of Salicet, however, neglected none of the ordinary surgical procedures that could be undertaken under the discouraging surgical circumstances in which he lived. The limitations of anesthesia, though there was much more of this aid than there has commonly been any idea of, and the frequent occurrence of suppuration must have been constant sources of disheartenment. His insistence on the use of the knife rather than on the cautery shows how much he appreciated the value of proper healing. It is from such a man that we might expect the advance by careful in-

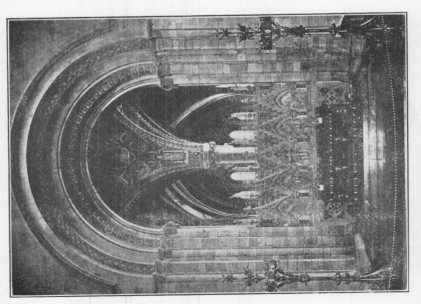

ENTRANCE TO SACRISTY (BOURGES)

SCREEN (HEREFORD)

vestigation as to just what tissues had been injured, with the idea of bringing them together in such juxtaposition as would prevent loss of function and encourage rapid and perfect union.

Perhaps to the ordinary individual William's reference of certain known venereal affections to their proper cause, will be the most astonishing in this marvelous list of anticipations of what is supposed to be very modern. The whole subject of venereal disease in anything like a scientific treatment of it is supposed to date from the early part of the Sixteenth Century. There is even question in certain minds as to whether the venereal diseases did not come into existence, or at least were not introduced from America or from some other distant country that the Europeans had been exploring about this time. William's studies in this subject, however, serve to show that nothing escaped his watchful eye and that he was in the best sense of the word a careful observer and must have been an eminently suggestive and helpful teacher.

What has thus been learned about him will serve of itself and without more ado, to stamp all that has been said about the unpractical character of the medical teaching of the medieval universities as utterly unfounded. Because men have not taken the trouble to look up the teaching of these times, and because their works were until recent years buried in old folios, difficult to obtain and still more difficult to read when obtained, it has been easy to ignore their merit and even to impugn the value of their teaching completely. William of Salicet was destined, moreover, to be surpassed in some ways by his most distinguished pupil, Lanfranc, who taught at the University of Paris at the end of the Thirteenth Century. Of Lanfranc, in the address already quoted from, Professor Allbutt has one very striking paragraph that shows how progressive was the work of this great French surgeon, and how fruitful had been the suggestive teaching of his great master. He says:

"Lanfranc's 'Chirurgia Magna' was a great work, written by a reverent but independent follower of Salicet. He distinguished between venous and arterial hemorrhage, and used styptics (rabbit's fur, aloes, and white of egg was a popular styptic in elder surgery), digital compression for an hour, or in severe cases ligature. His chapter on injuries of the head is one of the classics of medieval surgery. Clerk (cleric) as he was, Lanfranc nevertheless saw but the more clearly the danger of separating surgery from medicine."

Certain assertions in this paragraph deserve, as in the case of Lanfranc's master, to be discussed, because of their anticipations of what is sometimes thought to be very modern in surgery. The older surgeons are supposed to have feared hemorrhage very much. It is often asserted that they knew little or nothing about the ligature and that their control of hemorrhage was very inadequate. As a matter of fact, however, it was not primary hemorrhage that the old surgeons feared, but secondary hemorrhage. Suppuration often led to the opening of an important artery, and this accident, as can well be understood, was very much dreaded. Surgeons would lose their patients before they could come to their relief. How thoroughly Lanfranc knew how to control primary hemorrhage can be appreciated from the quotation just made from Dr. Allbutt's address. The ligature is sometimes said to have been an invention of Ambroise Paré, but, as a matter of fact, it had been in use for at least three centuries before his time, and perhaps even longer.

Usually it is considered that the difficult chapter of head injuries, with all the problems that it involves in diagnosis and treatment, is a product of the Nineteenth Century. Hence do we read, with all the more interest, Allbutt's declaration that Lanfranc wrote what is practically a classical monograph, on the subject. It is not so surprising, then, to find that the great French surgeon was far ahead of his generation in other matters, or that he should even have realized the danger of separating surgery from medicine. Both the Regius professors of medicine at the two great English universities, Cambridge and Oxford, have, since the beginning of the Twentieth Century, made public expression of their opinion that the physician should see more of the work of the surgeon, and should not depend on the autopsy room for his knowledge of the results of internal disease. Professor Osler, particularly, has emphasized his colleague, Professor Allbutt's opinion in this matter. That a surgical professor at the University of Paris, in the Thirteenth Century, should have anticipated these two leaders of medical thought in the Twentieth Century, would not be so surprising, only that unfortunately the history of medieval teaching has, because of prejudice and a lamentable tradition, not been read aright.

Occasionally one finds a startling bit of anticipation of what is most modern, in medicine as well as in surgery. For instance, toward the end of the Thirteenth Century, a distinguished English professor of medicine, known as Gilbert, the Englishman, was teaching at Montpelier, and among other things, was insisting that the rooms of patients suffering from smallpox should be hung entirely with red curtains, and that the doors and the windows should be covered with heavy red hangings. He claimed that this made the disease run a lighter course, with lessened mortality, and with very much less disfigurement. Smallpox was an extremely common disease in the Thirteenth Century, and he probably had many chances for observation. It is interesting to realize that one of the most important observations made at the end of the Nineteenth Century by Dr. Finsen, the Danish investigator whose studies in light and its employment in therapeutics, drew to him the attention of the world, and eventually the Nobel prize of $40,000 for the greatest advance in medicine was, that the admission of only red light to the room of smallpox patients modified the disease very materially, shortened its course, often prevented the secondary fever, and almost did away completely with the subsequent disfigurement.

It is evident that these men were searching and investigating for themselves, and not following blindly in the footsteps of any master. It has often been said that during the Middle Ages it was a heresy to depart, ever so little, from the teaching of Galen. Usually it is customary to add that the first writer to break away from Galen, effectually, was Vesalius, in his De Fabrica Corporis Humani, published toward the end of the second quarter of the Sixteenth Century. It may be said, in passing, that, as a matter of fact, Vesalius, though he accomplished much by original investigation, did not break so effectually with Galen as would have been for the best in his own work, and, especially, for its influence on his successors. He certainly did not set an example of independent research

and personal observation, any more fully, than did the medical
teachers of the Thirteenth Century already mentioned, and
some others, like Mondaville and Arnold of Villanova, whose
names well deserve to be associated with them.

One reason why it is such a surprise to find how thoroughly
practical was the teaching of the Thirteenth Century university medical schools, is because it has somehow come to be a
very general impression that medicine was taught mainly by
disputations, and by the consultation of authorities, and that
it was always more important to have a passage of Galen to
support a medical notion, than to have an original observation.
This false impression is due to the fact that the writers of the
history of medical education have, until recent years, drawn
largely on their imaginations, and have not consulted the old-
time medical books.   In spite of the fact that printing was not
discovered for more than two centuries later, there are many
treatises on medicine that have come down to us from this
early time, and the historians of medicine now have the opportunity, and are taking the trouble, to read them with a consequent alteration of old-time views, as to the lack of encouragement for original observation, in the later Middle Ages.
These old tomes are not easy reading, but nothing daunts a
German investigator bound to get to the bottom of his subject, and such men as Pagel and Puschmann have done much
to rediscover for us medieval medicine.   The French medical
historians have not been behind their German colleagues and
magnificent work has been accomplished, especially by the republication of old texts.   William of Salicet's surgery was republished by Pifteau at Toulouse in 1898.   Mondaville's Surgery was republished under the auspices of the Society for the
Publication of old French Texts in 1897 and 1898.   These re-
publications have made the works of the old-time surgeons
readily available for study by all interested in our great predecessors in medicine, all over the world.   Before this, it has
always been necessary to get to some of the libraries in which
the old texts were preserved, and this, of course, made it extremely difficult for the ordinary teacher of the history of medicine to know anything about them.   Besides, old texts are such
difficult reading that few, except the most earnest of students,

have patience for them, and they are so time-taking as to be practically impossible for modern, hurried students.

Unfortunately, writers of the history of medicine filled up this gap in their knowledge, only too frequently, either out of their imaginations. or out of their inadequate authorities, with the consequence of inveterating the old-time false impression with regard to the absence of anything of medical or surgical interest, even in the later Middle Ages.

Another and much more serious reason for the false impression with regard to the supposed blankness of the middle age in medical progress, was the notion, quite generally accepted, and even yet not entirely rejected, by many, that the Church was opposed to scientific advance in the centuries before the reformation so-called, and that even the sciences allied to medicine, fell under her ban. For instance, there is not a history of medicine, so far as I know, published in the English language, which does not assert that Pope Boniface VIII., by a Bull promulgated at the end of the Thirteenth Century, forbade the practise of dissection. To most people, it will, at once, seem a natural conclusion, that if the feeling against the study of the human body by dissection had reached such a pass as to call forth a papal decree in the matter, at the end of the century, all during the previous hundred years, there must have been enough ecclesiastical hampering of anatomical work to prevent anything like true progress, and to preclude the idea of any genuinely progressive teaching of anatomy.

There is not the slightest basis for this bit of false history except an unfortunate, it is to be hoped not intentional, misapprehension on the part of historical writers as to the meaning of a papal decree issued by Boniface VIII. in the year 1300. He forbade, under pain of excommunication, the boiling of bodies and their dismemberment in order that thus piecemeal they might be transported to long distances for burial purposes. It is now well known that the Bull was aimed at certain practises which had crept in, especially among the Crusaders in the East. When a member of the nobility fell a victim to wounds or to disease, his companions not infrequently dismembered the body, boiled it so as to prevent putrefaction, or at least delay decay, and then transported it long distances to his home, in or-

der that he might have Christian burial in some favorite grave-
yard, and that his friends might have the consolation of knowing where his remains rested. The body of the Emperor Frederick Barbarosa, who died in the East, is said to have been
thus treated. Boniface was one of the most broadly educated
men of his time, who had been a great professor of canon and
civil law at Paris when younger, and realized the dangers involved in such a proceeding from a sanitary standpoint, and he
forbade it, requiring that the bodies should be buried where the
persons had died. He evidently considered that the ancient
custom of consecrating a portion of earth for the purpose of
burial in order that the full Christian rites might be performed,
was quite sufficient for noble as for common soldier.

For this very commendable sanitary regulation Boniface has
been set down by historians of medicine as striking a death
blow at the development of anatomy for the next two centuries.
As a matter of fact, however, anatomy continued to be studied
in the universities after this Bull as it had been before, and it
is evident that never by any misapprehension as to its meaning
was the practise of dissection lessened. Curiously enough
the history of human dissection can only be traced with absolute certainty from the time immediately after this Bull. It
is during the next twenty-five years at the University of Bologna, which was always closely in touch with the ecclesiastical
authorities in Italy and especially with the Pope, that the
foundations of dissection, as the most important practical department of medical teaching, were laid by Mondino, whose
book on dissection continued to be the text book used in most
of the medical schools for the next two centuries. Guy de
Chauliac who studied there during the first half of the Fourteenth Century says he saw many dissections made there. It
was at Montpellier, about the middle of the century, when the
Popes were at Avignon not far away, that Guy de Chauliac
himself made attendance at dissections obligatory for every
student, and obtained permission to use the bodies of criminals
for dissection purposes. At the time Chauliac occupied the post
of chamberlain to the Popes. All during the Fourteenth and
Fifteenth centuries constant progress was making in anatomy,
especially in Italy, and some of it was accomplished at Rome

by distinguished teachers of anatomy who had been summoned by the popes to their capital in order to add distinction to the teaching staff at the famous Papal School of Science, the Sapienza, to which were attached during the next two centuries many of the distinguished scientific professors of the time.

This story with regard to the papal prohibition of dissection has no foundation in the history of the times. It has had not a little to do, however, with making these times very much misunderstood and one still continues to see printed references to the misfortune, which is more usually called a crime, that prevented the development of a great humanitarian science because of ecclesiastical prejudice. This story with regard to anatomy, however, is not a whit worse than that which is told of chemistry in almost the same terms. At the beginning of the Fourteenth Century Pope John XXII. is said to have issued a Bull forbidding chemistry under pain of excommunication, which according to some writers in the matter is said to have included the death penalty. It has been felt in the same way as with regard to anatomy, that this was only the culmination of a feeling in ecclesiastical circles against chemistry which must have hampered its progress all during the Thirteenth Century.

An examination of the so-called Bull with regard to chemistry, it is really only a decree, shows even less reason for the slander of Pope John XXII. than of Boniface VIII. John had been scarcely a year on the papal throne when he issued this decree forbidding "alchemies" and inflicting a punishment upon those who practised them. The first sentence of the title of the document is: "Alchemies are here prohibited and those who practise them or procure their being done are punished." This is evidently all of the decree that those who quoted it as a prohibition of chemistry seem ever to have read. Under the name "alchemies," Pope John, as is clear from the rest of the document, meant a particular kind of much-advertised chemical manipulations. He forbade the supposed manufacture of gold and silver. The first sentence of his decree shows how thoroughly he recognized the falsity of the pretensions of the alchemists in this matter. "Poor themselves," he says, "the alchemists promise riches which are not forthcoming." He then forbids them further to impose upon the poor people whose confidence they abuse and whose good money they take to return them only base-metal or none at all.

The only punishment inflicted for the doing of these "alchemies" on those who might transgress the decree was not death or imprisonment, but that the pretended makers of gold and silver should be required to turn into the public treasury as much gold and silver as had been paid them for their alchemies, the money thus paid in to go to the poor. As in the case of the Bull with regard to anatomy, it is very clear that by no possible misunderstanding at the time was the development of the science of chemistry hindered by this papal document. Chemistry had to a certain extent been cultivated at the University of Paris, mainly by ecclesiastics. Both Aquinas and his master Albertus wrote treatises on chemical subjects. Roger Bacon devoted much time to it as is well known, and for the next three centuries the history of chemistry has a number of names of men who were not only unhampered by the ecclesiastical authorities, but who were themselves usually either ecclesiastics, or high in favor with the churchmen of their time and place. This is true of Hollandus, of Arnold of Villanova, of Basil Valentine, and finally of the many abbots and bishops to whom Paracelsus in his time acknowledged his obligations for aid in his chemical studies.

Almost needless to say it has been impossible, in a brief sketch of this kind limited to a single chapter, to give anything like an adequate idea of what the enthusiastic graduate students and professors of the Thirteenth Century succeeded in accomplishing. It is probably this department of University life, however, that has been least understood, or rather we should say most persistently misunderstood. The education of the time is usually supposed to be eminently unpractical, and great advances in the departments of knowledge that had important bearings on human life and its relations were not therefore thought possible. It is just here, however, that sympathetic interpretation and the pointing out of the coordination of intellectual work often considered to be quite distinct from university influences were needed. It is hoped then that this short sketch will prove sufficient to call the attention of modern educators to a field that has been neglected, or at least has received very little cultivation compared to its importance, but which must be sedulously worked, if our generation is to under-stand with any degree of thoroughness the spirit manifested and the results attained by the medieval universities.

DOUBLE FLYING BUTTRESS (RHEIMS)

VI

THE BOOK OF THE ARTS AND POPULAR
EDUCATION.

The most important portion of the history of the Thirteenth Century and beyond all doubt the most significant chapter in the book of its arts, is to be found in the great Gothic Cathedrals, so many of which were erected at this time and whose greatest perfection of finish in design and in detail came just at the beginning of this wonderful period. We are not concerned here with the gradual development of Gothic out of the older Romanesque architectural forms, nor with the Oriental elements that may have helped this great evolution. All that especially concerns us is the fact that the generations of the Thirteenth Century took the Gothic ideas in architecture and applied them so marvelously, that thereafter it could be felt that no problem of structural work had been left unsolved and no feature of ornament or decoration left untried or at least unsuggested. The great center of Gothic influence was the North of France, but it spread from here to every country in Europe, and owing to the intimate relations existing between England and France because of the presence of the Normans in both countries, developed almost as rapidly and with as much beauty and effectiveness as in the mother country.

It is in fact in England just before the Thirteenth Century, that the spirit which gave rise to the Cathedrals can be best observed at work and its purposes most thoroughly appreciated. The great Cathedral at Lincoln had some of its most important features before the beginning of the Thirteenth Century and this was doubtless due to the famous St. Hugh of Lincoln, who was a Frenchman by birth and whose experience in Normandy in early life enabled him successfully to set about the creation of a Gothic Cathedral in the country that had become his by adoption. Hugh himself

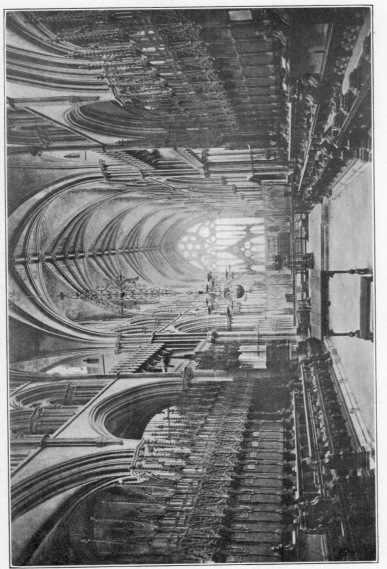

ANGEL CHOIR (LINCOLN)

was so great of soul, so deeply interested in his people and their
welfare, so ready to make every sacrifice for them even to the
extent of incurring the enmity of his King (even Froude
usually so unsympathetic to medieval men and things has
included him among his Short Studies of Great Subjects), that
one cannot help but think that when he devoted himself to the
erection of the magnificent Cathedral, he realized very well
that it would become a center of influence, not only religious
but eminently educational, in its effects upon the people of his
diocese. The work was begun then with a consciousness of the
results to be attained and the influence of the Cathedral must
not be looked upon as accidental. He must have appreciated
that the creating of a work of beauty in which the people themselves shared, which they looked on as their own property, to
which they came nearly every second day during the year for
religious services, would be a telling book out of which they
would receive more education than could come to them in any
other way.

Of course we cannot hope in a short chapter or two to convey
any adequate impression of the work that was done in and for
the Cathedrals, nor the even more important reactionary influence they had in educating the people. Ferguson says :*
"The subject of the cathedrals, their architecture and decoration is, in fact, practicably inexhaustible. . . . Priests and
laymen worked with masons, painters, and sculptors, and all
were bent on producing the best possible building, and improving every part and every detail, till the amount of thought and
contrivance accumulated in any single structure is almost
incomprehensible. If any one man were to devote a lifetime
to the study of one of our great cathedrals—assuming it to
be complete in all its medieval arrangements—it is question-
able whether he would master all its details, and fathom all
the reasonings and experiments which led to the glorious
result before him. And when we consider that not in the great
cities alone, but in every convent and in every parish, thoughtful professional men were trying to excel what had been done
and was doing, by their predecessors and their fellows, we shall

* Ferguson—History of Architecture. N. Y., Dodd, Mead & Co.

understand what an amount of thought is built into the walls
of our churches, castles, colleges, and dwelling houses. If any
one thinks he can master and reproduce all this, he can hardly
fail to be mistaken. My own impression is that not one tenth
part of it has been reproduced in all the works written on the
subject up to this day, and much of it is probably lost and never
again to be recovered for the instruction and delight of future
ages."

This profound significance and charming quality of the
cathedrals is usually unrecognized by those who see them only
once or twice, and who, though they are very much interested in
them for the moment, have no idea of the wealth of artistic
suggestion and of thoughtful design so solicitously yet happily
put into them by their builders. People who have seen them
many times, however, who have lived in close touch with them,
who have been away from them for a time and have come back
to them, find the wondrous charm that is in these buildings. Architects and workmen put their very souls into them and they
will always be of interest. It is for this reason, that the casual
visitor at all times and in all moods finds them ever a source of
constantly renewed pleasure, no matter how many times they
may be seen.

Elizabeth Robbins Pennell has expressed this power of
Cathedrals to please at all times, even after they have been often seen and are very well known, in a recent number of the
Century, in describing the great Cathedral of Notre Dame,
"Often as I have seen Notre Dame," she says, "the marvel of
it never grows less. I go to Paris with no thought of time for
it, busy about many other things and then on my way over one
of the bridges across the river perhaps, I see it again on its
island, the beautiful towers high above the houses and
palaces and the view now so familiar strikes me afresh with all
the wonder of my first impression."

This is we think the experience of everyone who has the
opportunity to see much of Notre Dame. The present writer
during the course of his medical studies spent many months
in daily view of the Cathedral and did a good deal of work
at the old Morgue, situated behind the Cathedral. Even at
the end of his stay he was constantly finding new beauties in

the grand old structure and learning to appreciate it more and more as the changing seasons of a Paris fall and winter and spring, threw varying lights and shadows over it. It was like a work of nature, never growing old, but constantly displaying some new phase of beauty to the passers-by. Mrs. Pennell resents only the restorations that have been made. Generations down even to our time have considered that they could rebuild as beautifully as the Thirteenth Century constructors; some of them even have thought that they could do better, doubtless, yet their work has in the opinion of good critics served only to spoil or at least to detract from the finer beauty of the original plan. No wonder that R. M. Stevenson, who knew and loved the old Cathedral so well, said: "Notre Dame is the only un-Greek thing that unites majesty, elegance, and awfulness." Inasmuch as it does so it is a typical product of this wonderful Thirteenth Century, the only serious rival the Greeks have ever had. But of course it does not stand alone. There are other Cathedrals built at the same time at least as handsome and as full of suggestions. Indeed in the opinion of many critics it is inferior in certain respects to some three or four of the greatest Gothic Cathedrals.

It cannot be possible that these generations builded so much better than they knew, that it is only by a sort of happy accident that their edifices still continue to be the subject of such profound admiration, and such endless sources of pleasure after seven centuries of experience. If so we would certainly be glad to have some such happy accident occur in our generation, for we are building nothing at the present time with regard to which we have any such high hopes. Of course the generations of Cathedral builders knew and appreciated their own work. The triumph of the Thirteenth Century is therefore all the more marked and must be considered as directly due to the environment and the education of its people. We have then in the study of their Cathedrals the keynote for the modern appreciation of the character and the development of their builders.

It will be readily understood, how inevitably fragmentary must be our consideration of the Cathedrals, yet there is the consolation that they are the best known feature of Thirteenth

Century achievement and that consequently all that will be necessary will be to point out the significance of their construction as the basis of the great movement of education and uplift in the century. Perhaps first a word is needed with regard to the varieties of Gothic in the different countries of Europe and what they meant in the period.

Probably, the most interesting feature of the history of Gothic architecture, at this period, is to be found in the circumstance that, while all of the countries erected Gothic structures along the general lines which had been laid down by its great inventors in the North and Center of France, none of the architects and builders of the century, in other countries, slavishly followed the French models. English Gothic is quite distinct from its French ancestor, and while it has defects it has beauties, that are all its own, and a simplicity and grandeur, well suited to the more rugged character of the people among whom it developed. Italian Gothic has less merits, perhaps, than any of the other forms of the art that developed in the different nations. In Italy, with its bright sunlight, there was less crying need for the window space, for the provision of which, in the darker northern countries, Gothic was invented, but, even here the possibilities of decorated architecture along certain lines were exhausted more fully than anywhere else, as might have been expected from the esthetic spirit of the Italians. German Gothic has less refinement than any of the other national forms, yet it is not lacking in a certain straightforward strength and simplicity of appearance, which recommends it. The Germans often violated the French canons of architecture, yet did not spoil the ultimate effect. St. Stephen's in Vienna has many defects, yet as a good architectural authority has declared it is the work of a poet, and looks it.

A recent paragraph with regard to Spanish Gothic in an article on Spain, by Havelock Ellis, illustrates the national qualities of this style very well. As much less is generally known about the special development of Gothic architecture in the Spanish peninsula, it has seemed worth while to quote it at some length:

"Moreover, there is no type of architecture which so admirably embodies the romantic spirit as Spanish Gothic. Such a statement implies no heresy against the supremacy of French Gothic. But the very qualities of harmony and balance of finely tempered reason, which make French Gothic so exquisitely satisfying, softened the combination of mysteriously grandiose splendor with detailed realism, in which lies the essence of Gothic as the manifestation of the romantic spirit. Spanish Gothic at once by its massiveness and extravagance and by its realistic naturalness, far more potently embodies the spirit of medieval life. It is less esthetically beautiful but it is more romantic. In Leon Cathedral, Spain possesses one of the very noblest and purest examples of French Gothic—a church which may almost be said to be the supreme type of the Gothic ideal, of a delicate house of glass finely poised between buttresses; but there is nothing Spanish about it. For the typical Gothic of Spain we must go to Toledo and Burgos, to Tarragona and Barcelona. Here we find the elements of stupendous size, of mysterious gloom, of grotesque and yet realistic energy, which are the dominant characters, alike of Spanish architecture and of medieval romance."

Those who think that the Gothic architecture came to a perfection all its own by a sort of wonderful manifestation of genius in a single generation, and then stayed there, are sadly mistaken. There was a constant development to be noted all during the Thirteenth Century. This development was always in the line of true improvement, while just after the century closed degeneration began, decoration became too important a consideration, parts were over-loaded with ornament, and the decadence of taste in Gothic architecture cannot escape the eye even of the most untutored. All during the Thirteenth Century the tendency was always to greater lightness and elegance. One is apt to think of these immense structures as manifestations of the power of man to overcome great engineering difficulties and to solve immense structural problems, rather than as representing opportunities for the expression of what was most beautiful and poetic in the intellectual aspirations of the generations. But this is what they were, and their architects were poets, for in the best sense of the etymology of the word they were creators. That their raw material was stone and mortar rather than words was only an accident of their environment. Each of the architects succeeded in expressing himself with wonderful individuality in his own work in each Cathedral.

The improvements introduced by the Thirteenth Century people into the architecture that came to them, were all of a very practical kind, and were never suggested for the sake of merely adding to opportunities for ornamentation. In this matter, skillful combinations of line and form were thought out and executed with wonderful success. At the beginning of the century, delicate shafts of marble, highly polished, were employed rather freely, but as these seldom carried weight, and were mainly ornamental in character, they were gradually eliminated, yet, without sacrificing any of the beauty of structure since combinations of light and shade were secured by the composition of various forms, and the use of delicately rounded mouldings alternated with hollows, so as to produce forcible effects in high light and deep shadow. In a word, these architects and builders, of the Thirteenth Century, set themselves the problem of building effectively, making every portion count in the building itself, and yet, securing ornamental effects out of actual structure such as no other set of architects have ever been able to surpass, and, probably, only the Greek architects of the Periclean period ever equaled. Needless to say, this is the very acme of success in architectural work, and it is for this reason that the generations of the after time have all gone back so lovingly to study the work of this period.

It might be thought, that while Gothic architecture was a great invention in its time and extremely suitable for ecclesiastical or even educational edifices of various kinds, its time of usefulness has passed and that men's widening experience in structural work, ever since, has carried him far away from it. As a matter of fact, most of our ecclesiastical buildings are still built on purely Gothic lines, and a definite effort is made, as a rule, to have the completed religious edifice combine a number of the best features of Thirteenth Century Gothic. With what success this has been accomplished can best be appreciated from the fact, that none of the modern structures attract anything like the attention of the old, and the Cathedrals of this early time still continue to be the best asset of the towns in which they are situated, because of the number of visitors they attract. Far from considering Gothic architecture outlived, architects still apply themselves to it with devotion because of the practical suggestions which it contains, and there are those of wide experience, who still continue to think it the most wonderful example of architectural development that has ever come, and even do not hesitate to foretell a great future for it.

Reinach, in his Story of Art Throughout the Ages,* has been so enthusiastic in this matter that a paragraph of his opinion must find a place here. Reinach, it may be said, is an excellent authority, a member of the Institute of France, who has made special studies in comparative architecture, and has written works that carry more weight than almost any others of our generation:

"If the aim of architecture, considered as an art, should be to free itself as much as possible from subjection to its materials, it may be said that no buildings have more successfully realized this ideal than the Gothic churches. And there is more to be said in this connection. Its light and airy system of construction, the freedom and slenderness of its supporting skeleton, afford, as it were, a presage of an art that began to develop in the Nineteenth Century, that of metallic architecture. With the help of metal, and of cement reinforced by metal bars, the moderns might equal the most daring feats of the Gothic architects. It would even be easy for them to surpass them, without endangering the solidity of the structure, as did the audacities of Gothic art. In the conflicts that obtain between the two elements of construction, solidity and open space, everything seems to show that the principle of free spaces will prevail, that the palaces and houses of the future will be flooded with air and light, that the formula popularized by Gothic architecture has a great future before it, and that following the revival of the Graeco-Roman style from

* Scribners, New York, 1905.

the Sixteenth Century, to our own day, we shall see a yet more enduring renaissance of the Gothic style applied to novel materials."

It would be a mistake, however, to think that the Gothic Cathedrals were impressive only because of their grandeur and immense size. It would be still more a mistake to consider them only as examples of a great development in architecture. They are much more than this; they are the compendious expression of the art impulses of a glorious century. Every single detail of the Gothic Cathedrals is not only worthy of study but deserving of admiration, if not for itself, then always for the inadequate means by which it was secured, and most of these details have been found worthy of imitation by subsequent generations. It is only by considering the separate details of the art work of these Cathedrals that the full lesson of what these wonderful people accomplished can be learned. There have been many centuries since, in which they would be entirely unappreciated. Fortunately, our own time has come back to a recognition of the greatness of the art impulse that was at work, perfecting even what might be considered trivial portions of the cathedrals, and the brightest hope for the future of our own accomplishment is founded on this belated appreciation of old-time work.

It has been said that the medieval workman was a lively symbol of the Creator Himself, in the way in which he did his work. It mattered not how obscure the portion of the cathedral at which he was set, he decorated it as beautifully as he knew how, without a thought that his work would be appreciated only by the very few that might see it. Trivial details were finished with the perfection of important parts. Microscopic studies in recent years have revealed beautiful designs on pollen grains and diatoms which are far beneath the possibilities of human vision, and have only been discovered by lens combinations of very high powers of the compound microscope. Always these beauties have been there though hidden away from any eye. It was as if the Creator's hand could not touch anything without leaving it beautiful as well as useful. To as great extent as it is possible

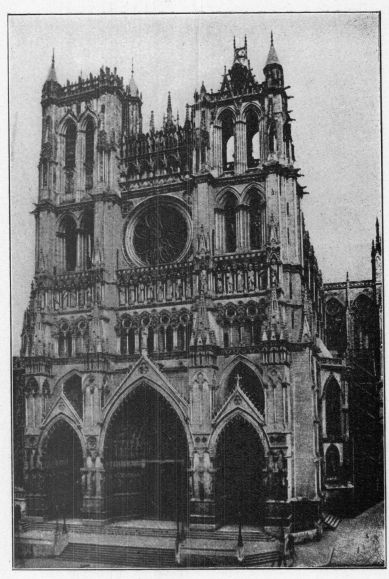

CATHEDRAL (AMIENS)

perhaps for man to secure such a desideratum, the Thirteenth Century workman succeeded in this same purpose. It is for this reason more than even for the magnificent grandeur of the design and the skilful execution with inadequate means, that makes the Gothic Cathedral such a source of admiration and wonder.

To take first the example of sculpture. It is usually considered that the Thirteenth Century represented a time entirely too early in the history of plastic art for there to have been any fine examples of the sculptor's chisel left us from it. Any such impression, however, will soon be corrected if one but examines carefully the specimens of this form of art in certain Cathedrals. As we have said, probably no more charmingly dignified presentation of the human form divine in stone has ever been made than the figure of Christ above the main door of the cathedral of Amiens, which the Amiennois so lovingly call their "beautiful God." There are some other examples of statuary in the same cathedral that are wonderful specimens of the sculptor's art, lending itself for decorative purposes to architecture. This is true for a number of the Cathedrals. The statues in themselves are not so beautiful, but as portions of a definite piece of structural work such as a doorway or a facade, they are wonderful models of how all the different arts became subservient to the general effect to be produced. It was at Rheims, however, that sculpture reached its acme of accomplishment, and architects have been always unstinted in their praise of this feature of what may be called the Capitol church of France.

Those who have any doubts as to the place of Gothic art itself in art history and who need an authority always to bolster up the opinion that they may hold, will find ample support in the enthusiastic opinion of an authority whom we have quoted already. The most interesting and significant feature of his ardent expression of enthusiasm is his comparison of Romanesque with Gothic art in this respect. The amount of ground covered from one artistic mode to the other is greater than any other advance in art that has ever been made. After all, the real value of the work of the period must be judged, rather by the amount of progress that has been made than by the stage of advance actually reached, since it is development rather than accomplishment that counts in the evolution of the race. On the other hand it will be found that Reinach's opinion of the actual attainments of Gothic art are far beyond anything that used to be thought on the subject a half century ago, and much higher than any but a few of the modern art critics hold in the matter. He says:

"In contrast to this Romanesque art, as yet in bondage to convention, ignorant or disdainful of nature, the mature Gothic art of the Thirteenth Century appeared as a brilliant revival or realism. The great sculptors who adorned the Cathedrals of Paris, Amiens, Rheims, and Chartres with their works, were realists in the highest sense of the word. They sought in Nature not only their knowledge of human forms, and of the draperies that cover them, but also that of the principles of decoration. Save in the gargoyles of cathedrals and in certain minor sculptures, we no longer find in the Thirteenth Century those unreal figures of animals, nor those ornaments, complicated as nightmares, which load the capitals of Romanesque churches; the flora of the country, studied with loving attention, is the sole, or almost the sole source from which decorators take their motives. It is in this charming profusion of flowers and foliage that the genius of Gothic architecture is most freely displayed. One of the most admirable of its creations is the famous Capital of the Vintage in Notre Dame at Rheims, carved about the year 1250. Since the first century of the Roman Empire art had never imitated Nature so perfectly, nor has it ever since done so with a like grace and sentiment."

Reinach defends Gothic Art from another and more serious objection which is constantly urged against it by those who know only certain examples of it, but have not had the advantage of the wide study of the whole field of artistic endeavor in the Thirteenth Century, which this distinguished member of the Institute of France has succeeded in obtaining. It is curious what unfounded opinions have come to be prevalent in art circles because, only too often, writers with regard to the Cathedrals have spent their time mainly in the large cities, or along the principal arteries of travel, and have not realized

CATHEDRAL (RHEIMS)

that some of the smaller towns contained work better fitted to illustrate Gothic Art principles than those on which they depended for their information. If only particular phases of the art of any one time, no matter how important, were to be considered in forming a judgment of it, that judgment would almost surely be unfavorable in many ways because of the lack of completeness of view. This is what has happened unfortunately with regard to Gothic art, but a better spirit is coming in this matter, with the more careful study of periods of art and the return of reverence for the grand old Middle Ages.

Reinach says: "There are certain prejudices against this admirable, though incomplete, art which it is difficult to combat. It is often said, for instance, that all Gothic figures are stiff and emaciated. To convince ourselves of the contrary we need only study the marvelous sculpture of the meeting between Abraham and Melchisedech, in Rheims Cathedral; or again in the same Cathedral, the Visitation, the seated Prophet, and the standing Angel, or the exquisite Magdalen of Bordeaux Cathedral. What can we see in these that is stiff, sickly, and puny? The art that has most affinity with perfect Gothic is neither Romanesque nor Byzantine, but the Greek art of from 500 to 450 B. C. By a strange coincidence, the Gothic artists even reproduce the somewhat stereotyped smile of their forerunners." Usually it is said that the Renaissance brought the supreme qualities of Greek plastic art back to life, but here is a thoroughly competent critic who finds them exhibited long before the Fifteenth Century, as a manifestation of what the self-sufficient generations of the Renaissance would have called Gothic, meaning thereby, barbarous art.

What has been said of sculpture, however, can be repeated with even more force perhaps with regard to every detail of construction and decoration. Builders and architects did make mistakes at times, but, even their mistakes always reveal an artist's soul struggling for expression through inadequate media. Many things had to be done experimentally, most things were being done for the first time. Everything had an originality of its own that made its execution something more than merely a secure accomplishment after previous careful tests. In spite of this state of affairs, which might be expected sadly to interfere with artistic execution, the Cathedrals, in the main, are full of admirable details not only worthy of imitation, but that our designers are actually imitating or at least finding eminently suggestive at the present time.

To begin with a well known example of decorative effect which is found in the earliest of the English Cathedrals, that of Lincoln. The nave and choir of this was finished just at the beginning of the Thirteenth Century. The choir is so beautiful in its conception, so wonderful in its construction, so charming in its finish, so satisfactory in all its detail, though there is very little of what would be called striving after effect in it, that it is still called the Angel Choir.

The name was originally given it because it was considered to be so beautiful even during the Thirteenth Century, that visitors could scarcely believe that it was constructed by human hands and so the legend became current that it was the work of angels. If the critics of the Thirteenth Century, who had the opportunity to see work of nearly the same kind being constructed in many parts of England, judged thus highly of it, it is not surprising that modern visitors should be unstinted in their praise. It is interesting to note as representative of the feeling of a cultured modern scientific mind that Dr. Osler said not long ago, in one of his medical addresses, that probably nothing more beautiful had ever come from the hands of man than this Angel Choir at Lincoln. As to who were the designers, who conceived it, or the workmen who executed it, we have no records. It is not unlikely that the famous Hugh of Lincoln, the great Bishop to whom the Cathedral owes its foundation and much of its splendor, was responsible to no little extent for this beautiful feature of his Cathedral church. The workmen who made it were artist-artisans in the best sense of the word and it is not surprising that other beautiful archtectural features should have flourished in a country where such workmen could be found.

Almost as impressive as the Angel Choir was the stained glass work at Lincoln. The rose windows are among the most beautiful ever made and one of them is indeed considered a gem of its kind. The beautiful colors and wonderful effectiveness of the stained glass of these old time Cathedrals cannot be appreciated unless the windows themselves are actually seen. At Lincoln there is a very impressive contrast that one can scarcely help calling to attention and that has been very frequently the subject of comment by visitors. During the Parliamentary time, unfortunately, the stained glass at Lincoln fell under the ban of the Puritans. The lower windows were almost completely destroyed by the soldiers of Cromwell's army. Only the rose windows owing to their height were preserved from the destroyer. There was an old sexton at the Cathedral, however, for whom the stained glass had become as the apple of his eye. As boy and man he had lived in its beautiful colors as they broke the light of the rising and the setting sun and they were too precious to be neglected even when lying upon the pavement of the Cathedral in fragments. He gathered the shattered pieces into bags and hid them away in a dark corner of the crypt, saving them at least from the desecration of being trampled to dust.

Long afterwards, indeed almost in our own time, they were found here and were seen to be so beautiful that regardless of the fact that they could not be fitted together in anything like their former places, they were pieced into windows and made to serve their original purpose once more? It so happened that new stained glass windows for the Cathedral of Lincoln were ordered during the Nineteenth Century. These were made at an unfortunate time in stained glass making and are as nearly absolutely unattractive, to say nothing worse, as it is possible to make stained glass. The contrast with the antique windows, fragmentary as they are, made up of the broken pieces of Thirteenth Century glass is most striking. The old time colors are so rich that when the sun shines directly on them they look like jewels. No one pays the slightest attention, unless perhaps the doubtful compliment of a smile be given, to the modern windows which were, however, very costly and the best that could be obtained at that time.

More of the stained glass of the Thirteenth Century is preserved at York where, because of the friendship of General Ireton, the town and the Cathedral were spared the worst ravages of the Parliamentarians. As a consequence York still possesses some of the best of its old time windows. It is probable that there is nothing more beautiful or wonderful in its effectiveness than the glass in the Five Sisters window at York. This is only an ordinary lancet window of five compartments—hence the name—in the west front of the Cathedral. There are no figures on the window, it is only a mass of beautiful greyish green tints which marvelously subdues the western setting sun at the vesper hour and produces the most beautiful effects in the interior of the Cathedral. Here if anywhere one can realize the meaning of the expression dim religious light. In recent years, however, it has become the custom for so many people to rave over the Five Sisters that we are spared the necessity of more than mentioning it. Its tints far from being injured by time have probably been enriched. There can be no doubt at all, however, of the artistic tastes and esthetic genius of the man who designed it. The other windows of the Cathedral were not unworthy of this truimph of art. How truly the Cathedral was a Technical School can be appreciated from the fact that it was able to inspire such workmen to produce these wondrous effects.

Experts in stained glass work have often called attention to the fact that the windows constructed in the Thirteenth Century were not only of greater artistic value but were also more solidly put together. Many of the windows made in the century still maintain their places, in spite of the passage of time, though later windows are sometimes dropping to pieces. It might be thought that this was due to the fact that later stained glass workers were more delicate in the construction of their windows in order not to injure the effect of the stained glass. To some extent this is true, but the stained glass workers of the Thirteenth Century preserve the effectiveness of their artistic pictures in glass, though making the frame work very substantial. This is only another example of their ability to combine the useful with the beautiful so characteristic of the century, stamping practically every phase of its accomplishment and making their work more admirable because its usefulness does not suffer on account of any strained efforts after supposed beauties.

Though it is somewhat out of place here we cannot refrain

from pointing out the educational value of this stained glass work.

Some of the stories on these windows gave details of many passages from the Bible, that must have impressed them upon the people much more than any sermon or reading of the text could possibly have accomplished. They were literally sermons in glass that he who walked by had to read whether he would or not. When we remember that the common people in the Middle Ages had no papers to distract them, and no books to turn to for information, such illustrations as were provided by the stained glass windows, by the painting and the statuary decorations of the Cathedrals, must have been studied with fondest devotion even apart from religious sentiment and out of mere inquisitiveness. The famous "prodigal" window at Chartres is a good example of this. Every detail of the story is here pictorially displayed in colors, from the time when the young man demands his patrimony through all the various temptations he met with in being helped to spend it, there being a naive richness of detail in the matter of the temptations that is quite medieval, from the boon companions who first led him astray to the depths of degradation which he finally reached before he returned to his father,—even the picture of the fatted calf is not lacking.

On others of these windows there are the stories of the Patron Saints of certain crafts. The life of St. Crispin the shoemaker is given in rather full detail. The same is true of St. Romain the hunter who was the patron of the furriers. The most ordinary experiences of life are pictured and the methods by which these were turned to account in making the craftsman a saint, must have been in many ways an ideally uplifting example for fellow craftsmen whenever they viewed the window. This sort of teaching could not be without its effect upon the poor. It taught them that there was something else in life besides money getting and that happiness and contentment might be theirs in a chosen occupation and the reward of Heaven at the end of it all, for at the top of these windows the hand of the Almighty is introduced reaching down from Heaven to reward his faithful servants. It is just by such presentation of ideals even to the poor, that

the Thirteenth Century differs from the modern time in which
even the teaching in the schools seems only to emphasize the
fact that men must get money, honestly if they can, but must
get money, if they would have what is called success in life.

Another very interesting feature of these windows is the
fact that they were usually the gifts of the various Guilds and
so represented much more of interest for the members. It
is true that in France, particularly, the monarchs frequently presented stained glass windows and in St. Louis time this was so
common that scarcely a French Cathedral was without one or
more testimonials of this kind to his generosity; but most of
the windows were given by various societies among the people
themselves. How much the construction of such a window
when it was well done, would make for the education in taste
of those who contributed to the expense of its erection, can
scarcely be over-estimated. There was besides a friendly rivalry in this matter in the Thirteenth Century, which served to
bring out the talents of local artists and by the inevitably suggested comparisons eventually served to educate the taste of the
people.

It must not be thought, however, that it was only in
stained glass and painting and sculpture—the major arts—
that these workmen attained their triumphs. Practically every
detail of Cathedral construction is a monument to the artistic genius of the century, to the wonderful inspiration afforded
the workmen and to the education provided by the Guilds
which really maintained, as we shall see, a kind of Technical
School with the approbation and the fostering care of the
ecclesiastics connected with the Cathedrals. An excellent example of a very different class of work may be noted in the
hinges of the Cloister door of the Cathedral at York. Personally I have seen three art designers sketching these at the
same time only one of whom was an Englishman, another coming from the continent and the third from America. The
hinge still swings the heavy oak door of the Thirteenth Century. The arborization of the metal as it spreads out from the
main shaft of the hinge is beautifully decorative in effect.
A little study of the hinge seems to show that these branching
portions were so arranged as to make the mechanical mo-

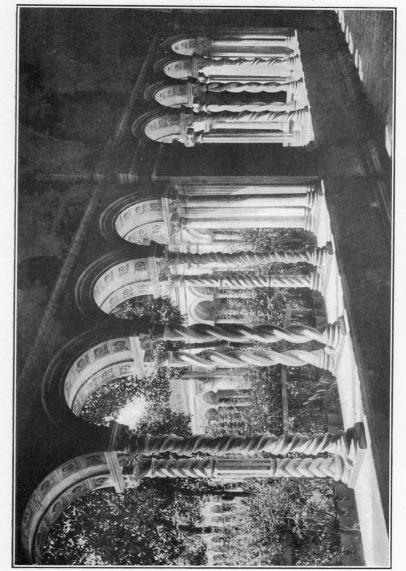

CLOISTER OF ST. PAUL'S (WITHOUT THE WALLS, ROME)

ment of the swinging door less of a dead weight than it would have been if the hinge were a solid bar of iron. Besides the spreading of the branches over a wide surface serves to hold the woodwork of the door thoroughly in place. While the hinge was beautiful, then it was eminently useful from a good many standpoints, and trivial though it might be considered to be, it was in reality a type of all the work accomplished in connection with these Thirteenth Century Cathedrals. According to the old Latin proverb *"omne tulit punctum qui miscuit utile dulci,"* he scores every point who mingles the useful with the beautiful, and certainly the Thirteenth Century workman succeeded in accomplishing the desideratum to an eminent degree. This mingling of the useful and the beautiful is of itself a supreme difference between the Thirteenth Century generations and our own. Mr. Yeats, the well known Irish poet, in bidding farewell to America some years ago said to a party of friends, that no country could consider itself to be making real progress in culture until the very utensils in the kitchen were beautiful as well as useful. Anything that is merely useful is hideous, and anyone who can handle such things with impunity has not true culture. In the Thirteenth Century they never by any chance made anything that was merely useful, especially not if it was to be associated with their beloved Cathedral.

An excellent example of this can be found in their Chalices and other ceremonial utensils which were meant for Divine Service. As we have said elsewhere The Craftsman, the journal of the Arts and Crafts Movement in this country not long since compared a Chalice of the Thirteenth Century with the prize cups which are offered for yacht races and other competitions in this country. We may say at once that the form which the Chalice received during the Thirteenth Century is that which constitutes to a great extent the model for this sacred vessel ever since and the comparison with the modern design is therefore all the more interesting. In spite of the fact that money is no object as a rule in the construction of many of the modern prize cups, they compare unfavorably according to the writer in The Craftsman with the old time chalices. There is a tendency to over ornamentation which

spoils the effectiveness of the lines of the metal work in many
cases and there is also only too often, an attempt to introduce
forms of plastic art which do not lend themselves well to this
class of work. It is in design particularly that the older workman excels his modern colleague though usually there are
suggestions from several sources for present day work. In
a word the Thirteenth Century Chalice was much more admirable than the modern piece of metal work, because the lines
were simpler, the combination of beauty with utility more
readily recognizable and the obtrusiveness of the ornamentation much less marked.

This same thing is true for other even coarser forms of
metal work in connection with the Cathedrals, and anyone
who has seen some of the beautiful iron screens built for
Cathedral choirs in the olden times will realize that even the
worker in iron must have been an artist as well as a blacksmith.
The effect produced, especially in the dim light of the Cathedral, is often that of delicate lace work. To appreciate the
strength of the screen one must actually test it with the
hands. This of itself represents a very charming adaptation
of what might be expected to be rough work meant for protective purposes into a suitable ornament. Some of the
gates of the old churchyards are very beautiful in their designs and have often been imitated in quite recent years, for
the gates of country places, for our modern millionaires. The
Reverend Augustus Jessop who has written much with regard to the times before the Reformation, says that he has
found in his investigations, that not infrequently such gates were
made by the village blacksmiths. Most of the old parish records are lost because of the suppression of the parishes as
well as the monasteries in Henry the Eighth's time. Some of
the original documents are, however, preserved and among
them are receipts from the village blacksmith, for what we now
admire as specimens of artistic ironwork and corresponding
receipts from the village carpenter, for woodwork that we
now consider of equally high order. There were carved bench
ends and choir stalls which seem to have been produced in
this way. Just how these generations of the Thirteenth Century, in little towns of less than ten thousand inhabitants, suc-

ceeded in raising up artisans in numbers, capable of doing such fine work, and yet content to make their living at such ordinary occupations, is indeed hard to understand. It must not be forgotten, moreover, that though there was not much furniture during the Thirteenth Century what little there was, was as a rule very carefully and artistically made. Thirteenth Century benches and tables are famous. Cathedrals and castles worked together in inspiring and giving occupation to these wonderful workmen.

It was not only the workmen engaged in the construction of the edifices proper who made the beautiful things and created marvelously artistic treasures during this century. All the adornments of the Cathedrals and especially everything associated in any intimate way with the religious service was sure to be executed with the most delicate taste. The vestments of the time are some of the most beautiful that have ever been made. The historians of needlework tell us that this period represents the most flourishing era of artistic accomplishment with the needle of all modern history. One example of this has secured a large share of notoriety in quite recent years. An American millionaire bought the famous piece of needlework known as the Cope of Ascoli. This is an example of the large garment worn over the shoulders in religious processions and at benediction. The price paid for the garment is said to have been $60,000. This was not considered extortionate or enforced, as the Cope was declared by experts to be one of the finest pieces of needlework in the world. The jewels which originally adorned it had been removed so that the money was paid for the needlework itself. After a time it became clear that the Cope had been stolen before being sold, and accordingly it was returned to the Italian government who presented the American millionaire with a medal for his honesty.

We have spoken of the Cathedrals as great stone books, in which he who ran, might read, even though he were not able to read in the technical sense of the term. This has been an old-time expression with regard to the Cathedrals, but not even its inventor perhaps, and certainly not most of those who have repeated it have realized how literally true was the saying. I have elsewhere quoted from Reinach's Story of Art Through-out the Ages as an authority on the subject. His re-statement of the intellectual significance for the people of the Cathedrals of their towns, in which it must be remembered that they had a personal interest because in a sense they were really theirs, and they felt their ownership quite as much as a modern member of a parish feels with regard to his church, emphasizes and illuminates this subject to a wonderful degree. The realization that the information of the time was deliberately woven into these great stone structures, mainly of course for decorative purposes, but partly also with the idea of educating the people, is a startling confirmation of the idea that education was the most important and significant work of this great century.

"The Gothic Cathedral is a perfect encyclopedia of human knowledge. It contains scenes from the Scriptures and the legends of saints; motives from the animal and vegetable kingdom; representations of the seasons of agricultural labor, of the arts and sciences and crafts, and finally moral allegories, as, for instance, ingenious personifications of the virtues and the vices. In the Thirteenth Century a learned Dominican, Vincent of Beauvais, was employed by St. Louis to write a great work which was to be an epitome of all the knowledge of his times. This compilation, called The Mirror of the World, is divided into four parts: The Mirror of Nature, The Mirror of Science, the Moral Mirror, and the Historical Mirror. A contemporary archaeologist, M. E. Male, has shown that the works of art of our great cathedrals are a translation into stone of the Mirror of Vincent of Beauvais, setting aside the episodes from Greek and Roman History, which would have been out of place. It was not that the imagers had read Vincent's work; but that, like him, they sought to epitomise all the knowledge of their contemporaries. The first aim of their art is not to please, but to teach; they offer an encyclopedia for the use of those who cannot read, translated by sculptor or glass-painter into a clear and precise language, under the lofty direction of the Church which left nothing to chance. It was present always and everywhere, advising and superintending the artist, leaving him to his own devices only when he

CATHEDRAL (CHARTRES)

CATHEDRAL (BOURGES)

modelled the fantastic animals of the gargoyles, or borrowed decorative motives from the vegetable kingdom."*

As to how much the cathedrals held of meaning for those who built them and worshiped in them, only a careful study of the symbolism of the time will enable the present-day admirer to understand. Modern generations have lost most of their appreciation of the significance of symbolism. The occupation of mind with the trivial things that are usually read in our day, leaves little or no room for the study of the profounder thought an artist may care to put into his work, and so the modern artist tells his story as far as possible without any of this deeper significance, since it would only be lost. In the Thirteenth Century, however, everything artistic had a secondary meaning. Literature was full of allegories, even the Arthur Legends were considered to be the expression of the battle of a soul with worldly influences as well as a poetic presentation of the story of the old time British King. The Gothic Cathedrals were a mass of symbolism. This will perhaps be best understood from the following explanation of Cathedral symbolism, which we take from the translation of Durandus's work on the meaning of the Divine Offices, a further account of which will be found in the chapter on The Prose of the Century.

"Far away and long ere we can catch the first view of the city itself, the three spires of its Cathedral, rising high above its din and turmoil, preach to us of the Most High and Undivided Trinity. As we approach, the Transepts, striking out crosswise, tell of the Atonement. The Communion of Saints is set forth by the chapels clustering around Choir and Nave: the mystical weathercock bids us to watch and pray and endure hardness; the hideous forms that are seen hurrying from the eaves speak the misery of those who are cast out of the church; spire, pinnacle, and finial, the upward curl of the sculptured foliage, the upward spring of the flying buttress, the sharp rise of the window arch, the high thrown pitch of the roof, all these, overpowering the horizontal tendency of string course and parapet, teach us, that vanquishing earthly desires, we also should ascend in heart and mind. Lessons of holy

* **Reinach—The Story of Art Throughout the Ages, Scribner's, 1904.**

wisdom are written in the delicate tracery of the windows;
the unity of many members is shadowed forth by the multiplex
arcade; the duty of letting our light shine before men, by the
pierced and flowered parapet that crowns the whole.

We enter. The triple breadth of Nave and Aisles, the triple
height of Pier arch, Triforium, and Clerestory, the triple length
of Choir, Transepts, and Nave, again set forth the HOLY
TRINITY. And what besides is there that does not tell of our
Blessed SAVIOUR? that does not point out "HIM First" in
the two-fold western door; "HIM Last" in the distant altar;
"HIM Midst," in the great Rood; "HIM Without End," in
the monogram carved on boss and corbel, in the Holy Lamb, in
the Lion of the tribe of Judah, in the Mystic Fish? Close by
us is the font; for by regeneration we enter the Church; it
is deep and capacious; for we are buried in Baptism with
CHRIST; it is of stone, for HE is the Rock; and its spiry
cover teaches us, if we be indeed risen from its waters with
HIM, to seek those things which are above. Before us in
long-drawn vista are the massy piers, which are the Apostles
and Prophets—they are each of many members, for many are
the Graces in every Saint, there is beautifully delicate foliage
round the head of all; for all were plentiful in good works.
Beneath our feet are the badges of worldly pomp and glory,
the graves of Kings and Nobles and Knights; all in the Presence of God as dross and worthlessness. Over us swells
the vast valley of the high pitched roof; from the crossing and
interlacing of its curious rafters hang fadeless flowers and
fruits which are not of earth; from its hammer-beams project
wreaths and stars such as adorn heavenly beings; in its
center stands the LAMB as it has been slain; from around
HIM the celestial Host, Cherubim and Seraphim, Thrones,
Principalities, and Powers, look down peacefully on the wor-
shipers below. Harpers there are among them harping with
their harps; for one is the song of the Church in earth and in
Heaven. Through the walls wind the narrow cloister galleries;
emblems of the path by which holy hermits and anchorets
whose conflicts were known only to their GOD, have reached
their Home. And we are compassed about with a mighty
cloud of witnesses; the rich deep glass of the windows teems

with saintly forms, each in its own fair niche, all invested with the same holy repose; there is the glorious company of the Apostles; the goodly fellowship of the Prophets; the noble army of Martyrs; the shining band of Confessors; the jubilant chorus of the Virgins; there are Kings, who have long since changed an earthly for an heavenly crown; and Bishops who have given in a glad account to the Shepherd and Bishop of souls. But on none of these things do we rest; piers, arch behind arch, windows, light behind light, arcades, shaft behind shaft, the roof, bay behind bay, the Saints around us, the Heavenly Hierarchy above with dignity of preeminence still increasing eastward, each and all, lead on eye and soul and thought to the Image of the Crucified Saviour as dispayed on the great East window. Gazing steadfastly on that we pass up the Nave, that is through the Church Militant, till we reach the Rood Screen, the barrier between it and the Church Triumphant, and therein shadowing forth the death of the Faithful. High above it hangs on His Triumphant Cross the image of Him who by His death hath overcome death; on it are portrayed Saints and Martyrs, His warriors who, fighting under their LORD have entered into rest and inherit a tearless eternity. They are to be our examples, and the seven lamps above them typify those graces of the SPIRIT, by Whom alone we can tread in their steps. The screen itself glows with gold and crimson; with gold, for they have on their heads goden crowns; with crimson, for they passed the Red Sea of Martyrdom, to obtain them. And through the delicate network, and the unfolding Holy Doors, we catch faint glimpses of the Chancel beyond. There are the massy stalls; for in Heaven is everlasting rest; there are the Sedilia, emblems of the seats of the Elders round the Throne; there is the Piscina; for they have washed their robes and made them white; and there heart and soul and life of all, the Altar with its unquenched lights, and golden carvings, and mystic steps, and sparkling jewels; even CHRIST Himself, by Whose only Merits we find admission to our Heavenly Inheritance. Verily, as we think on the oneness of its design, we may say: Jerusalem edificatur ut civitas cujus participatio ejus in idipsum."

It is because of all this wealth of meaning embodied in them, that the Cathedrals of this old time continue to be so interesting and so unfailingly attractive even to our distant and so differently constituted generation.*

We cannot close this chapter on the Book of the Arts leaving the impression that only the Church Architecture of the time deserves to be considered in the category of great art influences. There were many municipal buildings, some stately castles, and a large number of impressively magnificent Abbeys and Monasteries, besides educational and charitable institutions built at this same time. The town halls of some of the great Hansa towns, that is, the German free cities that were members of the Hanseatic League, present some very striking examples of the civil architecture of the period. It has the same characteristics that we have discussed in treating of the Cathedrals. While wonderfully impressive it was eminently suitable for the purpose for which it was intended and the decorations always forming integral parts of the structure, sounded the note of the combination of beauty with utility which is so characteristic of every phase of the art accomplishment of the century.

Some of the castles would deserve special description by themselves but unfortunately space forbids more than a passing mention. Certain castellated fortresses still standing in England and Ireland come from the time of King John, and are excellent examples of the stability and forceful character of this form of architecture in the Thirteenth Century. It is interesting to find that when we come to build in the Twentieth Century in America, the armories which are to be used for the training of our militia and the storage of arms and ammunition, many of the ideas used in their construction are borrowed from this olden time. There is a famous castle in Limerick, Ireland, built in John's time which constitutes an ex-

---

*Those who care to realize to some degree all the wonderful symbolic meaning of the ornamentation of some of these cathedrals, should read M. Huysman's book La Cathedrale, which has, we believe, been translated into English. Needless to say it has been often in our hands in compiling this chapter, and the death of its author as this chapter is going through the press poignantly recalls all the beauty of his work.

DURHAM CASTLE AND CATHEDRAL

KING JOHN'S CASTLE (LIMERICK)

cellent example of this and which has doubtlessly often been studied and more or less imitated.

One portion of Kenilworth Castle in England dates from the Thirteenth Century and has been often the subject of careful study by modern architects. The same thing might be said of many others.

With regard to the English Abbeys too much cannot be said in praise of their architecture and it has been the model for large educational and municipal buildings ever since. St. Mary's Abbey at York, though only a few scattered fragments of its beauties are to be seen and very little of its walls still stand, is almost as interesting as Yorkminster, the great Cathedral itself. There were many such abbeys as this built in England during the Thirteenth Century—more than a dozen of them at least and probably a full score. All of them are as distinguished in the history of architecture as the English Cathedrals. It will be remembered that what is now called Westminster Abbey was not a Cathedral church, but only a monastery church attached to the Abbey of Westminster and this, the only well preserved example of its class furnishes an excellent idea of what these religious institutions signify in the Thirteenth Century. They meant as much for the art impulse as the Cathedrals themselves.

One feature of these monastic establishments deserves special mention. The cloisters were usually constructed so beautifully as to make them veritable gems of the art of the period. These cloisters were the porticos usually surrounding a garden of the monastery within which the Monks could walk, shaded from the sun, and protected from the rain and the snow. They might very easily have been hideously useful porches, especially as they were quite concealed from the outer world as a rule, and those not belonging to the order were not admitted to them except on very special occasions. The name cloister signifies an enclosed place and lay persons were not ordinarily admitted to them. Those who know anything about them will recall what beautiful constructive work was put into them. Certain examples as that of St. John Lateran in Rome and the Cloister of St. Paul's without the walls some five miles from Rome, constructed during the

Thirteenth Century and under the influence of the same great art movement as gave the Cathedrals, are the most beautiful specimens that now remain. The only thing that they can be compared with is the famous Angel Choir at Lincoln which indeed they recall in many ways.

The pictures of these two Cloisters which we present will give some idea of their beauty. To be thoroughly appreciated, however, they must be seen, for there is a delicacy of finish about every detail that makes them an unending source of admiration and brings people back again and again to see them, yet always to find something new and apparently unnoticed before. It might be thought that the studied variety in the columns so that no two are of exactly the same form, would produce a bizarre effect. The lack of symmetry that might result from this same feature could be expected to spoil their essential beauty. Neither of these effects has been produced, however. The Cloisters were, moreover, not purple patches on monasteries, but ever worthy portions of very beautiful buildings.

All of these buildings were furnished as regards their metal work, their wood work, and the portions that lent themselves to decoration, in the same spirit as the Cathedrals themselves. The magnificent tables and benches of the Thirteenth Century are still considered to be the best models of simplicity of line with beauty of form and eminent durability in the history of furniture making. The fashion for Colonial furniture in our own time has brought us nearer to such Thirteenth Century furniture making than has been true at any other time in history. Here once more there was one of these delightful combinations of beauty and utility which is so characteristic of the century. Even the kitchen utensils were beautiful as well as useful and the Irish poet might have been satisfied to his heart's content.

Certain other architectural forms were wonderfully developed during the Thirteenth Century and the opening years of the Fourteenth Century while men trained during the former period were still at work. Giotto's tower, for instance, must be considered a Thirteenth Century product since its architect was well past thirty-five years of age before the Thirteenth

PALAZZO VECCHIO (ARNULFO, FLORENCE)
CAMPANILE (GIOTTO)

GIOTTO'S TOWER (FLORENCE)

Century closed and all his artistic character had been formed under its precious inspiration. It is a curious reflection on modern architecture, that some of the modern high business buildings are saved from being hideous just in as much as they approach the character of some of these tower-like structures of the Thirteenth Century. The first of New York's skyscrapers which is said to have escaped the stigma of being utterly ugly, as most of them are, because of their appeal to mere utility, was the New York Times Building which is just Giotto's tower on a large scale set down on Broadway at the beginning of the Twentieth Century. Seen from a mile away the effect is exactly that of the great Florentine architect's beautiful structure and this was of course the deliberate intention of the modern architect. Anyone who would think, however, that our modern business building with its plain walls recalls in any adequate sense its great pattern, should read what Mr. Ruskin has said with regard to the wealth of meaning that is to be found in Giotto's tower. Into such structures just as into the Cathedrals, the architects and builders of the time succeeded in putting a whole burden of suggestion, which to the generations of the time in which they were built, accustomed to the symbolism of every art feature in life around them, had a precious wealth of significance that we can only appreciate after deep study and long contemplation. We have felt that only the quotation from Mr. Ruskin himself can fully illustrate what we wish to convey in this matter.

"Of these representations of human art under heavenly guidance, the series of basreliefs which stud the base of this tower of Giotto's must be held certainly the chief in Europe. At first you may be surprised at the smallness of their scale in proportion to their masonry; but this smallness of scale enabled the master workmen of the tower to execute them with their own hands; and for the rest, in the very finest architecture, the decoration of most precious kind is usually thought of as a jewel, and set with space round it—as the jewels of a crown, or the clasp of a girdle."

VII

ARTS AND CRAFTS—GREAT TECHNICAL SCHOOLS.

The most interesting social movement in our time is undoubtedly that of the arts and crafts. Its central idea is to lift the workmen up above the mere machine that he is likely to become, as the result of the monotonous occupation at some trade that requires him only to do a constantly repeated series of acts, or direct one little portion of machinery and so kills the soul in him. Of course, the other idea that a generation of workmen shall be created, who will be able to make beautiful things for the use of the household as well as the adornment of the house is another principal purpose. Too many people have mistaken this entirely secondary aim of the movement for its primary end. It is because of the effect upon the workman himself of the effort to use his intellect in the designing, his taste in the arrangement, and his artisan skill for the execution of beautiful things, that the arts and crafts movement has its appeal to the generality of mankind.

The success of the movement promises to do more to solve social problems than all the socialistic agitation that is at present causing so much dismay in some quarters and raising so many hopes that are destined to be disappointed in the hearts of the laboring classes. The solution of the problem of social unrest is to be found, not in creating new wants for people and giving them additional wages that will still further stimulate their desire to have many things that will continue to be in spite of increased wages beyond their means, but rather to give them such an interest in their life work that their principal source of pleasure is to be found in their occupation. Unfortunately work has come to be looked upon as a drudgery and as men must spend the greater portion of their lives, at least the vast majority of them must, in doing something that will enable them to make a living, it is clear that unhappiness and discontent will still continue. Blessed is the man who has found his work, blessed is the man to whom his work appeals with so much interest that he goes from it with a longing to be able to finish what he has been at, and comes back to it with a prospect that now he shall be able to accomplish what time and perhaps fatigue would not allow him to proceed with the day before.

This is the best feature of the promises held out by the arts and crafts movement, that men shall be interested in the work they do. This may seem to some people an unrealizable idea, and a poetic aspiration rather than a possible actuality. A little study of what was accomplished in this line during the Thirteenth Century, will surely prove even to the most skeptical how much of success is capable of being realized in this matter. The men who worked around the Cathedrals were given opportunities to express themselves and the best that was in them as no class of workmen before or since have ever had the opportunity. Every single portion of the Cathedral was to be made as beautiful as the mind of man could conceive, his taste could plan and his hands could achieve. As a consequence the carpenter had the chance to express himself in the woodwork, the village blacksmith the opportunity to display his skill in such small ironwork as the hinges or the latch for the door and every workman felt called upon to do the best that was in him.

It is easy to understand under these circumstances with what interest the men must have applied themselves to their tasks. They were, as a rule, the designers as well as the executors of the work assigned them. They planned and executed in the rough and tried, then modified and adapted, until finally as we know of most of the Cathedrals, their finished product was as nearly perfect in most particulars as it is ordinarily given to man to achieve. Their aim above all was to make such a combination of utility with beauty of line yet simplicity of finish, as would make their work worthy counterparts of all the other portions of the Cathedral. The sense of competition must have stirred men to the very depths of their souls and yet it was not the heartless rivalry that crushes when it succeeds, but the inspiring emulation that makes one do as well as or better than others, though not necessarily in such a way as to belittle others' efforts by contrast or humble them by triumph.

In these old medieval days England used to be called Merrie England and it is easy to understand that workmen would be profoundly merry at heart, when they had the consciousness of accomplishing such good work. Men must have almost tardily quitted their labor in the evening while they hoped and strove to accomplish something that would be worthy of the magnificent building in which so many of their fellow workmen were achieving triumphs of handicraftsmanship. Each went home to rest for the night, but also to dream over what he might be able to do and awoke in the morning with the thought that possibly to-day would see some noteworthy result. This represents the ideal of the workman's life. He has an interest quite apart from the mere making of money. The picture of the modern workman by contrast looks vain and sordid. The vast majority of our workmen labor merely because they must make enough money to-day, in order that they may be able to buy food enough so as to get strength to work to-morrow. Of interest there is very little. Day after day there is the task of providing for self and others. Only this and nothing more. Is it any wonder that there should be social unrest and discontentment? How can workmen be merry unless with the artificial stimulus of strong drink, when there is nothing for them to look forward to except days and weeks and years of labor succeeding one another remorselessly, and with no surcease until Nature puts in her effective demand for rest, or the inevitable end comes.

It would be idle to say that these men who knew how to make the beautiful things for these cathedrals were not conscious of the perfection of the work that they were accomplishing. The very fact that each in his own line was achieving such beautiful results must have stamped him as thoroughly capable of appreciating the work of others. The source of pleasure that there must have been therefore, in some twenty towns in England alone, to see their Cathedral approaching completion, must have been of itself a joy far beyond anything we can imagine as possible for the workmen of the present day. The interest in it was supreme and was only heightened by the fact that it was being done by relatives and friends and brother workmen, even

FOUNTAIN (PERUGIA). [TOWN PUMP]

LAVATOIO (TODI). [PUBLIC WASH HOUSE]

though they might be rivals, and that whatever was done was redounding first to the glory of the Lord to whom they turned with so much confidence in these ages of faith, and secondly, and there was scarcely less satisfaction in the thought, to the reputation of their native town and their fellow-townsmen.

This is the feature of the life of the lower classes in the Thirteenth Century which most deserves to be studied in our time. We hear much of people being kept in ignorance and in servitude. Men who talk this way know nothing at all of the lives of the towns of the Middle Ages and are able to appreciate not even in the slightest degree the wonderful system of education, that made life so much fuller of possibilities for intellectual development for all classes and for happiness in life, than any other period of which we know. This phase of the Thirteenth Century is at once the most interesting, the most significant for future generations, and the most important in its lessons for all time.

We have been following up thus far the exemplification in the Thirteenth Century of John Ruskin's saying, that if you wish to get at the real significance of the achievements of a period in history, you must read the book of its deeds, the book of its arts and the book of its words. We have been turning over a few of the pages of the book of the deeds of the Thirteenth Century in studying the history of the establishment of the universities and of the method and content of university teaching. After all the only deeds that ought to count in the history of mankind are those that are done for men—that have accomplished something for the uplift of mankind. History is unfortunately occupied with deeds of many other kinds, and it is perhaps the saddest blot on our modern education, that it is mainly the history of deeds that have been destructive of man, of human happiness and in only too many cases of human rights and human liberties, that are supposed to be most worthy of the study of the rising generation. History as written for schools is to a great extent a satire on efforts for social progress.

We shall continue the study of the book of the deeds of the Thirteenth Century and its most interesting and important chapter, that of the education of the masses. We shall find in what was accomplished in educating the people of the Thirteenth Century, the model of the form of education which in spite of our self-complacency does not exist, but must come in our time, if our education is to fulfil its real purpose. Perhaps the most interesting phase of this question of the education of the masses will be the fact that in studying this book of the deeds, we shall have also to study once more the book of the arts of the Thirteenth Century. All their best accomplishment was linked with achievement and progress in art. Yet it was from the masses that the large number of artist-artisans of workmen with the true artistic spirit came, who in this time in nearly every part of Europe, created masterpieces of art in every department which have since been the admiration of the world.

We may say at once that the opportunity for the education of the masses was furnished in connection with the Cathedrals. In the light of what we read in these great stone books, it is a constant source of surprise that the Church should be said to have been opposed to education. Reinach in his Story of Art throughout the Ages says:

"The Church was not only rich and powerful in the Middle Ages; it dominated and directed all the manifestations of human activity. There was practically no art but the art it encouraged, the art it needed to construct and adorn its buildings, carve its ivories and its reliquaries, and paint its glass and its missals. Foremost among the arts it fostered was architecture, which never played so important a part in any other society. Even now, when we enter a Romanesque or Gothic church, we are impressed by the might of that vast force of which it is the manifestation, a force which shaped the destinies of Europe for a thousand years."

It was as the result of this demand for art that the technical schools naturally developed around the Cathedrals. To take the example of England alone, during the Thirteenth Century some twenty cathedrals were erected in various parts of the country. Most of these were built in what we would now call small towns, indeed some of them would be considered scarcely more than villages. There were no large cities, in praise be it spoken, during the Thirteenth Century, and it must not be forgotten that the whole population of England at the beginning of the century was scarcely more than two millions of people and did not reach three millions even at the end of it. Every rood of ground did not perhaps maintain its man, but every part of England had its quota of population so that there could not be many crowded centers. Even London probably at no time during the century had more than twenty-five thousand inhabitants and Oxford during the palmiest days of the University was perhaps the most populous place in the land.

There was a rivalry in the building of Cathedrals, and as the main portion of the buildings were erected in the short space of a single century, a feeling of intense competition was rife so that there was very little possibility of procuring workmen from other towns. Each town had to create not only its cathedral but the workmen who would finish it in all its details. When we consider that a Cathedral like Salisbury was practically completed in the short space of about twenty-five years, it becomes extremely difficult to understand just how this little town succeeded in apparently accomplishing the impossible. It has often been said that artists cannot be obtained merely because of a demand for them and that they are the slow creation of rather capricious nature. It is only another way of saying that the artist is born, not made. Nature then must have been in a particularly fruitful mood and tense during the Thirteenth Century, for there is no doubt at all of the wonderful artistic beauty of the details of these Gothic cathedrals. While nature's beneficence meant much, however, the training of the century probably meant even more and the special form of popular education which developed well deserves the attention of all other generations.

It may be said at once that education in our sense of teaching everybody to read and write there was none. There were more students at the universities to the number of the population than in the Twentieth Century as we have seen, but people who were not to devote themselves in after life to book learning, were not burdened with acquisitions of doubtful benefit, which might provide stores of useless information for them, or enable them to while away hours of precious time reading trash, or make them conceited with the thought that because they had absorbed some of the opinions of others on things in general, they had a right to judge of most things under the sun and a few other things besides. The circulation of our newspapers and the records of the books in demand at our libraries, show how much a knowledge of reading means for most of our population. Popular education of this kind may, and does benefit a few, but it works harm to a great many.

Of education in the sense of training the faculties so that the individual might express whatever was in him and especially that he might bring out what was best in him, there was much. Take again the example of England. There was considerably less in population than there is in Greater New York at the present time, yet there was some twenty places altogether in which they were building Cathedrals during this century, that would be monuments of artistic impulse and accomplishment for all future time. Any city in this country would be proud to have any one of these English cathedrals of the Thirteenth Century as the expression of its taste and power to execute. We have tried to imitate them more or less in many places. In order to accomplish our purpose in this matter, though, we deliberately did everything on a much smaller and less ambitious scale than the people of the small English towns of seven centuries ago, and our results do not bear comparison for a moment with theirs, we had to appeal to other parts of the country and even to Europe for architects and designers, and even had to secure the finished products of art from distant places. This too, in spite of the fact that we are seven centuries later and that our education is supposed to be developed to a high extent. If there were twenty places of instruction in Greater New York where architects and artist workers in iron and glass, and metal of all kinds, and wood and stone, were being trained to become such finished artisans as were to be found in twenty different little towns of England in the Thirteenth Century, we should be sure that our manual training schools and our architectural departments of universities and schools of design were wonderfully successful.

When we find this to be true of the England of the Thirteenth Century we can conclude that somehow better opportunities for art education must have been supplied in those times than in our own, and though we do not find the mention or records of formal schools, we must look patiently for the methods of instruction that enabled these generations to accomplish so much. Needless to say such attainments do not come spontaneously in a large number of people, but must be carefully fostered and are the result of that greatest factor in education, environment. It will not be hard to find where the ambitious youth of England even of the workman class found opportunities for technical education of the highest character in these little towns. This was never merely theoretic, though, it was sufficiently grounded in principle to enable men to solve problems in architecture and engineering, in decoration and artistic arrangement, such as are still sources of anxiety for modern students of these questions.

To take but a single example, it will be readily appreciated that the consideration of the guilds of builders of the Cathedrals as constituting a great technical school, is marvelously emphasized by certain recent observations with regard to architects' and builders' methods in the Cathedrals. There is a passage in Evelyn's Diary in which he describes certain corrections that were introduced into Old St. Paul's Cathedral, London (the Gothic edifice predecessor of the present classical structure), in order to remove appearances of dissymmetry and certain seeming mistakes of construction. This passage was always so misunderstood that editors usually considered it to be defective in some way and as the classical critics always fall back on an imperfect text for insoluble difficulties, so somehow Evelyn was considered as either not having understood what he intended to say, or else the printer failed to put in all the words that he wrote. It was the modern readers, however, not Evelyn nor his printer who were mistaken. Mr. Goodyear of the Brooklyn Institute of Arts and Sciences has proved by a series of photographs and carefully made observations, that many of the old Gothic Cathedrals have incorporated into them by their builders, optical corrections which correspond to those made by the Greeks in their building in the classical period, which have been the subject of so much admiration to the moderns.

The medieval architects and builders knew nothing of these classical architectural refinements. They learned for themselves by actual experience the necessity for making such optical corrections and then introduced them so carefully, that it is not until the last decade or so that their presence has been realized. It is only by an educational tradition of the greatest value that the use of such a refinement could become as general as Professor Goodyear has found it to be. Besides the practical work then, and the actual exercise of craftsmanship and of design which the apprentices obtained from the guild, there was evidently a body of very definite technical information conveyed to them, or at least to certain chosen spirits among them, which carried on precious traditions from place to place. This same state of affairs must of course have existed with regard to stained glass work, the making of bells and especially the finer work in the precious metals. Practical metallurgy must have been studied quite as faithfully as in any modern technical school, at least so far as its practical purposes and application were concerned. Here we have the secret of the technical schools revealed.

It is extremely interesting to study the details of the very practical organization by which this great educational movement in the arts and crafts was brought about. It was due entirely to the trades' and merchants' guilds of the time. In the cathedral towns the trades' guilds preponderated in influence. There gathered around each of these cathedrals during the years when work was most active, numbers of workmen engaged at various occupations requiring mechanical skill and long practice at their trade. These workmen were all affiliated with one another and they were gradually organized into trades' unions that had a certain independent existence. There was the guild of the stone workers; the guild of the metal workers—in some places divided into a guild of iron workers and a guild of gold workers, or workers in precious metals; there was the guild of the wood workers and then of the various other forms of occupation connected with the supplying of finished or unfinished materials for the cathedral. In association with these were established guilds of tailors, bakers, butchers, all affiliated in a merchants' guild which maintained the rights of its members as well as the artisans' guilds. Some idea of the number and variety of these can be obtained from the list given in the chapter on the Origin of the Drama.

RELIQUARY (LIMOGES)

CRUCIFIX (SIENA)

These were the workmen who not only accomplished such brilliant results in art work, but also succeeded in training other workmen so admirably for every line of artistic endeavor.

It is somewhat difficult to understand just how a village carpenter did wood-carving of so exquisite a design and such artistic finish of detail that it has remained a subject of admiration for centuries. It is quite as difficult to understand how one of the village blacksmiths of the time made a handsome gate, that has been the constant admiration of posterity ever since, or designed huge hinges for doors that artists delight to copy, or locks and latches and bolts that are transported to our museums to be looked at with interest, not only because they are antiques, but for the wonderful combination of the beautiful and the useful which they illustrate. We are assured, however, by the Rev. Augustus Jessop, that he has seen in the archives of the old English parishes, some of the receipts for the bills of these village workmen for the making of these beautiful specimens of arts and crafts. (See Appendix.)

The surprise grows greater when we realize that these beautiful objects were made not alone in one place or even in a few places, but in nearly every town of any size in England and France and Italy and Germany and Spain at various times during the Thirteenth Century, and that at any time a town of considerably less than ten thousand inhabitants seemed to be able to obtain among its own inhabitants, men who could make such works of art not as copies nor in servile imitation of others, but with original ideas of their own, and make them in such perfection that in many cases they have remained the models for future workmen for many centuries. Even the bells for the cathedrals seem to have keen cast in practically all cases in the little town in which they were to be used. It may be added that these bells of the Thirteenth Century represent the highest advances in bell making that have ever been attained and that their form and composition have simply been imitated over and over again since that time. Even the finer precious metal work such as chalices and the various sacred vessels and objects used in the church services, were not obtained from a distance but were made at home.

An article that appeared a few years ago in The Craftsman

(Syracuse, N. Y.), a magazine published in the interests of the
Arts and Crafts movement, called attention to how much more
beautifully the Thirteenth Century workman in the precious
metals accomplished his artistic purpose than does the corresponding workman of the present day. A definite comparison
was made between some typical chalices of the Thirteenth Century and some prize cups which were made without regard to
cost, as rewards for yachting and other competitions in the
Twentieth Century. The artist workman of the olden time
knew how to combine the beautiful with the useful, to use decoration just enough not to offend good taste, to make the lines of
his work eminently artistic and in general to turn out a fine
work of art. The modern prize cup is usually made by one of
the large firms engaged in such work who employ special designers for the purpose, such designs ordinarily passing
through the trained hands of a series of critics before being
accepted and only after this are turned over to the modern skilled workmen to be executed in metal. All this ought
to assure the more artistic results; that they do not according to the writer in the Craftsman, demonstrates how
much such success is a matter of men and of individual taste
rather than of method. We have already called attention to the
fact that in needlework and in other arts connected with the
provision of church ornaments and garments, the success of the
Thirteenth Century workers was quite as great. The Cope of
Ascoli considered by experts to be one of the most beautiful
bits of needlework ever made is an example of this. Many
other examples are to be found in the treasuries of churches
and monasteries, in spite of the ravages of time and only too often of intolerant and unfortunate destruction by so-called re-
formers, who could see no beauty in even the most beautiful
things if they ran counter to certain of their religious prejudices.

The training necessary for the production of such beautiful
objects of handicraftsmanship was obtained through the guilds
themselves. The boy in the small town who thought that he
had a liking for a certain trade or craft was received as an ap-
prentice in it. If during the course of a year or more he demonstrated his aptness for his chosen craft, he was allowed to con-

tinue his labor of assisting the workmen in various ways, and indeed very early in the history of the guilds was bound over to some particular workman, who usually supplied him with board and clothing, though with no other remuneration during his years of apprenticeship. After four or five years, always, however, with the understanding that he had shown a definite talent for his chosen trade, he was accepted among the workmen of the lowest grade, the journeymen, who usually went traveling in order to perfect their knowledge of the various methods by which their craft maintained itself and the standard of its workmanship in the different parts of the country.

During these three years of "journeying" a striking development was likely to take place in the mind of the ambitious young workman. His *wanderjahre* came just at the most susceptible period, sometime betwen 17 and 25, they continued for three years or more, and the young workman if at all ambitious was likely to see many men and methods and know much of the cities and towns of his country before he returned to his native place. Sometimes these craft-wanderings took him even into France, where he learned methods and secrets so different to those at home.

After these years if he wished to settle down in his native town or in some other, having brought evidence of the accomplishment of his apprenticeship and then of his years as a journeyman, he became an applicant for full membership in the guild to which his years of training had been devoted. He was not admitted, however, until he had presented to the officials of the organization a piece of work showing his skill. This might be only a hinge, or a lock for a door, but on the other hand it might be a design for an important window or a delicate piece of wood or stone-carving. If it was considered worthy of the standard of workmanship of the guild it was declared to be a masterpiece. This is where the fine old English word masterpiece comes from. The workman was then admitted as a master workman and became a full member of the guild.

This membership carried with it a number of other rights besides that of permission to work as a master-workman at full wages whenever the guild was employed. Guilds had certain privileges conferred on them by the towns in which they lived,

by the nobles for whom they worked and the ecclesiastical authorities on whose various church structures they were employed. At the beginning of the Thirteenth Century at least,
feudal ideas prevailed to such an extent that no one was supposed to enjoy any rights or privileges except those which had
been conferred on him by some authority. Besides the workmen of the same guild were bound together by ties, so that any
injury inflicted on one of them was considered to be done to
the whole body. When human rights were much less recognized than has come to be the case since, this constituted an important source of protection against many forms of injury and
infringement of rights.

Besides the privileges, however, the guild possessed certain
other decided advantages which made membership desirable,
even though it involved the fulfilment of certain duties. In the
various towns in England, after the introduction during the
Thirteenth Century of the practice of having mystery plays in
the various towns, the guild claimed and obtained the privilege
of giving these at various times during the year. The guild of
the goldsmiths would give the performance of one portion of
the Old Testament; the guild of the tailors another; the guild
of the butchers and so on for each of the trades and crafts still
another, so that during the year a whole cycle of the mysteries
of the Christian religion in type and in reality were exhibited
to the people of each region. Almost needless to say, on such
festive occasions, for the plays were given on important feast
days, the people from the countryside flocked in to see them and
the influence was widespread. What was most important, however, was the influence on those who took part in the plays, of
such intimate contact for a prolonged period with the simplicity
of style, the sublimity of thought, the concentration of purpose
and the effectiveness of expression of the Scriptures and the
Scripture narratives even in their dramatized form.

The fact of actually taking part in these performances meant
ever so much more than merely viewing them as an outsider. It
is doubtless to this intimate relationship with the great truths
of Christianity that the profound devotion so characteristic of
the accomplishments of the arts and crafts, during the Thirteenth Century must be to no little extent attributed. Their

MADONNA (CIMABUE, FLORENCE)

beautiful work could only have come from men of profoundest faith, but also it could not have come from those who were ignorant of the basis of what they accepted on faith. In other words, there was a mental training with regard to some of the sublimest truths of life and its significance, the creation of a Christian philosophy of life, that made the workman see clearly the great truths of religion and so be able to illustrate them by his handiwork. Education of a higher order than this has never been conceived of, and the very lack of tedious formality in it only made it all the more effectual in action.

Other duties were involved in membership in the guild. All the members were bound to attend church services regularly and to perform what is known as their religious duties at periodic intervals, that is, the rule of the guild required them to go to mass on Sundays and holy days, to abstain from manual labor on such days unless there was absolute necessity for it and to go to confession and communion several times a year. Besides they were bound to contribute to the support of such of their fellow-members as were sick and unable to work or as had been injured. A very interesting phase of this duty toward sick members existed at least in some parts of the country. A workman was supposed to pass one night at certain intervals on his turn in helping to nurse a fellow-workman who was seriously hurt or who was very ill. It was considered that the family were quite worn out enough with the care of the sick man during the day, and so one of his brother guildsmen came to relieve them of this duty at night. It is a custom that is still maintained in certain country places but which of course has passed out of use entirely in our unsympathetic city life. In a word, there was a thorough education not only in the life work that made for wages and family support, but also in those precious social duties that make for happiness and contentment in life.

VIII

GREAT ORIGINS IN PAINTING.*

At the commencement of the Thirteenth Century the movement of emancipation in every phase of thought and life in
Italy went on apace with an extraordinary ardor. After a very
serious struggle the Italian republics were on the point of forc-
ing the German Empire to recognize them. Everywhere in the
first enthusiasm of their independence which had been achieved
by valiant deeds and aspirations after liberty as lofty as any in
modern times, the cities, though united in confederations they
were acting as independent rivals, brought to all enterprises, lay
or religious foundations, commercial or educational institutions,
a wonderful youthful activity and enterprise. The papacy allied with them favored this movement in its political as well as
its educational aspects and strengthened the art movement of
the time. Christianity under their guidance, by the powerful
religious exhaltation which it inspired in the hearts of all men,
became a potent factor in all forms of art. From Pope Innocent
III to Boniface VIII probably no other series of Popes have
been so misunderstood and so misrepresented by subsequent
generations, as certainly the Popes of no other century did so
much to awaken the enthusiasm of Christians for all modes of
religious development, and be it said though credit for this is

---

* Most of this chapter is taken from the work on Italian painting (La
Peinture Italienne depuis les origines jusqu'a la fin du xv Siecle, par
Georges Lafenestre, Paris Ancienne Maison Quantin Libraries-Imprime-
ries Reunies, May & Motteroz, Directeurs, rue Saint-Benoit. Nou-
velle Edition), which forms one of the series of text books for instruction in art at L'Ecole Des Beaux-Arts—the famous French Government
Art School in Paris. It may be said that this collection of art manuals is
recognized as an authority on all matters treated of, having been crowned
by the Academie Des Beaux-Arts with the prize Bordin. There is no
better source of information with regard to the development of the arts
and none which can be more readily consulted nor with more assurance
as to the facts and opinions exposed.

only too often refused them, also for educational, charitable and social betterment.

The two great church institutions of the time that were destined to act upon the people more than any others were the Franciscan and Dominican orders—the preachers and the friars minor, who were within a short time after their formation to have such deep and widespread influence on all strata of society. Both of these orders from their very birth showed themselves not only ready but anxious to employ the arts as a means of religious education and for the encouragement of piety. Their position in this matter had an enormous influence on art and on the painters of the time. The Dominicans, as became their more ambitious intellectual training and their purpose as preachers of the word, demanded encyclopedic and learned compositions; the Franciscans asked for loving familiar scenes such as would touch the hearts of the common people. Both aided greatly in helping the artist to break away from the old fashioned formalism which was no longer sufficient to satisfy the new ardors of men's souls. In this way they prepared the Italian imagination for the double revolution which was to come.

It was the great body of legends which grew up about St. Francis particularly, all of them bound up with supreme charity for one's neighbor, with love for all living creatures even the lowliest, with the tenderest feelings for every aspect of external nature, which appealed to the painters as a veritable light in the darkness of the times. It was especially in the churches founded by the disciples of "the poor little man of Assisi," that the world saw burst forth before the end of the century, the first grand flowers of that renewal of art which was to prove the beginning of modern art history. It is hard to understand what would have happened to the painters of the time without the spirit that was brought into the world by St. Francis' beautifully simple love for all and every phase of nature around him. This it was above all that encouraged the return to nature that soon supplanted Oriental formalism. It was but due compensation that the greatest works of the early modern painters should have been done in St. Francis' honor. Besides this the most important factor in art was the revival of the thirst for knowledge, which arose among the more intellectual portions of the communities and developed an enthusiasm for antiquity which was only a little later to become a veritable passion.

The most important phase of Italian art during the Thirteenth Century is that which developed at Florence. It is with this that the world is most familiar. It began with Cimabue, who commenced painter, in the quaint old English phrase, not long before the middle of the century and whose great work occupies the second half of it. There are not wanting some interesting traditions of certain other Florentine painters before his time as Marchisello, of the early part of the century, Lapo who painted, in 1261, the facade of the Cathedral at Pistoia, and Fino di Tibaldi who painted a vast picture on the walls of the Municipal Palace about the middle of the century, but they are so much in the shadow of the later masters' work as to be scarcely known. Everywhere Nature began to reassert herself. The workers in Mosaic even, who were occupied in the famous baptistry at Florence about the middle of the century, though they followed the Byzantine rules of their art, introduced certain innovations which brought the composition and the subjects closer to nature. These are enough to show that there was a school of painting and decoration at Florence quite sufficient to account for Cimabue's development, without the necessity of appealing to the influence over him of wandering Greek artists as has sometimes been done.

Though he was not the absolute inventor of all the new art modes as he is sometimes supposed to be, Cimabue was undoubtedly a great original genius. Like so many others who have been acclaimed as the very first in a particular line of thought or effort, his was only the culminating intelligence which grasped all that had been done before, assimilated it and made it his own. As a distinct exception to the usual history of such great initiators, this father of Italian painting was rich, born of a noble family, but of a character that was eager for work and with ambition to succeed in his chosen art as the mainspring of life. At his death, as the result of his influence, artists had acquired a much better social position than had been theirs before, and one that it was comparatively easy for his successors to maintain. His famous Madonna which was subsequently borne in triumph from his studio to the Church of

Santa Maria Novella, placed the seal of popular approval on the new art, and the enthusiasm it evoked raised the artist for all time from the plane of a mere worker in colors to that of a member of a liberal profession. Even before this triumph his great picture had been deemed worthy of a visit by Charles of Anjou, the French King, who was on a visit to Florence, and according to tradition ever afterwards the portion of the city in which it had been painted and through which it was carried in procession, bore by reason of these happy events the name Borgo Allegri—Ward of Joy.

This picture is still in its place in the Rucellai chapel and is of course the subject of devoted attention on the part of visitors. Lafenestre says of it, that this monument of Florentine art quite justifies the enthusiasm of contemporaries if we compare it with the expressionless Madonnas that preceded it. There is an air of beneficent dignity on the features quite unlike the rigidity of preceding art, and there is besides an attractive suppleness about the attitude of the body which is far better proportioned than those of its predecessors. Above all there is a certain roseate freshness about the colors of the flesh which are pleasant substitutes for the pale and greenish tints of the Byzantines. It did not require more than this to exalt the imaginations of the people delivered from their old-time conventional painting. It was only a ray of the dawn after a dark night, but it announced a glorious sunrise of art and the confident anticipations of the wondrous day to come, aroused the depths of feeling in the peoples' hearts. Life and nature went back into art once more; no wonder their re-apparition was saluted with so much delight.

Two other Madonnas painted by him, one at Florence in the Academy, the other in Paris in the Louvre, besides his great Mosaic in the apse of the Cathedral at Pisa, serve to show with what prudence Cimabue introduced naturalistic qualities into art, while always respecting the tradition of the older art and preserving the solemn graces and the majestic style of monumental painting. The old frescoes of the upper church at Assisi which represent episodes in the life of St. Francis have also been attributed to Cimabue, but evidently were done by a number of artists probably under his direction. It is easy to see from them what an important role the Florentine artist played in directing the gropings of his assistant artists.

After Cimabue the most important name at Florentine in the Thirteenth Century is that of his friend, Gaddo Gaddi, whose years of life correspond almost exactly with those of his great contemporary. His famous Coronation of the Virgin at Santa Maria de Fiore in Florence shows that he was greatly influenced by the new ideas that had come into art. Greater than either of these well-known predecessors, however, was Giotto the friend of Dante, whose work is still considered worthy of study by artists because of certain qualities in which it never has been surpassed nor quite outgrown. From Giotto, however, we shall turn aside for a moment to say something of the development of art in other cities of Italy, for it must not be thought that Florence was the only one to take up the new art methods which developed so marvelously during the Thirteenth Century.

Even before the phenomenal rise of modern art in Florence, at Pisa, at Lucca and especially at Siena, the new wind of the spirit was felt blowing and some fine inspirations were realized in spite of hampering difficulties of all kinds. The Madonna of Guido in the Church of St. Dominic at Siena is the proof of his emancipation. Besides him Ugolino, Segna and Duccio make up the Siena school and enable this other Tuscan city to dispute even with Florence the priority of the new influence in art. At Lucca Bonaventure Berlinghieri flourished and there is a famous St. Francis by him only recently found, which proves his right to a place among the great founders of modern art. Giunta of Pisa was one of those called to Assisi to paint some of the frescoes in the upper church. He is noted as having striven to make his figures more exact and his colors more natural. He did much to help his generation away from the conventional expressions of the preceding time and he must for this reason be counted among the great original geniuses in the history of art.

The greatest name in the art of the Thirteenth Century is of course that of Giotto. What Dante did for poetry and Villani for history, their compatriot and friend did for painting. Ambrogio de Bondone familiarly called Ambrogiotto (and with the abbreviating habit that the Italians have always had for the names of all those of whom they thought much shortened to

Giotto, as indeed Dante's name had been shortened from Durante) was born just at the beginning of the last quarter of the Thirteenth Century. According to a well-known legend he was guarding the sheep of his father one day and passing his time sketching a lamb upon a smooth stone with a soft pebble when Cimabue happened to be passing. The painter struck by the signs of genius in the work took the boy with him to Florence, where he made rapid progress in art and soon surpassed even his master. The wonderful precocity of his genius may be best realized from the fact that at the age of twenty he was given the commission of finishing the decorations of the upper Church at Assisi, and in fulfilling it broke so completely with the Byzantine formalism of the preceding millenium, that he must be considered the liberator of art and its deliverer from the chains of conventionalism into the freedom of nature.

It is no wonder that critics and literary men have been so unstinted in his praise. Here is an example:

"In the Decamerone it is said of him 'that he was so great a genius that there was nothing in nature he had not so reproduced that it was not only like the thing, but seemed to be the thing itself.' Eulogies of this tenor on works of art are, it is quite true, common to all periods alike, to the most accomplished of classical antiquity as well as to the most primitive of the Middle Age; and they must only be accepted relatively, according to the notion entertained by each period of what constitutes truth and naturalness. And from the point of view of his age, Giotto's advance towards nature, considered relatively to his predecessors, was in truth enormous. What he sought was not merely the external truth of sense, but also the inward truth of the spirit. Instead of solemn images of devotion, he painted pictures in which the spectator beheld the likeness of human beings in the exercise of activity and intelligence. His merit lies, as has been well said, in 'an entirely new conception of character and facts.' " *

* History of Ancient, Early Christian and Medieval Painting from the German of the late Dr. Alfred Woltmann, Professor at the Imperial University of Strasburg, and Karl Woertmann, Professor at the Royal Academy of Arts, Dusselford. Edited by Sidney Colvin, M. A., Dodd, Mead & Co., N. Y., 1894.

Lafenestre, in his history of Italian painting for the Beaux-Arts of Paris already referred to, says that what has survived of Giotto's work justifies the enthusiasm of his contemporaries. None of his predecessors accomplished anything like the revolution that he worked. He fixed the destinies of art in Italy at the moment when Dante fixed those of literature. The stiff, confused figures of the mosaics and manuscripts grew supple under his fingers and the confusion disappeared. He simplified the gestures, varied the expression, rectified the proportions. Perhaps the best example of his work is that of the Upper Church of Assisi, all accomplished before he was thirty. What he had to represent were scenes of life almost contemporary yet already raised to the realm of poetry by popular admiration. He interpreted the beautiful legend of the life of the Saint preserved by St. Bonaventure, and like the subject of his sketches turned to nature at every step of his work. If his figures are compared with those of the artists of the preceding generations, their truth to life and natural expressions easily explain the surprise and rapture of his contemporaries.

Beautiful as are the pictures of the Upper Church, however, ten years after their completion Giotto's genius can be seen to have taken a still higher flight by the study of the pictures on the vast ceilings of the Lower Church. The four compartments contain the Triumph of Chastity, the Triumph of Poverty, the Triumph of Obedience, and the Glorification of St. Francis. The ideal and the real figures in these compositions are mingled and grouped with admirable clearness and inventive force. To be appreciated properly they must be seen and studied *in situ*. Many an artist has made the pilgrimage to Assisi and none has come away disappointed. Never before had an artist dared to introduce so many and such numerous figures, yet all were done with a variety and an ease of movement that is eminently pleasing and even now are thoroughly satisfying to the artistic mind. After his work at Assisi some of the best of Giotto's pictures are to be found in the Chapel of the Arena at Padua. Here there was a magnificent opportunity and Giotto took full advantage of it. The whole story of Christ's life is told in the fourteen episodes of the life of his Mother which were painted here by Giotto. For their sake Padua as well as

ST. FRANCIS' MARRIAGE WITH POVERTY (GIOTTO, ASSISI)

Assisi has been a favorite place of pilgrimage for artists ever since and never more so than in our own time.

No greater tribute to the century in which he lived could possibly be given than to say that his genius was recognized at once, and he was sought from one end of Italy to another by Popes and Kings, Republics and Princes, Convents and Municipalities, all of which competed for the privilege of having this genius work for them with ever increasing enthusiasm. It is easy to think and to say that it is no wonder that such a transcendent genius was recognized and appreciated and received his due reward. Such has not usually been the case in history, however. On the contrary, the more imposing the genius of an artist, or a scientist, or any other great innovator in things human, the more surely has he been the subject of neglect and even of misunderstanding and persecution. The very fact that Giotto lifted art out of the routine of formalism in which it was sunk might seem to be enough to assure failure of appreciation. Men do not suddenly turn round to like even great innovations, when they have long been satisfied with something less and when their principles of criticism have been formed by their experience with the old.

We need not go farther back than our own supposedly illuminated Nineteenth Century to find some striking examples of this. Turner, the great English landscapist, failed of appreciation for long years and had to wait till the end of his life to obtain even a small meed of reward. The famous Barbizon School of French Painters is a still more striking example. They went back to nature from the classic formalism of the early Nineteenth Century painters just as Giotto went back to nature from Byzantine conventionalism. The immediate rewards in the two cases were very different and the attitude of contemporaries strikingly contrasted. Poor Millet did his magnificent work in spite of the fact that his family nearly starved. Only that Madame Millet was satisfied to take more than a fair share of hardships for herself and the family in order that her husband might have the opportunity to develop his genius after his own way, we might not have had the magnificent pictures which Millet sold for a few paltry francs that barely kept the wolf from the door, and for which the next generation has been paying almost fabulous sums.

All through the Thirteenth Century this characteristic will be found that genius did not as a rule lack appreciation. The greater the revolution a genuinely progressive thinker and worker tried to accomplish in human progress, the more sure was he to obtain not only a ready audience, but an enthusiastic and encouraging following. This is the greatest compliment that could be paid to the enlightenment of the age. Men's minds were open and they were ready and willing to see things differently from what they had been accustomed to before. This constitutes after all the best possible guarantee of progress. It is, however, very probably the last thing that we would think of attributing to these generations of the Thirteenth Century, who are usually said very frankly to have been wrapped up in their own notions, to have been only too ready to accept things on authority rather than by their own powers of observation and judgment, and to have been clingers to the past rather than lookers to the present and the future. Giotto's life shows better than any other how much this prejudiced view of the Thirteenth Century and perforce of the Middle Age needs to be corrected.

During forty years Giotto responded to every demand, and made himself suffice for every call, worked in nearly every important city of Italy, enkindling everywhere he went the new light of art. Before the end of the century he completed a cartoon for the famous picture of the Boat of Peter which was to adorn the Facade of St. Peter's. He was in Rome in 1300, the first jubilee year, arranging the decorations at St. John Lateran. The next year he was at Florence, working in the Palace of the Podesta. And so it went for full two score years. He was at Pisa, at Lucca, at Arezzo, at Padua, at Milan, then he went South to Urbino, to Rome and then even to Naples. Unfortunately the strain of all this work proved too much for him and he was carried away at the comparatively early age of sixty in the midst of his artistic vigor and glory.

The art of the Middle Ages and especially at the time of the beginnings of modern art in the Thirteenth Century, is commonly supposed to be inextricably bound up with certain in-

ESPOUSAL OF ST. CATHERINE (GADDI, PUPIL OF XIII CENTURY).

fluences which place it beyond the pale of imitation for modern life. It has frequently been said, that this art besides being too deeply mystical and pietistic, is so remote from ordinary human feelings as to preclude a proper understanding of it by the men of our time and certainly prevent any deep sympathy. The pagan element in art which entered at the time of the Renaissance and which emphasized the joy of life itself and the pleasure of mere living for its own sake, is supposed to have modified this sadder aspect of things in the earlier art, so that now no one would care to go back to the pre-Renaissance day. There has been so much writing of this kind that has carried weight, that it is no wonder that the impression has been deeply made. It is founded almost entirely on a misunderstanding, however. Reinach whom we have quoted before completely overturns this false notion in some paragraphs which bring out better than any others that we know something of the true significance of the Thirteenth Century art in this particular.

Those who think that Gothic art was mainly gloomy in character, or if not absolutely sad at heart that it always expressed the sadder portion of religious feelings, who consider that the ascetic side of life was always in the ascendant and the brighter side of things seldom chosen, for pictorial purposes, should recall that the Gothic Cathedrals themselves are the most cheery and lightsome buildings, that indeed they owe their character as creations of a new idea in architecture to the determined purpose of their builders to get admission for all possible light in the dreary Northern climates. The contradiction of the idea that Gothic art in its essence was gloomy will at once be manifest from this. Quite apart from this, however, if Gothic art be studied for itself and in its subjects, that of the Thirteenth Century particularly will be found far distant from anything that would justify the criticism of over sadness. Reinach (in his Story of Art Throughout the Middle Ages) has stated this so clearly that we prefer simply to quote the passage which is at once authoritative and informing:

"It has also been said that Gothic art bears the impress of ardent piety and emotional mysticism, that it dwells on the suffering of Jesus, of the Virgin, and of the martyrs with harrowing persistency. Those who believe this have never studied

Gothic art. It is so far from the truth that, as a fact, the Gothic art of the best period, the Thirteenth Century, never represented any sufferings save those of the damned. The Virgins are smiling and gracious, never grief stricken. There is not a single Gothic rendering of the Virgin weeping at the foot of the cross. The words and music of the Stabat Mater, which are sometimes instanced as the highest expression of the religion of the Middle Ages, date from the end of the Thirteenth Century at the very earliest, and did not become popular till the Fifteenth Century. Jesus himself is not represented as suffering, but with a serene and majestic expression. The famous statue known as the Beau Dieu d'Amiens may be instanced as typical."

GROUP FROM THE VISITATION
(RHEIMS)

IX

LIBRARIES AND BOOKMEN.

As the Thirteenth Century begins some 250 years before the art of printing was introduced, it would seem idle to talk of libraries and especially of circulating libraries during this period and quite as futile to talk of bookmen and book collectors. Any such false impression, however, is founded entirely upon a lack of knowledge of the true state of affairs during this wonderful period. A diocesan council held in Paris in the year 1212, with other words of advice to religious, recalled to them the duty that they had to lend such books as they might possess, with proper guarantee for their return, of course, to those who might make good use of them. The council, indeed, formally declared that the lending of books was one of the works of mercy. The Cathedral chapter of Notre Dame at Paris was one of the leaders in this matter and there are records of their having lent many books during the Thirteenth Century. At most of the abbeys around Paris there were considerable libraries and in them also the lending custom obtained. This is especially true of the Abbey of St. Victor of which the rule and records are extant.

Of course it will be realized that the number of books was not large, but on the other hand it must not be forgotten that many of them were works of art in every particular, and some of them that have come down to us continue to be even to the present day among the most precious bibliophilic treasures of great state and city libraries. Their value depends not alone on their antiquity but on their perfection as works of art. In general it may be said that the missals and office books, and the prayer books made for royal personages and the nobility at this time, are yet counted among the best examples of bookmaking the world has ever seen. It is not surprising that such should be the case since these books were mainly meant for use in the Cathedrals and the chapels, and these edifices were so beautiful in every detail that the generations that erected them

could not think of making books for use in them, that would
be unworthy of the artistic environment for which they were
intended.   With the candlesticks, the vessels, and implements
used in the ceremonial surpassing works of art, with every form
of decoration so nearly perfect as to be a source of unending
admiration, with the vestments and altar linens specimens of
the most exquisite handiwork of their kind that had ever been
made, the books associated with them had to be excellent in
execution, expressive of the most refined taste and finished with
an attention utterly careless of the time and labor that might be
required, since the sole object was to make everything as absolutely beautiful as possible.   Hence there is no dearth of wonderful examples of the beautiful bookmaking of this century
in all the great libraries of the world.

The libraries themselves, moreover, are of surpassing interest because of their rules and management, for little as it might
be expected this wonderful century anticipated in these matters
most of our very modern library regulations.   The bookmen of
the time not only made beautiful books, but they made every
provision to secure their free circulation and to make them
available to as many people as was consonant with proper care
of the books and the true purposes of libraries.   This is a chapter of Thirteenth Century history more ignored perhaps than
any other, but which deserves to be known and will appeal to
our century more perhaps than to any intervening period.

The constitutions of the Abbey St. Victor of Paris give us
an excellent idea at once of the solicitude with which the books
were guarded, yet also of the careful effort that was made to
render them useful to as many persons as possible.   One of the
most important rules at St. Victor was that the librarian should
know the contents of every volume in the library, in order to be
able to direct those who might wish to consult the books in their
selection, and while thus sparing the books unnecessary handling also save the readers precious time.   We are apt to think
that it is only in very modern times that this training of librarians to know their books so as to be of help to the readers was
insisted on.   Here, however, we find it in full force seven centuries ago.   It would be much more difficult in the present day
to know all the books confided to his care, but some of the

librarians at St. Victor were noted for the perfection of their knowledge in this regard and were often consulted by those who were interested in various subjects.

In his book on the Thirteenth Century* M. A. Lecoy de la Marche says that in France, at least, circulating libraries were quite common. As might be expected of the people of so practical a century, it was they who first established the rule that a book might be taken out provided its value were deposited by the borrower. Such lending libraries were to be found at the Sorbonne, at St. Germain des Prés, as well as at Notre Dame. There was also a famous library at this time at Corbie but practically every one of the large abbeys had a library from which books could be obtained. Certain of the castles of the nobility, as for instance that of La Ferte en Ponthieu, had libraries, with regard to which there is a record, that the librarian had the custom of lending certain volumes, provided the person was known to him and assumed responsibility for the book.

Some of the regulations of the libraries of the century have an interest all their own from the exact care that was required with regard to the books. The Sorbonne for instance by rule inflicted a fine upon anyone who neglected to close large volumes after he had been making use of them. Many a librarian of the modern times would be glad to put into effect such a regulation as this. A severe fine was inflicted upon any library assistant who allowed a stranger to go into the library alone, and another for anyone who did not take care to close the doors. It seems not unlikely that these regulations, as M. Lecoy de la Marche says, were in vigor in many of the ecclesiastical and secular libraries of the time.

Some of the regulations of St. Victor are quite as interesting and show the liberal spirit of the time as well as indicate how completely what is most modern in library management was anticipated. The librarian had the charge of all the books of the community, was required to have a detailed list of them and each year to have them in his possession at least three times. On him was placed the obligation to see that the books were not destroyed in any way, either by parasites of any kind or by

* Le Treizieme Siecle Litteraire et Scientifique, Lille, 1857.

dampness. The librarian was required to arrange the books in such a manner as to make the finding of them prompt and easy. No book was allowed to be borrowed unless some pledge for its safe return were left with the librarian. This was emphasized particularly for strangers who must give a pledge equal to the value of the book. In all cases, however, the name of the borrower had to be taken, also the title of the book borrowed, and the kind of pledge left. The larger and more precious books could not be borrowed without the special permission of the superior.

The origin of the various libraries in Paris is very interesting as proof that the mode of accumulating books was nearly the same as that which enriches university and other such libraries at the present time. The library of La St. Chapelle was founded by Louis IX, and being continuously enriched by the deposit therein of the archives of the kingdom soon became of first importance. Many precious volumes that were given as presents to St. Louis found their way into this library and made it during his lifetime the most valuable collection of books in Paris. Louis, moreover, devoted much time and money to adding to the library. He made it a point whenever on his journeys he stopped at abbeys or other ecclesiastical institutions, to find out what books were in their library that were not at La Saint Chapelle and had copies of these made. His intimate friendship with Robert of Sorbonne, with St. Thomas of Aquin, with Saint Bonaventure, and above all with Vincent of Beauvais, the famous encyclopedist of the century, widened his interest in books and must have made him an excellent judge of what he ought to procure to complete the library. It was, as we shall see, Louis' munificent patronage that enabled Vincent to accumulate that precious store of medieval knowledge, which was to prove a mine of information for so many subsequent generations.

From the earliest times certain books, mainly on medicine, were collected at the Hotel Dieu, the great hospital of Paris, and this collection was added to from time to time by the bequests of physicians in attendance there. This was doubtless the first regular hospital library, though probably medical books had also been collected at Salernum. The principal colleges of the universities also made collections of books, some of them very valuable, though as a rule, it would seem as if no attempt was made to procure any other books than those which were absolutely needed for consultation by the students. The best working library at Paris was undoubtedly that of the Sorbonne, of which indeed its books were for a long time its only treasures. For at first the Sorbonne was nothing but a teaching institution which only required rooms for its lectures, and usually obtained these either from the university authorities or from the Canons of the Cathedral and possessed no property except its library. From the very beginning the professors bequeathed whatever books they had collected to its library and this became a custom. It is easy to understand that within a very short time the library became one of the very best in Europe. While most of the other libraries were devoted mainly to sacred literature, the Sorbonne came to possess a large number of works of profane literature. Interesting details with regard to this library of the Sorbonne and its precious treasures have been given by M. Leopold Delisle, in the second volume of Le Cabinet des Manuserits, describing the MSS. of the Bibliothèque Nationale at Paris. According to M. Lecoy de la Marche, this gives an excellent idea of the persevering efforts which must have been required, to bring together so many bibliographic treasures at a time when books were such a rarity, and consequently enables us better almost than anything else, to appreciate the enthusiasm of the scholars of these early times and their wonderful efforts to make the acquisition of knowledge easier, not only for their own but for succeeding generations. When we recall that the library of the Sorbonne was, during the Thirteenth Century, open not only to the professors and students of the Sorbonne itself, but also to those interested in books and in literature who might come from elsewhere, provided they were properly accredited, we can realize to the full the thorough liberality of spirit of these early scholars. Usually we are prone to consider that this liberality of spirit, even in educational matters, came much later into the world.

In spite of the regulations demanding the greatest care, it is easy to understand that after a time even books written on vellum or parchment would become disfigured and worn under the ardent fingers of enthusiastic students, when comparatively so few copies were available for general use. In order to replace these worn-out copies every abbey had its own scriptorium or writing room, where especially the younger monks who were gifted with plain handwriting were required to devote certain hours every day to the copying of manuscripts. Manuscripts were borrowed from neighboring libraries and copied, or as in our modern day exchanges of duplicate copies were made, so as to avoid the risk that precious manuscripts might be subject to on the journeys from one abbey to another. How much the duty of transcription was valued may be appreciated from the fact, that in some abbeys every novice was expected to bring on the day of his profession as a religious, a volume of considerable size which had been carefully copied by his own hands.

Besides these methods of increasing the number of books in the library, a special sum of money was set aside in most of the abbeys for the procuring of additional volumes for the library by purchase. Usually this took the form of an ecclesiastical regulation requiring that a certain percentage of the revenues should be spent on the libraries. Scholars closely associated with monasteries frequently bequeathed their books and besides left money or incomes to be especially devoted to the improvement of the library. It is easy to understand that with all these sources of enrichment many abbeys possessed noteworthy libraries. To quote only those of France, important collections of books were to be found at Cluny, Luxeuil, Fleury, Saint-Martial, Moissac, Mortemer, Savigny, Fourcarmont, Saint Père de Charters, Saint Denis, Saint-Maur-des-Fossés, Saint Corneille de Compiègne, Corbie, Saint-Amand, Saint-Martin de Tournai, where Vincent de Beauvais said that he found the greatest collections of manuscripts that existed in his time, and then especially the great Parisian abbeys already referred to, Saint-Germain-des-Prés, Saint Victor, Saint-Martin-des-Champs, the precious treasures of which are well known to all those who are familiar with the Bibliotheque Nationale of Paris, of whose manuscript department their relics constitute the most valuable nucleus.

Some of the bequests of books that were made to libraries at this time are interesting, because they show the spirit of the testators and at the same time furnish valuable hints as to the consideration in which books were held and the reverent care of their possessors for them. Peter of Nemours, the Bishop of Paris, when setting out on the crusades with Louis IX. bequeathed to the famous Abbey of St. Victor, his Bible in 22 volumes, which was considered one of the finest copies of the scriptures at that time in existence. To the Abbey of Olivet he gave his Psalter with Glosses, besides the Epistles of St. Paul and his Book of Sentences, by which is evidently intended the well-known work with that title by the famous Peter Lombard. Finally he gave to the Cathedral of Paris all the rest of his books. Besides these he had very little to leave. It is typical of the reputation of Paris in that century and the devotion of her churchmen to learning and culture, that practically all of the revenues that he considered due him for his personal services had been invested in books, which he then disposed of in such a way as would secure their doing the greatest possible good to the largest number of people. His Bible was evidently given to the abbey of St. Victor because it was the sort of work that should be kept for the occasional reference of the learned rather than the frequent consultation of students, who might very well find all that they desired in other and less valuable copies. His practical intention with regard to his books can be best judged from his gift to Notre Dame, which, as we have noted already possessed a very valuable library that was allowed to circulate among properly accredited scholars in Paris.

According to the will of Peter Ameil, Archbishop of Narbonne, which is dated 1238, he gave his books for the use of the scholars whom he had supported at the University of Paris and they were to be deposited in the Library at Notre Dame, but on condition that they were not to be scattered for any reason nor any of them sold or abused. The effort of the booklover to keep his books together is characteristic of all the centuries since, only most people will be surprised to find it manifesting itself so early in bibliophilic history. The Archbishop reserved from his books, however, his Bible for his own church. Before his death he had given the Dominicans in his diocese many books from his library. This churchman of the first half of the

Thirteenth Century seems evidently to deserve a prominent place among the bookmen of all times.

There are records of many others who bequeathed libraries and gave books during their lifetime to various institutions, as may be found in the Literary History of France,* already mentioned as well as in the various histories of the University of Paris. Many of these gifts were made on condition that they should not be sold and the constantly recurring last wish of these old booklovers is that their collections should be kept together. The libraries of Paris were also in the market for books, however, and there is proof that the Sorbonne purchased a number of volumes because the cost price of them was noted inside the cover quite as libraries do in our own days. When we realize the forbidding cost of them, it is surprising that there should be so much to say about them and so many of them constantly changing hands. An ordinary folio volume probably cost from 400 to 500 francs in our values, that is between $80 and $100.

While the older abbeys of the Benedictines and other earlier religious orders possessed magnificent collections of books, the newer orders of the Thirteenth Century, the Mendicants, though as their name indicates they were bound to live by alms given them by the faithful, within a short time after their foundation began to take a prominent part in the library movement. It was in the southern part of France that the Dominicans were strongest and so there is record of regulations for libraries made at Toulouse in the early part of the Thirteenth Century. In Paris, in 1239, considerable time and discussion was devoted in one of the chapters of the order to the question of how books should be kept, and how the library should be increased. With regard to the Franciscans, though their poverty was, if possible, stricter, the same thing is known before the end of the century. In both orders arrangements were made for the copying of important works and it is, of course, to the zeal and enthusiasm of the younger members of these orders for this copying work, that we owe the preservation by means of a large number of manuscript copies, of the

* Histoire Litteraire de la France, by the Benedictines of St. Maur.

MONUMENT OF CARD. DE BRAY (ARNULFO)

voluminous writings of such men as Albertus Magnus, St. Thomas, Duns Scotus and others.

While the existence of libraries of various kinds, and even circulating libraries, in the Thirteenth Century may seem definitely settled, it will appear to most people that to speak of book collecting at this time must be out of place. That fad is usually presumed to be of much later origin and indeed to be comparatively recent in its manifestations. We have said enough already, however, of the various collections of books in libraries especially in France to show that the book collector was abroad, but there is much more direct evidence of this available from an English writer. Richard de Bury's Philobiblon is very well known to all who are interested in books for their own sake, but few people realize that this book practically had its origin in the Thirteenth Century. The writer was born about the beginning of the last quarter of that century, had completed his education before its close, and it is only reasonable to attribute to the formative influences at work in his intellectual development as a young man, the germs of thought from which were to come in later life the interesting book on bibliophily, the first of its kind, which was to be a treasure for book-lovers ever afterwards.

Philobiblon tells us, among other things, of Richard's visits to the continent on an Embassy to the Holy See and on subsequent occasions to the Court of France, and the delight which he experienced in handling many books which he had never seen before, in buying such of them as his purse would allow, or his enthusiasm could tempt from their owners and in conversing with those who could tell him about books and their contents. Such men were the chosen comrades of his journeys, sat with him at table, as Mr. Henry Morley tells us in his English Writers (volume IV, page 51), and were in almost constant fellowship with him. It was at Paris particularly that Richard's heart was satisfied for a time because of the great treasures he found in the magnificent libraries of that city. He was interested, of course, in the University and the opportunity for intellectual employment afforded by Academic proceedings, but above all he found delight in books, which monks and monarchs and professors and churchmen of all kinds and scholars and students had gathered into this great intellectual capital of Europe at that time. Anyone who thinks the books were not valued quite as highly in the Thirteenth Century as at the present time should read the Philobiblon. He is apt to rise from the reading of it with the thought that it is the modern generations who do not properly appreciate books.

One of the early chapters of Philobiblon argues that books ought always to be bought whatever they cost, provided there are means to pay for them, except in two cases, "when they are knavishly overcharged, or when a better time for buying is expected." "That sun of men, Solomon," Richard says, "bids us buy books readily and sell them unwillingly, for one of his proverbs runs, 'Buy the truth and sell it not, also wisdom and instruction and understanding.' " Richard in his own quaint way thought that most other interests in life were only temptations to draw men away from books. In one famous paragraph he has naively personified books as complaining with regard to the lack of attention men now display for them and the unworthy objects, in Richard's eyes at least, upon which they fasten their affections instead, and which take them away from the only great life interest that is really worth while—books.

"Yet," complain books, "in these evil times we are cast out of our place in the inner chamber, turned out of doors, and our place taken by dogs, birds, and the two-legged beast called woman. But that beast has always been our rival, and when she spies us in a corner, with no better protection than the web of a dead spider, she drags us out with a frown and violent speech, laughing us to scorn as useless, and soon counsels us to be changed into costly head-gear, fine linen, silk and scarlet double dyed, dresses and divers trimmings, linens and woolens. And so," complain the books still, "we are turned out of our homes, our coats are torn from our backs, our backs and sides ache, we lie about disabled, our natural whiteness turns to yellow—without doubt we have the jaundice. Some of us are gouty, witness our twisted extremities. Our bellies are griped and wrenched and are consumed by worms; on each side the dirt cleaves to us, nobody binds up our wounds, we lie ragged and weep in dark corners, or meet with Job upon a dunghill, or, as seems hardly fit to be said, we are hidden in abysses of the sewers. We are sold also like slaves, and lie as unredeemed pledges in taverns. We are thrust into cruel butteries, to be cut up like sheep and cattle; committed to Jews, Saracens, heretics and Pagans, whom we always dread as the plague, and by whom some of our forefathers are known to have been poisoned."

Richard De Bury must not be thought to have been some mere wandering scholar of the beginning of the Fourteenth Century, however, for he was, perhaps, the most important historical personage, not even excepting royalty or nobility, of this era and one of the striking examples of how high a mere scholar might rise in this period quite apart from any achievement in arms, though this is usually supposed to be almost the only basis of distinguished reputation and the reason for advancement at this time. While he was only the son of a Norman knight, Aungervyle by name, born at Bury St. Edmund's, he became the steward of the palace and treasurer of the royal wardrobe, then Lord Treasurer of England and finally Lord Keeper of the Privy Seal. While on a mission to the Pope he so commended himself to the Holy See that it was resolved to make him the next English bishop. Accordingly he was made Bishop of Durham shortly after and on the occasion of his installation there was a great banquet at which the young King and Queen, the Queen Mother Isabelle, the King of Scotland, two Archbishops, five bishops, and most of the great English lords were present. At this time the Scots and the English were actually engaged in war with one another and a special truce was declared, in order to allow them to join in the celebration of the consecration of so distinguished an individual to the See of Durham near the frontier.

Before he was consecrated Bishop, Richard De Bury had been for some time the treasurer of the kingdom. Before the end of the year in which he was consecrated he became Lord Chancellor, at a time when the affairs of the kingdom needed a master hand and when the French and the Scots were seriously disturbing English peace and prosperity. He resigned his office of Chancellor, as Henry Morley states, only to go abroad in the royal service as ambassador that he might exercise his own trusted sagacity in carrying out the peaceful policy he had advised. During this diplomatic mission to the continent he visited the courts of Paris, of Flanders, of Hainault and of Germany. He succeeded in making terms of peace between the English king and the Counts of Hainault and Namur, the Marquis of Juliers and the Dukes of Brabant and Guelders. This would seem to indicate that he must be considered as one of the most prominent men of Europe at this time.

His attitude toward books is then all the more noteworthy. Many people were surprised that a great statesman like Gladstone in the Nineteenth Century, should have been interested in so many phases of thought and of literature and should himself have been able to find the time to contribute important works to English letters. Richard De Bury was at least as important a man in his time as Gladstone in ours, and occupied himself as much with books as the great English commoner. This is what will be the greatest source of surprise to those who in our time have been accustomed to think, that the great scholars deeply interested in books who were yet men of practical worth in helping their generation in its great problems, are limited to modern times and are least of all likely to be found in the heart of the Middle Ages. In spite of his occupations as a politician and a bookman, Richard De Bury was noted for his faithfulness in the fulfilment of his duties as a churchman and a bishop. It is worthy of note that many of the important clergymen of England, who were to find the highest church preferment afterwards, were among the members of his household at various times and that the post of secretary to the bishop, particularly, was filled at various times by some of the best scholars of the period, men who were devoted friends to the bishop, who dedicated their works to him and generally added to the reputation that stamped him as the greatest scholar of England and one of the leading lights of European culture of his time.

This is not so surprising when we realize that to be a member of Richard's household was to have access to the best library in England, and that many scholars were naturally ambitious to have such an opportunity, and as the results showed many took advantage of it. Among Richard of Durham's chaplains were Thomas Bradwardine who afterwards became Archbishop of Canterbury. Richard Fitzraufe, subsequently Archbishop of

Armagh, Walter Seagrave, afterwards Bishop of Chichester, and Richard Bentworth, who afterwards became Bishop of London Among the distinguished scholars who occupied the post were Robert Holcot, John Manduit, the astronomer of the Fourteenth Century, Richard Kilmington, a distinguished English theologian, and Walter Burley, a great commentator on Aristotle, who dedicated to the bishop, who had provided him with so many opportunities for study, his Commentaries upon the Politics and Ethics of the ancient Greek philosopher.

That Richard's love for books and the time he had necessarily devoted to politics did not dry up the fountains of charity in his heart, nor cause him to neglect his important duties as the pastor of the people and especially of the poor, we know very well from certain traditions with regard to his charitable donations. According to a standing rule in his household eight quarters of wheat were regularly every week made into bread and given to the poor. In his alms giving Richard was as careful and as discriminating as in his collection of books, and he used a number of the regularly organized channels in his diocese to make sure that his bounty should be really helpful and should not encourage lack of thrift. This is a feature of charitable work that is supposed to be modern, but the personal service of the charitably inclined in the Thirteenth Century, far surpassed in securing this even the elaborate organization of charity in modern times. Whenever the bishop traveled generous alms were distributed to the poor people along the way. Whenever he made the journey between Durham and New Castle eight pounds sterling were set aside for this purpose; five pounds for each journey between Durham and Stockton or Middleham, and five marks between Durham and Auckland. Money had at that time at least ten times the purchasing power which it has at present, so that it will be easy to appreciate the good bishop's eminent liberality.

That Richard was justified in his admiration of the books of the time we know from those that remain, for it must not be thought for a moment that because the making of books was such a time-taking task in the Thirteenth Century, they were not therefore made beautiful. On the contrary, as we shall see shortly, no more beautiful books have ever been made than at this time. This of itself would show how precious in the eyes of the collectors of the time their books were, since they wanted to have them so beautifully made and were satisfied to pay the high prices that had to be demanded for such works of art. Very few books of any size cost less than the equivalent of $100 in our time and illuminated books cost much higher than this, yet seem never to have been a drug on the market. Indeed, considering the number of them that are still in existence to this day, in spite of the accidents of fire, and water, and war, and neglect, and carelessness, and ignorance, there must have been an immense number of very handsome books made by the generations of the Thirteenth Century.

While illumination was not an invention of the Thirteenth Century, as indeed were very few of the great art features of the century, during this time book decoration was carried to great perfection and reached that development which artists of the next century were to improve on in certain extrinsic features, though the intrinsic qualities were to remain those which had been determined as the essential characteristics of this branch of art in the earlier time. The Thirteenth Century, for instance, saw the introduction of the miniature as a principal feature and also the drawing out of initials in such a way as to make an illuminated border for the whole side of the page. After the development thus given to the art in the Thirteenth Century further evolution could only come in certain less important details. In this the Thirteenth Century generations were accomplishing what they had done in practically everything else that they touched, laying foundations broad and deep and giving the superstructure the commanding form which future generations were only able to modify to slight degree and not always with absolute good grace.

Humphreys in his magnificent volume on The Illuminated Books of the Middle Ages, which according to its title contains an account of the development and progress of the art of illumination as a distinct branch of pictorial ornamentation from the Fourth to the Seventeenth centuries,* has some very strik-

*The Illuminated Books of the Middle Ages, by Henry Noel Humphreys Longman. Green, Brown and Longmans, London, 1848.

ing words of praise for Thirteenth Century illuminations and the artists who made them. He says:

"Different epochs of the art of illumination present widely different and distinct styles; the most showy and the best known, though the least pure and inventive in design, being that of the middle and end of the Fifteenth Century; whilst the period perhaps the least generally known, that of the Thirteenth Century, may be considered as the most interesting and original, many of the best works of that period displaying an astonishing variety and profusion of invention. The manuscript, of which two pages form the opposite plate, may be ranked among the most elaborate and profusely ornamented of the fine books of that era; every page being sufficient to make the fortune of the modern decorator by the quaint and unexpected novelties of inventions which it displays at every turn of its intricate design."

The illuminations of the century then are worthy of the time and also typical of the general work of the century. It is known by experts for its originality and for the wealth of invention displayed in the designs. Men did not fear that they might exhaust their inventive faculty, nor display their originality sparingly, in order that they might have enough to complete other work. As the workmen of the Cathedrals, the artist illuminators devoted their very best efforts to each piece of work that came to their hands, and the results are masterpieces of art in this as in every other department of the period. The details are beautifully wrought, showing the power of the artist to accomplish such a work and yet his designs are never overloaded, at least in the best examples of the century, with details of ornamentation that obscure and minimize the effect of the original design. This fault was to be the error of his most sophisticated successors two centuries later.

Nor must it be thought the high opinion of the century is derived from the fact that only a very few examples of its illumination and bookmaking are now extant, and that these being the chosen specimens give the illumination of the century a higher place than it might otherwise have. Many examples have been preserved and some of them are the most beautiful books that were made. Paris was particularly the home of this form of art in the Thirteenth Century, and indeed the school established there influenced all the modes of illumination everywhere, so much so that Dante speaks of the art with the epithet "Parisian," as if it were exclusively done there. The incentive to the development of this form of art came from St. Louis who, as we have said, was very much interested in books. His taste as exhibited in La Sainte Chapelle was such as to demand artistic excellence of high grade in this department of art, which has many more relations with the architecture of the period, and especially with the stained glass, than might possibly be thought at the present time, for most of the decoration of books partook of the character of the architectural types of the moment.

Among the most precious treasures from the century are three books which belonged to St. Louis himself. One of these is the Hours or Office Book; a second, is his Psalter, which contains some extremely beautiful initials; a third, which is in the Library of the Arsenal at Paris, is sometimes known as the Prayer Book of St. Louis himself, though a better name for it would be the Prayer Book of Queen Blanche, for it was made at Louis' orders for his mother, the famous Blanche of Castile, and is a worthy testimonial of the affectionate relations which existed between mother and son.

Outside of Paris there are preserved many books of great value that come from this century. One of them, a Bestiarum or Book of Beasts, is in the Ashmoleam Museum at Oxford. This is said to be a very beautiful example of the illumination of the Thirteenth Century, but it is even more interesting because it shows the efforts of the artists of the time to copy nature in the pictures of animals as they are presented. There is said to be an acuity of observation and a vigor of representation displayed in the book which is highly complimentary to the powers of the Thirteenth Century artists.

Even these brief notes of the books and libraries of the Thirteenth Century, will serve to make clear how enthusiastic was the interest of the generations of this time in beautiful books and in collections of them that were meant for show as well as for practical usefulness. There is perhaps nothing more amusing in the attitude of modern generations with regard to the Middle Ages, than the assumption that all the methods of education and of the distribution of knowledge worth while talking about, are the inventions of comparatively modern times. The fact that libraries were also a creation of that time and that most of the regulations which are supposed to be the first fruit of quite recent science in the circulation of books had been adopted by these earlier generations, is commonly ignored utterly, though it is a precious bit of knowledge that cannot help but increase our sympathy with those bookmen of the olden times, who thought so much of their books, yet wished to share the privilege of their use with all those who would employ them properly, and who, in their great practical way succeeded in working out the scheme by which many people could have the opportunity of consulting the treasures they thought so much of, without risk of their loss or destruction, even though use might bring some deterioration of their value.

DECORATION THIRTEENTH CENTURY MS.

X

THE CID, THE HOLY GRAIL, THE NIBELUNGEN.

Anyone who has studied even perfunctorily the Books of the Arts and of the Deeds of the Thirteenth Century, who has realized its accomplishments in enduring artistic creations, sublime and exemplary models and inspirations for all after time, who has appreciated what it succeeded in doing for the education of the classes and of the masses, the higher education being provided for at least as large a proportion of the people as in our present century, while the creation of what were practically great technical schools that culled out of the masses the latent geniuses who could accomplish supreme artistic results in the arts and crafts and did more and better for the masses than any subsequent generation, can scarcely help but turn with interest to read the Book of the Words of the period and to find out what forms of literature interested this surprising people. One is almost sure to think at the first moment of consideration that the literature will not be found worthy of the other achievements of the times. In most men's minds the Thirteenth Century does not readily call up the idea of a series of great works in literature, whose influence has been at all as profound and enduring as that of the universities in the educational order, or of the Cathedrals in the artistic order.

This false impression, however, is due only to the fact that the literary creations of the Thirteenth Century are so diverse in subject and in origin, that they are very seldom associated with each other, unless there has been actual recognition of their contemporaneousness from deliberate calling to mind of the dates at which certain basic works in our modern literatures were composed. It is not the least surprise that comes to the student of the Thirteenth Century, to find that the great origins of what well deserves the name of classic modern literature, comprising a series of immortal works in prose and poetry, were initiated by the contemporaries of the makers of the universities and the builders of the Cathedrals. If we stop to think for a moment it must be realized, that generations who succeeded in expressing themselves so effectively in other departments of esthetics could scarcely be expected to fail in literature alone, and they did not. From the Cid in Spain, through the Arthur Legends in England, the Nibelungen in Germany, the Minnesingers and the Meistersingers in the southern part of what is now the German Empire, the Trouvères in North France, the Troubadours in South France and in Italy, down to Dante, who was 35 before the century closed, there has never been such a mass of undying literature written within a little more than a single hundred years, as came during the period from shortly before 1200 down to 1300. Great as was the Fifth Century before Christ in this matter, it did not surpass the Thirteenth Century after Christ in its influence on subsequent generations.

We have already pointed out in discussing the Cathedrals that one of the most characteristic features of the Gothic architecture was the marvelous ease with which it lent itself to the expression of national peculiarities. Norman Gothic is something quite distinct from German Gothic which arose in almost contiguous provinces, but so it is also from English Gothic; these two were very closely related in origin and undoubtedly the English Cathedrals owe much to the Norman influence so prevalent in England at the end of the Twelfth Century, and the beginning of the Thirteenth Century. Italian Gothic has the principal characteristic peculiarities of the architectural style which passes under the name developed to a remarkable degree, and yet its finished product is far distant from any of the three other national forms that have been mentioned, yet is not lacking in a similar interest. Spanish Gothic has an identity of its own that has always had a special appeal for the traveler. Any one who has ever visited the shores of the Baltic sea and has seen what was accomplished in such places as Stralsund, Greifswald, Lubeck, and others of the old Hansa towns, will appreciate still more the power of Gothic to lend itself to the feelings of the people and to the materials that they had at hand. Here in the distant North they were far away from any sources of the stone that would ordinarily be deemed absolutely necessary for Gothic construction. How effectively they used brick for ecclesiastical edifices can only be realized by those who have seen the remains of the Gothic monuments of this portion of Europe.

The distinguishing mark of all these different styles is the eminent opportunity for the expression of nationality which they afford. It might be expected that since they were all Gothic, most of them would be little better than servile copies, or at best scarce more than good imitations of the great originals of the North of France. As a matter of fact, the assertion of national characteristics, far from destroying the effectiveness of Gothic, rather added new beauties to this style of architecture. This was true even occasionally when mistakes were made by architects and designers. As Ferguson has said in his History of Architecture, St. Stephen's at Vienna is full of architectural errors and yet the attractiveness of the Cathedral remains. It was a poet who designed it and something of his poetic soul gleams out of the material structure after the lapse of centuries.

In nearly this same way the literatures of the different countries during the Thirteenth Century are eminently national and mirror with quite wonderful appropriateness the characteristics of the various people. This is true even when similar subjects, as for instance the Graal stories, are treated from nearly the same standpoint by the two Teutonic nations, the Germans and the English. Parsifal and Galahad are national as well as poetic heroes with a distinction of character all their own. As we shall see, practically every nation finds in this century some fundamental expression of its national feeling that has been among its most cherished classics ever since.

The first of these in time is the Cid, which was written in Spain during the latter half of the Twelfth Century, but probably took its definite form just about the beginning of the Thirteenth. It might well be considered that this old-fashioned Spanish ballad would have very little of interest for modern readers, and yet there are very few scholars of the past century who have not been interested in this literary treasure. Critics of all nations have been unstinted in their praise of it. Since the Schlegels recalled world attention to Spanish litera-

SANTA MARIA SOPRA MINERVA (ROME'S GOTHIC CHURCH).

ture, it has been considered almost as unpardonable for anyone who pretended to literary culture not to have read the Cid, as it would be not to have read Don Quixote.

As is true of all the national epics founded upon a series of ballads which had been collecting in the mouth of the people for several centuries before a great poetic genius came to give them their supreme expression, there has been some doubt expressed as to the single authorship of Cid. We shall find the same problem to be considered when we come to discuss the Nibelungen Lied. A half a century ago or more the fashion of the critics for insisting on the divided authorship of such poems was much more prevalent than it is at present. At that time a great many scholars, following the initiative of Wolf and the German separatist critics, declared even that the Homeric poems were due to more than one mind. There are still some who cling to this idea with regard to many of these primal national epics, but at present·most of the literary men are quite content to accept the idea of a single authorship. With regard to the Cid in this matter Mr. Fitzmaurice Kelly, in his Short History of Spanish Literature in the Literatures of the World Series, says very simply:

"There is a unity of conception and of language which forbids our accepting the Poema (del Cid) as the work of several hands; and the division of the poem into several cantares is managed with a discretion which argues a single artistic intelligence. The first part closes with a marriage of the hero's daughters; the second with the shame of the Infantes de Carrion, and the proud announcement that the Kings of Spain are sprung from Cid's loins. In both the singer rises to the level of his subject, but his chiefest gust is in the recital of some brilliant deed of arms."

The Spanish ballad epic is a characteristic example of the epics formed by the earliest poetic genius of a country, on the basis of the patriotic stories of national origin that had been accumulating for centuries. Of course the Cid had to be the Christian hero who did most in his time against the Moslem in Spain. So interesting has his story been made, and so glorious have been his deeds as recorded by the poets, that there has been even some doubt of his existence expressed, but that he was a genuine historical character seems to be clear. Many people will recall the Canons' argument in the forty-ninth chapter of Don Quixote in which Cervantes, evidently speaking for himself, says: "That there was a Cid no one will deny and likewise a Bernardo Del Carpio, but that they performed all the exploits ascribed to them, I believe there is good reason to doubt." The Cid derives his name from the Arabic Seid which means Lord and owes his usual epithet, El Campeador (champion), to the fact that he was the actual champion of the Christians against the Moors at the end of the Eleventh Century. How gloriously his warlike exploits have been described may be best appreciated from the following description of his charge at Alcocer:

'With bucklers braced before their breasts, with lances pointing low,
With stooping crests and heads bent down above the saddle-bow,
All firm of hand and high of heart they roll upon the foe.
And he that in good hour was born, his clarion voice rings out,
And clear above the clang of arms is heard his battle-shout,
'Among them, gentlemen! Strike home for the love of charity!
The Champion of Bivar is here—Ruy Diaz—I am he!'
Then bearing where Bermuez still maintains unequal fight,
Three hundred lances down they come, their pennons flickering white;
Down go three hundred Moors to earth, a man to every blow;
And, when they wheel, three hundred more, as charging back they go,
It was a sight to see the lances rise and fall that day;
The shivered shields and riven mail, to see how thick they lay;
The pennons that went in snow-white come out a gory red;
The horses running riderless, the riders lying dead;
While Moors call on Muhamed, and 'St. James!' the Christians cry."

While the martial interest of such early poems would be generally conceded, it would usually be considered that they would be little likely to have significant domestic, and even

what might be called romantic, interests. The Cid's marriage
is the result of not what would exactly be called a romance
nowadays, though in ruder times there may have been a certain
sense of sentimental reparation in it at least. He had killed
in fair fight the father of a young woman, who being thus left
without a protector appealed to the king to appoint one for her.
In the troublous Middle Ages an heiress was as likely to be
snapped up by some unsuitable suitor, more literally but with
quite as much haste, as in a more cultured epoch. The king
knew no one whom he could trust so well with the guardianship
of the rich and fair young orphan than the Cid, of whose
bravery and honor he had had many proofs. Accordingly he
suggested him as a protector and the Cid himself generously
realizing how much the fair Jimena had lost by the death of
her father consented, and in a famous passage of the poem, a
little shocking to modern ideas, it must be confessed, frankly
states his feelings in the matter:

"And now before the altar the bride and bridegroom stand,
And when to fair Jimena the Cid stretched forth his hand,
He spake in great confusion: 'Thy father have I slain
Not treacherously, but face to face, my just revenge to gain
For cruel wrong; a man I slew, a man I give to thee;
In place of thy dead father, a husband find in me.'
And all who heard well liked the man, approving what he said;
Thus Rodrigo the Castilian his stately bride did wed."

There are tender domestic scenes between the Cid and his
wife and his daughters, which serve to show how sincere was
his affection and with what sympathetic humanity a great poet
knew how to depict the tender natural relations which have an
interest for all times. Some of these domestic scenes are not
unworthy to be placed beside Homer's picture of the parting of
Hector and Andromache, though there is more naive self-consciousness in the work of the Spanish bard, than in that of his
more artistic colleague of the Grecian olden times. There is
particularly a famous picture of the duties of noble ladies in
Spain of this time and of the tender solicitude of a father for
his daughters' innocence, that is quite beyond expectation at

the hands of a poet whose forte was evidently war and its alarms, rather than the expression of the ethical qualities of home life. The following passage, descriptive of the Cid's parting from his wife, will give some idea of these qualities better than could be conveyed in any other way:

"Thou knowest well, señora, he said before he went,
To parting from each other our love doth not consent;
But love and joyance never may stand in duty's way,
And when the king commandeth the noble must obey.
Now let discretion guide thee, thou art of worthy name;
While I am parted from thee, let none in thee find blame.
Employ thy hours full wisely, and tend thy household well,
Be never slothful, woe and death with idleness do dwell.
Lay by thy costly dresses until I come again.
For in the husband's absence let wives in dress be plain;
And look well to thy daughters, nor let them be aware,
Lest they comprehend the danger because they see thy care,
And lose unconscious innocence. At home they must abide,
For the safety of the daughter is at the mother's side.
Be serious with thy servants, with strangers on thy guard,
With friends be kind and friendly, and well thy household
       ward,
To no one show my letters, thy best friends may not see,
Lest reading them they also may guess of thine to me.
And if good news they bring thee, and woman-like dost seek
The sympathy of others, with thy daughters only speak.

*   *   *   *

Farewell, farewell, Jimena, the trumpet's call I hear!
One last embrace, and then he mounts the steed without a
       peer."

The touch of paternal solicitude and prudence in the passage we have put in italics is so apparently modern, that it can scarcely fail to be a source of surprise, coming as it does from that crude period at the end of the Twelfth Century when such minute psychological observation as to young folks' ways would be little expected, and least of all in the rough warrior hero or his poet creator, whose notions of right and wrong are, to judge from many passages of the poem, so much coarser than those of our time.

After the Cid in point of time, the next enduring poetic work that was destined to have an influence on all succeeding generations, was the series of the Arthur Legends as completed in England. As in the case of the Cid these stories of King Arthur's Court, his Knights and his Round Table, had been for a long time the favorite subject of ballad poets among the English people. Just where they originated is not very clear, though it seems most likely that the original inspiration came from Celtic sources. These old ballads, however, had very little of literary form and it was not until the end of the Twelfth and the beginning of the Thirteenth Century that they **were cast in their present** mold, after having passed through the alembic of the mind of a great poetic and literary genius, which refined away the dross and left only the pure gold of supremely sympathetic human stories. To whom we owe this transformation is not known with absolute certainty, though the literary and historical criticism of the last quarter of a century seems to have made it clear that the work must be attributed to Walter Map or Mapes, an English clergyman who died during the first decade of the Thirteenth Century.

His claims to the authorship of the Graal legend in its artistic completeness and to the invention of the character of Lancelot, which is one of the great triumphs of the Arthur legends as they were told at this time, have been much discussed by French and English critics. This discussion has perhaps been best summarized by Mr. Henry Morley, the late Professor of Literature at the University of London, whose third volume of English writers contains an immense amount of valuable information with regard to the literary history, not alone of England at this time but practically of all the countries of Europe. Mr. Morley's plan was conceived with a breath of view that makes his work a very interesting and authoritative guide in the literary matters of the time. His summation of the position of critical opinion with regard to the authorship of the Arthur Legends deserves to be quoted in its entirety:

"The Arthurian Romances were, according to this opinion,

all perfectly detached tales, till in the Twelfth Century Robert de Borron (let us add, at Map's suggestion) translated the first Romance of the St. Graal as an introduction to the series, and shortly afterwards Walter Map added his Quest of the Graal, Lancelot, and Mort Artus. The way for such work had been prepared by Geoffrey of Monmouth's bold setting forward of King Arthur as a personage of history, in a book that was much sought and discussed, and that made the Arthurian Romances a fresh subject of interest to educated men.

"But M. Paulin Paris, whose opinions, founded upon a wide acquaintance with the contents of old MSS. I am now sketching, and in part adopting, looked upon Walter Map as the soul of this work of Christian spiritualisation. Was the romance of the St. Graal Latin before it was French? He does not doubt that it was. He sees in it the mysticism of the subtlest theologian. It was not a knight or a jongleur who was so well read in the apocryphal gospels, the legends of the first Christian centuries, rabbinical fancies, and old Greek mythology; and there is all this in the St. Graal. There is a theory, too, of the sacrifice of the mass, an explanation of the Saviour's presence in the Eucharist, that is the work, he says, of the loftiest and the most brilliant imagination. These were not matters that a knight of the Twelfth Century would dare to touch. They came from an ecclesiastic and a man of genius. But if so, why should we refuse credit to the assertion, repeated in every MS. that they were first written in Latin? The earliest MSS. are of a date not long subsequent to the death of Walter Map, Latinist, theologian, wit, and Chaplain to King Henry II., who himself took the liveliest interest in Breton legends. King Henry, M. Paris supposes, wished them to be collected, but how? Some would prefer one method, some another; Map reconciled all. He satisfied the clergy, pleased the scholar, filled the chasms in the popular tales, reconciled contradictions, or rejected inconsistencies, and by him also the introductory tale of the Graal was first written in Latin for Robert de Borron to translate into French."

The best literary appreciation of Map's genius, apart, of course, from the fact that all generations ever since have acknowledged the supreme human interest and eminently sympathetic quality of his work, is perhaps to be found in certain remarks of the modern critics who have made special studies in these earlier literary periods. Prof. George Saintsbury, of the University of Edinburgh, for instance, in the second volume of Periods of English Literature,* has been quite unstinted in his praise of this early English writer. He has not hesitated even to say in a striking passage that Map, or at least the original author of the Launcelot story, was one of the greatest of literary men and deserves a place only next to Dante in this century so preciously full of artistic initiative.

"Whether it was Walter Map, or Chrestien de Troyes, or both, or neither to whom the glory of at once completing and exalting the story is due, I at least have no pretension to decide. Whoever did it, if he did it by himself, was a great man indeed—a man second to Dante among the men of the Middle Age. Even if it was done by an irregular company of men, each patching and piecing the other's efforts, the result shows a marvelous 'wind of the spirit' abroad and blowing on that company."

Prof. Saintsbury then proceeds to show how much even readers of Mallory miss of the greatness and especially of the sympathetic humanity of the original poem, and in a further passage states his firm conviction that the man who created Lancelot was one of the greatest literary inventors and sympathetic geniuses of all times, and that his work is destined, because the wellsprings of its action are so deep down in the human heart, to be of interest to generations of men for as long as our present form of civilization lasts.

"Perhaps the great artistic stroke in the whole legend, and one of the greatest in all literature, is the concoction of a hero who should be not only

'Like Paris handsome, and like Hector brave,'

but more heroic than Paris and more interesting than Hector—not only a 'greatest knight,' but at once the sinful lover of his queen and the champion who should himself all but achieve and in the person of his son actually achieve, the sacred ad-

---

*The Flourishing of Romance and the Rise of Allegory, by George Saintsbury, Professor of Rhetoric and English Literature in the University of Edinburgh (New York, Charles Scribner & Sons, 1897).

venture of the Holy Graal. If, as there seems no valid reason to disbelieve, the hitting upon this idea, and the invention or adoption of Lancelot to carry it out, be the work of Walter Mapes (or Map), then Walter Mapes is one of the great novelists of the world, and one of the greatest of them. If it was some unknown person (it could hardly be Chrestien, for in Chrestien's form the Graal interest belongs to Percevale, not to Lancelot or Galahad), then the same compliment must be paid to that person unknown. Meanwhile the conception and execution of Lancelot, to whomsoever they may be due, are things most happy. Entirely free from the faultlessness which is the curse of the classical hero; his unequaled valor not seldom rewarded only by reverses; his merits redeemed from mawkishness by his one great fault, yet including all virtues that are themselves most amiable, and deformed by no vice that is actually loathsome; the soul of goodness in him always warring with his human frailty—Sir Lancelot fully deserves the noble funeral eulogy pronounced over his grave, felt by all the elect to be, in both senses, one of the first of all extant pieces of perfect English prose."

To appreciate fully how much Walter Map accomplished by his series of stories with regard to King Arthur's Court, it should be remembered that poets and painters have in many generations ever since found subjects for their inspiration within the bounds of the work which he created. After all, the main interest of succeeding poets who have put the legends into later forms, has centered more in the depth of humanity that there is in the stories, than in the poetic details for which they themselves have been responsible. In succeeding generations poets have often felt that these stories were so beautiful that they deserved to be retold in terms readily comprehensible to their own generation. Hence Malory wrote his Morte D' Arthur for the Fifteenth Century, Spenser used certain portions of the old myths for the Sixteenth, and the late Poet-laureate set himself once more to retell the Idyls of the King for the Nineteenth Century. Each of these was adding little but new literary form, to a work that genius had drawn from sources so close to the heart of human nature, that the stories were always to remain of enduring interest.

For the treasure of poesy with which humanity was enriched when he conceived the idea of setting the old ballads of King Arthur into literary form, more must be considered as due to the literary original writer than to any of his great successors. This is precisely the merit of Walter Map. Of some of his less ambitious literary work we have many examples that show us how thoroughly interested he was in all the details of human existence, even the most trivial. He had his likes and dislikes, he seems to have had some disappointed ambition that made him rather bitter towards ecclesiastics, he seems to have had some unfortunate experiences, especially with the Cistercians, though how much of this is assumed rather than genuine, is hard to determine at this modern day. Many of the extremely bitter things he says with regard to the Cistercians might well be considered as examples of that exaggeration, which in certain minds constitutes one modality of humor, rather than as serious expressions of actual thought. It is hard, for instance, to take such an expression as the following as more than an example of this form of jesting by exaggeration. Map heard that a Cistercian had become a Jew. His comment was: "If he wanted to get far from the Cistercians why didn't he become a Christian."

From England the transition to Germany is easy. Exactly contemporary with the rise of the Arthur Legends in England to that standard of literary excellence that was to give them their enduring poetic value, there came also the definite arrangement and literary transformation of the old ballads of the German people, into that form in which they were to exert a lasting influence upon the German language and national feeling. The date of the Nibelungen Lied has been set down somewhat indefinitely as between 1190 and 1220. Most of the work was undoubtedly accomplished after the beginning of the Thirteenth Century and in the form in which we have it at present, there seems to be no doubt that much was done after the famous meeting of the Meistersingers on the Wartburg—the subject of song and story and music drama ever since, which took place very probably in the year 1207. With regard to the Nibelungen Lied, as in the case of the other great literary arrangements of folk-ballads, there has been question as to the

singleness of authorship.   Here, however, as with regard to
Homer and the Cid, the trend of modern criticism has all been
towards the attribution of the poem to one writer, and the internal evidence of similarity of expression constantly maintained, a certain simplicity of feeling and naïveté of repetition
seems to leave no doubt in the matter.

As regards the merits of the Nibelungen Lied as a great work
of literature, there has been very little doubt in the English-
speaking world at least, because of the enthusiastic recognition
accorded it by German critics and the influence of German
criticism in all branches of literature over the whole Teutonic
race during the Nineteenth Century.   English admiration for
the poem began after Carlyle's introduction of it to the English
reading public in his essays.   Since this time it has come to be
very well known and yet, notwithstanding all that has been said
about it no English critic has expressed more fully the place
of the great German poem in world literature, than did this
enthusiastic pro-German of the first half of the Nineteenth
Century.

For those for whom Carlyle's Essays are a sealed book because of loss of interest in him with the passage of time, the
citation of some of his appreciative critical expressions may be
necessary.

"Here in the old Frankish (Oberdeutsch) dialect of the
Nibelungen, we have a clear decisive utterance, and in a real
system of verse, not without essential regularity, great liveliness
and now and then even harmony of rhythm. Doubtless we must
often call it a diffuse diluted utterance; at the same time it is
genuine, with a certain antique garrulous heartiness, and has
a rhythm in the thoughts as well as the words. The simplicity
is never silly; even in that perpetual recurrence of epithets,
sometimes of rhymes, as where two words, for instance lip
(body), lif (leib) and wip (woman), weib (wife) are in-
dissolubly wedded together, and the one never shows itself
without the other following—there is something which reminds
us not so much of poverty, as of trustfulness and childlike innocence.   Indeed a strange charm lies in those old tones, where,
in gay dancing melodies, the sternest tidings are sung to us;
and deep floods of sadness and strife play lightly in little

purling billows, like seas in summer. It is as a meek smile, in whose still, thoughtful depths a whole infinitude of patience, and love, and heroic strength lie revealed. But in other cases too, we have seen this outward sport and inward earnestness offer grateful contrasts, and cunning excitement; for example, in Tasso; of whom, though otherwise different enough, this old Northern Singer has more than once reminded us. There too, as here, we have a dark solemn meaning in light guise; deeds of high temper, harsh self-denial, daring and death, stand embodied in that soft, quick-flowing joyfully-modulated verse. Nay farther, as if the implement, much more than we might fancy, had influenced the work done, these two poems, could we trust our individual feeling, have in one respect the same poetical result for us; in the Nibelungen as in the Gerusalemme, the persons and their story are indeed brought vividly before us, yet not near and palpably present; it is rather as if we looked on that scene through an inverted telescope, whereby the whole was carried far away into the distance, the life-large figures compressed into brilliant miniatures, so clear, so real, yet tiny, elf-like and beautiful as well as lessened, their colors being now closer and brighter, the shadows and trivial features no longer visible. This, as we partly apprehend, comes of singing epic poems; most part of which only pretend to be sung. Tasso's rich melody still lives among the Italian people; the Nibelungen also is what it professes to be, a song."

The story of the Nibelungen would ordinarily be supposed to be so distant from the interests of modern life, as scarcely to hold the attention of a reader unless he were interested in it from a scholarly or more or less antiquarian standpoint. For those who think thus, however, there is only one thing that will correct such a false impression and that is to read the Nibelungen itself. It has a depth of simplicity and a sympathetic human interest all its own but that reminds one more of Homer than of anything else in literature, and Homer has faults but lack of interest is not one of them. From the very beginning the story of the young man who does not think he will marry, and whose mother does not think that any one is good enough for him, and of the young woman who is sure that no one will come that will attract enough of her attention so as to compel her to subject herself to the yoke of marriage, are types of what is so permanent in humanity, that the readers' attention is at once caught. After this the fighting parts of the story become the center of interest and hold the attention in spite of the refining influences that later centuries are supposed to have brought to humanity.

Hence it is that Prof. Saintsbury in the second volume of his Periods of European Literature, already quoted from, is able to say much of the modern interest in the story. "There may be," as he says, "too many episodic personages—Deitrich of Bern, for instance, has extremely little to do in this galley. But the strength, thoroughness, and in its own savage way, charm of Kriemhild's character, and the incomparable series of battles between the Burgundian princes and Etzel's men in the later cantos—cantos which contain the very best poetical fighting in the history of the world—far more than redeem this. The Nibelungen Lied is a very great poem; and with Beowulf (the oldest but the least interesting on the whole), Roland (the most artistically finished in form), and the poem of the Cid (the cheerfullest and perhaps the fullest of character), composes a quartette of epics with which the literary story of the great European literary nations most appropriately begins. In bulk, dramatic completeness, and a certain furia, the Nibelungen Lied, though the youngest and probably the least original is the greatest of the four."

Less need be said of the Nibelungen than of the Cid or Walter Map's work because it is more familiar, and even ordinary readers of literature have been brought more closely in touch with it because of its relation to the Wagnerian operas. Even those who know the fine old German poems only passingly, will yet realize the supreme genius of their author, and those who need to have the opinions of distinguished critics to back them before they form an estimate for themselves, will not need to seek far in our modern literature to find lofty praises of the old German epic.

With even this brief treatment no reader will doubt that there is in these three epics, typical products of the literary spirit of three great European nations whose literatures rising high above these deep firm substructures, were to be of the greatest

influence in the development of the human mind, and yet were
to remain practically always within the limits of thought and
feeling that had been traced by these old founders of literature
of the early Thirteenth Century, whose work, like that of their
contemporaries in every other form of artistic expression, was
to be the model and the source of inspiration for future generations.

PASTORAL STAFF

XI

MEISTERSINGERS, MINNESINGERS, TROUVÈRES, TROUBADOURS.

It would be a supreme mistake to think because the idea of literature in the Thirteenth Century is usually associated with the Arthur Legends, the Nibelungen and Dante, that all of the literary content of the century was inevitably serious in character or always epical in form. As a matter of fact the soul of wit and humor had entered into the body social, as we shall see in subsequent chapters, and the spirit of gaiety and the light-hearted admiration for nature found as frequent expression as at any time in history. With these as always in literary history there came outbursts of love in lyric strains that were not destined to die. While the poets of South Germany and of Italy sang of love that was of the loftiest description, never mingled with anything of the merely sensual, their tuneful trifles are quite as satisfying to the modern ear in both sense and sound as any of the more elaborate *vers de societé* of the modern times. The German poets particularly did not hesitate to emphasize the fact that sensuality had no part in Minne —their pretty term for love—and yet they sang with all the natural grace and fervid rapture of the Grecian poets of the old pagan times, worshiping at the shrines of fleshly goddesses, or singing to the frail beauties of an unmoral period. Nothing in the history of literature is better proof that ideal love can, unmixed with anything sensual, inspire lyric outbursts of supreme and enduring beauty, than the poems of the Minnesingers and of some of the French and Italian Troubadours ot this period. It is easier to understand Dante's position in this matter after reading the poems of his predecessors in the Thirteenth Century.

For this feeling of the lofty character of the love they sang was not, in spite of what is sometimes said, confined only to the Germans, though as is well known from time immemorial the

Teutonic feeling towards woman was by racial influence of higher character than that of the southern Nations. As Mr. H. J. Chaytor says in the introduction to his Troubadours of Dante, there came a gradual change over the mind of the Troubadour about the beginning of the Thirteenth Century and "seeing that love was the inspiring force to good deeds," the later Troubadours gradually dissociated their love from the object which had aroused it. Among them, "as among the Minnesingers, love is no longer sexual passion, it is rather the motive to great works, to self-surrender, to the winning an honorable name as Courtier and Poet." Mr. Chaytor then quotes the well known lines from Bernart de Ventadorn, one of the Troubadours to whom Dante refers, and whose works Dante seems to have read with special attention since their poems contain similar errors of mythology.

> "for indeed I know
> Of no more subtle passion under heaven
> Than is the maiden passion for a maid,
> Not only to keep down the base in man,
> But teach high thought and amiable words,
> And courtliness and the desire of fame,
> And love of truth and all that makes a man."

A sentiment surely that will be considered as true now as it ever was, be the time the Thirteenth Century or earlier or later, and that represents the best solution of social problems that has ever been put forward—nature's own panacea for ills that other remedies at best only palliate.

In the early Nineteenth Century Carlyle said of this period what we may well repeat here:

"We shall suppose that this Literary Period is partially known to all readers. Let each recall whatever he has learned or figures regarding it; represent to himself that brave young heyday of Chivalry and Minstrelsy when a stern Barbarossa, a stern Lion-heart, sang sirventes, and with the hand that could wield the sword and sceptre twanged the melodious strings, when knights-errant tilted, and ladies' eyes rained bright influences; and, suddenly, as at sunrise, the whole earth had grown vocal and musical. Then truly was the time of singing come; for princes and prelates, emperors and squires, the wise and the simple, men, women and children, all sang and rhymed or delighted in hearing it done. It was a universal noise of Song; as if the Spring of Manhood had arrived, and warblings from every spray, not, indeed, without infinite twitterings also, which, except their gladness, had no music, were bidding it welcome."

This is the keynote of the Century—song, blithesome and gay as the birds, solemn and harmonious as the organ tones that accord so well with the great Latin hymns—everywhere song.

"Believers," says Tieck, the great collector of Thirteenth Century poetry, "sang of Faith; Lovers of Love; Knights described knightly actions and battles; and loving, believing knights were their chief audience. The Spring, Beauty, Gaiety, were objects that could never tire; great duels and deeds of arms carried away every hearer, the more surely the stronger they were painted; and as the pillars and dome of the Church encircled the flock, so did Religion, as the Highest, encircle Poetry and Reality; and every heart, in equal love, humbled itself before her."

The names of the Meistersingers are well-known to musical lovers at least, because of the music drama of that name and the famous war of the Wartburg. The most familiar of all of them is doubtless Walter von der Vogelweide who, when he was asked where he found the tuneful melodies of his songs, said that he learned them from the birds. Those who recall Longfellow's pretty ballad with regard to Walter and his leaving all his substance to feed the birds over his grave near Nuremberg's minster towers, will not find it surprising that this Meistersinger's poetry breathes the deepest love of Nature, and that there is in it a lyric quality of joy in the things of Nature that we are apt to think of as modern, until we find over and over again in these bards, that the spirit of the woods and of the fields and of the spring time, meant as much for them as for any follower of the Wordsworth school of poetry in the more conscious after-time. This from Walter with regard to the May will serve to illustrate very well this phase of his work.

Gentle May, thou showerest fairly
　Gifts afar and near;
Clothest all the woods so rarely,
　And the meadows here;
O'er the heath new colors glow;
Flowers and clover on the plain,
Merry rivals, strive amain
Which can fastest grow.

Lady! part me from my sadness,
　Love me while 'tis May;
Mine is but a borrowed gladness
　If thou frown alway;
Look around and smile anew!
All the world is glad and free;
Let a little joy from thee
Fall to my lot too!

Walter could be on occasion, however, as serious as any of the Meistersingers and is especially known for his religious poems. It is not surprising that any one who set woman on so high a pedestal as did Walter, should have written beautiful poems to the Blessed Virgin. He was the first, so it is said, to express the sentiment: "Woman, God bless her, by that name, for it is a far nobler name than lady." Occasionally he can be seriously didactic and he has not hesitated even to express some sentiments with regard to methods of education. Among other things he discusses the question as to whether children should be whipped or not in the process of education and curiously enough takes the very modern view that whipping is always a mistake. In this, of course, he disagrees with all the practical educators of his time, who considered the rod the most effective instrument for the education of children and strictly followed the scriptural injunction about sparing the rod and spoiling the child. Walter's opinion is for that reason all the more interesting:

"Children with rod ruling—
'Tis the worst of schooling.
Who is honor made to know,
Him a word seems as a blow."

The birds were always a favorite subject for poetic inspiration on the part of the Minnesingers. Bird music rapt poetic souls into ecstasies in which the passage of time was utterly unnoticed. It is from the Thirteenth Century that comes the beautiful legend with regard to the monk who, having wondered how time could be kept from dragging in Heaven, was permitted to listen to the song of a bird one day in the forest and when he awoke from his rapture and went back to his convent found that a hundred years had passed, that all of the monks of his acquaintance were dead, and while his name was found on the rolls of the monastery, after it there was a note that he had disappeared one day and had never been heard of afterwards. Almost in the same tenor as this is a pretty song from Dietmar von Eist, written at the beginning of the Thirteenth Century, and which was a type of the charming songs that were to be so characteristic of the times:

> There sat upon the linden-tree
>   A bird, and sung its strain;
> So sweet it sung that as I heard
>   My heart went back again.
> It went to one remember'd spot,
>   It saw the rose-tree grow,
> And thought again the thoughts of love,
>   There cherished long ago.
>
> A thousand years to me it seems
>   Since by my fair I sate;
> Yet thus to be a stranger long
>   Is not my choice, but fate;
> Since then I have not seen the flowers,
>   Nor heard the birds' sweet song;
> My joys have all too briefly past,
>   My griefs been all too long.

Hartman von Aue was a contemporary of Walter's and is best known for his romantic stories. It is rather curiously interesting to find that one of the old chroniclers considers it a great mark of distinction that, though Hartman was a knight, he was able to read and write whatever he found written in books. It must not be forgotten, however, that not all of these poets could read and write, and that indeed so distinguished a literary man as Wolfram von Eschenbach, the author of Percival, the story on which Wagner founded his opera of Parsifal, could neither read nor write. He had developed a very wonderful memory and was able to store faithfully his poems in the course of their composition so that he was above the need of pen and paper. Hartman is most famous for having written the story of Poor Henry, which Longfellow has chosen so effectively for his Golden Legend. Hartman's appreciation of women can be judged from the following lines, which accord her an equal share in her lord's glory because of her sufferings in prayer at home.

> Glory be unto her whose word
> Sends her dear lord to bitter fight;
> Although he conquer by his sword,
> She to the praise has equal right;
> He with the sword in battle, she at home with
> prayer,
> Both win the victory, and both the glory share.

Occasionally one finds, as we have said, among the little songs of the Minnesingers of the time such tuneful trifles as could be included very appropriately in a modern collection of *vers de société,* or as might even serve as a love message on a modern valentine or a Christmas card. The surprise of finding such things at such a time will justify the quotation of one of them from Brother Wernher, who owes his title of brother not to his membership in any religious order, very probably, but to the fact that he belonged to the brotherhood of the poets of the time.

> Since creation I was thine;
> Now forever thou art mine.
> I have shut thee fast
> In my heart at last.
> I have dropped the key
> In an unknown sea.
> Forever must thou my prisoner be!

Wolfram von Eschenbach was the chief of a group of poets who at the close of the Twelfth and beginning of the Thirteenth centuries gathered about the Landgraf Hermann of Thuringen in his court on the Wartburg, at the foot of which lies Eisenach, in the present Grand Duchy of Saxe-Weimar. They shaped tales of knightly adventure, blended with reflection, spiritual suggestion, and a grace of verse that represented the best culture of the court, and did not address itself immediately to the people. Wolfram was a younger son of one of the lower noble Bavarian families settled at Eschenbach, nine miles from Ausbach, in Middle Franconia. He had a poor little home of his own, Wildenberg, but went abroad to seek adventures as a knight, and tell adventures as a poet welcome to great lords, and most welcome to the lavish friend of poets, Hermann of Thuringen, at whose court on the Wartburg he remained twenty years, from 1195 to 1215, in which latter year his "Parzival" was finished. From some passages in his poem it may safely be inferred that he was happily married, and had children. The Landgraf Hermann died in 1216, and was succeeded by Ludwig, husband of St. Elizabeth.

We cannot ascribe to English writers alone the spiritualizing of the Grail Legends, when there is Wolfram's "Parzival" drawing from the same cycle of myths a noble poem of the striving to bind earthly knighthood to the ever-living God. While Gawain, type of the earthly knight wins great praise in love and chivalry, Parzival—Percival—finds his way on from childhood up, through humble searchings of the spirit, till he is ruler in the kingdom of the soul, where he designs that Lohengrin, his eldest son, shall be his successor, while Kardeiss, his younger son, has rule over his earthly possessions.

How beautifully the Minnesingers could enter into the spirit of nature and at the same time how much the spirit of Spring has always been prone to appeal to poetic sensibilities may be judged from the following song of Conrad of Kirchberg, which is translated very closely and in the same meter as the original old high German poem. It is very evident that none of the spirit of Spring was lost on this poet of the olden time, nor on the other hand that any possibility of poetic expression was missed by him. There is a music in the lilt of the verselets, eminently suggestive of the lyric effect that the new birth of things had on the poet himself and that he wished to convey to his readers. Of this, however, every one must judge for himself and so we give the poem as it may be found in Roscoe's edition of Sismondi's Literature of the South of Europe.

> May, sweet May, again is come;
> May, that frees the land from gloom.
> Up, then, children, we will go
> Where the blooming roses grow,
> In a joyful company
> We the bursting flowers will see;
> Up! your festal dress prepare!
> Where gay hearts are meeting, there
> May hath pleasures most inviting.
> Heart, and sight, and ear delighting:
> Listen to the bird's sweet song,
> Hark! how soft it floats along!
> Courtly dames our pleasures share,
> Never saw I May so fair;
> Therefore, dancing will we go:
> Youths rejoice, the flowrets blow;
> Sing ye! join the chorus gay!
> Hail this merry, merry May!

At least as beautiful in their tributes to their lady loves and their lyric descriptions of the beauties of Spring, were the Troubadours whose tuneful trifles, sometimes deserving of much more serious consideration than the application of such a term to them would seem to demand, have come down to us though the centuries. One of the best known of these is Arnaud de Marveil, who was born in very humble circumstances but who succeeded in raising himself by his poetic genius to be the companion of ruling princes and the friend of the high nobility. Among the provencals he has been called the great Master of Love, though this is a name which Petrarch reserves especially for Arnaud Daniel, while he calls Marveil the less famous of the Arnauds. An example of his work as the Poet of Love, that is typical of what is usually considered to have

been the favorite mode of the Troubadour poets runs as follows:

> All I behold recalls the memory
> Of her I love. The freshness of the hour
> Th' enamell'd fields, the many coloured flower,
> Speaking of her, move me to melody.
> Had not the poets, with their courtly phrase,
>   Saluted many a fair of meaner worth,
> I could not now have render'd thee the praise
>   So justly due, of "Fairest of the Earth."
> To name thee thus had been to speak thy name,
> And waken, o'er thy cheek, the blush of modest shame."

An example of the love of nature which characterizes some
of Arnaud de Marveil's work will serve to show how
thoroughly he entered into the spirit of the spring-time and
how much all the sights and sounds of nature found an echo
in his poetic spirit. The translation of this as of the preceding
specimen from Arnaud is taken from the English edition of
the Historical View of the Literature of the South of Europe
by Sismondi, and this translation we owe to Thomas Roscoe,
the well known author of the life of Lorenzo the Magnificent,
who considering that Sismondi does not furnish enough of
specimens of this Troubadour poet, inserts the following verses,
for the translation of which he acknowledges himself indebted
to the kindness of friends, a modest concealment doubtless of
his own work:

> Oh! how sweet the breeze of April,
>   Breathing soft as May draws near!
> While, through nights of tranquil beauty,
>   Songs of gladness meet the ear:
> Every bird his well-known language
>   Uttering in the morning's pride,
> Revelling in joy and gladness
>   By his happy partner's side.
>
> When, around me, all is smiling,
>   When to life the young birds spring,

Thoughts of love, I cannot hinder,
 Come, my heart inspiriting—
Nature, habit, both incline me
 In such joy to bear my part:
With such sounds of bliss around me
 Could I wear a sadden'd heart?

His description of his lady love is another example of his worship of nature in a different strain, which serves to show that a lover's exaggeration of the qualities of his lady is not a modern development of *la belle passion*.

Fairer than the far-famed Helen,
 Lovelier than the flow'rets gay,
Snow-white teeth, and lips truth-telling,
 Heart as open as the day;
Golden hair, and fresh bright roses—
 Heaven, who formed a thing so fair,
Knows that never yet another
 Lived, who can with thee compare.

A single stanza from a love-song by Bertrand De Born will show better than any amount of critical appreciation how beautifully he can treat the more serious side of love. While the Troubadours are usually said to have sung their love strains in less serious vein than their German brother poets of the North, this has the ring of tenderness and truth about it and yet is not in these qualities very different from others of his songs that are well known. The translation we have chosen is that made by Roscoe who has rendered a number of the songs of the Troubadours into English verse that presents an excellent equivalent of the original. Bertrand is insisting with his lady-love that she must not listen to the rumors she may hear from others with regard to his faithfulness.

I cannot hide from thee how much I fear
The whispers breathed by flatterers in thine ear
 Against my faith. But turn not, oh, I pray!
That heart so true, so faithful, so sincere,
So humble and so frank, to me so dear,
 Oh, lady! turn it not from me away.

At times one is surprised to find pretty tributes to nature even in the midst of songs that are devoted to war. The two things that were nearest the hearts of these Troubadour poets were war and their lady-loves, but the beauties of nature became mixed up not only with their love songs but also with their battle hymns, or at least with their ardent descriptions of military preparations and the glories of war. An excellent example of this is to be found in the following stanza written by William of Saint Gregory, a Troubadour who is best known for his songs of war rather than of tenderness.

> The beautiful spring delights me well,
>   When flowers and leaves are growing;
> And it pleases my heart to hear the swell
>   Of the birds' sweet chorus flowing
>   In the echoing wood;
> And I love to see all scattered around
> Pavilions and tents on martial ground;
>   And my spirit finds it good
> To see on the level plains beyond
> Gay knights and steeds caparison'd.

Occasionally the Troubadours indulge in religious poetry though usually not of a mystical or profoundly devotional character. Even the famous Peyrols, who is so well known for his love songs, sometimes wandered into religious poetry that was not unworthy to be placed beside his lyric effusions on other topics. Peyrols is best known perhaps for his lamentations over King Richard the Lion Heart's fate, for he had been with that monarch on the crusade, and like most of the Troubadours who went with the army, drank in deep admiration for the poetic king. After his visit to the Holy Land on this occasion one stanza of his song in memory of that visit runs as follows :*

> I have seen the Jordan river,
>   I have seen the holy grave.
> Lord! to thee my thanks I render
>   For the joys thy goodness gave,

*Translated by Roscoe.

Showing to my raptured sight
The spot whereon thou saw'st the light.

Vessel good and favoring breezes,
   Pilot, trusty, soon shall we
Once more see the towers of Marseilles
   Rising o'er the briny sea.
Farewell, Acre, farewell, all,
Of Temple or of Hospital:

Now, alas! the world's decaying.
   When shall we once more behold
Kings like lion-hearted Richard,
   France's monarch, stout and bold?

TOWER OF THE SCALIGERS
(VERONA)

XII

GREAT LATIN HYMNS AND CHURCH MUSIC.

One of the most precious bequests of the Thirteenth Century to all the succeeding centuries is undoubtedly the great Latin hymns. These sublime religious poems, comparable only to the Hebrew psalms for their wondrous expression of the awe and devotion of religious feeling, present the beginnings of rhymed poetry, yet they have been acclaimed by competent modern critics as among the greatest poems that ever came from the mind of man. They come to us from this period and were composed, most of them at least, during the Thirteenth Century itself, a few, shortly before it, though all of them received during this century the stamp of ecclesiastical and popular approval, which made them for many centuries afterward the principal medium of the expression of congregational devotion and the exemplar and incentive for vernacular poetry. It is from these latter standpoints that they deserve the attention of all students of literature quite apart from their significance as great expressions of the mind of these wondrous generations.

These Latin hymns have sometimes been spoken of with perhaps a certain degree of contempt as "rhymed Latin poetry," as if the use of rhyme in conjunction with Latin somehow lowered the dignity of the grand old tongue in which Cicero wrote his graceful periods and Horace sang his tuneful odes. As a matter of fact, far from detracting from the beauties of Latin expression, these hymns have added new laurels to the glory of the language and have shown the wonderful possibilities of the Roman speech in the hands of generations long after the classical period. If they served no other purpose than to demonstrate beyond cavil how profoundly the scholars of this generation succeeded in possessing themselves of the genius of the Latin language, they would serve to contradict the foolish critics who talk of the education of the period as superficial, or as negligent of everything but scholastic philosophy and theology.

At least one distinguished philologist, Professor F. A. March, who has now for the better part of half a century occupied the chair of comparative philology at Lafayette College, does not hesitate to say that the Latin hymns represent an expression of the genius of the Latin people and language, more characteristic than the classical poetry even of the golden or silver ages. "These hymns," he says, "were the first original poetry of the people in the Latin language, unless perhaps those Latin critics may be right who think they find in Livy a prose rendering of earlier ballads. The so-called classic poetry was an echo of Greece, both in substance and in form. The matter and meters were both imitated and the poems were composed for the lovers of Grecian art in the Roman Court. It did not spring from the people, but the Christian hymns were proper folk poetry, the Bible of the people—their Homeric poems. Their making was not so much speech as action. They were in substance festive prayers, the simplest rythmic offering of thanks and praise to the Giver of Light and of rest both natural and spiritual, at morning and evening and at other seasons, suited to the remembrance and rythmical rehearsal of the truths of the Bible." Prof. March's opinion has been echoed by many another enthusiastic student of these wonderful hymns. It is only those who do not know them who fail to grow enthusiastic about them.

This of itself would stamp these great poems as worthy of careful study. There is, however, an additional reason for modern interest in them. These hymns were sung by the whole congregation at the many services that they attended in the medieval period. In this regard it seems well to recall, that it was the custom to go to church much oftener then than at present. Besides the Sundays there were many holy days of obligation, that is, religious festivals on which attendance at Church was obligatory, and in addition a certain number of days of devotion on which, because of special reverence for some particular saint, or in celebration of some event in the life of the Lord or his saints, the people of special parts of the country found themselves drawn to attendance on church services. It seems probable that instead of the sixty or so times a year that is now obligatory, people went to Church during the Thirteenth Century more than a hundred times in the year. Twice a week then, at least, there was the uplifting cultural influence of this congregational singing of wonderful hymns that are among the greatest poems ever written and that belong to literature of the very highest order. The educational value of such intimate contact with what is best in literary expression could scarcely fail to have a distinct effect upon the people. It is idle to say that the hymns being in Latin they were not understood, since the language of them was close akin to the spoken tongues, the subjects were eminently familiar mysteries of religion and constant repetition and frequent explanation must have led to a very general comprehension even by the least educated classes. For anyone with any pretension to education they must have been easy to understand, since Latin was practically a universal language.

It is not always realized by the students whose interests have been mainly confined to modern literature, in what estimation these Latin hymns have been held by those who are in the best position to be able to judge critically of their value as poetry. Take for example the Dies Irae, confessedly the greatest of them, and it will be found that many of the great poets and literary men of the Nineteenth Century have counted it among their favorite poems. Such men as Goethe, Friedrich and August Schlegel, Scott, Milman and Archbishop Trench were enthusiastic in its praise; while such geniuses as Dryden, Johnson and Jeremy Taylor, and the musicians Mozart and Hayden, avowed supreme admiration for it. Herder, Fichte and August Schlegel besides Crashaw, Drummond, Roscommon, Trench and Macaulay gave the proof of their appreciation of the great Thirteenth Century hymn by devoting themselves to making translations of it, and Goethe's use of it in Faust and Scott's in the Lay of the Last Minstrel, show how much poets, whose sympathies were not involved in its religious aspects, were caught by its literary and esthetic merit.

In very recent times the Latin hymns have been coming more to their own again and such distinguished critics as Prof. Henry Morley, and Prof. George Saintsbury, have not hesitated to express their critical appreciation of these hymns as great

ST, FRANCIS PROPHESIES CELANO'S DEATH (GIOTTO)

literature. Prof. Saintsbury says in his volume of the Thirteenth Century literature:*

"It will be more convenient to postpone to a later chapter of this volume a consideration of the exact way in which Latin sacred poetry affected the prosody of the vernacular; but it is well here to point out that almost all the finest and most famous examples of the medieval hymns, with perhaps the sole exception of the Veni Sancte Spiritus, date from the Twelfth and Thirteenth centuries. Ours (that is, from this period) are the stately rhythms of Adam of St. Victor, and the softer ones of St. Bernard the Greater. It was at this time that Jacopone da Todi, in the intervals of his eccentric vernacular exercises, was inspired to write the Stabat Mater. From this time comes that glorious descant of Bernard of Morlaix, in which, the more its famous and very elegant English paraphrase is read beside it (Jerusalem the Golden), the more does the greatness and the beauty of the original appear.

"And from this time comes the greatest of all hymns, and one of the greatest of all poems, the Dies Irae. There have been attempts—more than one of them—to make out that the Dies Irae is no such wonderful thing after all; attempts which are, perhaps, the extreme examples of that cheap and despicable paradox which thinks to escape the charge of blind docility by the affectation of heterodox independence. The judgment of the greatest (and not always of the most pious) men of letters of modern times may confirm those who are uncomfortable without authority in a different opinion. Fortunately there is not likely ever to be lack of those who, authority or no authority, in youth and in age, after much reading or without much, in all time of their tribulation and in all time of their wealth, will hold these wonderful triplets, be they Thomas of Celano's or another's, as nearly or quite the most perfect wedding of sound to sense that they know."

This seems almost the limit of praise but Prof. Saintsbury can say even more than this: "It would be possible, indeed, to

* The Flourishing of Romance and the Rise of Allegory, Volume II. of. Periods of European Literature, Edited by George Saintsbury, New York, Scribners, 1899.

illustrate a complete dissertation on the methods of expression in serious poetry from the fifty-one lines of the Dies Irae. Rhyme, alliteration, cadence, and adjustment of vowel and consonant values—all these things receive perfect expression in it, or, at least, in the first thirteen stanzas, for the last four are a little inferior. It is quite astonishing to reflect upon the careful art or the felicitous accident of such a line as:

Tuba mirum spargens sonum,

with the thud of the trochee falling in each instance in a different vowel; and still more on the continuous sequence of five stanzas, from *Judex ergo* to *non sit cassus,* in which not a word could be displaced or replaced by another without loss. The climax of verbal harmony, corresponding to and expressing religious passion and religious awe, is reached in the last—

Quaerens me sedisti lassus,
Redemisti crucem passus:
Tantus labor non sit cassus!

where the sudden change from the dominant *e* sounds (except in the rhyme foot) of the first two lines to the *a's* of the last is simply miraculous and miraculously assisted by what may be called the internal sub-rhyme of *sedisti* and *redemisti.* This latter effect can rarely be attempted without a jingle: there is no jingle here, only an ineffable melody. After the Dies Irae, no poet could say that any effect of poetry was, as far as sound goes, unattainable, though few could have hoped to equal it, and perhaps no one except Dante and Shakespeare has fully done so."

Higher praise than this could scarcely be given and it comes from an acknowledged authority, whose interests are moreover in secular rather than religious literature, and whose enthusiastic praise is therefore all the more striking. Here in America, Schaff, whose critical judgment in religious literature is unquestionable and whose sympathies with the old church and her hymns were not as deep as if he had been a Roman Catholic, has been quite as unstinted in laudation.

"This marvelous hymn is the acknowledged masterpiece of Latin poetry, and the most sublime of all uninspired hymns.

. . The secret of its irresistible power lies in the awful grandeur of the theme, the intense earnestness and pathos of the poet, the simple majesty and solemn music of its language, the stately meter, the triple rhyme, and the vowel assonances, chosen in striking adaptation to the sense—all combining to produce an overwhelming effect, as if we heard the final crash of the universe, the commotion of the opening graves, the trumpet of the archangel summoning the quick and the dead, and saw the 'king of tremendous majesty' seated on the throne of justice and of mercy, and ready to dispense everlasting life and everlasting woe."

Neale says of Thomas Aquinas' great hymn the Pange Lingua: "This hymn contests the second place among those of the Western Church, with the 'Vexilla Regis,' the 'Stabat Mater,' the 'Jesu Dulcis Memoria,' the 'Ad Regias Agni Dapes,' the 'Ad Supernam,' and one or two others, leaving the 'Dies Irae' in its unapproachable glory," thus furnishing another precious testimony to the hymn we have been discussing, which indeed only needs to be read to be appreciated, since it will inevitably tempt to successive readings and these bring with them ever and ever increasing admiration, showing in this more than in any other way that it is a work of sublime genius.

With regard to rhyme particularly the triumph of art and the influence of the Latin hymns is undoubted. This latest beauty of poetry reached its perfection of expression in the Latin hymns. It is rather curious to trace its gradual development. It constitutes the only feature of literature which apparently did not come to us from the East. The earlier specimens of poetry of which we know anything among the Oriental nations other than the Hebrews, are beautiful examples of the possibilities of rhythm and the beginnings of meter. As poetry goes westward meter becomes as important as rhythm in poetry and these two qualities differentiated it from prose. Both of these literary modes, however, are eastern in origin. Rhyme comes from the distant West and seems to have originated in the alliteration invented by the Celtic bards. The vowel assonance was after a time completed by the addition of consonantal assonance and then the invention of rhyme was completed. The first fully rhymed hymns seem to have been written by the

Irish monks and carried over to the Continent by them on their Christianizing expeditions, after the irruption of the barbarians had obliterated the civilization of Europe. During the Tenth and Eleventh centuries rhyme developed mainly in connection with ecclesiastical poetry. During the Twelfth and Thirteenth centuries it reached an acme of evolution which has never been surpassed during all the succeeding generations.

It must not be thought that, because so much attention is given to the Dies Irae, this constitutes the only supremely great hymn of the Thirteenth Century. There are at least five or six others that well deserve to be mentioned in the same breath. One of them, the famous Stabat Mater of Jacopone da Todi, has been considered by some critics as quite as beautiful as the Dies Irae in poetic expression, though below it as poetry because of the lesser sublimity of its subject. Certainly no more marvelously poetic expression of all that is saddest in human sorrow has ever been put into words, than that which is to be found in these stanzas of the Franciscan Monk who had himself known all the depths of human sorrow and trial. Most people know the opening stanzas of it well enough to scarce need their presentation and yet it is from the poem itself, and not from any critical appreciation of it, that its greatness must be judged.

Stabat mater dolorosa
Juxta crucem lacrymosa,
Dum pendebat filius,
Cuius animan gementem,
Contristantem et dolentem
Pertransivit gladius.

O quam tristis et afflicta
Fuit illa benedicta
Mater unigeniti,
Quae mœrebat et dolebat
Et tremebat, dum videbat
Nati poenas inclyti.

Quis est homo, qui non fleret,
Matrem Christi si videret,
In tanto supplicio?

MADONNA AND CHILD (CAMPO SANTO, PISA, GIOV. PIS.)

> Quis non posset contristari,
> Piam matrem contemplari
> Dolentem cum filio!

As in the case of the Dies Irae there have been many translations of the Stabat Mater, most of them done by poets whose hearts were in their work and who were accomplishing their purpose as labors of love. While we realize how many beautiful translations there are, it is almost pitiful to think what poor English versions are sometimes used in the devotional exercises of the present day. One of the most beautiful translations is undoubtedly that by Denis Florence MacCarthy, who has been hailed as probably the best translator into English of foreign poetry that our generation has known, and whose translations of Calderon present the greatest of Spanish poets, in a dress as worthy of the original as it is possible for a poet to have in a foreign tongue. MacCarthy has succeeded in following the intricate rhyme plan of the Stabat with a perfection that would be deemed almost impossible in our harsher English, which does not readily yield itself to double rhymes and which permits frequency of rhyme as a rule only at the sacrifice of vigor of expression. The first three stanzas, however, of the Stabat Mater will serve to show how well MacCarthy accomplished his difficult task:

> By the cross, on which suspended,
> With his bleeding hands extended,
>   Hung that Son she so adored,
> Stood the mournful Mother weeping,
> She whose heart, its silence keeping,
>   Grief had cleft as with a sword.

> O, that Mother's sad affliction—
> Mother of all benediction—
>   Of the sole-begotten One;
> Oh, the grieving, sense-bereaving,
> Of her heaving breast, perceiving
>   The dread sufferings of her Son.

> What man is there so unfeeling,
> Who, his heart to pity steeling,
>   Could behold that sight unmoved?

> Could Christ's Mother see there weeping,
> See the pious Mother keeping
>   Vigil by the Son she loved?

A very beautiful translation in the meter of the original
was also made by the distinguished Irish poet, Aubrey de Vere.
The last two stanzas of this translation have been considered
as perhaps the most charmingly effective equivalent in English
for Jacopone's wonderfully devotional termination that has
ever been written.

> May his wounds both wound and heal me;
> His blood enkindle, cleanse, anneal me;
>   Be his cross my hope and stay:
> Virgin, when the mountains quiver,
> From that flame which burns for ever,
>   Shield me on the judgment-day.

> Christ, when he that shaped me calls me,
> When advancing death appalls me,
>   Through her prayer the storm make calm:
> When to dust my dust returneth
> Save a soul to thee that yearneth;
>   Grant it thou the crown and palm.

Even distinguished professors of philosophy and theology
occasionally indulged themselves in the privilege of writing
these Latin hymns and, what is more surprising, succeeded in
making poetry of a very high order. At least two of the most
distinguished professors in these branches at the University
of Paris in the latter half of the Thirteenth Century, must be
acknowledged as having written hymns that are confessedly
immortal, not because of any canonical usage that keeps them
alive, but because they express in very different ways, in wondrously beautiful language some of the sublimest religious
thoughts of their time. These two are St. Bonaventure, the
Franciscan, and St. Thomas of Aquin, the Dominican. St.
Bonaventure's hymns on the Passion and Cross of Christ represent what has been most beautifully sung on these subjects in all
the ages. St. Thomas' poetic work centers around the Blessed
Sacrament in whose honor he was so ardent and so devoted

that the composition of the office for its feast was confided to him by the Pope. The hymns he wrote, far from being the series of prosy theological formulas that might have been expected perhaps under such circumstances, are great contributions to a form of literature which contains more gems of purest ray in its collection than almost any other. St. Thomas' poetic jewels shine with no borrowed radiance, and their effulgence is not cast into shadow even by the greatest of their companion pieces among the Latin hymns of a wonderfully productive century. Neale's tribute to one of them has already been quoted in an earlier part of this chapter.

It has indeed been considered almost miraculous, that this profoundest of thinkers should have been able to attain within the bounds of rhyme and rhythm, the accurate expression of some of the most intricate theological thoughts that have ever been expressed, and yet should have accomplished his purpose with a clarity of language, a simplicity and directness of words, a poetic sympathy of feeling, and an utter devotion, that make his hymns great literature in the best sense of the word. One of them at least, the Pange Lingua Gloriosi, has been in constant use in the church ever since his time, and its two last stanzas beginning with Tantum Ergo Sacramentum, are perhaps the most familiar of all the Latin hymns. Few of those most familiar with it realize its place in literature, the greatness of its author, or its own marvelous poetic merits.

It must not be forgotten that at the very time when these hymns were most popular the modern languages were just assuming shape. Even at the end of the Thirteenth Century none of them had reached anything like the form that it was to continue to hold, except perhaps the Italian and to some extent the Spanish. When Dante wrote his Divine Comedy at the beginning of the Fourteenth Century, he was tempted to use the Latin language, the common language of all the scholars of his day, and the language ordinarily used for any ambitious literary project for nearly a century later. It will not be forgotten that when Petrarch in the Fourteenth Century wrote his epic, Africa, on which he expected his fame as a poet to rest, he preferred to use the Latin language. Fortunately Dante was large enough of mind to realize, that the vulgar tongue of the Italians would prove the best instrument for the expression of the thoughts he wished to communicate, and so he cast the Italian language into the mold in which it has practically ever since remained.

His very hesitation, however, shows how incomplete as yet were these modern languages considered by the scholars who used them. It was at this very formative period, however, that the people on whose use of the nascent modern languages their future character depended, were having dinned into their ears in the numerous church services, the great Latin hymns with their wonderful finish of expression. Undoubtedly one of the most effective factors of whatever of sweetness there is in the modern tongues, must be attributed to this influence exerted all unconsciously upon the minds of the people. The rhythm and the expressiveness of these magnificent poems could scarcely fail to stamp itself to some degree upon the language, crude though it might be, of the people who had become so familiar with them. It is, then, to no small extent because of the influence of these Latin hymns that our modern languages possess a rythmic melodiousness that in time enabled them to become the instruments for poetic diction in such a way as to satisfy all the requirements of the modern ear in rhyme, and rhythm, and meter. A striking corresponding effect upon the exactness of expression in the modern languages, it will be noticed, is pointed out in the chapter on the Prose of the Century as representing, according to Professor Saintsbury, the greatest benefit that was derived from the exaggerated practise of dialectic disputation in the curriculum of the medieval Universities.

Those who would think that the Thirteenth Century was happy in creative genius but lacking in the critical faculty that would enable it to select the best, not only of the hymns presented by its own generations but also of those which came from the preceding centuries, should make themselves acquainted with the history of these Latin hymns. Just before the Thirteenth Century the monks of the famous Abbey of St. Victor took up the writing of hymns with wonderful success and two of them, Adam and Hugh, became not only the favorites of their own but of succeeding generations. The Thirteenth

Century received the work of these men and gave them a vogue which has continued down to our own time. Some of the hymns that were thus acclaimed and made popular are among the greatest contributions to this form of literature, and while they have had periods of eclipse owing to bad taste in the times that followed, the reputation secured during the Thirteenth Century has always been sufficient to recall them to memory and bring men again to a realization of their beauty when a more esthetic generation came into existence.

One of the hymns of the immediately preceding time, which attained great popularity during the Thirteenth Century—a popularity that reflects credit on those among whom it is noted as well as upon the great hymn itself—was Bernard of Cluny's or Bernard of Morlaix's hymn, concerning the contempt of the world, many of the ideas of which were to be used freely in the book bearing this title written by the first Pope of the century, Innocent III, whose name is usually, though gratuitously associated with quite other ideas than those of contempt for worldly grandeur. The description of the New Jerusalem to come, which is found at the beginning of this great poem, is the basis of all the modern religious poems on this subject. Few hymns have been more praised. Schaff, in his Christ in Song says: "This glowing description is the sweetest of all the new Jerusalem Hymns of Heavenly Homesickness which have taken their inspiration from the last two chapters of Revelation." The extreme difficulty of the meter which its author selected and which would seem almost to preclude the possibility of expressing great connected thought, especially in so long a poem, became under the master hand of this poetic genius, whose command of the Latin language is unrivaled, the source of new beauties for his poem. Besides maintaining the meter of the old Latin hexameters he added double rhymes in each line and yet had every alternate line also end in a rhyme. To appreciate the difficulty this must be read.

Hora novissima, tempora pessima sunt, vigilemus,
Ecce minaciter imminet arbiter ille supremus
Imminet, imminet ut mala terminet, aequa coronet,
Recta remuneret, anxia liberet, aethera donet,

Auferat aspera duraque pondera mentis onustae,
Sobria muniat, improba puniat, utraque juste.

Hic breve vivitur, hic breve plangitur, hic breve fletur;
Non breve vivere, non breve plangere retribuetur;
O retributio! stat brevis actio, vita perennis;
O retributio! coelica mansio stat lue plenis;
Quid datur et quibus? aether egentibus et cruce dignis,
Sidera vermibus, optima sontibus, astra malignis.

There are many versions, but few translators have dared to attempt a close imitation of the original meter. Its beauty is so great, however, that even the labor required for this has not deterred some enthusiastic admirers. Our English tongue, however, does not lend itself readily to the production of hexameters, though in these lines the rhyme and rhythm has been caught to some extent:

"These are the latter times, these are not better times;
Let us stand waiting;
Lo! how with, awfulness, He, first in lawfulness,
Comes arbitrating."

Even from this it may be realized that Doctor Neale is justified in his enthusiastic opinion that "it is the most lovely, in the same way that the Dies Irae is the most sublime, and the Stabat Mater the most pathetic, of medieval poems."

While it scarcely has a place here properly, a word must be said with regard to the music of the Thirteenth Century. It might possibly be thought that these wondrous rhymes had been spoiled in their effectiveness by the crude music to which they were set. To harbor any such notion, however, would only be another exhibition of that intellectual snobbery which concludes that generations so distant could not have anything worth the consideration of our more developed time. The music of the Thirteenth Century is as great a triumph as any other feature of its accomplishment. It would be clearly absurd to suppose, that the people who created the Cathedrals and made every element associated with the church ceremonial so beautiful as to attract the attention of all generations since, could have failed to develop a music suitable to these magnificent fanes. As a matter of fact no more suitable music for congregational singing than the Gregorian Chant, which reached the acme of its development in the Thirteenth Century, has been invented, and the fact that the Catholic Church, after having tried modern music, is now going back to this medieval musical mode for devotional expression, is only a further noteworthy tribute to the enduring character of another phase of Thirteenth Century accomplishment.

Rockstro, who wrote the article on Plain Chant for Grove's Dictionary of Music and for the Encyclopedia Britannica, declared that no more wonderful succession of single notes, had even been strung into melodies so harmoniously adapted to the expression of the words with which they were to be sung, than some of these Plain Chants of the Middle Ages and especially of the Thirteenth Century. No more sublimely beautiful musical expression of all the depths there are in sadness has ever found its way into music, than what is so simply expressed in the Lamentations as they are sung in the office called Tenebrae during Holy Week. Even more beautiful in its joyousness is the marvelous melody of the Exultet which is sung in the Office of Holy Saturday. This latter is said to be the sublimest expression of joyful sound that has ever come from the human heart and mind. In a word, in music as in every other artistic department, the men of the Thirteenth Century reached a standard that has never been excelled and that remains to the present day as a source of pleasure and admiration for intellectual men, and will continue to be so for numberless generations yet unborn.

Nor must it be thought that the Thirteenth Century men and women were satisfied with Church music alone. About the middle of the century part singing came into use in the churches at the less formal ceremonials, and soon spread to secular uses. As the Mystery Plays gave rise to the modern drama, so church music gave birth to the popular music of the time. In England, particularly, about the middle of the century, various glee songs were sung, portions of which have come down to us, and a great movement of folk music was begun. Before the end of the century the interaction of church and secular music had given rise to many of the modes of modern musical development, and the musical movement was as substantially begun as were any of the other great artistic and intellectual movements which this century so marvelously initiated. This subject, of course, is of the kind that needs to be studied in special works if any satisfactory amount of information is to be obtained, but even the passing hint of it which we have been able to give will enable the reader to realize the important place of the Thirteenth Century in the development of modern music.

BLESSED VIRGIN ENTOMBED (NOTRE DAME, PARIS)

XIII

THREE MOST READ BOOKS OF THE CENTURY.

Three books were more read than any others during the Thirteenth Century, that is, of course, apart from Holy Scriptures, which contrary to the usually accepted notion in this matter, were frequently the subject of study and of almost daily contact in one way or another by all classes of people. These three books were, Reynard the Fox, that is the series of stories of the animals in which they are used as a cloak for a satire upon man and his ways, called often the Animal Epic; the Golden Legend, which impressed Longfellow so much that he spent many years making what he hoped might prove for the modern world a bit of the self-revelation that this wonderful old medieval book has been for its own and subsequent generations; and, finally, the Romance of the Rose, probably the most read book during the Thirteenth and Fourteenth and most of the Fifteenth centuries in all the countries of Europe. Its popularity can be well appreciated from the fact that, though Chaucer was much read, there are more than three times as many manuscript copies of The Romance of the Rose in existence as of Chaucer's Canterbury Tales, and it was one of the earliest books to see the light in print.*

* It was a favorite occupation some few years ago to pick out what were considered the ten best books. Sir John Lubbock first suggested, that it would be an interesting thing to pick out the ten books which, if one were to be confined for life, should be thought the most likely to be of enduring interest. If this favorite game were to be played with the selection limited to the authors of a single century, it is reasonably sure that most educated people would pick out the thirteenth century group of ten for their exclusive reading for the rest of life, rather than any other. An experimental list of ten books selected from the thirteenth century writers would include the Cid, the Legends of King Arthur, the Nibelungen Lied, the Romance of the Rose, Reynard the Fox, the Golden Legend, the Summa of St. Thomas Aquinas, Parsifal or Perceval by Wolfram von Eschenbach, Durandus's Symbolism and Dante. As will readily be appreciated by anyone who knows literature well, these are eminently books of enduring interest. When it is considered that in making this list no call is made upon Icelandic Literature nor Provençal Literature, both of which are of supreme interest, and both reached their maturity at this time, the abounding literary wealth of the century will be understood.

It has become the fashion in recent years, to take the pains from time to time to find out which are the most read books. The criterion of worth thus set up is not very valuable, for unfortunately for the increase in readers, there has not come a corresponding demand for the best books nor for solid literature. The fact that a book has been the best seller, or the most read for a time, usually stamps it at once as trivial or at most as being of quite momentary interest and not at all likely to endure. It is all the more interesting to find then, that these three most read books of the Thirteenth Century, have not only more than merely academic interest at the present time, but that they are literature in the best sense of the word. They have always been not only a means of helping people to pass the time, the sad office to which the generality of books has been reduced in our time, but a source of inspiration for literary men in many generations since they first became popular.

The story of Reynard the Fox is one of the most profoundly humorous books that was ever written. Its satire was aimed at its own time yet it is never for a moment antiquated for the modern reader. At a time when, owing to the imperfect development of personal rights, it would have been extremely dangerous to satirize as the author does very freely, the rulers, the judges, the nobility, the ecclesiastical authorities and churchmen, and practically all classes of society, the writer, whose name has, unfortunately for the completeness of literary history, not come down to us, succeeded in painting all the foibles of men and pointing out all the differences there are between men's pretensions and their actual accomplishments. All the methods by which the cunning scoundrel could escape justice are exploited. The various modes of escaping punishment by direct and indirect bribery, by pretended repentance and reformation, by cunning appeal to the selfishness of judges, are revealed with the fidelity to detail of a modern muckraker; yet, all of it with a humanly humorous quality which, while it takes away nothing from the completeness of the exposure, removes most of the bitterness that probably would have made the satire fail of its purpose. While every class in the community of the time comes in for satirical allusions, that give us a better idea of how closely the men and the women of the time resembled those of our own, than is to be found in any other single literary work that has been preserved for us from this century, or, indeed, any other, the series of stories seemed to be scarcely more than a collection of fables for children, and probably was read quite unsuspectingly by those who are so unmercifully satirized in it, though doubtless, as is usually noted in such cases, each one may have applied the satire of the story as he saw it to his neighbor and not to himself.

A recent editor has said very well of Reynard the Fox that it is one of the most universal of books in its interest for all classes. Critics have at all times been ready to praise and few if any have found fault. It is one of the books that answers well to what Cardinal Newman declared to be at least the accidental definition of a classic; it pleases in childhood, in youth, in middle age and even in declining years. It is because of the eternal verity of the humanity in the book, that with so much truth Froude writing of Reynard can say: "It is not addressed to a passing mode of folly or of profligacy, but it touches the perennial nature of mankind, laying bare our own sympathies, and tastes, and weaknesses, with as keen and true an edge as when the living world of the old Suabian poet winced under its earliest utterance."

The writer who traced the portraits must be counted one of the great observers of all time. As is the case with so many creative artists of the Thirteenth Century, though this is truer elsewhere than in literature, the author is not known. Perhaps he thought it safer to shroud his identity in friendly obscurity, rather than expose himself to the risks the finding of supposed keys to his satire might occasion. Too much credit must not be given to this explanation, however, though some writers have made material out of it to exploit Church intolerance, which the conditions do not justify. We are not sure who wrote the Arthur Legends, we do not know the author of the Cid, even all-pervasive German scholarship has not settled the problem of the writer of the Nibelungen, and the authorship of the Dies Irae is in doubt, though all of these would be sources of honor and praise rather than danger. Authors had evidently not as yet become sophisticated to the extent of seeking immortality for their works. They even seem to have been indifferent as to whether their names were associated with them or not. Enough for them apparently to have had the satisfaction of doing, all else seemed futile.

The original of Reynard the Fox was probably written in the Netherlands, though it may be somewhat difficult for the modern mind to associate so much of wit and humor with the Dutchmen of the Middle Ages. It arose there about the time that the Cid came into vogue in Spain, the Arthur Legends were being put into shape in England, and the Nibelungen reaching its ultimate form in Germany. Reynard thus fills up the geographical chart of contemporary literary effort for the Thirteenth Century, since France and Italy come in for their share in other forms of literature, and no country is missing from the story of successful, enduring accomplishment in letters. It was written from so close to the heart of Nature, that it makes a most interesting gift book even for the Twentieth Century child, and yet will be read with probably even more pleasure by the parents. With good reason another recent editor has thus summed up the catholicity of its appeal to all generations:

"This book belongs to the rare class which is equally delightful to children and to their elders. In this regard it may be compared to 'Gulliver's Travels,' 'Don Quixote' and 'Pilgrim's Progress.' For wit and shrewd satire and for pure drollery both in situations and descriptions, it is unsurpassed. The animals are not men dressed up in the skin of beasts, but are throughout true to their characters, and are not only strongly realized but consistently drawn, albeit in so simple and captivating a way that the subtle art of the narrator is quite hidden, and one is aware only of reading an absorbingly interesting and witty tale." To have a place beside Gulliver, the old Spanish Knight and Christian, shows the estimation in which the book is held by those who are best acquainted with it.

The work is probably best known through the version of it which has come to us from the greatest of German poets, Goethe, whose Reineke Fuchs has perhaps had more sympathetic readers and a wider audience than any other of Goethe's works. The very fact that so deeply intellectual a literary man should have considered it worth his while to devote his time to making a modern version of it, shows not only the estimation in which he held it, but also affords excellent testimony to its worth as literature, for Goethe, unlike most poets, was a fine literary critic, and one who above all knew the reasons for the esthetic faith that was in him. Animal stories in every age, however, have been imitations of it much more than is usually imagined. While the author probably obtained the hint for his work from some of the old-time fables as they came to him by tradition, though we have no reason to think that Æsop was familiar to him and many for thinking the Greek fabulist was not, he added so much to this simple literary mode, transformed it so thoroughly from child's literature to world literature, that the main merit of modern animal stories must be attributed to him. Uncle Remus and the many compilations of this kind that have been popular in our own generation, owe much more to the animal Epic than might be thought possible by one not familiar with the original Thirteenth Century work.

Every language has a translation of the Animal Epic and most of the generations since have been interested and amused by the quaint conceits, which enable the author to picture so undisguisedly, men and women under animal garb. It discloses better than any other specimen of the literature of the time that men and women do not change even in the course of centuries, and that in the heart of the Middle Ages a wise observer could see the foibles of humanity just as they exist at the present time. Any one who thinks that evolution after seven centuries should have changed men somewhat in their ethical aspects, at least, made their aspirations higher and their tendencies less commonplace, not to say less degenerative, should read one of the old versions of Reynard the Fox and be convinced that men and women in the Thirteenth Century were quite the same as we are familiar with them at the present moment.

The second of the most read books of the century is the famous Legenda Aurea or, as it has been called in English, the Golden Legend, written by Jacobus de Voragine, the distinguished Dominican preacher and writer (born during the first half of the Thirteenth Century, died just at its close), who, after rising to the higher grades in his own order, became the Archbishop of Genoa. His work at once sprang into popular favor and continued to be perhaps the most widely read book, with the exception of the Holy Scriptures, during the Fourteenth and Fifteenth centuries. It was one of the earliest books printed in Italy, the first edition appearing about 1570, and it is evident that it was considered that its widespread popularity would not only reimburse the publisher, but would help the nascent art of printing by bringing it to the attention of a great many people. Its subject is very different from that of the modern most read books; librarians do not often have to supply lives of Saints nowadays, though some similarities of material with that of books now much in demand help to account for its vogue.

Jacobus de Voragine's work consisted of the lives of the greater Saints of the Church since the time of Christ, and detailed especially the wonderful things that happened in their lives, some of which of course were mythical and all of them containing marvelous stories. This gave prominence to many legends that have continued to maintain their hold upon the popular imagination ever since. With all this adventitious interest, however, the book contained a solid fund of information with regard to the lives of the Saints, and besides it taught the precious lessons of unselfishness and the care for others of the men who had come to be greeted by the title of Saint. The work must have done not a little to stir up the faith, enliven the charity, and build up the characters of the people of the time, and certainly has fewer objections than most popular reading at any period of the world's history. For young folks the wonderful legends afforded excellent and absolutely innocuous exercise of the functions of the imagination quite as well as our own modern wonder books or fairy tales, while the stories themselves presented many descriptive portions out of which subjects for decorative purposes could readily be obtained. It must be set down as another typical distinction of the Thirteenth Century and an addition to its greatness, that it should have made the Golden Legend popular and thus preserved it for future generations, who became

ST. CHRISTOPHER (ALTO RELIEVO, VENICE)

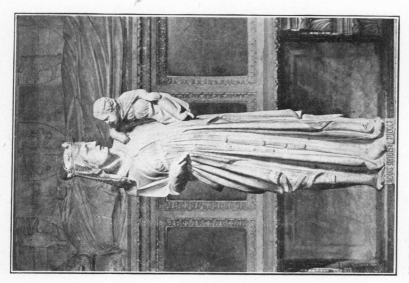

MADONNA AND CHILD (GIOV. PISANO, PADUA)

deeply interested in it, as in most of the other precious heritages they received from this great original century.

The third of the most read books of the century, The Romance of the Rose, is not so well known except by scholars as is the Animal Epic or perhaps even the Golden Legend. Anyone who wants to understand the burden of the time, however, and who wishes to put himself in the mood and the tense to comprehend not only the other literature of the era, and in this must be included even Dante, but also the social, educational, and even scientific movements of the period, must become familiar with it. It has been well said that a knowledge and study of the three most read books of the century, those which we have named, will afford a far clearer insight into the daily life and the spirit working within the people for whom they were written, than the annals of the wars or political struggles that were waged during the same period between kings and nobles. For this clearer insight a knowledge of the Romance of the Rose is more important than of the others. It provides a better introduction to the customs and habits, the manners of thought and of action, the literary and educational interests of the people of the Thirteenth Century, than any mere history, however detailed, could. In this respect it resembles Homer who, as Froude declares, has given us a better idea of Greek life than a whole encyclopedia of classified information would have done. The intimate life stories of no other periods in history are so well illustrated, nor so readily to be comprehended, as those of Homer and the authors of the medieval Romaunt.

The Romance of the Rose continued to be for more than two centuries the most read book in Europe. Every one with any pretense to scholarship or to literary taste in any European country considered it necessary to be familiar with it, and without exaggeration what Lowell once declared with regard to Don Quixote, that it would be considered a mark of lack of culture to miss a reference to it in any country in Europe, might well have been repeated during the Fourteenth and Fifteenth centuries of the Romance of the Rose. It has in recent years been put into very suitable English dress by Mr. F. S. Ellis and published among the Temple Classics, thus placing it within easy reach of English readers. Mr. Ellis must certainly be considered a suitable judge of the interest there is in the work. He spent several years in translating its two and twenty thousand six hundred and eight lines and yet considers that few books deserve as much attention as this typical Thirteenth Century allegory. He says:

"The charge of dulness once made against this highly imaginative and brilliant book, successive English writers, until quite recent times have been content to accept the verdict, though Professor Morley and others have of late ably repelled the charge. If further testimony were necessary as to the falsity of the accusation, and the opinion of one who has found a grateful pastime in translating it might be considered of any weight, he would not hesitate to traverse the attribution of dulness, and to assert that it is a poem of extreme interest, written as to the first part with delicate fancy, sweet appreciation of natural beauty, clear insight, and skilful invention, while J. de Meun's continuation is distinguished by vigor, brilliant invention, and close observation of human nature. The Thirteenth Century lives before us."

The Rose is written on a lofty plane of literary value, and the fact that it was so popular, speaks well for the taste of the times and for the enthusiasm of the people for the more serious forms of literature. Not that the Romance of the Rose is a very serious book itself, but if we compare it with the popular publications which barely touch the realities of life in the modern time, it will seem eminently serious. In spite of the years that have elapsed since its original publication it has not lost all its interest, even for a casual reader, and especially for one whose principal study is mankind in its varying environment down the ages, for it presents a very interesting picture of men and their ways in this wonderful century. Here, as in the stories of Reynard the Fox, one is brought face to face with the fact that men and women have not changed and that the peccadillos of our own generation have their history in the Middle Ages also. Take, for instance, the question of the too great love of money which is now the subject of so much writing and sermonizing. One might think that at least this was modern. Here, however, is what the author of the Romance of the Rose has to say about it:

> Three cruel vengeances pursue
> These miserable wretches who
> Hoard up their worthless wealth: great toil
> Is theirs to win it; then their spoil
> They fear to lose; and lastly, grieve
> Most bitterly that they must leave
> Their hoards behind them. Cursed they die
> Who living, lived but wretchedly;
> For no man, if he lack of love,
> Hath peace below or joy above.
> If those who heap up wealth would show
> Fair love to others, they would go
> Through life beloved, and thus would reign
> Sweet happy days. If they were fain,
> Who hold so much of good to shower around
> Their bounty unto those they found
> In need thereof, and nobly lent
> Their money, free from measurement
> Of usury (yet gave it not
> To idle gangrel men), I wot
> That then throughout the land were seen
> No pauper carl or starveling quean.
> But lust of wealth doth so abase
> Man's heart, that even love's sweet grace
> Bows down before it; men but love
> Their neighbors that their love may prove
> A profit, and both bought and sold
> Are friendships at the price of gold.
> Nay, shameless women set to hire
> Their bodies, heedless of hell-fire;

It is after reading a passage like this in a book written in the Thirteenth Century that one feels the full truth of that expression of the greatest of American critics, James Russell Lowell, which so often comes back to mind with regard to the works of this century, that to read a classic is like reading a commentary on the morning paper. When this principle is applied the other way, I suppose it may be said, that when a book written in the long ago sounds as if it were the utterance of some one aroused by the evils round him in our modern life, then it springs from so close to the heart of nature that it is destined to live and have an influence far beyond its own time. The Romance of the Rose, written seven centuries ago, now promises to have renewed youth in the awakening of interest in our Gothic ancestors and their accomplishments, before the over-praised renaissance came to trouble the stream of thought and writing.

Other passages serve to show how completely the old-time poet realized all the abuses of the desire for wealth, and how much it makes men waste their lives over unessentials, instead of trying to make existence worth while for themselves and others. Here is an arraignment of the strenuous life of business every line of which is as true for us as it was for the poet's generation:

> 'Tis truth (though some 'twill little please)
> To hear the trader knows no ease;
> For ever in his soul a prey
> To anxious care of how he may
> Amass more wealth: this mad desire
> Doth all his thought and actions fire,
> Devising means whereby to stuff
> His barns and coffers, for 'enough'
> He ne'er can have, but hungreth yet
> His neighbors' goods and gold to get.
> It is as though for thirst he fain
> Would quaff the volume of the Seine
> At one full draught, and yet should fail
> To find its waters of avail
> To quench his longing. What distress,
> What anguish, wrath, and bitterness
> Devour the wretch! fell rage and spite
> Possess his spirit day and night,
> And tear his heart; the fear of want
> Pursues him like a spectre gaunt.
> The more he hath, a wider mouth
> He opes, no draught can quench his drouth.

The old poet pictures the happiness of the poor man by contrast, and can in conclusion depict even more pitilessly the real poverty of spirit of the man who "having, struggleth still to get" and never stops to enjoy life itself by helping his fellows:

> Light-heart and gay
> Goes many a beggar by the way,
> But little heeding though his back
> Be bent beneath a charcoal sack.
> They labor patiently and sing,
> And dance, and laugh at whatso thing
> Befalls, for havings care they nought,
> But feed on scraps and chitlings bought
> Beside St. Marcel's, and dispend
> Their gains for wassail, then, straight wend
> Once more to work, not grumblingly,
> But light of heart as bird on tree
> Winning their bread without desire
> To fleece their neighbors. Nought they tire
> Of this their round, but week by week
> In mirth and work contentment seek;
> Returning when their work is done
> Once more to swill the jovial tun.
> And he who what he holds esteems
> Enough, is rich beyond the dreams
> Of many a dreary usurer,
> And lives his life-days happier far;
> For nought it signifies what gains
> The wretched usurer makes, the pains
> Of poverty afflict him yet
> Who having, struggleth still to get.

The pictures are as true to life at the beginning of the Twentieth Century as they were in the latter half of the Thirteenth.   There are little touches of realism in both the pictures, which show at once how acute an observer, how full of humor his appreciation, and yet how sympathetic a writer the author of the Romance was, and at the same time reveal something of the sociological value of his work. It discloses what is so easily concealed under the mask of formal historical writing and tells us of the people rather than of the few great ones among them, or those whom time and chance had made leaders of men. It seems long to read but as a recent translator has said, it represents only the file of a newspaper for eighteen months, and while it talks of quite as trivial things as the modern newspaper, the information is of a kind that is likely to do more good, and prove of more satisfaction, than the passing crimes and scandals that now occupy over-anxious readers.

CENTRAL TOWER (LINCOLN)

XIV

SOME THIRTEENTH CENTURY PROSE.

It would be unpardonable to allow the notion to be entertained that it was only in poetry that the writers of the Thirteenth Century succeeded in creating works of enduring influence. Some of the prose writings of the time are deeply interesting for many reasons. Modern prose was in its formative period, and the evolution of style, as of other things in the making, is proverbially worthy of more serious study than even the developed result. The prose writings of the Thirteenth Century were mainly done in Latin, but that was not for lack of command over the vernacular tongues, as we shall see, but because this was practically a universal language. This century had among other advantages that subsequent ages have striven for unsuccessfully, our own most of all, a common medium of expression for all scholars at least. There are, however, the beginnings of Prose in all the modern languages and it is easy to understand that the Latin of the time had a great influence on the vernacular and that the modes of expression which had become familiar in the learned tongue, were naturally transferred to the vulgar speech, as it was called, whenever accuracy of thought and nicety of expression invited such transmutation.

With regard to the Latin of the period it is the custom of many presumably well-educated men to sniff a little and say deprecatingly, that after all much cannot be expected from the writers of the time, since they were dependent on medieval or scholastic Latin for the expression of their ideas. This criticism is supposed to do away with any idea of the possibility of there having been a praiseworthy prose style, at this time in the Middle Ages. In the chapter on the Latin Hymns, we call attention to the fact that this same mode of criticism was supposed to preclude all possibility of rhymed Latin, as worthy to occupy a prominent place in literature. The widespread encourage-

ment of this false impression has, as a matter of fact, led to a
neglect of these wonderful poems, though they may in the
opinion of competent critics, even be considered as representing
the true genius of the Latin language and its powers of poetic
expression better than the Greek poetic modes, which were
adopted by the Romans, but which, with the possible exception
of their two greatest poets, never seem to have acquired that
spontaneity that would characterize a native outburst of language vitality.

As for the philosophic writers of the century that great
period holds in this, as in other departments, the position of
the palmiest time of the Middle Ages. To it belongs Alexander Hales, the Doctor Irrefragabilis who disputes with Aquinas
the prize for the best example of the Summa Theologiae;
Bonaventure the Mystic, and writer of beautiful hymns; Roger
Bacon, the natural philosopher; Vincent of Beauvais, the
encyclopedist. While of the four, greatest of all, Albertus
Magnus, the "Dumb Ox of Cologne," was born seven years
before its opening, his life lasted over four-fifths of it; that of
Aquinas covered its second and third quarters; Occam himself,
though his main exertions lie beyond this century, was probably
born before Aquinas died; while John Duns Scotus hardly outlived the century's close by a decade. Raymond Lully, one of
the most characteristic figures of Scholasticism and of the
medieval period (with his "great art" of automatic philosophy), who died in 1315, was born as early as 1235. Peter
the Spaniard, Pope and author of the Summulae Logicales,
the grammar of formal logic for ages as well of several
medieval treatises that have attracted renewed attention in our
day, died in 1277.

With regard to what was accomplished in philosophic and
theologic prose, examples will be found in the chapter on St.
Thomas Aquinas, which prove beyond all doubt the utter
simplicity, the directness, and the power of the prose of the
Thirteenth Century. In the medical works of the time there
was less directness, but always a simplicity that made them
commendable. In general, university writers were influenced
by the scholastic methods and we find it reflected constantly in
their works. In the minds of many people this would be

enough at once to condemn it. It will usually be found, however, as we have noted before, that those who are readiest to
condemn scholastic writing know nothing about it, or so little
that their opinion is not worth considering. Usually they have
whatever knowledge they think they possess, at second hand.
Sometimes all that they have read of scholastic philosophy are
some particularly obscure passages on abstruse subjects,
selected by some prejudiced historian, in order to show how
impossible was the philosophic writing of these centuries of
the later Middle Ages.

There are other opinions, however, that are of quite different
significance and value. We shall quote but one of them, written by Professor Saintsbury of the University of Edinburgh,
who in his volume on the Flourishing of Romance and the Rise
of Allegory (the Twelfth and Thirteenth centuries) of his
Periods of European Literature, has shown how sympathetically the prose writing of the Thirteenth Century may appeal
even to a scholarly modern, whose main interests have been
all his life in literature. Far from thinking that prose was
spoiled by scholasticism, Prof. Saintsbury considers that scho!-
asticism was the fortunate training school in which all the
possibilities of modern prose were brought out and naturally
introduced into the budding languages of the time. He says:

"However this may be" (whether the science of the Nineteenth Century after an equal interval will be of any more
positive value, whether it will not have even less comparative
interest than that which appertains to the scholasticism of the
Thirteenth Century) "the claim modest, and even meager as it
may seem to some, which has been here once more put forward
for this scholasticism—the claim of a far-reaching educative
influence in mere language, in mere system of arrangement and
expression, will remain valid. If at the outset of the career
of modern languages, men had thought with the looseness of
modern thought, had indulged in the haphazard slovenliness
of modern logic, had popularized theology and vulgarized
rhetoric, as we have seen both popularized and vulgarized
since, we should indeed have been in evil case. It used to be
thought clever to moralize and to felicitate mankind over the
rejection of the stays, the fetters, the prison in which its

thought was medievally kept. The justice or the injustice, the taste or the vulgarity of these moralizings, of these felicitations, may not concern us here. But in expression, as distinguished from thought, the value of the discipline to which these youthful languages was subjected is not likely now to be denied by any scholar who has paid attention to the subject. It would have been perhaps a pity if thought had not gone through other phases; it would certainly have been a pity if the tongues had been subjected to the fullest influence of Latin constraint. But that the more lawless of them benefited by that constraint there can be no doubt whatever. The influence of form which the best Latin hymns of the Middle Ages exercised in poetry, the influence in vocabulary and in logical arrangement which scholasticism exercised in prose are beyond dispute: and even those who will not pardon literature, whatever its historic and educative importance be, for being something less than masterly in itself, will find it difficult to maintain the exclusion of the Cur Deus Homo, and impossible to refuse admission to the Dies Irae."

Besides this philosophic and scientific prose, there were two forms of writing of which this century presents a copious number of examples. These are the chronicles and biographies of the time and the stories of travelers and explorers. These latter we have treated in a separate chapter. The chronicles of the time deserve to be studied with patient attention by anyone who wishes to know the prose writers of the century and the character of the men of that time and their outlook on life. It is usually considered that chroniclers are rather tiresome old fogies who talk much and say very little, who accept all sorts of legends on insufficient authority and who like to fill up their pages with wonderful things regardless of their truth. In this regard it must not be forgotten that in times almost within the memory of men still alive, Herodotus now looked upon deservedly as the Father of History and one of the great historical writers of all time, was considered to have a place among these chroniclers, and his works were ranked scarcely higher, except for the purity of their Greek style.

The first of the great chroniclers in a modern tongue was the famous Geoffrey de Villehardouin, who was not only a writer of, but an actor in the scenes which he describes. He was enrolled among the elite of French Chivalry, in that Crusade at the beginning of the Thirteenth Century, which resulted in the foundation of the Greco-Latin Empire. His book entitled "The Conquest of Constantinople," includes the story of the expedition during the years from 1198 to 1207. Modern war correspondents have seldom succeeded in giving a more vivid picture of the events of which they were witnesses than this first French chronicler of the Thirteenth Century. It is evident that the work was composed with the idea that it should be recited, as had been the old poetic Chansons de Geste, in the castles of the nobles and before assemblages of the people, perhaps on fair days and other times when they were gathered together. The consequence is that it is written in a lively straightforward style with direct appeals to its auditors.

It contains not a few passages of highly poetic description which show that the chronicler was himself a literary man of no mean order and probably well versed in the effusions of the old poets of this country. His description of the fleet of the Crusaders as it was about to set sail for the East and then his description of its arrival before the imposing walls of the Imperial City, are the best examples of this, and have not been surpassed even by modern writers on similar topics.

Though the French writer was beyond all doubt not familiar with the Grecian writers and knew nothing of Xenophon, there is a constant reminder of the Greek historian in his work. Xenophon's simple directness, his thorough-going sincerity, the impression he produces of absolute good faith and confidence in the completeness of the picture, so that one feels that one has been present almost at many of the scenes described, are all to be encountered in his medieval successor. Villehardouin went far ahead of his predecessors, the chroniclers of foregoing centuries, in his careful devotion to truth. A French writer has declared that to Villehardouin must be ascribed the foundation of historical probity. None of his facts, stated as such, has ever been impugned, and though his long speeches must necessarily have been his own composition, there seems no doubt that they contain the ideas which had been expressed on various occasions, and besides were composed with due reference to the character of the speaker and convey something of his special style of expression.

Prof. Saintsbury in his article in the Encyclopedia Britannica on Villehardouin, sums up very strikingly the place that this first great vernacular historian's book must occupy.

He says: "It is not impertinent, and at the same time an excuse for what has been already said, to repeat that Villehardouin's book, brief as it is, is in reality one of the capital books of literature, not merely for its merit, but because it is the most authentic and the most striking embodiment in the contemporary literature of the sentiments which determined the action of a great and important period of history. There are but very few books which hold this position, and Villehardouin's is one of them. If every other contemporary record of the crusades perished, we should still be able by aid of this to understand and realize what the mental attitude of crusaders, of Teutonic Knights, and the rest was, and without this we should lack the earliest, the most undoubtedly genuine, and the most characteristic of all such records. The very inconsistency with which Villehardouin is chargeable, the absence of compunction with which he relates the changing of a sacred religious pilgrimage into something by no means unlike a mere filibustering raid on a great scale, add a charm to the book. For, religious as it is, it is entirely free from the very slightest touch of hypocrisy or, indeed, of self-consciousness of any kind. The famous description of the Crusades, *gesta Dei per Francos,* was evidently to Villehardouin a plain matter-of-fact description and it no more occurred to him to doubt the divine favor being extended to the expeditions against Alexius or Theodore than to doubt that it was shown to expeditions against Saracens and Turks."

It was especially in the exploitation of biographical material that the Thirteenth Century chroniclers were at their best. Any one who recalls Carlyle's unstinted admiration of Jocelyn of Brakelonds' life of Abbot Sampson in his essays Past and Present, will be sure that at least one writer in England had succeeded in pleasing so difficult a critic in this rather thorny mode of literary expression. It is easy to say too much or too little about the virtues and the vices of a man whose biography one has chosen to write. Jocelyn's simple, straightforward story

PONTE ALLE GRAZIE (FLORENCE, LAPO)

PORTA ROMANA (FLORENCE, N. PISANO)

would seem to fulfil the best canons of modern criticism in this
respect. Probably no more vivid picture of a man and his ways
was ever given until Boswell's Johnson. Nor was the English
chronicler alone in this respect. The Sieur de Joinville's biographical studies of the life of Louis IX. furnish another example of this literary mode at its best, and modern writers of
biography could not do better than go back to read these intimate pictures of the life of a great king, which are not flattered
nor overdrawn but give us the man as he actually was.

The English biographic chronicler of the olden time could
picture exciting scenes without any waste of words. A specimen of his work will serve to show the merit of his style. After reading it one is not likely to be surprised that Carlyle
should have so taken the Chronicler to heart nor been so enthusiastic in his praise. It is the very type of that impression-
ism in style that has once more in the course of time become
the fad of our own day.

"The abbot was informed that the church of Woolpit was
vacant, Walter of Coutances being chosen to the bishopric of
Lincoln. He presently convened the prior and great part of
the convent, and taking up his story thus began: 'You well
know what trouble I had in respect of the church of Woolpit;
and in order that it should be obtained for your exclusive use
I journeyed to Rome at your instance, in the time of the schism
between Pope Alexander and Octavian. I passed through Italy
at that time when all clerks bearing letters of our lord the Pope
Alexander were taken. Some were imprisoned, some hanged,
and some, with nose and lips cut off, sent forward to the pope,
to his shame and confusion. I, however, pretended to be
Scotch; and putting on the garb of a Scotchman, and the gesture of one, I often brandished my staff, in the way they use
that weapon called a gaveloc, at those who mocked me, using
threatening language, after the manner of the Scotch. To
those that met and questioned me as to who I was, I answered
nothing, but, "Ride ride Rome, turne Cantwereberei." This
did I to conceal myself and my errand, and that I should get
to Rome safer in the guise of a Scotchman.

" 'Having obtained letters from the pope, even as I wished,
on my return I passed by a certain castle, as my way led me

from the city; and behold the officers thereof came about me, laying hold upon me, and saying, "This vagabond who makes himself out to be a Scotchman is either a spy or bears letters from the false pope Alexander." And while they examined my ragged clothes, and my boots, and my breeches, and even the old shoes which I carried over my shoulders, after the fashion of the Scotch, I thrust my hand into the little wallet which I carried, wherein was contained the letter of our lord the pope, placed under a little cup I had for drinking. The Lord God and St. Edmund so permitting, I drew out both the letter and the cup together, so that, extending my arm aloft, I held the letter underneath the cup. They could see the cup plain enough, but they did not see the letter; and so I got clear out of their hands, in the name of the Lord. Whatever money I had about me they took away; therefore I had to beg from door to door, without any payment, until I arrived in England.' "

Another excellent example of the biographic prose of the century, though this is the vernacular, is Joinville's life of St. Louis, without doubt one of the precious biographical treasures of all times. It contains a vivid portrait of Louis IX., made by a man who knew him well personally, took part with him in some of the important actions of the book, and in general was an active personage in the affairs of the time. Those who think that rapid picturesque description such as vividly recalls deeds of battle was reserved for the modern war correspondent, should read certain portions of Joinville's book. As an example we have ventured to quote the page on which the seneschal historian himself recounts the role which he played in the famous battle of Mansourah, at which, with the Count de Soissons and Pierre de Neuville, he defended a small bridge against the enemy under a hail of arrows.

He says: "Before us there were two sergeants of the king, one of whom was named William de Boon and the other John of Gamaches. Against these the Turks who had placed themselves between the river and the little tributary, led a whole mob of villains on foot, who hurled at them clods of turf or whatever came to hand. Never could they make them recoil upon us, however. As a last resort the Turks sent forward a foot soldier who three times launched Greek fire at them. Once William de Boon received the pot of green fire upon his buckler. If the fire had touched anything on him he would have been entirely burned up. We at the rear were all covered by arrows which had missed the Sergeants. It happened that I found a waist-coat which had been stuffed by one of the Saracens. I turned the open side of it towards me and made a shield out of the vest which rendered me great service, for I was wounded by their arrows in only five places though my horse was wounded in fif-teen. One of my own men brought me a banner with my arms and a lance. Every time then that we saw that they were press-ing the Royal Sergeants we charged upon them and they fled. The good Count Soissons, from the point at which we were, joked with me and said 'Senechal, let us hoot out this rabble, for by the headdress of God (this was his favorite oath) we shall talk over this day you and I many a time in our ladies' halls.' "

We have said that the writing of the Thirteenth Century must have been done to a great extent for the sake of the women of the time, and that its very existence was a proof that the women possessed a degree of culture, that might not be realized from the few details that have been preserved to us of their education and habits of life. In this last passage of Joinville we have the proof of this, since evidently the telling of the stories of these days of battle was done mainly in order that the women folks might have their share in the excitement of the campaign, and might be enabled vividly to appreciate what the dangers had been and how gloriously their lords had triumphed. At every period of the world's history it was true that literature was mainly made for women and that some of the best portions of it always concerned them very closely.

We have purposely left till last, the greatest of the chroniclers of the Thirteenth Century, Matthew Paris, the Author of the Historia Major, who owes his surname doubtless to the fact that he was educated at the University of Paris. Instead of trying to tell anything about him from our own slight personal knowledge, we prefer to quote the passage from Green's History of the English People, in which one of the greatest of our modern English historians pays such a magnificent tribute to his colleague of the earlier times :

"The story of this period of misrule has been preserved for us by an annalist whose pages glow with the new outburst of patriotic feeling which this common expression of the people and the clergy had produced. Matthew Paris is the greatest, as he is in reality the last of our monastic historians. The school of St. Albans survived indeed till a far later time, but the writers dwindle into mere annalists whose view is bounded by the Abbey precincts, and whose work is as colorless as it is jejune. In Matthew the breadth and precision of the narrative, the copiousness of his information on topics whether national or European, the general fairness and justice of his comments, are only surpassed by the patriotic fire and enthusiasm of the whole. He had succeeded Roger of Wendover as Chronicler of St. Albans; and the Greater Chronicle, with the abridgement of it which has long passed under the name of Matthew of Westminster, a "History of the English," and the "Lives of the Earlier Abbots," were only a few among the voluminous works which attest his prodigious industry. He was an eminent artist as well as a historian, and many of the manuscripts which are preserved are illustrated by his own hand. A large circle of correspondents—bishops like Grosseteste, ministers like Hubert de Burgh, officials like Alexander de Swinford—furnished him with minute accounts of political and ecclesiastical proceedings. Pilgrims from the East and Papal agents brought news of foreign events to his scriptorium at St. Albans. He had access to and quotes largely from state documents, charters, and exchequer rolls. The frequency of the royal visits to the abbey brought him a store of political intelligence and Henry himself contributed to the great chronicle which has preserved with so terrible a faithfulness the memory of his weakness and misgovernment. On one solemn feast-day the King recognized Matthew, and bidding him sit on the middle step between the floor and the throne, begged him to write the story of the day's proceedings. While on a visit to St. Albans he invited him to his table and chamber, and enumerated by name two hundred and fifty of the English barons for his information. But all this royal patronage has left little mark on his work. *"The case,"* as he says, *"of historical writers is hard, for if they tell the truth they provoke*

men, and if they write what is false they offend God." With
all the fullness of the school of court historians, such as Benedict or Hoveden, Matthew Paris combines an independence
and patriotism which is strange to their pages. He denounces
with the same unsparing energy the oppression of the Papacy
and the King. His point of view is neither that of a courtier
nor of a Churchman, but of an Englishman, and the new
national tone of his chronicle is but an echo of the national
sentiment which at last bound nobles and yeomen and Churchmen together into an English people."

We of the Twentieth Century are a people of information
and encyclopedias rather than of literature, so that we shall
surely appreciate one important specimen of the prose writing
of the Thirteenth Century since it comprises the first modern
encyclopedia. Its author was the famous Vincent of Beauvais.
Vincent consulted all the authors, sacred and profane, that he
could possibly lay hands on, and the number of them was
indeed prodigious. It has often been said by men supposed to
be authorities in history, that the historians of the Middle Ages
had at their disposition only a small number of books, and that
above all they were not familiar with the older historians.
While this was true as regards the Greek, it was not for the
Latin historical writers. Vincent of Beauvais has quotations
from Cæsar's De Bello Gallico, from Sallust's Catiline and
Jugurtha, from Quintus Curtius, from Suetonius and from
Valerius Maximus and finally from Justin's Abridgement of
Trogus Pompeius.

Vincent had the advantage of having at his disposition the
numerous libraries of the monasteries throughout France, the
extent of which, usually unrealized in modern times, will be
appreciated from our special chapter on the subject. Besides
he consulted the documents in the chapter houses of the Cathedrals especially those of Paris, of Rouen, of Laon, of Beauvais
and of Bayeux, which were particularly rich in collections of
documents. It might be thought that these libraries and
archives would be closely guarded. Far from being closed to
writers from the outer world they were accessible to all to such
an extent, indeed, that a number of them are mentioned by
Vincent as public institutions.

His method of collecting his information is interesting, because it shows the system employed by him is practically that which has obtained down to our own day. He made use for his immense investigation of a whole army of young assistants, most of whom were furnished him by his own order, the Dominicans. He makes special mention in a number of places of quotations due to their collaboration. The costliness of maintaining such a system would have made the completion of the work absolutely impossible were it not for the liberality of King Louis IX., who generously offered to defray the expenses of the composition. Vincent has acknowledged this by declaring in his prefatorial letter to the King that, "you have always liberally given assistance even to the work of gathering the materials."

Vincent's method of writing is quite as interesting as his method of compilation of facts. The great Dominican was not satisfied with being merely a source of information. The philosophy of history has received its greatest Christian contribution from St. Augustine's City of God. In this an attempt was made to trace the meaning and causal sequence of events as well as their mere external connection and place in time. In a lesser medieval way Vincent tried deliberately to imitate this and besides writing history attempted to trace the philosophy of it. For him, as for the great French philosophic historian Bossuet in his Universal History five centuries later, everything runs its provided race from the creation to the redemption and then on toward the consummation of the world. He describes at first the commencements of the Church from the time of Abel, through its progress under the Patriarchs, the Prophets, Judges, Kings, and leaders of the people, down to the Birth of Christ. He traces the history of the Apostles and of the first Disciples, though he makes it a point to find place for the famous deeds of the great men of Pagan antiquity. He notes the commencement of Empires and Kingdoms, their glory, their decadence, their ruin, and the Sovereigns who made them illustrious in peace and war. There was much that was defective in the details of history as they were traced by Vincent, much that was lacking in completeness, but the intention was evidently the best, and patience and labor were devoted to the sour-

ST. CATHARINE'S (LÜBECK)

ST. ANTONY'S AND CLOISTERS (PADUA)

ces of history at his command. Perhaps never more than at the present moment have we been in a position to realize that history at its best can be so full of defects even after further centuries of consultation of documents and printed materials, that we are not likely to be in the mood to blame this first modern historian very much. As for the other portions of his encyclopedia, biographic, literary and scientific, they were not only freely consulted by his contemporaries and successors, but we find traces of their influence in the writings and also in the decorative work of the next two centuries. We have already spoken of the use of his book in the provision of subjects for the ornamentation of Cathedrals and the same thing might be said of edifices of other kinds.

Nor must it be thought that Vincent has only a historic or ecclesiastical interest. Dr. Julius Pagel, in his Chapter on Medicine in the Middle Ages in Puschmann's Hand-Book of the History of Medicine,* says, "that there were three writers whose works were even more popular than those of Albertus Magnus. These three were Bartholomew, the Englishman; Thomas, of Cantimprato, and Vincent, of Beauvais, the last of whom must be considered as one of the most important contributors to the generalization of scientific knowledge, not alone in the Thirteenth but in the immediately succeeding centuries. His most important work was really an encyclopedia of the knowledge of his time. It was called the Greater Triple Mirror and there is no doubt that it reflected the knowledge of his period. He had the true scientific spirit and constantly cites the authorities from whom his information was derived. He cites hundreds of authors and there is scarcely a subject that he does not touch on. One book of his work is concerned with human anatomy, and the concluding portion of it is an abbreviation of history carried down to the year 1250."

It might be considered that such a compend of information would be very dry-as-dust reading and that it would be fragmentary in character and little likely to be attractive except to a serious student. Dr. Pagel's opinion does not agree with this *a priori* impression. He says with regard to it: "The lan-

---

* Puschmann, Hand-Buch der Geschichte der Medizin, Jena, Fischer, 1902.

guage is clear, readily intelligible, and the informaton is conveyed usually in an excellent, simple style. Through the introduction of interesting similes the contents do not lack a certain taking quality, so that the reading of the work easily becomes absorbing." This is, I suppose, almost the last thing that might be expected of a scientific teacher in the Thirteenth Century, because, after all, Vincent of Beauvais must be considered as one of the schoolmen, and they are supposed to be eminently arid, but evidently, if we are to trust this testimony of a modern German physician, only by those who have not taken the trouble to read them.

One of the most important works of Thirteenth Century prose is the well-known Rationale Divinorum Officiorum (Significance of the Divine Offices) written by William Durandus, the Bishop of Mende, in France, whose tomb and its inscription in the handsome old Gothic Cathedral of Santa Maria Sopra Minerva, in Rome, shares with the body of St. Catherine of Sienna the honor of attracting so many visitors. The book has been translated into English under the title, The Symbolism of Churches and Church Ornaments, and has been very widely read. It was very popular in the Thirteenth Century, and the best possible idea of its subsequent reputation can be gathered from the fact, that the Rationale was the first work from the pen of an uninspired writer to be accorded the privilege of being printed. The Editio Princeps, a real first edition of supreme value, appeared from the press of John Fust in 1459. The only other books that had been printed at that time were the Psalters of 1457 and 1459. This edition is, of course, of the most extreme rarity. According to the English translators of Durandus the beauty of the typography has seldom been exceeded.

The style of Durandus has been praised very much by the critics of succeeding centuries for its straightforwardness, simplicity and brevity. Most of these qualities it evidently owes to the hours spent by its author in the reading of Holy Scriptures. Durandus fashioned his style so much on the sacred writings that most of his book possesses something of the impressive character of the Bible itself. The impression derived from it is that of reading a book on a religious subject written in an eminently suitable tone and spirit. Most of this impression must be attributed without doubt to the fact, that Durandus has not only formed his style on the Scriptures, but has actually incorporated Scriptural expressions in his writings to such an extent as to make them mostly a scriptural composition. This, far from being a fault, appears quite appropriate in his book because of its subject and the method of treatment. A quotation from the proeme (as it is in the quaint spelling of the English translation) will give the best idea of this.

"All things, as pertain to offices and matters ecclesiastical, be full of divine significations and mysterious, and overflow with celestial sweetness; if so be that a man be diligent in his study of them, and know how to draw HONEY FROM THE ROCK, AND OIL FROM THE HARDEST STONE. But who KNOWETH THE ORDINANCES OF HEAVEN, OR CAN FIX THE REASONS THEREOF UPON THE EARTH? for he that prieth into their majesty, is overwhelmed by the glory of them. Of a truth THE WELL IS DEEP, AND I HAVE NOTHING TO DRAW WITH: unless he giveth it unto me WHO GIVETH TO ALL MEN LIBERALLY, AND UPBRAIDETH NOT: so that WHILE I JOURNEY THROUGH THE MOUNTAINS I may DRAW WATER WITH JOY OUT OF THE WELLS OF SALVATION. Wherefore albeit of the things handed down from our forefathers, capable we are not to explain all, yet if among them there be any thing which is done without reason it should be forthwith put away. Wherefore, I, WILLIAM, by the alone tender mercy of God, Bishop of the Holy Church which is in Mende, will knock diligently at the door, if so be that THE KEY OF DAVID will open unto me: that the King may BRING ME INTO HIS TREASURE? and shew unto me the heavenly pattern which was shewed unto Moses in the mount: so that I may learn those things which pertain to Rites Ecclesiastical whereof they teach and what they signify: and that I may be able plainly to reveal and make manifest the reasons of them, by HIS help, WHO HATH ORDAINED STRENGTH OUT OF THE MOUTH OF BABES AND SUCKLINGS: WHOSE SPIRITS BLOWETH WHERE IT

LISTETH: DIVIDING TO EACH SEVERALLY AS IT WILL to the praise and glory of the Trinity."

This passage alone of Durandus would serve as an excellent refutation of the old-time Protestant tradition, fortunately now dying out though not as yet entirely eradicated, which stated so emphatically that the Bible was not allowed to be read before Luther's time.

Those who wish to obtain a good idea of Durandus' style and the way he presents his material, can obtain it very well from his chapter on Bells, the first two paragraphs of which we venture to quote. They will be found quite as full of interesting information in their way as any modern writer might have brought together, and have the dignity and simplicity of the best modern prose.

"Bells are brazen vessels, and were first invented in Nola, a city of Campania. Wherefore the larger bells are called Campanae, from Campania the district, and the smaller Nolae, from Nola the town.

"You must know that bells, by the sound of which the people assembleth together to the church to hear, and the Clergy to preach, IN THE MORNING THE MERCY OF GOD AND HIS POWER BY NIGHT do signify the silver trumpets, by which under the Old Law the people was called together unto sacrifice. (Of these trumpets we shall speak in our Sixth Book.) For just as the watchmen in a camp rouse one another by trumpets, so do the Ministers of the Church excite each other by the sound of bells to watch the livelong night against the plots of the Devil. Wherefore our brazen bells are more sonorous than the trumpets of the Old Law, because then GOD was known in Judea only, but now in the whole earth. They be also more durable: For they signify that the teaching of the New Testament will be more lasting than the trumpets and sacrifices of the Old Law, namely, even unto the end of the world.

"Again bells do signify preachers, who ought after the likeness of a bell to exhort the faithful unto faith: the which was typified in that the LORD commanded Moses to make a vestment for the High Priest who entered into the Holy of Holies. Also the cavity of the bell denoteth the mouth of the preacher, according to the saying of the Apostle, I AM BECOME AS SOUNDING BRASS ON A TINKLING CYMBAL."

Of course there are what we would be apt to consider exaggerations of symbolic meanings and far-fetched explanations and references, but this was of the taste of the time and has not in subsequent centuries been so beyond the canons of good taste as at present. Durandus goes on to tell that the hardness of the metal of the bell signifies fortitude in the mind of the preacher, that the wood of the frame on which the bell hangeth doth signify the wood of our Lord's Cross, that the rope by which the bell is strung is humility and also showeth the measure of life, that the ring in the length of the rope is the crown of reward for perseverance unto the end, and then proceeds to show why and how often the bells are rung and what the significance of each ringing is. He explains why the bells are silent for three days before Easter and also during times of interdict, and gives as the justification for this last the quotation from the Prophet "I WILL MAKE THY TONGUE CLEAVE TO THE ROOF OF THY MOUTH FOR THEY ARE A REBELLIOUS HOUSE."

Even these few specimens of the prose of the Thirteenth Century, will serve to show that the writers of the period could express themselves with a vigor and directness which have made their books interesting reading for generations long after their time, and which stamp their authors as worthy of a period that found enduring and adequate modes of expression for every form of thought and feeling.

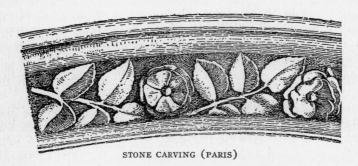

STONE CARVING (PARIS)

XV

ORIGIN OF THE DRAMA.

_____

The last place in the world, perhaps, that one would look for a great impulse to the development of the modern drama, which is entirely a new invention, an outgrowth of Christian culture and has practically no connection with the classic drama, would be in the life of St. Francis of Assisi. His utter simplicity, his thorough-going and cordial poverty, his sincere endeavor all during his life to make little of himself, might seem quite enough to forbid any thought of him as the father of a literary movement of this kind. "The poor little man of God," however, as he liked to call himself, in his supreme effort to get back to nature and out of the ways of the conventional world, succeeded in accomplishing a number of utterly unexpected results. His love for nature led to his wonderful expression of his feelings in his favorite hymn, one of the first great lyrical outbursts in modern poetry, a religious poem which as we shall see in the chapter on the Father of the Renaissance, Renan declares can only be appreciated properly by comparing it with the old Hebrew psalms, beside which it is worthy to be placed.

Those who know the life of St. Francis best will easily appreciate how dramatic, though unconsciously so, were all the actions of his life. After all, his utter renunciation of all things, his taking of holy poverty to be his bride, his address to the birds, his sisters, his famous question of the butcher as to why he killed his brothers, the sheep, his personification of the sun and the moon and even of the death of the body as his brothers and sisters, are all eminently dramatic moments. His life is full of incidents that lent themselves, because of their dramatic quality, to the painters of succeeding centuries as the subjects of their striking pictures. Before the end of the century Giotto had picked out some of the most interesting of these for the decorative illustration of the upper church at Assisi. During the succeeding century, the author of the Little Flowers of St. Francis, embodied many of these beautiful scenes in his little work, where they have been the favorite reading of poets for many centuries since.

It should not be such a surprise as it might otherwise be, then, to find that St. Francis may be considered in one sense as the father of the modern drama. The story is a very pretty one and has an additional value because it has been illustrated by no less a brush than that of Giotto. One Christmas Eve just at the beginning of the Thirteenth Century, St. Francis gathered round him some of the poor people living outside of the town of Assisi, in order to recall vividly to them the great event which had taken place on that night so many centuries before. A little figure of a child, dressed in swaddling clothes, was laid on some straw in a manger with the breath of the nearby animals to warm it. To this manger throne of the Child King of Bethlehem, there came in adoration, after the hymns that recalled the angels' visit, first some of the shepherds from the surrounding country and then some of the country people who represented the kings from the East with their retinues, bringing with them their royal gifts. After this little scene, probably one of the first Nativity plays that had ever been given, St. Francis, according to the old legend, took the little image in his arms and in an excess of devotion pressed it to his heart. According to the old-time story, the infant came to life in his embrace and putting its little arms around his neck embraced him in return. Of course our modern generation is entirely too devoted to "common sense" to accept any such pretty, pious story as this as more than a beautiful poetic legend. The legend has provided a subject for poet and painter many a time in subsequent centuries. Perhaps never has it been used with better effect than by Giotto, whose representation is one of the favorite pictures on the wall of the upper church of Assisi. Whether the little baby figure of the play actually came to life in his arms or not we do not know, but one thing is certain, that infant modern dramatic literature did come to life at the moment and that before the end of the Thirteenth Century it was to have a vigor and an influence that made it

one of the great factors in the social life of the period. The
Franciscans were soon spread over the world. With filial reverence they took with them all the customs of their loved Father of Assisi, and especially such as appealed to the masses
and brought home to them in a vivid way the great truths of
religion. By the middle of the century many of the towns had
cycles of mystery plays given at various times during the year,
associated with the different feasts and illustrating and enforcing the lessons of the liturgy for the people in a manner so
effective that it has probably never been equaled before or
since.

While the most potent factor in the dissemination of the
early religious drama can be traced to Francis and the Franciscans, they were but promoters of a movement already well
begun. Mystery plays were attempted before the Thirteenth
Century in England and in North France. There is a well-
known story from Matthew Paris, who wrote about the middle of the Thirteenth Century, of one Geoffrey who afterwards
became Abbot of St. Albans. While yet a secular he borrowed
certain precious religious vestments to be used in some sort of
a miracle play in honor of St. Catherine. During the performance of the play, these vestments were destroyed by fire and
Geogory was so much afflicted by the misfortune that in a spirit
of reparation he became a religious in the Abbey of St. Albans.
This must have been about the beginning of the Twelfth Century. Towards the end of this century mystery plays were
not infrequent, though not in anything like the developed form
nor popular character which they acquired during the Thirteenth Century. Fitz Stephen, writing the life of St. Thomas
a Becket, towards the end of the Twelfth Century, contrasts the
holier plays of London in his days with the theatrical spectacles of ancient Rome. The plays he mentioned were, however,
scarcely more than slight developments of Church ceremonial
with almost literal employment of scripture and liturgical language.

The first cycle of mystery plays of which there is definite
mention is that of Chester. According to the proclamation of
the Chester plays, the representation of this cycle dates in some
form from the mayoralty of John Arneway, who was the

ST. FRANCIS' NATIVITY PLAY (GIOTTO)

Mayor of Chester, between 1268 and 1276. Of the series of plays as given in the Thirteenth Century there are few remains. It is probable, even, that at this early date they were not acted in English but in French. English plays were probably first given in some of the Cathedral towns along the east coast of England, and perhaps York should have the credit of this innovation. It is easy to understand how the simpler dramatic additions to the ritual of the Church would inevitably develop in the earnest and very full religious life of the people which came with the building of the cathedrals, the evolution of Church ceremonial and the social life fostered by the trade-guilds of the time. While we have none of the remains of the actual plays of the Thirteenth Century, there is no doubt that an excellent idea of their form and content can be gathered from the English mystery plays, that have recently been edited in modern form and which serve to show the characteristics of the various cycles.

It might perhaps be thought that these mystery plays would not furnish any great amount of entertainment for the populace, especially after they had seen them a certain number of times. The yearly repetition might naturally be expected to bring with it before long a satiety that would lead to inattention. As is well known, however, there is an enduring interest about these old religious stories that makes them of much greater attractiveness than most ordinary historical traditions. Many a faithful reader of the Bible finds constantly renewed interest in the old Biblical stories in spite of frequent repetition.

Their significance to the eye of faith in the Middle Ages gave them, beyond any doubt, that quality which in any literary work will exemplify and fulfil Horace's dictum, *decies repetita placebit*. Besides, it must not be forgotten that the men and women of the Thirteenth Century had not the superficial facilities of the printing press to cloy their intellectual curiosity, and by trivial titillation make them constantly crave novelty.

It must not be thought, in spite of the fact that these were religious plays, that they were always so serious as to be merely instructive without being amusing. A large fund of amusement was injected into the old biblical stories by the writers of the different cycles and undoubtedly the actors themselves added certain personal elements in this matter, which still further enhanced some of the comical aspects of the solemn stories. Nearly always the incidents of the Scriptural narrative though followed more or less literally, were treated with a large humanity that could scarcely fail to introduce elements of humor into the dramatic performances. Such liberties, however, were taken only with characters not mentioned by the Bible—the inventions of the writers. A series of quotations from the Chester Cycle of Plays will best illustrate this. We give them in the quaint spelling of the oldest version extant.

The scene we quote is from the play dealing with Noah's flood and pictures Noah's wife as a veritable shrew.

NOYE—
    Wyffe, in this vessel we shall be kepte:
    My children and thou, I woulde in ye lepte.
NOYE'S WIFFE—
    In fayth, Noye, I hade as leffe thou slepte!
      For all thy frynishe fare,
    I will not doe after thy reade.
NOYE—
    Good wyffe, doe nowe as I thee bydde.
NOYE'S WIFFE—
    Be Christe! not or I see more neede,
      Though thou stande all the daye and stare.
NOYE—
    Lorde, that wemen be crabbed aye,
    And non are meke, I dare well saye,
    This is well seene by me to daye,
      In witnesse of you ichone (each one).
    Goodwiffe, lett be all this beare,
    That thou maiste in this place heare;
    For all the wene that thou arte maister,
      And so thou arte, by Sante John!

All Noah's artful concession of his wife's mastery in the household does not avail to move her and so he tries objurgation.

NOYE—
    Wiffe, come in: why standes thou their?
    Thou arte ever frowarde, I dare well sweare;
    Come in, one Godes halfe! tyme yt were,
      For feare leste that we drewne.

Noye's Wiffe—
> Yes, sir, sette up youer saile,
> And rowe fourth with evill haile,
> For withouten (anye) fayle
>   I will not oute of this towne;
> But I have my gossippes everyechone,
> One foote further I will not gone:
> The shall not drowne, by Sainte John!
>   And I may save ther life.
> The loven me full well, by Christe!
> But thou lett them into thy cheiste, (ark)
> Elles rowe nowe wher thee leiste,
>   And gette thee a newe wiffe.

It is evident that he will not succeed so Noah, wise doubtless with the wisdom of experience, forbears to urge but appeals to her sons to bring her.

Noye—
> Seme, sonne, loe! thy mother is wrawe:
> Forsooth, such another I doe not knowe.

Sem—
> Father, I shall fetch her in, I trowe,
>   Withoutten anye fayle.—
> Mother, my father after thee sends,
> And byddes thee into yeinder shippe wende.
> Loke up and see the wynde,
>   For we bene readye to sayle.

Noye's Wiffe—
> Seme, goe againe to hym, I saie;
> I will not come theirin to daye.

Noye—
> Come in, wiffe, in twentye devilles waye!
>   Or elles stand there without.

Ham—
> Shall we all feche her in?

Noye—
> Yea, sonnes, in Christe blessinge and myne!
> I woulde you hied you be-tyme,
>   For of this flude I am in doubte.

Jeffatte—
> Mother, we praye you all together,
> For we are heare, youer owne childer,
> Come into the shippe for feare of the weither,
>   For his love that you boughte!

NOYE'S WIFFE—
>> That will not I, for all youer call,
>> But I have my gossippes all.

SEM—
>> In faith, mother, yett you shalle,
>>> Wheither thou wylte or (nought).
>
> (*Her sons bring her in; as she steps aboard she is greeted by Noah.*)

NOYE—
>> Welckome, wiffe, into this botte.

NOYE'S WIFFE—
>> Have thou that for thy note! (*Giving her husband a cuff on the head*).

NOYE—
>> Ha, ha! Marye, this is hotte!
>>> It is good for to be still.
>> Ha! children, me thinkes my botte remeves,
>> Our tarryinge heare highlye me greves,
>> Over the lande the watter spreades;
>>> God doe as he will.

This quotation will give a good idea of the human interest of these Mystery Plays and serve to show that they did not fail in dramatic power for any lack of humor or acute observation. It would be easy to illustrate this much more amply. The opportunities to enjoy these plays were abundant. We have said that the Chester Cycle is the one of which there is earliest mention. The method of its presentation has been described by Mr. Henry Morley in the fourth volume of his English Writers. He says:

"There were scaffolds erected for spectators in those places to which the successive pageants would be drawn; and a citizen who on the first day saw in any place the first pageant (that of the Fall of Lucifer), if he kept his place and returned to it in good time on each successive morning, would see the Scripture story, as thus told, pass in its right order before him. Each pageant was drawn on four or six wheels, and had a room in which the actors and properties were concealed, under the upper room or stage on which they played."

Mr. Morley then describes the action of the various parts of the cycle, showing how clearly the lessons of the Old Testament history and its symbolic and typical meaning were pointed out so that the spectators could not miss them.

How completely the story of the Bible was told may be judged from the order of the Pageants of the Play of Corpus Christi, in the time of the mayoralty of William Alne, in the third year of the reign of King Henry V., compiled by Roger Burton, town clerk.

1. TANNERS.
    God the Father Almighty creating and forming the heavens, angels and archangels, Lucifer and the angels that fell with him to hell.
2. PLASTERERS.
    God the Father, in his own substance, creating the earth and all which is therein, in the space of five days.
3. CARDMAKERS.
    God the Father creating Adam of the clay of the earth and making Eve of Adam's rib, and inspiring them with the breath of life.
4. FULLERS.
    God forbidding Adam and Eve to eat of the tree of life.
5. COOPERS.
    Adam and Eve and a tree betwixt them; the serpent deceiving them with apples; God speaking to them and cursing the serpent, and with a sword driving them out of paradise.
6. ARMOURERS.
    Adam and Eve, an angel with a spade and distaff assigning them work.
7. GAUNTERS (Glovers).
    Abel and Cain offering victims in sacrifice.
8. SHIPWRIGHTS.
    God warning Noah to make an Ark of floatable wood.
9. PESSONERS (Fishmongers) and MARINERS.
    Noah in the Ark, with his wife; the three sons of Noah with their wives; with divers animals.
10. PARCHMENT-MAKERS, BOOKBINDERS.
    Abraham sacrificing his son, Isaac, on an altar, a boy with wood and an angel.
11. HOSIERS.
    Moses lifting up the serpent in the wilderness; King Pharaoh; eight Jews wondering and expecting.
12. SPICERS.
    A Doctor declaring the sayings of the prophets of the future birth of Christ. Mary; an angel saluting her; Mary saluting Elizabeth.
13. PEWTERERS, FOUNDERS.
    Mary, Joseph wishing to put her away; an angel speaking to them that they go to Bethlehem.

14. TYLERS.

Mary, Joseph, a midwife; the Child born, lying in a manger betwixt an ox and an ass, and an angel speaking to the shepherds, and to the players in the next pageant.

15. CHANDLERS.

The shepherds talking together, the star in the East; an angel giving the shepherds the good tidings of the Child's birth.

16, 17. ORFEVERS (Goldsmiths), GOLDBEATERS, MONEYMAKERS.

The three kings coming from the East, Herod asking them about the child Jesus; the son of Herod, two counsellors, and a messenger. Mary with the Child, a star above. and the three kings offering gifts.

How completely the people of each town were engaged in the presentation of the plays, can be judged from the following supplementary list of the other trade guilds that took parts. Many of them bear quaint names, which are now obsolete They included the girdellers, makers of girdles; nailers, sawyers, lorymers (bridle makers), the spurriers (makers of spurs), the fevers or smiths, the curriers, the plumbers, the pattern-makers, the bottlers, the cap-makers, the skinners, the bladesmiths, the scalers, the buckle-makers, the cordwainers, the bowyers (makers of bows), the fletchers (arrow-featherers), the tilemakers, the hayresters (workers in horse hair), the bollers (bowl-makers), the tunners, the sellers or saddlers; the fuystours (makers of saddle tree), the verrours (glaziers), the broggours (brokers), the dubbers (refurbishers of clothes), the luminers or illuminators, the scriveners, the drapers, the potters, the weavers, the hostlers and mercers. The men of no occupation, however menial it may seem to us, were barred. Each of these companies had a special pageant with a portion of the Old or New Testament to represent and in each succeeding year spent much of their spare time in preparing for their dramatic performance, studying and practising their parts and making everything ready for competition with their brother craftsmen in the other pageants. Only those who know the supreme educative value of dramatic representations for those actively interested in them, will appreciate all that these plays meant for popular education in the best sense of the word, but all can readily understand how much they stood for in popular occupation of mind with high thoughts and how much they must have acted as a preventive of debasing dissipations.

It is extremely interesting to follow out some of the details of the management of these Mystery Plays. We shall find in even the meagre accounts that we have of them, sufficient to show us that men were not expected to work for nothing, nor even to be satisfied with what compensation there might be in the honor of being chosen for certain parts, nor in the special banquets that were provided for the actors after the performances. A definite salary was paid to each of the actors according to the importance of the part he took. Not only this, but the loans of garments for costume purposes, or of furniture or other material for stage properties, was repaid by definite sums of money. These are not large, but, considering the buying power of money at that time and the wages paid workmen, which enabled them to live at least as well, comparatively, as modern workmen, the compensation is ample. Mr. Morley, in the fourth volume of his "English Writers," has given us some of these details and as they have a special social interest and the old documents rejoice in a comic literalness of statement, they deserve citation.

When about to set up a play, each guild chose for itself a competent manager, to whom it gave the rule of the pageant, and voted a fixed sum for its expenses. The play-book and the standing wardrobe and other properties were handed over to him, and he was accountable, of course, for their return after the close of the performances. The manager had to appoint his actors, to give them their several parts written out for them (perhaps by the prompter, who was a regular official), and to see to the rehearsals, of which there would be two for an old play and at least five for a new one.

At rehearsal time, as well as during the great performance the actors ate and drank at the cost of the guild, ending all with a supper, at which they had roast beef and roast goose, with wine for the chiefs, and beer for the rest. The actors were paid, of course, according to the length of their parts and quantity of business in them, not their dignity. Thus in a play setting forth the Trial and Crucifixion of our Lord, the actors of Herod and Caiaphas received each 3s. 4d.; the representative of Annas, 2s. 2d.; and of Christ 2s.; which was also the sum paid to each actor in the parts of His executioners, and 6d. more than was paid for acting the Devil or Judas. In the united plays of the "Descent into Hell" and the "Ascension," the payment was to the actor who represented Christ, 1s. 6d.; and 1s. 4d. to him who played the Devil. In one play we find this gradation of the scale of payment to performers:— "Paid, for playing of Peter, xvid.; to two damsels, xiid.; to the demon, vid.; to Fawston for hanging Judas, ivd.; paid to Fawston for cock-crowing, ivd."

Of the costume of the actors, and of the stage furniture a tolerably clear notion is also to be drawn from the Coventry account-books, of which Mr. Sharp printed all that bears upon such questions. They record, of course, chiefly repairs and renewals of stage properties and wardrobe. "In one year Pilate has a new green cloak, in another a new hat. Pilate's wife was Dame Procula, and we have such entries as, 'For mending of Dame Procula's garments, viid.' 'To reward to Mrs. Grimsby for lending of her gear for Pilate's wife, xiid.' 'For a quart of wine for hiring Porcula's gown, iid.' No actor had naked hands. Those not in masks had their faces prepared by a painter. The costume of each part was traditional, varied little in the course of years, and much of it was originally designed after the pictures and painted sculpture in the churches. As in those medieval decorations, gilding was used freely; the performer of Christ wore a gilt peruke and beard, so did Peter, and probably all the Apostles or saints who would be represented on church walls with a gilt nimbus." Christ's coat was of white sheep-skin, painted and gilded, with a girdle and red sandals. The part of the High Priests Caiaphas and Annas were often played in ecclesiastical robes hired from a church, a practice (one sad result of which because of fire has already been noted) that was eventually condemned as likely to lead to disrespect for sacred objects. Herod, who wore a mask, was set up as a sceptred royal warrior in a gilt and silvered helmet, in armour and gown of blue satin, with such Saracen details of dress as the Crusaders connected with the worship of Mahomet, including the crooked faulchion, which was gilt. The tormentors of Christ wore jackets of black

PALAZZO BUONDELMONTE (FLORENCE)

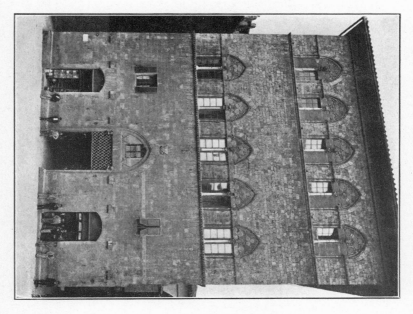

PALAZZO TOLOMEI (SIENA)

buckram with nails and dice upon them. The Virgin Mary was crowned, as in her images. The angels wore white surplices and wings. The devil also had wings, and was played in an appropriate mask and leather dress trimmed with feathers and hair. He was, as the Prologue to the Chester Plays describes him, "the devil in his feathers all ragged and rent," or, as the Coventry account-books show, carried three pounds of hair upon his hose.

There was probably no greater impulse for social uplift and for real education of the masses than these mystery and morality plays, in which the people took part themselves and in which, as a consequence of the presence of friends in the various roles, the spectators had a livelier interest than would have been otherwise the case under even the most favorable circumstances, or with elaborate presentation. In recent years there has come the realization that the drama may thus be made a real educational influence. Unfortunately at the present time, whatever of influence it has is exerted almost exclusively upon the better-to-do classes, who have so many other opportunities for educational uplift. These plays during the Thirteenth Century brought the people intimately into contact with the great characters of Old Testament and New Testament history, and besides giving them precious religious information, which of itself, however, might mean very little for true education, helped them to an insight into character and to a right appreciation of human actions and a sympathy with what was right even though it entailed suffering, such as could not have otherwise been obtained.

Of course it is easy to say that such dramas constantly repeated, the subjects always the same and only the cast varying from year to year, would become intolerably familiar and might after a time degenerate into the merely contemptible. As a matter of fact, however, they did not. These old stories of religious heroes were written so close to the heart of nature, involved so intimately all the problems of life that they are of undying interest. Their repetition was only from year to year and this did not give the opportunity for the familiarity which breeds contempt. Besides, though the plays in the various cycles existed in definite forms there seems no doubt that certain changes were made by the players themselves and by the managers of the plays from time to time, and indeed such changes of the text of a play as we know from present-day experience, are almost inevitable.

It might be urged, too, that the people themselves would scarcely be possessed of the histrionic talent necessary to make the plays effective. Ordinarily, however, as we know from our modern city life, much less of the actor's art is needed than of interest in the action, to secure the attention of the gallery. It must not be assumed too readily, however, that the guilds which were able to supply men for the great artistic decoration of the cathedrals of the Thirteenth Century, could not supply actors who would so enter into the artistic expression of a part as to represent it to the life. The actor is more born than made, in spite of the number of schools of acting that are supposed to be turning out successful rivals of Roscius, on recurring graduation days. It must not be forgotten that the only example of these mystery plays which is still left to us is the Passion Play at Oberammergau, and that is one of the world's greatest spectacles. On the last occasion when it was given about half a million of people from all over the world, many of them even from distant America and Australia, found their way into the Tyrolese Mountains in order to be present at it. It is only the old, old, old story of the Passion and death of the Lord. It is represented by villagers chosen from among the inhabitants of a little village of fourteen hundred inhabitants, who while they have a distinct taste for the artistic and produce some of the best wood-carving done anywhere in Europe, thus approximating very interestingly the Thirteenth Century peoples, are not particularly noted for their education, nor for their dramatic ability. No one who went up to see the Passion Play came away dissatisfied either with the interest of the play or with its manner of representation. It is distinctly an example of how well men and women do things when they are thoroughly interested in them, and when they are under the influence of an old-time tradition according to which they must have the ability to accomplish what is expected of them. Such a tradition actually existed during the Thirteenth and Fourteenth centuries, leading to a gradual development of dramatic power both in writers and actors, that eventually was to result in the magnificent outburst of dramatic genius during the Elizabethan period. For it must not be forgotten, that mystery and morality plays continued to hold the stage down almost, if not quite, to the time of Shakespeare's early manhood, and he probably saw the Coventry Cycle of plays acted.

While we have a certain number of these old-time plays, most of them, of course, have disappeared by time's attrition during the centuries before the invention of printing, when they were handed round only in manuscript form. Of some of these plays we shall have something to say after a moment, stopping only to call attention to the fact that in this literary mode of the mystery and morality plays, dramatic literature in English reached a height of development which has been equaled only by our greatest dramatic geniuses.

Within the last few years most of the large cities of the English-speaking world, besides the more important universities, have been given the opportunity to hear one of the great products of this form of literary activity. "Everyman" is probably as great a play as there is in English and comparable with the best work of Shakespeare, Marlowe and Jonson. Its author only took the four last things to be remembered— Death, Judgment, Heaven and Hell—the things which must come to *every man,* and wrote his story around them, yet he did it with such dramatic effectiveness as to make his drama a triumph of literary execution.

The Mystery Plays were as interesting in their way to the medieval generations as "Everyman" to us. As may be seen from the list quoted from Mr. Morley, practically all the significant parts of the Bible story were acted by these craftsmen. Too much can scarcely be said of the educational value of such dramatic exercises; the Bible itself with its deep religious teachings, with its simple but sublime style, with its beautiful poetry, entered for a time into the very lives of these people. No wonder that our English speech during these centuries became saturated with biblical thoughts and words. Anyone who has ever had any experience with amateur theatricals when a really great play was given, will be able to realize how much more thoroughly every quality, dramatic, literary, poetic, even lyric

and historical, that there might be in the drama, entered into
the hearts and minds of those who took part. It is this feature
that is especially deserving of attention with regard to these
mystery plays which began in the Thirteenth Century. The people's interest in them, lifted them out of themselves and their
trivial round of life into the higher life of this great religious
poetry. On the other hand the teachings of the Bible came down
from the distant plane on which they might otherwise have
been set and entered into the very life of the people. Their
familiarity with scripture made it a something not to be discussed merely, but to be applied in their everyday affairs.

Besides this, the organization of the company to give the
play and the necessity for the display and exercise of taste in
the costumes and of ingenuity in the stage settings, were of
themselves of great educative value. The rivalry that naturally existed between the various companies chosen from the
different guilds only added to the zest with which rehearsals
were taken up, and made the play more fully occupy the minds
of those actively engaged in its preparation. For several dull
winter months before Easter time there was an intense preoc-
cupation of mind with great thoughts and beautiful words, instead of with the paltry round of daily duties, which would
otherwise form the burden of conversation. Gossip and scandal
mongering had fewer opportunities since people's minds were
taken up by so much worthier affairs. The towns in which
the plays were given never had more than a few thousand inhabitants and most of them must have been personally interested in some way in the play. The Jesuits, whose acumen
for managing students is proverbial, have always considered
it of great importance to have their students prepare plays several times a year. Their reason is the occupation of mind
which it affords as well as the intellectual and elocutionary
training that comes with the work. What they do with pre-
meditation, the old guilds did unconsciously but even more effectively, and their success must be considered as one of the
social triumphs of this wonderful Thirteenth Century.

Only in recent years has the idea succeeded in making way
in government circles on the continent, that the giving of free
dramatic entertainments for the poor would form an excellent

addition to other educational procedures. Such performances have now been given for nearly a score of years in Berlin. After all, the subvention allowed by government to the
great theaters and opera houses in Europe is part of this
same policy, though unfortunately they are calculated to af-
fect only the upper classes, who need the help and the stimulus of great dramatic art and great music less than the lower
classes, who have so little of variety or of anything that makes
for uplift in their lives. In the Thirteenth Century this very
modern notion was anticipated in such a way as to benefit the
very poorest of the population, and that not only passively, that
is by the hearing of dramatic performances, but also actively, by
taking parts in them and so having all the details of the action
and the words impressed upon them.

CAPITAL (LINCOLN)

XVI

FRANCIS THE SAINT—THE FATHER OF THE RENAISSANCE.

The Renaissance is often thought of as a movement which originated about the middle of the Fifteenth Century. Careful students sometimes trace its origin back somewhat further. In recent years it has come to be realized, however, that the great intellectual development which came during the century after the fall of Constantinople in Italy, and gradually spread to all the civilized countries of Europe, had been preparing for at least two centuries and a half. While the period from the middle of the Fifteenth to the end of the Sixteenth Centuries well deserves the name of Renaissance, because one of the most important fructifying principles of the movement was the rebirth of Greek ideas into the modern world after the dispersion of Greek scholars by the Turkish advance into the Byzantine Empire, the term must not be allowed to carry with it the mistaken notion which only too often has been plausibly accepted, that there was a new birth of poetic, literary and esthetic ideas at this time, just as if there had been nothing worth considering in these lines before. Any such notion as this would be the height of absurdity in the light of the history of the previous centuries in Italy. It was a cherished notion of the people of the Renaissance themselves that they were the first to do artistic and literary work, hence they invented the term Gothic, meaning thereby barbarous, for the art of the preceding time, but in this they were only exercising that amusing self-complacency which each generation deems its right. Succeeding generations adopting their depreciative term have turned it into one of glory so that Gothic art is now in highest honor.

Fortunately in recent years there has come, as we have said, a growing recognition of the fact that the real beginning of modern art lies much farther back in history, and that the real father of the Italian Renaissance is a man whom very few people in the last three centuries have appreciated at his true worth. Undoubtedly the leader in that great return to nature, which constitutes the true basis of modern poetic and artistic ideas of all kinds, was St. Francis of Assisi. "The poor little man of God," as in his humility he loved to call himself, would surely be the last one to suspect that he should ever come to be thought of as the initiator of a great movement in literature and art. Such he was, however, in the highest sense of the term and because of the modern appreciation of him in this regard, publications concerning him have been more frequent during the last ten years than with regard to almost any other single individual. We have under our hand at the present moment what by no means claims to be a complete bibliography of St. Francis' life and work, yet we can count no less than thirty different works in various languages (not reckoning translations separate from the originals) which have issued from the press during the last ten years alone. This gives some idea of present day interest in St. Francis.

It must not be thought, however, that it is only in our time that these significant tributes have been paid him. Much of his influence in literature and art, as well as in life, was recognized by the southern nations all during the centuries since his death. That it is only during the last century that other nations have come to appreciate him better, and especially have realized his literary significance, has been their loss and that of their literatures. At the beginning of the Nineteenth Century Görres, the German historian who was so sympathetic towards the Middle Ages, wrote of St. Francis as one of the Troubadours, and even did not hesitate to add that without St. Francis at the beginning of the Thirteenth Century there would have been no Dante at the end. Renan, the well-known French rationalist historian and literateur, did not hesitate to proclaim St. Francis one of the great religious poets of all time and his famous Canticle of the Sun as the greatest religious poem since the Hebrew Psalms were written. It was from Renan that Matthew Arnold received his introduction to St. Francis as a literary man, and his own studies led him to write the famous passages in the Essays in Criticism, which are usually so much a source of surprise to those who think of Mr. Arnold as the rationalizing critic, rather than the sympathetic admirer of a medieval saint.

"In the beginning of the Thirteenth Century, when the clouds and storms had come, when the gay sensuous pagan life was gone, when men were not living by the senses and understanding, when they were looking for the speedy coming of Antichrist, there appeared in Italy, to the north of Rome, in the beautiful Umbrian country at the foot of the Appennines, a figure of the most magical power and charm, St. Francis. His century is, I think, the most interesting in the history of Christianity after its primitive age; more interesting than even the century of the Reformation; and one of the chief figures, perhaps the very chief, to which this interest attaches itself, is St. Francis. And why? Because of the profound popular instinct which enabled him, more than any man since the primitive age, to fit religion for popular use. He brought religion to the people. He founded the most popular body of ministers of religion that has ever existed in the Church. He transformed monachism by uprooting the stationary monk, delivering him from the bondage of property, and sending him, as a mendicant friar, to be a stranger and sojourner, not in the wilderness, but in the most crowded haunts of men, to console them and to do them good. This popular instinct of his is at the bottom of his famous marriage with poverty. Poverty and suffering are the condition of the people, the multitude, the immense majority of mankind; and it was towards this people that his soul yearned. "He listens," it was said of him, "to those to whom God himself will not listen."

The more one reads the English apostle of sweetness and light on Francis the greater the wonder grows. With a sympathy quite unexpected in the man for whom the Diety had become merely "a stream of tendency that makes for righteousness," he realized the influence that this supreme lover of a personal God had over his generation, and his brother poet soul flew to its affinity in spite of the apparently insurmountable obstacle of extreme aloofness of spiritual temperament.

Matthew Arnold proceeds:

"So in return, as no other man, St. Francis was listened to. When an Umbrian town or village heard of his approach, the

GLORIFICATION OF ST. FRANCIS (GIOTTO)

whole population went out in joyful procession to meet him, with green boughs, flags, music, and songs of gladness. The master, who began with two disciples, could in his own lifetime (and he died at forty-five) collect to keep Whitsuntide with him, in presence of an immense multitude, five thousand of his Minorites. He found fulfilment to his prophetic cry: "I hear in my ears the sound of the tongues of all the nations who shall come unto us; Frenchmen, Spaniards, Germans, Englishmen. The Lord will make of us a great people, even unto the ends of the earth."

When we reach the next paragraph the secret of this surprising paradoxical sympathy is out. It is the literary and esthetic side of St. Francis that has appealed to him, and like Renan he does not hesitate to give "the poor little man of God" a place among the great original geniuses of all time, associating his name with that of Dante.

"Prose could not satisfy this ardent soul, and he made poetry. Latin was too learned for this simple, popular nature, and he composed in his mother tongue, in Italian. The beginnings of the mundane poetry of the Italians are in Sicily, at the court of kings; the beginnings of their religious poetry are in Umbria, with St. Francis. His are the humble upper waters of a mighty stream: at the beginning of the Thirteenth Century, it is St. Francis, at the end, Dante. Now it happens that St. Francis, too, like the Alexandrian songstress, has his hymn for the sun, for Adonis; Canticle of the Sun, Canticle of the Creatures, the poem goes by both names. Like the Alexandrian hymn, it is designed for popular use, but not for use by King Ptolemy's people; artless in language, irregular in rhythm, it matches with the childlike genius that produced it, and the simple natures that loved and repeated it."

Probably the most satisfactory translation for those who may not be able to appreciate the original of this sublime hymn that has evoked so many tributes, is the following literal rendering into English in which a quite successful attempt to give the naif rhythm of the original Italian, which necessarily disappears in any formal rhymed translation, has been made by Father Paschal Robinson of the Order of St. Francis for his recent edition of the writings of St. Francis.*

*Philadelphia, The Dolphin Press, 1906.

"Here begin the praises of the Creatures which the Blessed Francis made to the praise and honor of God while he was ill at St. Damian's:

Most high, omnipotent, good Lord,
Praise, glory and honor and benediction all, are Thine.
To Thee alone do they belong, most High,
And there is no man fit to mention Thee.
Praise be to Thee, my Lord, with all Thy creatures,
Especially to my worshipful brother sun,
The which lights up the day, and through him dost
    Thou brightness give;
And beautiful is he and radiant with splendor great;
Of Thee, Most High, signification gives.
Praised be my Lord, for sister moon and for the stars,
In heaven Thou hast formed them clear and precious
    and fair.
Praised be my Lord for brother wind
And for the air and clouds and fair and every kind
    of weather,
By the which Thou givest to Thy creatures nourish-
    ment.
Praised be my Lord for sister water,
The which is greatly helpful and humble and precious
    and pure.
Praised be my Lord for brother fire,
By the which Thou lightest up the dark.
And fair is he and gay and mighty and strong.
Praised be my Lord for our sister, mother earth,
The which sustains and keeps us
And brings forth diverse fruits with grass and flowers
    bright.
Praised be my Lord for those who for Thy love for-
    give
And weakness bear and tribulation.
Blessed those who shall in peace endure,
For by Thee, Most High, shall they be crowned.
Praised be my Lord for our sister, the bodily death,
From the which no living man can flee.

Woe to them who die in mortal sin;
Blessed those who shall find themselves in Thy most
    holy will,
For the second death shall do them no ill.
Praise ye and bless ye my Lord, and give Him thanks,
And be subject unto Him with great humility."

Except for his place in literature and art, the lives of few men would seem to be of so little interest to the modern time as that of St. Francis of Assisi, yet it is for the man himself that so many now turn to him. His spirit is entirely opposed to the sordid principles that have been accepted as the basis of success in modern life. His idea was that happiness consisted in being free from unsatisfied desires rather than seeking to secure the satisfaction of his wishes. Duty was self-denial, not self-seeking under any pretext. He stripped himself literally of everything and his mystic marriage to the Lady Poverty was, so far as he was concerned, as absolute a reality, as if the union had been actual instead of imaginary. The commonplace details of his early years seem all the more interesting from these later developments, and have been the subject of much sympathetic study in recent years.

St. Francis' father was a cloth merchant and St. Francis had been brought up and educated as became the son of a man whose commercial journeys often took him to France. It was indeed while his father was absent on one of these business expeditions that Francis was born and on his father's return received from him the name of Francisco—the Frenchman—in joyful commemoration of his birth.

As he grew up he did not differ from the ordinary young man of his time, but seems to have taken the world and its pleasures quite as he found them and after the fashion of those around him. At the age of twenty-five he fell seriously ill and then, for the first time, there came to him the realization of the true significance of life. As Dean Stanley said shortly before his death, "life seemed different when viewed from the horizontal position." Life lived for its own sake was not worth while. To Francis there came the realization that when God Himself became man he lived his life for others. Francis set about literally imitating him. Enthusiastic students of his life consider him the great type of genuine Christian, the most real disciple of Christ who ever lived. Some money and goods that came into his hands having been disposed of for the poor, Francis' father made serious objection and Francis was brought before the ecclesiastical authorities. It was at this moment that he stripped himself of everything that he had, the Bishop even having to provide a cloak to cover his nakedness, and became the wonderful apostle to the poor that he remained during all the rest of his life. Curious as it must ever seem, it was not long before he had many who wished to imitate him and who insisted on becoming his disciples and followers. St. Francis had had no idea how infectious his example was to prove. Before his death his disciples could be numbered by the thousands and the great order of the Franciscans, that for centuries was to do so much work, had come into existence not by any conscious planning, but by the mere force of the great Christian principles that were the guiding factors in St. Francis' own life.

Ruskin in his Mornings in Florence in discussing Giotto's famous picture of St. Francis' renunciation of his inheritance, and his incurrence thereby of his father's anger, has a characteristic passage that sounds the very keynote of the Saint's life and goes to the heart of things. In it he explains the meaning of this apparently contradictory incident in St. Francis' life, since Francis' great virtue was obedience, yet here, apparently as a beginning of his more perfect Christian life, is an act of disobedience. After Ruskin's explanation, however, it is all the more difficult to understand the present generation's revival of interest in Francis unless it be attributed to a liking for contrast.

"That is the meaning of St. Francis' renouncing his inheritance; and it is the beginning of Giotto's gospel of Works. Unless this hardest of deeds be done first—this inheritance of mammon and the world cast away,—all other deeds are useless. You cannot serve, cannot obey, God and mammon. No charities, no obedience, no self-denials, are of any use while you are still at heart in conformity with the world. You go to church, because the world goes. You keep Sunday, because your neigh-

ST. FRANCIS (CHURCH OF THE FRARI, VENICE, NIC. PISANO)

bor keeps it. But you dress ridiculously because your neighbors ask it; and you dare not do a rough piece of work, because your neighbors despise it. You must renounce your neighbor, in his riches and pride, and remember him in his distress. That is St. Francis' 'disobedience.' "

In spite of Ruskin's charming explanation of St. Francis' place in history, and his elucidation of the hard passages in his life, most people will only find it more difficult, after these explanations, to understand the modern acute reawakening of interest in St. Francis. Our generation in its ardent devotion to the things of this world does not seem a promising field for the evangel, "Give up all thou hast and follow me." The mystery of St. Francis' attraction only deepens the more we know of him. An American Franciscan has tried to solve the problem and his words are worth quoting. Father Paschal Robinson, O. S. M., in his "The True St. Francis" says:—

"What is the cause of the present widespread homage to St. Francis? It is, of course, far too wide a question to allow the present writer to do more than make a few suggestions. First and foremost, we must ever reckon with the perennial charm of the Saint's personality, which seems to wield an ineffable influence over the hearts of men—drawing and holding those of the most different habits of mind, with a sense of personal sympathy. Perhaps no other man, unless it be St. Paul, ever had such wide reaching, all-embracing sympathy: and it may have been wider than St. Paul's, for we find no evidence in the great apostle of a love for nature and of animals. This exquisite Franciscan spirit, as it is called, which is the very perfume of religion—this spirit at once so humble, so tender, so devout, so akin to 'the good odor of Christ'—passed out into the whole world and has become a permanent source of inspiration. A character at once so exhalted and so purified as St. Francis was sure to keep alive an ideal; and so he does. From this one can easily understand St. Francis' dominance among a small but earnest band of enthusiasts now pointing the world back to the reign of the spirit. It was this same gentle idealism of St. Francis which inspired the art of the Umbrian people; it was this which was translated into the paintings of the greatest artists. No school of painting has ever been penetrated with such pure idealism as the Umbrian; and this inspiration, at once religious and artistic, came from the tomb of the *poverello* above which Giotto had painted his mystical frescoes. The earnest quasi-religious study of the medieval beginnings of western art has therefore rightly been set down as another cause for some of the latter-day pilgrimages to Assisi. In like manner, the scientific treatment of the Romance literature leads naturally to St. Francis as to the humble upper waters of a mighty stream; at the beginning of the Thirteenth Century is St. Francis, at the end is Dante. It was Matthew Arnold, we believe, who first held up the poor man of Assisi as a literary type—a type as distinct and formal as the author of the *Divine Comedy.* 'Prose,' he says, 'could not easily satisfy the saint's ardent soul, and so he made poetry.' 'It was,' writes Ozanam, 'the first cry of a nascent poetry which has grown and made itself heard through the world.' "

Considering how thoroughly impractical Francis seemed to be in his life, it can scarcely help but be a source of ever increasing wonder that he succeeded in influencing his generation so widely and so thoroughly. It is evident that there were many men of the time tired of the more or less strenuous life, which chained them either to the cares of business or tempted them for the sake of the bubble reputation into a military career. To these St. Francis' method of life came with an especially strong appeal. The example of his neglect of worldly things and of his so thoroughly maintained resolve not to be harassed by the ordinary cares of life, and especially not to take too much thought of the future, penetrated into all classes. While it made the rich realize how much of their lives they were living merely for the sake of others, it helped the poor to be satisfied, since here was a sublime and complete recognition of the fact that an existence without cares was better than one with many cares, such as were sure to come to those who wrought ever and anon increase of the goods of this world. Such ideas may seen to be essentially modern, but anyone who will turn to the chapter on The Three Most Read Books of the Century and read the passages from the "Romance of the Rose" on wealth and poverty, will know better than to think them anything but perennial.

Men gathered around St. Francis then and pleaded to be allowed to follow his mode of life. Some of the men who thus came to him were the choice spirits of the times. Thomas of Celano, who was to be one of the Master's favorite disciples and subsequently to be his most authoritative biographer, was one of the great literary geniuses of all times, the author of the sublime Dies Irae. While most of his first companions were men of such extreme simplicity of mind that the world has been rather in an amused than admiring attitude with regard to them, there can be no doubt that this simplicity was of itself an index not only of their genuine sincerity of heart, but of a greatness of mind that set them above the ordinary run of mankind and made them live poetry when they did not write it. The institute established by St. Francis was destined, in the course of the century, to attract to it some of the great men of every country. Besides Thomas of Celano there was, in Italy, Anthony of Padua, almost as famous as his master for the beauty of his saintly life; Jacopone Da Todi, the well-known author of the Stabat Mater, a hymn that rivals in poetic genius, the Dies Irae; Bonaventure, the great teacher of philosophy and theology at the University of Paris, and the writer of some of the sublimest treatises of mystical theology that were to be text books for the members of the Franciscan order, and of many other religious bodies for centuries after his death, indeed down to even our own times. There was Roger Bacon, in England, the famous teacher of science at Paris and at Oxford; and that Subtle Doctor, Duns Scotus, whose influence in philosophical speculation was destined never quite to disappear, and many others, the pick of the generations in which they lived, all proud to look up to Francis of Assisi as their father; all glad of the opportunity that the order gave them, to pass their lives in peace, far from the madding crowd with its strifes and competition, providing them constantly with opportunities to live their own lives, to find their own souls, to cultivate their own individualities untrammelled by worldly cares.

Francis' success in this matter and the propaganda of his influence will not be so surprising to Americans of this generation, if they will only recall what is still a precious memory in the minds of men who are yet alive, that efforts to found a community not unlike that of the Franciscans in certain ways, attracted widespread attention even in our own country half a century ago. After all, the men who gathered at Brook Farm had ideas and ideals not so distant from those cherished by St. Francis and the early members of the Franciscan Order. Their main effort was also to get away from worldly cares and have the opportunity to work out their philosophy of life far from the disturbing influence of city life, in the peaceful pursuit of only such agricultural efforts as might be necessary to ensure them simple sustenance, yet at the same time enforce from them such exercise in the open air as would guarantee the preservation of health. The men of Brook Farm were, in the eyes of their generation, quite as far from practical ideas as were the early Franciscans. It must not be forgotten, however, that these men who thus attempted in the Nineteenth Century what St. Francis succeeded in accomplishing in the Thirteenth, in their subsequent careers succeeded in impressing themselves very strongly upon the life of the American people. Much of what is best in our Nineteenth Century life would be lost if the Brook farmers and what they accomplished were to be removed from it. Men of ideals are usually also men of working ideas, as these two experiences in history would seem to show.

It was not alone for the men of his generation, however, that Francis was destined to furnish a refuge from worldly care and a place of peace and thoughtful life. We have already said that it was by chance, certainly without any conscious intention on Francis' part that the Franciscan order for men which is usually spoken of as the First Order came into existence. The last thing in the world very probably that would ever have entered into the mind of Francis when he began to lead the simple life of a poor little man of God, was the founding of a religious order for women. We tell elsewhere the story, of St. Clare's interest in St. Francis' mode of life and of the trials that she underwent in order to obtain permission and opportunity to fashion her own life in the same way. The problem was even more serious for women than for men. St. Francis considered that they should not be

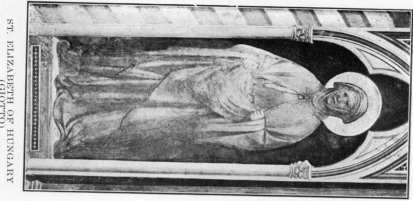

ST. ELIZABETH OF HUNGARY
(GIOTTO)

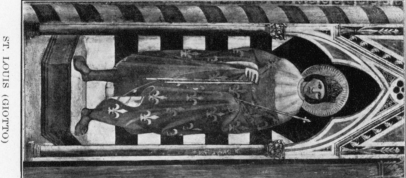

ST. LOUIS (GIOTTO)

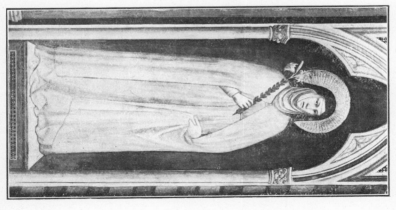

ST. CLAIRE (GIOTTO)

allowed to follow the Franciscan custom of going out to seek alms and yet required that they should live in absolute poverty, possessing nothing and supporting themselves only by the contributions of the faithful and the work of their hands. St. Clare attempted the apparently impossible and solved the problem of a new career for the women of her time.

It was not very long before St. Clare's example proved as infective as that of St. Francis himself. While in the beginning the members of her family had been the most strenuous objectors against her taking up such an unwonted mode of existence it was not long before she was joined in the monastery of St. Damian where her little community was living, by her sister who was to become almost as famous as herself under the name of St. Agnes, and by her mother and other near relatives, from Assisi and the neighborhood. This Second Order of St. Francis to which only women were admitted proved to have in it the germ of as active life as that of the first order. Before the end of the Thirteenth Century there were women Franciscans in every country in Europe. These convents furnished for women a refuge from the worried, hurried, over-busy life around them that proved quite as attractive as the similar opportunity for the men. For many hundreds of years down even to our own time, women were to find in the quiet obscurity of such Franciscan convents a peaceful, happy life in which they occupied themselves with simple conventual duties, with manual labor in their monastery gardens, with the making of needle work in which they became the most expert in the world, with the illuminating of missals and office books of such artistic beauty that they have become the most precious treasures of our great libraries, and with the long hours of prayer by which they hoped to accomplish as much in making the world better as if they devoted themselves to ardent efforts of reform which, of course, the circumstances of the time would not have permitted.

Finally there was the Third Order of St. Francis, which was to gather to itself so many of the distinguished people of the century whose occupations and obligations would not permit them to live the conventual life, but who yet felt that they must be attached by some bond to this beautiful sanctity that was entering into all the better life of the century. The Third Order was established so as to permit all the world to become Franciscans to whatever degree it considered possible, and to share in the sublime Christianity of the founder whom they all admired so much, even if they were not able to imitate his sublimer virtues. Into this Third Order of St. Francis most of the finer spirits of the time entered with enthusiasm. We need only recall that Louis IX. of France, the greatest Monarch of the century, considered it a special privilege to be a follower of the humble Francis, and that St. Elizabeth of Hungary, the daughter of a king, the wife and mother of a ruling prince, gave another example of the far-reachingness of Francis' work. Dante was another of the great members of the Third Order and was buried in the habit of St. Francis, glorying in the thought of the brotherhood this gave him with the saint he loved so much.

All down the centuries since, other distinguished men in many countries of Europe were proud to claim the same distinction. Modern science is supposed to be unorthodox in its tendencies and electricity is the most recent of the sciences in development. Three of the great founders in electricity, Volta, Galvani and Ampere, were members of the Third Order of St. Francis and at least one of them, Galvani, insisted on being buried in the habit of the order six centuries after the death of his father Francis in order to show how much he appreciated the privilege. There is no man who lived in the Thirteenth Century who influenced the better side of men more in all the succeeding ages down to and including our own time, than the poor little man of God of Assisi. He is just coming into a further precious heritage of uplift for the men of our time, that is surprising for those who are so buried in the merely material that they fail to realize how much the ideal still rules the minds of thinking men, but that seems only natural and inevitable to those who appreciate all the attractiveness there is in a simple life lived without the bootless hurry, the unattaining bustle and the over-strained excitement of the strenuous existence.

What St. Francis and his order accomplished in Italy another great Saint, Dominic, was achieving in the West. The fact that another order similar to that of St. Francis in many respects, yet differing from it in a number of essential particulars, should have arisen almost at the same time shows how profoundly the spirit of organization of effort had penetrated into the minds of these generations of the Thirteenth Century. While poverty was to be the badge of St. Dominic's followers as well as those of St. Francis, learning was to replace the simplicity which St. Francis desired for his sons. The order of preachers began at once to give many eminent scholars to the Church, and for three centuries there was not a single generation that did not see as Dominicans some of the most intellectual men of Europe. Leaders they were in philosophy, in the development of thought, in education, and in every phase of ecclesiastical life. The watch dogs of the Lord, (Domini Canes) they were called, punning on their name because everywhere they were in the van of defense against the enemies of Christianity. That the Thirteenth Century should have given rise to two such great religious orders stamps it as a wonderfully fruitful period for religion as well as for every other phrase of human development.

In order to understand what these great founders tried to do, the work of these two orders must be considered together. They have never ceased, during all the intervening seven centuries, to be the source of great influence in the religious world. They have proven refuges for many gentle spirits at all times and have been the homes of learning, as well as of piety. While occasionally their privileges have been abused, and men have taken advantage of the opportunities to be idle and luxurious, this has happened much seldomer than the world imagines. Not a single century has failed to show men among them whom the world honors as Saints, and whose lives have been examples of what can be accomplished by human nature at its best. They have been literally schools of unselfishness, and men have learned to think less of themselves and more of their labor by the contemplation of the lives of these begging friars. What they did for England, the Rev. Augustus Jessop, a non-conformist clergyman in England, has recently told very well, and the more one studies their history, the higher the estimation of them; and the more one knows of them, the less does one talk of their vices. Green in his "History of the English People" has paid them a tribute that it is well to remember :—

"To bring the world back again within the pale of the Church was the aim of two religious orders which sprang suddenly to life at the opening of the Thirteenth Century. The zeal of the Spaniard Dominic was aroused at the sight of the lordly prelates who sought by fire and sword to win the Albigensian heretics to the faith. 'Zeal,' he cried, 'must be met by zeal, lowliness by lowliness, false sanctity by real sanctity, preaching lies by preaching truth.' His fiery ardor and rigid orthodoxy were seconded by the mystical piety, the imaginative enthusiasm of Francis of Assisi. The life of Francis falls like a stream of tender light across the darkness of the time. In the frescoes of Giotto or the verse of Dante we see him take Poverty for his bride. He strips himself of all: he flings his very clothes at his father's feet, that he may be one with Nature and God. His passionate verse claims the moon for his sister and the sun for his brother ; he calls on his brother the Wind, and his sister the Water. His last faint cry was a 'Welcome, Sister Death.' Strangely as the two men differed from each other, their aim was the same, to convert the heathen, to extirpate heresy, to reconcile knowledge with orthodoxy, to carry the Gospel to the poor. The work was to be done by the entire reversal of the older monasticism, by seeking personal salvation in effort for the salvation of their fellow-men, by exchanging the solitary of the cloister for the preacher, the monk for a friar. To force the new 'brethren' into entire dependence on those among whom they labored the vow of Poverty was turned into a stern reality; the 'Begging Friars' were to subsist on the alms of the poor, they might possess neither money nor lands, the very houses in which they lived were to be held in trust for them by others. The tide of popular enthusiasm which welcomed their appearance swept before it the reluctance of Rome, the jealousy of the older orders, the opposition of the parochial priesthood. Thousands of brethren gathered in a few years around Francis and Dominic, and the begging preachers, clad in their coarse frock of serge, with the girdle of rope around their waist, wandered barefooted as missionaries over Asia, băttled with heresy in Italy and Gaul, lectured in the Universities, and preached and toiled among the poor."

SIDE CAPITAL (LINCOLN)

XVII

AQUINAS THE SCHOLAR.

No one of all the sons of the Thirteenth Century, not even Dante himself, so typifies the greatness of the mentality of the period as does Thomas, called from his birthplace Aquinas, or of Aquin, on whom his own and immediately succeeding generations because of what they considered his almost more than human intellectual acumen, bestowed the title of Angelical Doctor, while the Church for the supremely unselfish character of his life, formally conferred the title of Saint. The life of Aquinas is of special interest, because it serves to clarify many questions as to the education of the Thirteenth Century and to correct many false impressions that are only too prevalent with regard to the intellectual life of the period. Though Aquinas came of a noble family which was related to many of the Royal houses of Europe and was the son of the Count of Aquino, then one of the most important of the non-reigning noble houses of Italy, his education was begun in his early years and was continued in the midst of such opportunities as even the modern student might well envy.

It is often said that the nobility at this time, paid very little attention to the things of the intellect and indeed rather prided themselves on their ignorance of even such ordinary attainments as reading and writing. While this was doubtless true for not a few of them, Aquinas's life stands in open contradiction with the impression that any such state of mind was at all general, or that there were not so many exceptions as to nullify any such supposed rule. Evidently those who wished could and did take advantage of educational opportunities quite as in our day. Aquinas's early education was received at the famous monastery of Monte Cassino in Southern Italy, where the Benedictines for more than six centuries had been providing magnificent opportunities for the studious youth of Italy and for serious-minded students from all over Europe.

When he was scarcely more than a boy he proceeded to the University of Naples, which at that time, under the patronage of the Emperor Frederick II., was being encouraged not only to take the place so long held by Salernum in the educational world of Europe, but also to rival the renowned Universities of Paris and Bologna. Here he remained until he was seventeen years of age when he resolved to enter the Dominican Order, which had been founded only a short time before by St. Dominic, yet had already begun to make itself felt throughout the religious and educational world of the time.

Just as it is the custom to declare that as a rule, the nobility cared little for education, so it is more or less usual to proclaim that practically only the clergy had any opportunities for the higher education during the Thirteenth Century. Thomas had evidently been given his early educational opportunities, however, without any thought of the possibility of his becoming a clergyman. His mother was very much opposed to his entrance among the Dominicans, and every effort was made to picture to him the pleasures and advantages that would accrue to him because of his noble connections, in a life in the world. Thomas insisted, however, and his firm purpose in the matter finally conquered even the serious obstacles that a noble family can place in the way of a boy of seventeen, as regards the disposition of his life in a way opposed to their wishes.

The Dominicans realized the surpassing intelligence of the youth whom they had received and accordingly he was sent to be trained under the greatest teacher of their order, the famous Albert the Great, who was then lecturing at Cologne. Thomas was not the most brilliant of scholars as a young man and seems even to have been the butt of his more successful fellow-students. They are said to have called him the dumb one, or sometimes because of his bulkiness even as a youth, the dumb ox. Albert himself, however, was not deceived in his estimation of the intellectual capacity of his young student, and according to tradition declared, that the bellowings of this ox would yet be heard throughout all Christendom. After a few years spent at Cologne, Thomas when he was in his early twenties, accompanied Albert who had been called to

Paris. It was at Paris that Thomas received his bachelor's degree and also took out his license to teach—the doctor's degree of our time. After this some years further were spent at Cologne and then the greatness of the man began to dawn on his generation. He was called back to Paris and became one of the most popular of the Professors at that great University in the height of her fame, at a time when no greater group of men has perhaps ever been gathered together, than shared with him the honors of the professors' chairs at that institution.

"Albert the Great, Roger Bacon, St. Bonaventure, and St. Thomas Aquinas, form among themselves, so to speak, a complete representation of all the intellectual powers: they are the four doctors who uphold the chair of philosophy in the temple of the Middle Ages. Their mission was truly the reestablishment of the sciences, but not their final consummation. They were not exempt from the ignorances and erroneous opinions of their day, yet they did much to overcome them and succeeded better than is usually acknowledged in introducing the era of modern thought. Often, the majesty, I may even say the grace of their conceptions, disappears under the veil of the expressions in which they are clothed; but these imperfections are amply atoned for by superabundant merits. Those Christian philosophers did not admit within themselves the divorce, since their day become so frequent, between the intellect and the will; their lives were uniformly a laborious application of their doctrines. They realized in its plenitude the practical wisdom so often dreamed of by the ancients—the abstinence of the disciples of Pythagoras, the constancy of the stoics, together with humility and charity, virtues unknown to the antique world. Albert the Great and St. Thomas left the castles of their noble ancestors to seek obscurity in the cloisters of St. Dominic: the former abdicated, and the latter declined, the honors of the Church. It was with the cord of St. Francis that Roger Bacon and St. Bonaventure girded their loins; when the last named was sought that the Roman purple might be placed upon his shoulders, he begged the envoys to wait until he finished washing the dishes of the convent. Thus they did not withdraw themselves within the exclusive mysteries of an esoteric teaching; they opened the doors of their schools to the sons of shepherds and artisans, and, like their Master, Christ, they said: "Come all!" After having broken the bread of the word, they were seen distributing the bread of alms. The poor knew them and blessed their names. Even yet, after the lapse of six hundred years, the dwellers in Paris kneel round the altar of the Angel of the School, and the workmen of Lyons deem it an honor once a year to bear upon their brawny shoulders the triumphant remains of the 'Seraphic Doctor.'"

For most modern students and even scholars educated in secular universities the name of Aquinas is scarcely more than a type, the greatest of them, it is true, of the schoolmen who were so much occupied with distant, impractical and, to say the least, merely theoretic metaphysical problems, in the later Middle Ages. It is true that the renewed interest in Dante in recent years in English speaking countries, has brought about a revival of attention in Aquinas's work because to Dante, the Angelical Doctor, as he was already called, meant so much, and because the Divine Comedy has been declared often and often, by competent critics, to be the Summa Theologiae of St. Thomas of Aquin in verse. Even this adventitious literary interest, however, has not served to lift the obscurity in which Aquinas is veiled for the great majority of scholarly people, whose education has been conducted according to modern methods and present-day ideas.

As showing a hopeful tendency to recognize the greatness of these thinkers of the Middle Ages it is interesting to note that about five years ago one of St. Thomas's great works—the Summa Contra Gentiles—was placed on the list of subjects which a candidate may at his option offer in the final honor school of the *litterae humaniores* at Oxford. There has come a definite appreciation of the fact that this old time philosopher represents a phase of intellectual development that must not be neglected, and that stands for such educational influence as may well be taken advantage of even in our day of information rather than mental discipline. For the purposes of this course Father Rickaby, S. J., has prepared an annotated translation of the great philosophic work under the title, "Of

God and His Creatures," which was published by Burns and
Oates of London, 1905. This will enable those for whom the
Latin of St. Thomas was a stumbling block, to read the
thoughts of the great scholastic, in translation at least, and
it is to be hoped that we shall hear no more of the trifling
judgments which have so disgraced our English philosophical literature.

. The fact that Pope Leo XIII., by a famous papal bull, insisted that St. Thomas should be the standard of teaching in philosophy and theology in all the Catholic institutions of learning
throughout the world, aroused many thinkers to a realization
of the fact that far from being a thing of the dead and distant past, Thomas's voice was still a great living force in the
world of thought. To most people Leo XIII. appealed as an
intensely practical and thoroughly modern ruler, whose judgment could be depended on even with regard to teaching problems in philosophy and theology. There was about him none
of the qualities that would stamp him as a far-away mystic
whose thoughts were still limited by medieval barriers. The
fact that in making his declaration the Pope was only formulating as a rule, what had spontaneously become the almost
constant practice and tradition of Catholic schools and universities, of itself served to show how great and how enduring
was St. Thomas's influence.

In the drawing together of Christian sects that has inevitably come as a result of the attacks made upon Christianity
by modern materialists, and then later by those who would
in their ardor for the higher criticism do away with practically
all that is divine in Christianity, there has come a very general realization even on the part of those outside of her fold,
that the Roman Catholic Church occupies a position more
solidly founded on consistent logical premises and conclusions
than any of the denominations. Without her aid Christian
apologetics would indeed be in sad case. Pope Leo's declaration only emphasizes the fact, then, that the foundation stone
of Christian apologetics was laid by the great work of St.
Thomas, and that to him more than any other is due that wonderful coordination of secular and religious knowledge,
which appoints for each of these branches of knowledge its

proper place, and satisfies the human mind better than any other system of philosophic thought. This is the real panegyric of St. Thomas, and it only adds to the sublimity of it that it should come nearly six centuries and a half after his death. To only a bare handful of men in the history of the human race, is it given thus to influence the minds of subsequent generations for so long and to have laid down the principles of thought that are to satisfy men for so many generations. This is why, in any attempt at even inadequate treatment of the greatness of the Thirteenth Century, Thomas Aquinas, who was its greatest scholar, must have a prominent place. The present generation has had sufficient interest in him aroused, however, amply to justify such a giving of space.

When Leo XIII. made his recommendation of St. Thomas it was not as one who had merely heard of the works of the great medieval thinker, or knew them only by tradition, or had slightly dipped into them as a dilettante, but as one who had been long familiar with them, who had studied the Angelical Doctor in youth, who had pondered his wisdom in middle age, and resorted again and again to him for guidance in the difficulties of doctrine in maturer years, and the difficulties of morals such as presented themselves in his practical life as a churchman. It was out of the depths of his knowledge of him, that the great Pope, whom all the modern world came to honor so reverently before his death, drew his supreme admiration for St. Thomas and his recognition of the fact that no safer guide in the thorny path of modern Christian apologetics could be followed, than this wonderful genius who first systematized human thought as far as the relations of Creator to creature are considered, in the heyday of medieval scholarship and university teaching.

Those who have their knowledge of scholastic philosophy at second hand, from men who proclaim this period of human development as occupied entirely with fruitless discussion of metaphysical theories, will surely think that they could find nothing of interest for them in St. Thomas's writings. It is true the casual reader may not penetrate far enough into his writing to realize its significance and to appreciate its depth of knowledge, but the serious student finds constant details of supreme interest because of their applications to the most up-to-date problems. We venture to quote an example that will show this more or less perfectly according to the special philosophic interest of readers. It is St. Thomas's discussion of the necessity there was for the revelation of the truth of the existence of God. His statement of the reasons why men, occupied with the ordinary affairs of life, would not ordinarily come to this truth unless it were revealed to them, though they actually have the mental capacity to reach it by reason alone, will show how sympathetically the Saint appreciated human conditions as they are.

"If a truth of this nature were left to the sole inquiry of reason, three disadvantages would follow. One is that the knowledge of God would be confined to few. The discovery of truth is the fruit of studious inquiry. From this very many are hindered. Some are hindered by a constitutional unfitness, their natures being ill-disposed to the acquisition of knowledge. They could never arrive by study at the highest grade of human knowledge, which consists in the knowledge of God. Others are hindered by the claims of business and the ties of the management of property. There must be in human society some men devoted to temporal affairs. These could not possibly spend time enough in the learned lessons of speculative inquiry to arrive at the highest point of human inquiry, the knowledge of God. Some again are hindered by sloth. The knowledge of the truths that reason can investigate concerning God presupposes much previous knowledge; indeed almost the entire study of philosophy is directed to the knowledge of God. Hence, of all parts of philosophy that part stands over to be learned last, which consists of metaphysics dealing with (divine things). Thus only with great labour of study is it possible to arrive at the searching out of the aforesaid truth; and this labour few are willing to undergo for sheer love of knowledge.

"Another disadvantage is that such as did arrive at the knowledge or discovery of the aforesaid truth would take a long time over it on account of the profundity of such truth, and the many prerequisites to the study, and also because in youth and early manhood the soul, tossed to and fro on the waves of passion, is not fit for the study of such high truth; only in settled age does the soul become prudent and scientific, as the philosopher says. Thus if the only way open to the knowledge of God were the way of reason, the human race would (remain) in thick darkness of ignorance: as the knowledge of God, the best instrument for making men perfect and good, would accrue only to a few after a considerable lapse of time.

"A third disadvantage is that, owing to the infirmity of our judgment and the perturbing force of imagination, there is some admixture of error in most of the investigations of human reason. This would be a reason to many for continuing to doubt even of the most accurate demonstrations, not perceiving the force of the demonstration, and seeing the divers judgments, of divers persons who have the name of being wise men. Besides, in the midst of much demonstrated truth there is sometimes an element of error, not demonstrated but asserted on the strength of some plausible and sophistic reasoning that is taken for a demonstration. And therefore it was necessary for the real truth concerning divine things to be presented to men with fixed certainty by way of faith. Wholesome, therefore, is the arrangement of divine clemency, whereby things even that reason can investigate are commanded to be held on faith, so that all might be easily partakers of the knowledge of God, and that without doubt and error (Book I. cix)."

A still more striking example of Thomas's eminently sympathetic discussion of a most difficult problem, is to be found in his treatment of the question of the Resurrection of the Body. The doctrine that men will rise again on the last day with the same bodies that they had while here on earth, has been a stumbling block for the faith of a great many persons from the beginning of Christianity. In recent times the discovery of the indestructibility of matter, far from lessening the skeptical elements in this problem as might have been anticipated, has rather emphasized them. While the material of which man's body was composed is never destroyed, it is broken up largely into its original elements and is used over and over again in many natural processes, and even enters into the composition of other men's bodies during the long succeeding generations. Here is a problem upon which it would ordinarily be presumed at once, that a philosophic writer of the Thirteenth Century could throw no possible light. We venture to say, however, that the following passage which we quote from an article on St. Thomas in a recent copy of the *Dublin Review*, represents the best possible solution of the problem, even in the face of all our modern advance in science.

"What does not bar numerical unity in a man while he lives on uninterruptedly (writes St. Thomas), clearly can be no bar to the identity of the arisen man with the man that was. In a man's body, while he lives, there are not always the same parts in respect of matter but only in respect of species. In respect of matter there is a flux and reflux of parts. Still that fact does not bar the man's numerical unity from the beginning to the end of his life. The form and species of the several parts continue throughout life, but the matter of the parts is dissolved by the natural heat, and new matter accrues through nourishment. Yet the man is not numerically different by the difference of his component parts at different ages, although it is true that the material composition of the man at one stage of his life is not his material composition at another. Addition is made from without to the stature of a boy without prejudice to his identity, for the boy and the adult are numerically the same man."

In a word, Aquinas says that we recognize that the body of the boy and of the man are the same though they are composed of quite different material. With this in mind the problem of the Resurrection takes on quite a new aspect from what it held before. What we would call attention to, however, is not so much the matter of the argument as the mode of it. It is essentially modern in every respect. Not only does Thomas know that the body changes completely during the course of years, but he knows that the agent by which the matter of the parts is dissolved is "the natural heat," while "new matter accrues through nourishment." The passage contains a marvelous anticipation of present-day physiology as well as a distinct contribution to Christian apologetics. This coordination of science and theology, though usually thought to be lacking among scholastic philosophers, is constantly typical of their mode of thought and discussion, and this example, far from being exceptional, is genuinely representative of them, as all serious students of scholasticism know.

Perhaps the last thing for which the ordinary person would expect to find a great modern teacher recommending the reading of St. Thomas would be to find therein the proper doctrine with regard to liberty and the remedies for our modern social evils. Those who will recall, however, how well the generations of the Thirteenth Century faced social problems even more serious than ours—for the common people had no rights at all the beginning of the century, yet secured them with such satisfaction as to lay the foundation of the modern history of liberty—will realize that the intellectual men of the time must have had a much better grasp of the principles underlying such problems, than would otherwise be imagined. As a matter of fact, St. Thomas's treatment of Society, its rights and duties, and the mutual relationship between it and the individual, is one of the triumphs of his wonderful work in ethics. It is no wonder, then, that the great Pope of the end of the Nineteenth Century, whose encyclicals showed that he understood very thoroughly these social evils of our time, recognized their tendencies and appreciated their danger, recommended as a remedy for them the reading of St. Thomas. Pope Leo said:

"Domestic and civil society, even, which, as all see, is exposed to great danger from the plague of perverse opinions, would certainly enjoy a far more peaceful and a securer existence if more wholesome doctrine were taught in the academies and schools—one more in conformity with the teaching of the Church, such as is contained in the works of Thomas Aquinas.

"For the teachings of Thomas on the true meaning of liberty —which at this time is running into license—on the divine origin of all authority, on laws and their force, on the paternal and just rule of princes, on obedience to the higher powers, on mutual charity one towards another—on all of these and kindred subjects, have very great and invincible force to overturn those principles of the new order which are well known to be dangerous to the peaceful order of things and to public safety."

For this great Pope, however, there was no greater teacher of any of the serious philosophical, ethical and theological problems than this Saint of the Thirteenth Century. His position in the matter would only seem exaggerated to those who do not appreciate Pope Leo's marvelous practical intelligence, and Saint Thomas's exhaustive treatment of most of the questions that have always been uppermost in the minds of men. While, with characteristic humility, he considered himself scarcely more than a commentator on Aristotle, his natural genius was eminently original and he added much more of his own than what he took from his master. There can be no doubt that his was one of the most gifted minds in all humanity's history and that for profundity of intelligence he deserves to be classed with Plato and Aristotle, as his great disciple Dante is placed between Homer and Shakespeare. Those who know St. Thomas the best, and have spent their lives in the study of him, not only cordially welcomed but ardently applauded Pope Leo's commendation of him, and considered that lofty as was his praise there was not a word they would have changed even in such a laudatory passage as the following:

"While, therefore, we hold that every word of wisdom, every useful thing by whomsoever discovered or planned, ought to be received with a willing and grateful mind, We exhort you, Venerable Brethren, in all earnestness to restore the golden wisdom of St. Thomas, and to spread it far and wide for the defense and beauty of the Catholic faith, for the good of society, and for the advantage of all the sciences. The wisdom of St. Thomas, We say—for if anything is taken up with too great subtlety by the scholastic doctors, or too carelessly stated— if there is anything that ill agrees with the discoveries of a later age, or, in a word, improbable in whatever way, it does not enter Our mind, to propose that for imitation to Our age. Let carefully selected teachers endeavor to implant the doctrines of Thomas Aquinas in the minds of students, and set forth clearly his solidity and excellence over others. Let the academies already founded or to be founded by you illustrate and defend this doctrine, and use it for refutation of prevailing errors. But, lest the false for the true or the corrupt for the pure be drunk in, be watchful that the doctrine of Thomas be drawn from his own fountains, or at least from those rivulets which derived from the very fount, have thus far flowed, according to the established agreement of learned men, pure and clear; be careful to guard the minds of youth from those which are said to flow thence, but in reality are gathered from strange and unwholesome streams."

Tributes quite as laudatory are not lacking from modern secular writers and while there have been many derogatory remarks, these have always come from men who either knew Aquinas only at second hand, or who confess that they had been unable to read him understandingly. The praise all comes from men who have spent years in the study of his writings.

A recent writer in the Dublin *Review* (January, 1906) sums up his appreciation of one of St. Thomas's works, his masterly book in philosophy, as follows:

"The *Summa contra Gentiles* is an historical monument of the first importance for the history of philosophy. In the variety of its contents, it is a perfect encyclopedia of the learning of the day. By it we can fix the high-water mark of Thirteenth Century thought, for it contains the lectures of a doctor second to none in the great school of thought then flourishing—the University of Paris. It is by the study of such books that one enters into the mental life of the period at which they were written; not by the hasty perusal of histories of philosophy. No student of the Contra Gentiles is likely to acquiesce in the statement that the Middle Ages were a time when mankind seemed to have lost the power of thinking for themselves. Medieval people thought for themselves, thoughts curiously different from ours and profitable to study."

Here is a similar high tribute for Aquinas's great work on Theology from his modern biographer, Father Vaughan:

"The 'Summa Theologica' is a mighty synthesis, thrown into technical and scientific form, of the Catholic traditions of East and West, of the infallible dicta of the Sacred Page, and of the most enlightened conclusions of human reason, gathered from the soaring intuitions of the Academy, and the rigid severity of the Lyceum.

"Its author was a man endowed with the characteristic notes of the three great Fathers of Greek Philosophy: he possessed the intellectual honesty and precision of Socrates, the analytical keenness of Aristotle, and that yearning after wisdom and light which was the distinguishing mark of 'Plato the divine,' and which has ever been one of the essential conditions of the highest intuitions of religion."

As a matter of fact it was the very greatness of Thomas Aquinas, and the great group of contemporaries who were so close to him, that produced an unfortunate effect on subsequent thinking and teaching in Europe. These men were so surpassing in their grasp of the whole round of human thought, that their works came to be worshiped more or less as fetishes, and men did not think for themselves but appealed to them as authorities. It is a great but an unfortunate tribute to the scholastics of the Thirteenth Century that subsequent generations for many hundred years not only did not think that they could improve on them, but even hesitated to entertain the notion that they could equal them. Turner in his History of Philosophy has pointed out this fact clearly and has attributed to it, to a great extent, the decadence of scholastic philosophy.

"The causes of the decay of scholastic philosophy were both internal and external. The internal causes are to be found in the condition of Scholastic philosophy at the beginning of the Fourteenth Century. The great work of Christian syncretism had been completed by the masters of the preceding period; revelation and science had been harmonized; contribution had been levied on the pagan philosophies of Greece and Arabia, and whatever truth these philosophies had possessed had been utilized to form the basis of a rational exposition of Christian revelation. The efforts of Roger Bacon and of Alfred the Great to reform scientific method had failed; the sciences were not cultivated. There was, therefore, no source of development, and nothing was left for the later Scholastics except to dispute as to the meaning of principles, to comment on the text of this master or of that, and to subtilize to such an extent that Scholasticism soon became a synonym for captious quibbling. The great Thomistic principle that in philosophy the argument from authority is the weakest of all arguments was forgotten; Aristotle, St. Thomas, or Scotus became the criterion of truth, and as Solomon, whose youthful wisdom had astonished the world, profaned his old age by the worship of idols, the philosophy of the schools, in the days of its decadence, turned from the service of truth to prostrate itself before the shrine of a master. Dialectic, which in the Thirteenth Century had been regarded as the instrument of knowledge, now became an object of study for the sake of display; and to this fault of method was added a fault of style—an uncouthness and barbarity of terminology which bewilder the modern reader."

The appreciation of St. Thomas in his own time is the greatest tribute to the critical faculty of the century that could be made. "Genius is praised but starves," in the words of the old Roman poet. Certainly most of the geniuses of the world have met with anything but their proper meed of appreciation in their own time. This is not true, however, during our Thirteenth Century. We have already shown how the artists, and especially Giotto, (at the end of the Thirteenth Century Giotto was only twenty-four years old) were appreciated, and how much attention Dante began to attract from his contemporaries, and we may add that all the great scholars of the period had a following that insured the wide publication of their works, at a time when this had to be accomplished by slow and patient hand-labor. The appreciation for Thomas, indeed, came near proving inimical to his completion of his important works in philosophy and theology. Many places in Europe wanted to have the opportunity to hear him. We have only reintroduced the practise of exchanging university professors in very recent years. This was quite a common practise in the Thirteenth Century, however, and so St. Thomas, after having been professor at Paris and later at Rome, taught for a while at Naples and then at a number of the Italian universities.

Everywhere he went he was noted for the kindliness of his disposition and for his power to make friends. Looked upon as the greatest thinker of his time it would be easy to expect that there should be some signs of consciousness of this, and as a consequence some of that unpleasant self-assertion which so often makes great intellectual geniuses unpopular. Thomas, however, never seems to have had any over-appreciation of his own talents, but, realizing how little he knew compared to

the whole round of knowledge, and how superficial his thinking was compared to the depth of the mysteries he was trying,
not to solve but to treat satisfactorily, it must be admitted that
there was no question of conceit having a place in his life.
This must account for the universal friendship of all who came
in contact with him. The popes insisted on having him as a
professor at the Roman university in which they were so much
interested, and which they wished to make one of the greatest
universities of the time. Here Thomas was brought in contact with ecclesiastics from all over the world and helped to
form the mind of the time. Those who think the popes of the
Middle Ages opposed to education should study the records
of this Roman university.

Thomas became the great friend of successive popes, some
of whom had been brought in contact with him during his
years of studying and teaching at Rome and Paris. This gave
him many privileges and abundant encouragement, but finally
came near ruining his career as a philosophic writer and teacher, since his papal friends wished to raise him to high ecclesiastical dignities. Urban IV. seems first to have thought of
this but his successor Clement IV., one of the noblest churchmen of the period, who had himself wished to decline the
papacy, actually made out the Bull, creating Thomas Archbishop of Naples. When this document was in due course
presented to Aquinas, far from giving him any pleasure it
proved a source of grief and pain. He saw the chance to do
his life-work slipping from him. This was so evident to his
friend the Pope that he withdrew the Bull and St. Thomas
was left in peace during the rest of his career, and allowed
to prosecute that one great object to which he had dedicated
his mighty intellect. This was the summing up of all human
knowledge in a work that would show the relation of the
Creator to the creature, and apply the great principles of Greek
philosophy to the sublime truths of Christianity. Had Thomas
consented to accept the Archbishopric of Naples in all human
probability, as Thomas's great English biographer remarks,
the Summa Theologica would never have been written. It
seems not unlikely that the dignity was pressed upon him by
the Pope partly at the solicitation of powerful members of

his family, who hoped in this to have some compensation for their relative's having abandoned his opportunities for military and worldly glory. It is fortunate that their efforts failed, and it is only one of the many examples in history of the short-sightedness there may be in considerations that seem founded on the highest human prudence.

Thomas was left free then to go on with his great work, and during the next five years he applied every spare moment to the completion of his Summa. More students have pronounced this the greatest work ever written than is true for any other text-book that has ever been used in schools. That it should be the basis of modern theological teaching after seven centuries is of itself quite sufficient to proclaim its merit. The men who are most enthusiastic about it are those who have used it the longest and who know it the best.

St. Thomas's English biographer, the Very Rev. Roger Bede Vaughan, who is a worthy member of that distinguished Vaughan family who have given so many zealous ecclesiastics to the English Church and so many scholars to support the cause of Christianity, can scarcely say enough of this great work, nor of its place in the realm of theology. When it is recalled that Father Vaughan was not a member of St. Thomas's own order, the Dominicans, but of the Benedictines, it will be seen that it was not because of any *esprit de corps,* but out of the depths of his great admiration for the saint, that his words of praise were written:

"It has been shown abundantly that no writer before the Angelical's day could have created a synthesis of all knowledge. The greatest of the classic Fathers have been treated of, and the reasons of their inability are evident. As for the scholastics who more immediately preceded the Angelical, their minds were not ripe for so great and complete a work: the fullness of time had not yet come. Very possibly had not Albert the Great and Alexander (of Hales) preceded him, St. Thomas would not have been prepared to write his master-work; just as, most probably, Newton would never have discovered the law of gravitation had it not been for the previous labors of Galileo and of Kepler. But just as the English astronomer stands solitary in his greatness, though surrounded and succeeded by men of extraordinary eminence, so also the Angelical stands by himself alone, although Albertus Magnus was a genius, Alexander was a theological king, and Bonaventure a seraphic doctor. Just as the Principia is a work unique, unreachable, so, too, is the 'Summa Theologica' of the great Angelical. Just as Dante stands alone among the poets, so stands St. Thomas in the schools."

Probably the most marvelous thing about the life of St. Thomas is his capacity for work. His written books fill up some twenty folios in their most complete edition. This of itself would seem to be enough to occupy a lifetime without anything more. His written works, however, represent apparently only the products of his hours at leisure. He was only a little more than fifty when he died and he had been a university professor at Cologne, at Bologna, at Paris, at Rome, and at Naples. In spite of the amount of work that he was thus asked to do, his order, the Dominican, constantly called on him to busy himself with certain of its internal affairs. On one occasion at least he visited England in order to attend a Dominican Chapter at Oxford, and the better part of several years at Paris was occupied with his labors to secure for his brethren a proper place in the university, so that they might act as teachers and yet have suitable opportunities for the education and the discipline of the members of the Order.

Verily it would seem as though his days must have been at least twice as long as those of the ordinary scholar and student to accomplish so much; yet he is only a type of the monks of the Middle Ages, of whom so many people seem to think that their principal traits were to be fat and lazy. Thomas was fat, as we know from the picture of him which shows him before a desk from which a special segment has been removed to accommodate more conveniently a rather abnormal abdominal development, but as to laziness, surely the last thing that would occur to anyone who knows anything about him, would be to accuse him of it. Clearly those who accept the ancient notion of monkish laziness will never understand the Middle Ages. The great educational progress of the Thirteenth Century was due almost entirely to monks.

There is another extremely interesting side to the intellectual character of Thomas Aquinas which is usually not realized by the ordinary student of philosophy and theology, and still less perhaps by those who are interested in him from an educational standpoint. This is his poetical faculty. For Thomas as for many of the great intellectual geniuses of the modern time, the sacrament of the Holy Eucharist was one of the most wondrously satisfying devotional mysteries of Christianity and the subject of special devotion. In our own time the great Cardinal Newman manifested this same attitude of mind. Thomas because of his well-known devotion to the Blessed Sacrament, was asked by the Pope to write the office for the then recently established feast of Corpus Christi. There are always certain hymns incorporated in the offices of the different Feast days. It might ordinarily have been expected that a scholar like Aquinas would write the prose portions of the office, leaving the hymns for some other hand, or selecting hymns from some older sacred poetry. Thomas, however, wrote both hymns and prose, and, surprising as it may be, his hymns are some of the most beautiful that have ever been composed and remain the admiration of posterity.

It must not be forgotten in this regard that Thomas's career occurred during the period when Latin hymn writing was at its apogee. The Dies Irae and the Stabat Mater were both written during the Thirteenth Century, and the most precious Latin hymns of all times were composed during the century and a half from 1150 to 1300. Aquinas's hymns do not fail to challenge comparison even with the greatest of these. While he had an eminently devotional subject, it must not be forgotten that certain supremely difficult theological problems were involved in the expression of devotion to the Blessed Sacrament. In spite of the difficulties, Thomas succeeded in making not only good theology but great poetry. A portion of one of his hymns, the Tantum Ergo, has been perhaps more used in church services than any other, with the possible exception of the Dies Irae. Another one of his beautiful hymns that especially deserves to be admired, is less well known and so I have ventured to quote three selected stanzas of it, as an illustration

of Thomas's command over rhyme and rhythm in the Latin
tongue.

> Adoro te devote, latens Deitas,*
> Quae sub his figuris vere latitas.
> Tibi se cor meum totum subjicit,
> Quia te contemplans totum deficit.

> Visus, tactus, gustus, in te fallitur,
> Sed auditu solo tute creditur:
> Credo quidquid dixit Dei filius
> Nihil veritatis verbo verius.

And the less musical but wonderfully significative fourth
stanza—

> Plagas sicut Thomas non intueor,
> Deum tamen meum te confiteor,
> Fac me tibi semper magis credere,
> In te spem habere, te diligere.

Only the ardent study of many years will give anything like
an adequate idea of the great schoolman's universal genius.
I am content if I have conveyed a few hints that will help to
a beginning of an acquaintance with one of the half dozen
supreme minds of our race.

* The following translation made by Justice O'Hagan renders sense
and sound into English as adequately perhaps as is possible:

> Hidden God, devoutly I adore thee,
>   Truly present underneath these veils:
> All my heart subdues itself before thee,
>   Since it all before thee faints and fails.

> Not to sight, or taste, or touch be credit,
>   Hearing only do we trust secure;
> I believe, for God the Son hath said it—
>   Word of truth that ever shall endure.

. . . . .

> Though I look not on thy wounds with Thomas,
>   Thee, my Lord, and thee, my God, I call:
> Make me more and more believe thy promise,
>   Hope in thee, and love thee over all.

XVIII

ST. LOUIS THE MONARCH.

If large numbers of men are to be ruled by one of their number, as seems more or less inevitable in the ordinary course of things, then, without doubt, the best model of what such a monarch's life should be, is to be found in that of Louis IX., who for nearly half a century was the ruler of France during our period. Of all the rulers of men of whom we have record in history he probably took his duties most seriously, with most regard for others, and least for himself and for his family. There is not a single relation of life in which he is not distinguished and in which his career is not worth studying, as an example of what can be done by a simple, earnest, self-forgetful man, to make life better and happier for all those who come in contact with him.

His relations with his mother are those of an affectionate son in whom indeed, from his easy compliance with her wishes in his younger years one might suspect some weakness, but whose strength of character is displayed at every turn once he himself assumed the reins of government. After many years of ruling however, when his departure on the Crusade compelled him to be absent from the kingdom it was to her he turned again to act as his representative and the wisdom of the choice no one can question. As a husband Louis' life was a model, and though he could not accomplish the impossible, and was not able to keep the relations of his mother and his wife as cordial as he would have liked them to be, judging from human experience generally it is hard to think this constitutes any serious blot on his fair name. As a father, few men have ever thought less of material advantages for their children, or more of the necessity for having them realize that happiness in life does not consist in the possession of many things, but rather in the accomplishment of duty and in the recognition of the fact that the giving of happiness to others constitutes the best source of felicity for one's self. His letters and instructions to his children, as preserved for us by Joinville and other contemporaries, give us perhaps the most taking picture of the man that we have, and round out a personality, which, while it has in the telling French phrase "the defects of its virtues," is surely one of the most beautiful characters that has ever been seen upon earth, in a man who took an active and extremely important part in the great events of the world of his time.

The salient points of his character are his devotion to the three great needs of humanity as they present themselves in his time. He made it the aim of his life that men should have justice, and education, and when for any misfortune they needed it,—charity; and every portion of his career is taken up with successful achievement in these great departments of social action. It is well known that when he became conscious that the judges sometimes abused their power and gave sentences for partial reasons, the monarch himself took up the onerous duty of hearing appeals and succeeded in making the judges of his kingdom realize, that only the strictest justice would save them from the king's displeasure, and condign punishment. For an unjust judge there was short shrift. The old tree at Versailles, under which he used to hear the causes of the poor who appealed to him, stood for many centuries as a reminder of Louis' precious effort to make the dispensing of justice equal to all men. When the duty of hearing appeals took up too much of his time it was transferred to worthy shoulders, and so the important phase of jurisprudence in France relating to appeals, came to be thoroughly established as a part of the organic law of the kingdom.

As regards education, too much can not be said of Louis' influence. It is to him more than to anybody else that the University of Paris owes the success it achieved as a great institution of learning at the end of the Thirteenth Century. Had the monarch been opposed to the spread of education with any idea that it might possibly undermine his authority, had he even been indifferent to it, Paris would not have come to be the educational center of the world. As it was, Louis not only encouraged it in every way, but also acted as the patron of great

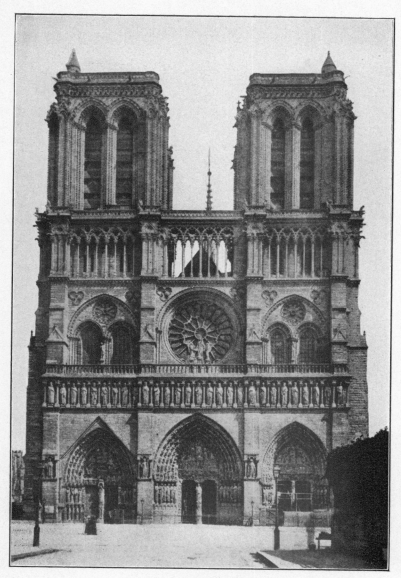

NOTRE DAME (PARIS)

subsidiary institutions which were to add to its prestige and enhance its facilities. Among the most noteworthy is the Sorbonne. La Sainte Chapelle deserves to be mentioned, however, and the library attached to it, which owed its foundation and development to Louis, were important factors in attracting students to Paris and in furnishing them interestingly suggestive material for thought and the development of taste during their residence there. His patronage of Vincent of Beauvais, the encyclopedist, was but a further manifestation of his interest in everything educational. His benefactions to the Hotel Dieu must be considered rather under the head of charity, and yet they also serve to represent his encouragement of medical education and of the proper care for the poor in educated hands.

Voltaire, to whom Louis' character as a supreme believer in revealed religion must have been so utterly unsympathetic, and whose position as the historical symbol of all that Voltaire most held in antipathy in medievalism, might have been expected to make the French philosopher avoid mention of him since he could not condemn, has been forced into some striking utterances in praise of Louis, one of which we quote:

"Louis IX appeared to be a prince destined to reform Europe, if she could have been reformed, to render France triumphant and civilized, and to be in all things a pattern for men. His piety which was that of an anchorite, did not deprive him of any kingly virtue. A wise economy took nothing from his liberality. A profound policy was combined with strict justice and he is perhaps the only sovereign who is entitled to this praise; prudent and firm in counsel, intrepid without rashness in his wars, he was as compassionate as if he had always been unhappy. No man could have carried virtue further."

Guizot, the French statesman and historian, whose unbending Calvinism made the men and institutions of the Middle Ages almost incomprehensible to him from their Catholic aspects, has much of good to say of Louis, though there is not wanting rather definite evidence of the reluctance of his admiration:

"The world has seen more profound politicians on the throne, greater generals, men of more mighty and brilliant intellect, princes who have exercised a more powerful influence over later generations and events subsequent to their own times; but it has never seen such a king as this St. Louis, never seen a man possessing sovereign power and yet not contracting the vices and passions which attend it, displaying upon the throne in such a high degree every human virtue purified and ennobled by Christian faith. St. Louis did not give any new or personal impulse to his age; he did not strongly influence the nature or the development of civilization in France; whilst he endeavored to reform the gravest abuses of the feudal system by the introduction of justice and public order, he did not endeavor to abolish it either by the substitution of a pure monarchy, or by setting class against class in order to raise the royal authority high above all. He was neither an egotist nor a scheming diplomatist; he was, in all sincerity, in harmony with his age and sympathetic alike with the faith, the institutions, the customs, and the tastes of France in the Thirteenth Century. And yet, both in the Thirteenth Century and in later times St. Louis stands apart as a man of profoundly original character, an isolated figure without any peer among his contemporaries or his successors. As far as it was possible in the Middle Ages, he was an ideal man, king, and Christian."

Guizot goes even further than this when he says, "It is reported that in the Seventeenth Century, during the brilliant reign of Louis XIV., Montecuculli, on learning of the death of his illustrious rival, Turenne, said to his officers, 'A man has died to-day who did honor to mankind.' St. Louis did honor to France, to royalty, to humanity, and to Christianity. This was the feeling of his contemporaries, and after six centuries it is still confirmed by the judgment of the historian."

Of Louis' wonderful influence for good as a ruler all historians are agreed in talking in the highest terms. His private life however, is even more admirable for our purpose of bringing out the greatness of the Thirteenth Century. Of course many legends and myths have gathered around his name, but still enough remains of absolutely trustworthy tradition and even documentary evidence, to make it very clear that he was a man among men, a nobleman of nature's making, who in any position of life would have acquitted himself with a perfection sure to make his life worthy of admiration. One of the most striking traits of his character is his love of justice, his insatiable desire to render to all men what was rightly theirs. A biographer has told the story that gives the most telling proof of this in relating the solicitude with which he tried to right all the wrongs not only of his own reign, but of those of his predecessors, before he set out on the Crusade. He wished to have the absolute satisfaction that he, nor his, owed any man any reparation, as the most precious treasure he could take with him on his perilous expedition. He wished even to undo any wrongs that might have been done in his name though he was entirely unconscious of them.

"As he wished to be in a state of grace at the moment of departure, and to take with him to the Holy Land a quiet conscience by leaving the kingdom in as happy a condition as possible, he resolved to carry out one of the noblest measures ever undertaken by a king. By his order, inquisitors were sent into all the provinces annexed to the royal dominion since the accession of Philip Augustus. All those who had been maltreated or despoiled by the bailiffs, seneschals, provosts, sergeants, and other representatives of the royal authority, came to declare their wrongs to these newly appointed judges, and to demand the reparation which was due to them; the number was great, since for forty years there had been much suffering in the country districts and even in the towns....The royal officers had too often acted as if they were in a conquered country; they believed themselves to be safe from observation, so that they might do as they pleased. The people had much to endure during these forty years, and it was a noble idea to make reparation freely and with elaborate care. No prince had been known, of his own accord and at his own cost, to redress the wrongs inflicted on the people during the reigns of his father and grandfather. This made an immense impression, which lasted for centuries. Blanche's son was not merely a good king, he became the unrivalled sovereign, the impeccable judge, the friend and consoler of his subjects."

It is no wonder that so inappeasable a lover of justice should commend that virtue above all others to his son. When we read his letters to that son who was to be his successor, in the light of Louis' own career, we appreciate with what utter

sincerity they were written. Louis realized that simple justice between men would undo more of the world's wrongs than
most of the vaunted cures for social ills, which are only too
often the result of injustice.

"Dear son," he writes in his Instruction, "if you come to
reign, do that which befits a king, that is, be so just as to devi-
ate in nothing from justice, whatever may befall you. If a poor
man goes to law with one who is rich, support the poor rather
than the rich man until you know the truth, and when the truth
is known, do that which is just. And if it happen that any man
has a dispute with yourself, maintain the cause of your adversary before the council so as not to appear partial to your own
cause, until the truth is known. Unless you do this, those who
are of the council may fear to speak against you, and this
ought not to be. . . . And if you find that you possess anything
unjustly acquired, either in your time or in that of your predecessors, make restitution at once, however great its value,
either in land, money, or any other thing. . . . If the matter is
doubtful and you cannot find out the truth, follow the advice
of trusty men, and make such an agreement as may fully deliver your soul and that of your predecessors. If you hear
that your predecessors have made restitution of anything, take
great trouble to discover if anything more should be restored,
and if you find that this is the case, restore it at once so as to
deliver your own soul and that of your predecessors."

"The education of his children, their future position and
well-being, engrossed the attention of the King as entirely,
and were subjects of as keen an interest, as if he had been a
father with no other task than the care of his children. After
supper they followed him to his apartment, where he made
them sit around him for a time whilst he instructed them in
their duty; he then sent them to bed. He would direct their
attention particularly to the good and bad actions of Princes
He used to visit them in their own apartment when he had
any leisure, inquire as to their progress, and like a second
Tobias, give them excellent instruction. . . . On Maundy Thursday, he and his children used to wash the feet of a dozen poor
persons, give them large alms, and afterward wait upon them
whilst they dined. The King together with his son-in-law

LA SAINTE CHAPELLE (PARIS)

CATHEDRAL (ORVIETO)

King Thibault, whom he loved and looked upon as his own son, carried the first poor man to the hospital of Compeigne, and his two oldest sons, Louis and Philippe, carried the second. They were accustomed to act with him in all things, showing him great reverence, and he desired that they and Thibault should also obey him implicitly in everything that he commanded."

Anyone who still retains any trace of the old-fashioned notion, which used to be unfortunately a commonplace among English speaking people, that the medieval Monks were unworthy of their great calling, and that the monasteries were the homes of lazy, fat-witted men whose only object in taking up the life was to secure an easy means of livelihood, will be thoroughly undeceived, if he but read with some attention the stories of Louis' relations to the monasteries. In all his journeys he stopped in them, he always asked to see their libraries, he insisted on not being treated better than the community and in every way he tried to show his esteem for them. There is a story which may or may not be true in the "Little Flowers of St. Francis," which comes from almost a contemporary source, however, that once on his travels he called on Brother Giles, the famous simple-minded companion of St. Francis, of whom so many delightfully humorous stories are told. Brother Giles received his affectionate greeting but said never a word in return. After the first words the King himself said nothing, but both sat and communed in silence for some time, and then the King departed apparently well-pleased with his visit. Needless to say when Brother Giles told the story of the King of France having called on him there was a commotion in the community. But by this time the King was far distant on his way.

Indeed Louis took so many opportunities to stop in monasteries and follow monastic regulations as to prayer and the taking of meals while there, that he quite disgusted some of the members of his retinue who were most with him. One of the ladies of the court in her impatience at him for this, is once said to have remarked under such indiscreet circumstances that it was reported to Louis, that she wished they had a man and not a monk for King. Louis is said to have asked her very gently if she would prefer that he spend most of his time in sport and in excesses of various kinds. Even such remarks, however, had no effect in turning him from his purpose to live as simply and as beneficently for others as possible. His genuine appreciation of the monks must be recognized from his wishes with regard to his children. On the other hand his readiness to secure their happiness as far as possible in the way they wished for themselves shows the tenderness of his fatherly heart. A modern biographer has said of him:—

"He was very anxious that his three children born in the East during the Crusade—Jean Tristan, Pierre, and Blanche— and even his eldest daughter Isabella, should enter the monastic life, which he looked upon as the most likely to insure their salvation; he frequently exhorted them to take this step, writing letters of the greatest tenderness and piety, especially to his daughter Isabella; but, as they did not show any taste for it, he did not attempt to force their inclinations. Thenceforth, he busied himself in making suitable marriages for them, and establishing them according to their rank; at the same time he gave them the most judicious advice as to their conduct and actions in the world upon which they were entering. When he was before Tunis and found that he was sick unto death, he gave the instructions which he had written out in French with his own hand to his eldest son, Philip. They are models of virtue, wisdom and paternal tenderness, worthy of a King and a Christian."

Perhaps the most interesting feature of St. Louis' life was his treatment of the poor. He used literally to recall the fact that they must stand to him in the place of God. "Whatever you do to the least of these you do even unto me" was a favorite expression frequently in his mouth. He waited on them personally and no matter how revolting their appearance would not be deterred from this personal service. It is easy to understand that his courtiers did not sympathize with this state of mind, though Louis used to encourage them not only by his example but by personal persuasion. Every Holy Thursday he used to wash the feet of twelve poor people at a public ceremonial, in honor of the washing of the feet of the Apostles by Christ. It must not be thought moreover, that such a pro-

APOSTLE (LA STE. CHAPELLE, PARIS)

ceeding was perhaps less repugnant to the feelings of the men of that time than they are to the present generation. It might be considered that the general paucity of means for maintaining personal cleanliness in medieval times would make the procedure less disgusting. As a proof of the contrary of this we have the words of Joinville who tells of the following conversation :—

"Many a time," says Joinville, "I have seen him cut their bread for them, and pour out their drink. One day he asked me if I washed the feet of the poor on Maundy Thursday. "Sire," I answered, "What, the feet of those dirty wretches! No indeed, I shall never wash them." "Truly," replied the King, "you have spoken ill, for you ought not to despise that which God intended for your instruction. I pray you, therefore, first of all for the love of God, and then by your love towards me, that you make a habit of washing their feet."

Even more striking than this however, was his attitude toward the lepers of the time. These poor creatures were compelled to live apart from the population and were not allowed to approach healthy individuals. They were of exceeding interest to Louis however, who took every opportunity to mitigate the trials and hardships of their existence. Whenever he met them on his journeys he insisted on abundant alms being given them, and gave orders that every possible provision for their welfare, consonant with the care that their affection should not be permitted to spread, be made for them. Over and over again he greeted them as his brothers and when his retinue feared to approach them, would himself go to them, in order to console them by his words and his exhibition of personal interest. There is an incident told of his having on one occasion, when a muddy stream intervened between him and some lepers, forded the stream alone in order to get to them, and neither any personal fear of contagion nor any natural repugnance was permitted to deter him from this sublime work of charity. It is no wonder that his people proclaimed him a saint, that is "one who thinks first of others and only second of himself," even during his lifetime.

The only supposed blot upon Louis' character is the denunciation by certain modern writers of what they call the fanaticism, which prompted him to go on the Crusades instead of remaining at home properly to care for his people. The opinion with regard to the place that must be assigned to the Crusades as a factor in history and national as well as European development, has changed very much in recent years. Formerly it was the custom almost entirely to condemn them and to look upon them as a serious mistake. Such ideas however, are only entertained by those who do not realize the conditions under which they were undertaken or the important results which flowed from them. Bishop Stubbs in his lectures on Medieval and Modern History, delivered while he was professor of History at Oxford, has been at some pains to correct this false notion, and his passage constitutes one of the best apologies for Louis' interest in the Crusades which could be written. He said :— ·

"The Crusades are not, in my mind, either the popular delusions that our cheap literature has determined them to be, nor papal conspiracies against kings and peoples, as they appear to Protestant controversialists; nor the savage outbreak of expiring barbarism, thirsting for blood and plunder, nor volcanic explosions of religious intolerance. I believe them to have been in their deep sources, and in the minds of their best champions, and in the main tendency of their results, capable of ample justification. They were the first great effort of medieval life to go beyond the pursuit of selfish and isolated ambitions; they were the trial-feat of the young world, essaying to use, to the glory of God and the benefit of man, the arms of its new knighthood. That they failed in their direct object is only what may be alleged against almost every great design which the great disposer of events has moulded to help the world's progress; for the world has grown wise from the experience of failure, rather than by the winning of high aims. That the good they did was largely leavened with evil may be said of every war that has ever been waged; that bad men rose by them while good men fell, is and must be true, wherever and whenever the race is to the swift and the battle to the strong. But that in the end they were a benefit to the world no one who reads can doubt; and that in their course they brought out a love for all that is heroic in human nature, the love of freedom, the honor of prowess, sympathy with sorrow, perseverance to the last, the chronicles of the age abundantly prove; proving, moreover, that it was by the experience of these times that the forms of those virtues were realized and presented to posterity."*

With the stigma of supposed imprudence or foolhardiness for having gone on the Crusade turned into a new cause for honor, Louis must be considered as probably the greatest monarch who ever occupied an important throne. Instead of being surprised that such a monarch should have come in the heart of the Middle Ages and during a century so distant as the Thirteenth, readers must now be ready to appreciate to some degree at least the fact, that his environment instead of being a hindrance in any sense of the word to the development of Louis' greatness, should rather be considered as one of the principal sources of it. Louis' character was representative of the men of that time and exhibits in their most striking form the qualities that were set up as ideals in that period. If the century had produced nothing else but Louis, it would have to be considered as a great epoch in history, for he was no mere accident but typically a son of his age. If this is but properly appreciated the true significance not only of Louis' life but the period in which he lived will be better understood than would be possible by any other means. Those who want to know the men of this wonderful century as they actually were should study Louis' life in detail, for we have been only able to hint at its most striking characteristics.

* Stubbs, "Seventeen Lectures on Medieval and Modern History," p. 180.

DECORATION THIRTEENTH CENTURY MS.

XIX

DANTE THE POET.

It is only too often the custom to talk of Dante as a solitary phenomenon in his time. Even Carlyle who knew well and properly appreciated many things in medieval life and letters and especially in the literary productions of the Thirteenth Century said, that in Dante "ten silent centuries found a voice." Anyone who has followed what we have had to say with regard to the Thirteenth Century will no longer think of Dante as standing alone, but will readily appreciate that he is only the fitting culmination of a great literary era. After having gone over even as hurriedly as has been necessary in our brief space, what was accomplished in every country of Europe in literature that was destined to live not only because of the greatness of the thoughts, but also for the ultimateness of its expression, we should expect some surpassing literary genius at the end of the period. It seems almost inevitable indeed that a supreme poet, whose name stands above all others but one or two at the most in the whole history of the race, should have lived in the Thirteenth Century, and should have summed up effectually in himself all the greatness of the century and enshrined its thoughts in undying verse for all future generations.

When Dante himself dares to place his name with those of the men whom he considered the five greatest poets of all time, it seems sublimest egotism. At first thought many will at once conclude that his reason for so doing was, that in the unlettered times his critical faculty was not well developed and as he knew that his work far surpassed that of his contemporaries, he could scarcely help but conclude that his place must be among the great poets. Any such thought however, is entirely due to lack of knowledge of the conditions of Dante's life and education. He had been in the universities of Italy, and in his exile had visited Paris and probably also Oxford. He knew the poets of his country well. He appreciated them

DANTE (GIOTTO)

highly. It was the consciousness of genius that made him place himself so high and not any faulty comparison with others. Succeeding generations have set him even higher than the place chosen by himself and now we breathe his name only with those of Homer and Shakespeare, considering that these three sublime immortals are so far above all other poets that there is scarcely a second to them.

Dante is the most universal of poets. He has won recognition from all nations, and he has been the favorite reading of the most diverse times and conditions of men. From the very beginning he has been appreciated, and even before his death men had begun to realize something of the supremacy of his greatness. Commentaries on his works that have been preserved down to our own day were written almost during his lifetime. Only supreme interest could have tempted men to multiply these by the hard labor of patient handwriting. Petrarch who as a young man, was his contemporary, recognized him as the Prince of Italian poets who had composed in their common tongue, and even was tempted to say that the subtle and profound conceptions of the Commedia could not have been written without the special gift of the Holy Ghost. Boccaccio was wont to speak of him as the Divine Poet, and tells us that he had learned that Petrarch deliberately held aloof from the Commedia, through fear of losing his originality if he came under the spell of so great a master.

Very few realize how great a poet Dante must be considered even if only the effusions of his younger years were to be taken as the standard of his poetical ability. Some of his sonnets are as beautiful of their kind as are to be found in this form of poetry. His description of his lady-love is famous among sonnets of lovers and may only be compared with some of the Sonnets from the Portuguese in our own day, or with one or two of Camoens' original sonnets in the Portuguese. for lofty praise of the beloved in worthy numbers. After reading Dante's sonnets it is easy to understand how a half century later Petrarch was able to raise the sonnet form to an excellence that was never to be surpassed. With a beginning like this it is no wonder that the sonnet became so popular in Europe during the next three centuries, and that every young poet, down to Shakespeare's time, had an attack of sonneteering just as he might have had an attack of the measles. The first one of a pair of sonnets that are considered supreme in their class deserves a place here as an example of Dante's poetic faculty in this form, for which he is so much less known than he ought to be.

He sees completely fullest bliss abound
   Who among ladies sees my Lady's face;
Those that with her do go are surely bound
   To give God thanks for such exceeding grace.
And in her beauty such strange might is found,
   That envy finds in other hearts no place;
So she makes them walk with her, clothed all round
   With love and faith and courteous gentleness.
The sight of her makes all things lowly be;
   Nor of herself alone she gives delight,
But each through her receiveth honor due.
   And in her acts is such great courtesy,
That none can recollect that wondrous sight,
   Who sighs not for it in Love's sweetness true.

It will be noted that Dante has nothing to say of the personal appearance of his beloved. This is true, however, of the whole series of poems to and about her. He never seems to have thought for a moment of her physical qualities. What he finds worthy to praise is her goodness which shines out from her features so that everyone rejoices in it, while a sweetness fills the heart as if a heavenly visitor had come. For him her supreme quality is that, with all her beauty, envy finds no place in others' hearts because she is so clothed around with love and faith and courteous gentleness. It has often been said that Shakespeare did not describe the physical appearances of his heroines because he realized that this meant very little, but then Shakespeare had to write for the stage and realized that blondes and brunettes, especially in the olden time, could not be made to order and that it was better to leave the heroine's physical appearance rather vague. It would be expected, however, that Dante, with his Southern temperament, would have dwelt on the physical perfections of his fair. The next sonnet, however, of the best known group emphasizes his abstraction of all physical influence in the matter and insists on her goodness and the womanly beauty of her character. It will be found in our chapter on Women of the Century.

In his earlier years Dante considered himself one of the Troubadours, and there can be no doubt that if he had never written the Divine Comedy, he still would have been remembered as one of the great poets who wrote of love in this Thirteenth Century. Not only does he deserve a place among the greatest of the Minnesingers, the Trouvères, and the Troubadours, but he is perhaps the greatest of them. That he should have sung as he did at the end of the century only shows that he was in the stream of literary evolution and not being merely carried idly along, but helping to guide it into ever fairer channels. Dante's minor poems would have made enduring fame for any poet of less genius than himself. His prose works deserve to be read by anyone who wishes to know the character of this greatest of poets, and also to appreciate what the educational environment of the Thirteenth Century succeeded in making out of good intellectual material when presented to it. Dante's works are the real treasury of information of the most precious kind with regard to the century, since they provide the proper standpoint from which to view all that it accomplished.

While Dante was a supreme singer among the poets of a great song time, it was only natural, in the light of what we know about the literary product of the rest of this century, that he should have put into epic form the supreme product of his genius. With the great national epics in every country of Europe—the Cid, the Arthur Legends, and the Nibelungen, at the beginning of this century, and the epical poems of the Meistersingers during its first half, it is not surprising, but on the contrary rather what might have been confidently looked for, that there should have arisen a great national epic in Italy before the end of the century. The Gothic art movement spread through all these countries, and so did the wind of the spirit of esthetic accomplishment which blew the flame of national literature in each country into a mighty blaze, that not only was never to be extinguished, but was to be a beacon light in the realm of national literatures forever after.

We have already said a word of the well-known contemporary admiration for the poet but it should be realized that due appreciation of Dante continued in Italy during all the time when Italian art and literature was at its highest. It dwindled only at periods of decadence and lack of taste. Cornelius' law with regard to Dante's influence on art is very well known. Italian art according to him, has been strong and vigorous just in proportion as it has worked under Dante's influence, while it became weak and sensuous as that influence declined. This has held true from the very beginning and has been as true for literature as for art. When the Italians became interested in trivialities and gave themselves up to weak imitations of the classics, or to pastoral poetry that was not a real expression of feeling but a passing fancy of literary folk, then Dante was for a time in obscurity. Even at the height of the Renaissance, however, when Greek was at the acme of its interest and the classics occupied so much attention that Dante might be expected to be eclipsed, the great thinkers and critics of the time still worshipped at the shrine of their great master of Italian verse. The best proof of this is to be found in Michael Angelo's famous sonnets in praise of Dante, the second of which would seem to exhaust all that can be said in praise of a brother poet.

Into the dark abyss he made his way;
  Both nether worlds he saw, and in the might
  Of his great soul beheld God's splendour bright,
And gave to us on earth true light of day:
Star of supremest worth with its clear ray,
  Heaven's secrets he revealed to us through our dim sight,
  And had for guerdon what the base world's spite
Oft gives to souls that noblest grace display,
Full ill was Dante's life-work understood,
  His purpose high, by that ungrateful state,
That welcomed all with kindness but the good.
  Would I were such, to bear like evil fate,
To taste his exile, share his lofty mood.
  For this I'd gladly give all earth calls great.

In the first of this pair of sonnets, however, Michael Angelo gave if possible even higher praise than this. It will be recalled that he himself, besides being the greatest of sculptors and one of the greatest of painters and architects in a wonderfully productive period, was also a very great poet. These sonnets to Dante, the one to his crucifix, and one to Vittoria Colonna, are the best proof of this. He knew how to chisel thoughts into wonderfully suitable words quite as well as marble into the beautiful forms that grew under his hands. With all his greatness, and he must have been conscious of it, he thinks that he would be perfectly willing to give up all that earth calls great, simply to share Dante's lofty mood even in his exile. No greater tribute has ever been paid by one poet to another than this, and Michael Angelo's genius was above all critical, never thoughtlessly laudatory. As emphasizing the highest enlightened taste of a great epoch this has seemed to deserve a place here also.

> What should be said of him speech may not tell;
>   His splendor is too great for men's dim sight;
>   And easier 'twere to blame his foes aright
> Than for his poorest gifts to praise him well.
> He tracked the path that leads to depths of Hell
>   To teach us wisdom, scaled the eternal height,
>   And heaven with open gates did him invite,
> Who in his own loved city might not dwell.
> Ungrateful country step-dame of his fate,
>   To her own loss: full proof we have in this
> That souls most perfect bear the greatest woe.
> Of thousand things suffice in this to state:
>   No exile ever was unjust as his,
> Nor did the world his equal ever know.

In England, in spite of distance of country, race and language, the appreciation of Dante began very early. Readers of Chaucer know the great Italian as the favorite poet of the Father of English poetry, and over and over again he has expressed the feeling of how much greater than anything he could hope to do was Dante's accomplishment. Readers will remember how Chaucer feels unable to tell the story of

Ugolino and his starving sons in the Hunger Tower, and refers those interested in the conclusion of the tale to Dante. After the religious revolt of the early Sixteenth Century Dante was lost sight of to a great extent. His temper was too Catholic to be appreciated by Puritan England, and the Elizabethans were too much occupied with their own creation of a great national literature, to have any time for appreciation of a foreigner so different in spirit from their times. With the coming of the Oxford Movement, however, Dante at once sprang into favor, and a number of important critical appreciations of him reintroduced him to a wide reading public in England, most of whom were among the most cultured of the island. This renewed interest in Dante gave rise to some of the best critical appreciations in any language. Dean Church's famous essay is the classic English monograph on Dante, and its opening paragraph sounds the keynote of critical opinion among English speaking people.

"The Divina Commedia is one of the landmarks of history. More than a magnificent poem, more than the beginning of a language and the opening of a national literature, more than the inspirer of art and the glory of a great people, it is one of those rare and solemn monuments of the mind's power which measure and test what it can reach to, which rise up ineffaceably and forever as time goes on, marking out its advance by grander divisions than its centuries, and adopted as epochs by the consent of all who come after. It stands with the Iliad and Shakespeare's Plays, with the writings of Aristotle and Plato, with the Novum Organon and the Principia, with Justinian's Code, with the Parthenon and St. Peter's. It is the first Christian Poem, and it opens European literature as the Iliad did that of Greece and Rome. And, like the Iliad, it has never become out of date; it accompanies in undiminished freshness the literature which it began."

No better introduction to Dante could be obtained than this from Dean Church. Those who have found it difficult to get interested in the great Florentine poet, and who have been prone to think that perhaps the pretended liking for him on the part of many people was an affectation rather than a sincere expression of opinion, should read this essay and learn some-

TORRE DEL FAME (DANTE, PISA)

PALAZZO PRETORIO (TODI)

thing of the wealth of sympathy there is in Dante for even the man of these modern times. Our Thirteenth Century poet is not easy to read but there is probably no reading in all the world that brings with it so much of intellectual satisfaction, so much of awakening of the best feelings in man, so many glimpses into the depths of his being, as some lines from Dante pondered under favorable circumstances. Like one of these Gothic cathedrals of the olden times he never grows old, but, on the contrary, every favorite passage seems to have a new message for each mood of the reader. This is particularly true for the spiritual side of man's being as has been pointed out by Dean Church in a well-known passage toward the end of his essay.

"Those who know the Divina Commedia best will best know how hard it is to be the interpreter of such a mind; but they will sympathize with the wish to call attention to it. They know, and would wish others also to know, not by hearsay, but by experience, the power of that wonderful poem. They know its austere yet submitting beauty; they know what force there is in its free and earnest and solemn verse to strengthen, to tranquillize, to console. It is a small thing that it has the secret of Nature and Man; that a few keen words have opened their eyes to new sights in earth, and sea, and sky; have taught them new mysteries of sound; have made them recognize, in distinct image of thought, fugitive feelings, or their unheeded expression, by look, or gesture, or motion; that it has enriched the public and collective memory of society with new instances, never to be lost, of human feeling and fortune; has charmed mind and ear by the music of its stately march, and the variety and completeness of its plan. But besides this, they know how often its seriousness has put to shame their trifling, its magnanimity their faint-heartedness, its living energy their indolence, its stern and sad grandeur rebuked low thoughts, its thrilling tenderness overcome sullenness and assuaged distress, its strong faith quelled despair, and soothed perplexity, its vast grasp imparted the sense of harmony to the view of clashing truth. They know how often they have found in times of trouble, if not light, at least that deep sense of reality, permanent though unseen, which is more than light can always give—in the view which it has suggested to them of the judgments and love of God."

As might have been expected from the fact of Dante's English popularity paralleling the Oxford Movement, both the great English Cardinals who were such prominent agents in that movement, looked upon him as a favorite author. Both of them have given him precious tributes. Newman's lofty compliment was the flattery of imitation when he wrote the Dream of Gerontius, that poem for poets which has told the men of our generation more about the immediate hereafter than anything written in these latter centuries. No poet of the intervening period, or of any other time, has so satisfactorily presented the after world as these writers so distant in time, so different in environment,—the one an Italian of the Thirteenth, the other an Englishman of the Nineteenth Century.

Cardinal Manning's tribute was much more formal though not less glorious. It occurs in the introduction to Father Bowden's English edition of the German critic Hettinger's appreciation of Dante, and deserves a place here because it shows how much a representative modern churchman thinks of the great Florentine poet.

"There are three works which always seem to me to form a triad of Dogma, of Poetry, and of Devotion,—The Summa of St. Thomas, The Divina Commedia, and the *Paradisus Animae* (a manual of devotional exercises by Horstius). All three contain the same outline of Faith. St. Thomas traces it on the intellect, Dante upon the imagination, and the *Paradisus Animae* upon the heart. The poem unites the book of Dogma and the book of Devotion, clothed in conceptions of intensity and of beauty which have never been surpassed nor equalled. No uninspired hand has ever written thoughts so high in words, so resplendent as the last stanza of the Divina Commedia. It was said of St. Thomas, '*Post Summan Thomae nihil restat nisi lumen gloriae*'—After the Summa of Thomas nothing is left except the light of glory. It may be said of Dante, '*Post Dantis Paradisum nihil restat nisi visio Dei,*'—After Dante's Paradise nothing is left except the vision of God."

Of course John Ruskin had a thorough-going admiration for so great a spiritual thinker as Dante and expressed it in no

uncertain terms. With his wonderful power to point out the
significance of unexpected manifestations of human genius,
Ruskin has even succeeded in minimizing one of the great objections urged against Dante, better perhaps than could be done
by anyone else, for English speaking people at least. For many
readers Dante is almost unbearable, because of certain grotesque elements they find in him. This has been the source
and cause of more unfavorable criticism than anything else in
the great Florentine's writings. Ruskin of course saw it but
appreciated it at its proper significance, and has made clear in
a passage that every Dante reader needs to go over occasionally, in order to assure himself that certain unusual things in
Dante's attitude toward life are an expression rather of the
highest human genius and its outlook on life, than some narrow limitation of medievalism. Ruskin said:—

"I believe that there is no test of greatness in nations, periods,
nor men more sure than the development, among them
or in them, of a noble grotesque, and no test of comparative
smallness or limitation, of one kind or another, more sure
than the absence of grotesque invention or incapability of
understanding it. I think that the central man of all the world,
as representing in perfect balance the imaginative, moral and
intellectual faculties, all at their highest is Dante; and in him
the grotesque reaches at once the most distinct and the most
noble development to which it was ever brought in the human
mind. Of the grotesqueness in our own Shakespeare I need
hardly speak, nor of its intolerableness to his French critics;
nor of that of Æschylus and Homer, as opposed to the lower
Greek writers; and so I believe it will be found, at all periods,
in all minds of the first order."

Great reverence for Dante might have been expected in Italy
but the colder Northern nations shared it.

In Germany modern admiration for Dante began with that
great wave of critical appreciation which entered into German
literature with the end of the Eighteenth and the beginning of
the Nineteenth Century. As might almost have been expected.
Frederick Schlegel was one of the first modern German admirers of Dante, though his brother August, whose translations
of Shakespeare began that series of German studies of Shakes-

peare which has been so fruitful during the past century, was also an open admirer of the medieval poet. Since then there has practically been no time when Germany has not had some distinguished Dante scholar, and when it has not been supplying the world with the products of profound study and deep scholarship with regard to him. The modern educational world has come to look so confidently toward Germany for the note of its critical appreciation, that the Dante devotion of the Germans will be the best possible encouragement for those who need to have the feeling, that their own liking is shared by good authorities, before they are quite satisfied with their appreciation. Dean Plumptre has summed up the Dante movement in Germany in a compendious paragraph that must find a place here.

"In the year 1824, Scartazzini, the great Dante scholar of the Nineteenth Century, recognizes a new starting point. The period of neglect of supercilious criticism comes to an end, and one of reverence, admiration and exhaustive study begins. His account of the labors of German scholars during the sixty years that have followed fills a large part of his volume. Translations of the Commedia by Kopisch, Kannegiesser, Witte, Philalethes (the nom de plume of John, King of Saxony), Josefa Von Hoffinger, of the Minor Poems by Witte and Krafft, endless volumes and articles on all points connected with Dante's life and character, the publications of the Deutsche Dante-Gesellschaft from 1867 to 1877, present a body of literature which has scarcely a parallel in history. It is no exaggeration to say that the Germans have taught Italians to understand and appreciate their own poet, just as they have at least helped to teach Englishmen to understand Shakespeare."

Nor must it be thought that only the literary lights of Germany thoroughly appreciated the great Florentine. The greater the genius of the man the more his admiration for Dante if he but once becomes interested in him. A noteworthy example of this is Alexander Von Humboldt the distinguished German scientist, who was generally looked upon as perhaps the greatest thinker in European science during the first quarter of the Nineteenth Century. He is said to have been very faithful in his study of Dante and has expressed his admiration in no

uncertain terms. Curiously enough he found much to admire
him for in matters scientific, for while it is not generally realized, Dante was an acute observer of Nature and has given expression in his works to many observations with regard to subjects that would now be considered within the scope of natural science, in a way to anticipate many supposedly modern
bits of information. With regard to this Humboldt said in his
Cosmos:—

"When the glory of the Aramaic Greek and Roman dominion—or I might almost say, when the ancient world had passed
away,—we find in the great and inspired founder of a new era,
Dante Alighieri, occasional manifestations of the deepest sensi-
bility to the charms of the terrestrial life of Nature, whenever
he abstracts himself from the passionate and subjective control
of that despondent mysticism which constituted the general circle of his ideas." How little Humboldt seems to have realized
in his own absorption in external nature, that the qualities he
blames in Dante are of the very essence of his genius, rounding
out his humanity to an interest in all man's relations, super-
natural as well as natural, and that without them he would not
be the world poet for all time that he is.

In America Dante came to his own almost as soon as literature obtained her proper place in our new country. The first
generation of distinctly literary men comprise the group at
Cambridge including Longfellow, Emerson, Oliver Wendell
Holmes, Charles Eliot Norton, James Russell Lowell, and
others of minor importance. It soon became a favorite occupation among these men to give certain leisure hours to Dante. The
Cambridge Dante society added not a little to the world's
knowledge of the poet. Longfellow's translation and edition
of Dante's works was a monumental achievement, for which
its author is likely to be remembered better by future generations than perhaps for any of his original work. Future generations are likely to remember James Russell Lowell for his
essays on Dante and Shakespeare better than for anything else.
His Dante monograph is as magnificently illuminating as
that of Dean Church's and perhaps even more satisfying to
critical readers. That these men should have been content
to give so much of their time to the study of the Thirteenth

Century poet shows in what appreciation he must be held by the rest of us if we would give him his due place in literature.

There are many misunderstandings with regard to Dante which apparently only some serious study of the poet serves to remove satisfactorily. Most people consider that he was a distant, prophetic, religious genius, and that his poetry has in it very little of sympathy for humanity. While it is generally conceded that he saw man projected on the curtain of eternity, and realized all his relationships to the universe and to his Creator better than perhaps any other poet of all time, it is usually thought that one must have something of the medieval frame of mind in order to read him with interest and admiration. Such impressions are largely the result of reading only a few lines of Dante, and, finding them difficult of thorough comprehension, allowing one's self to be forced to the conclusion that he is not of interest to the modern reader. The Inferno being the first part of Dante's great poem is the one oftenest read in this passing fashion and so many ideas with regard to Dante are derived from this portion, which is not only not the masterpiece of the work, but if taken alone, sadly misrepresents the genius of the poet. His is no morbid sentimentality and does not need the adventitious interest of supreme suffering.

As a matter of fact the Purgatorio is a much better introduction to Dante's real greatness, and is considered by the generality of Dante scholars as the more humanly sympathetic if not really the supreme expression of his creative faculty. The ascent of the Mount of Expiation with its constant note of hope and the gradually increasing facility of the ascent as the summit is approached, touches condolent cords in the human heart and arouses feelings that are close to what is best in human aspiration in spite of its consciousness of defect. Over and over again in the Purgatorio one finds evidence of Dante's wonderful powers of observation. The poet is first of all according to the etymology of the word a creator, one who gives life to the figments of his imagination so that we recognize them as vital manifestations of human genius, but is also the seer, the man who sees deeper into things and sees more of them than anyone else. Ordinarily Dante is considered by those who do not know him as not having been an observer of things human and around him in life. There are passages in his works, however, that entirely refute this.

The story that he went about the cities of North Italy during his exile, with countenance so gloomy and stare so fixed that men pointed to him and spoke of him as one who had visited Hell, and the other tradition, however well it may be founded, that the women sometimes pointed him out to their children and then used the memory of him as a bogy man to scare them into doing unpleasant things afterwards, would seem to indicate that he had occupied himself very little with the things around him, and that above all he had paid very little attention to the ways of childhood. He has shown over and over again, especially in the Purgatorio, that the simplest and most natural actions of child-life had been engraved upon his heart for he uses them with supreme truth in his figures. He knows how

> "An infant seeks his mother's breast
> When fear or anguish vex his troubled heart,"—

but he knows too, how the child who has done wrong, confesses its faults.

> "As little children, dumb with shame's keen smart,
> Will listening stand with eyes upon the ground,
> Owning their faults with penitential heart,
> So then stood I."

There is a passage in the Inferno in which he describes so vividly the rescue of a child from the flames by its mother that Plumptre has even ventured to suggest that Dante himself may have been the actual subject of the rescue. Because it helps to an appreciation of Dante's intensity of expression and poignancy of vision the passage itself, with Plumptre's comment, seems deserving of quotation:

> "Then suddenly my Guide his arms did fling
> Around me, as a mother, roused by cries,
> Sees the fierce flames around her gathering
> And takes her boy, nor ever halts but flies,
> Caring for him than for herself far more,
> Though one scant shift her only robe supplies."

It must not be thought, however, that Dante's quality as an observer was limited to the actions of human beings. His capacity to see many other things is amply manifested in his great poem. Even the smallest of living things, that would surely be thought beneath his notice, became the subject of similies that show how much everything in nature interested the spirit of genius. The passage with regard to the ants has often been quoted, and is indeed a surprising manifestation of nature study at an unexpected time and from an entirely unanticipated quarter. Dante saw the souls of those who were so soon to enter into the realm of blessedness, and who were already in the last circle of purgatory, greeting each other with the kiss of peace and his picturesque simile for it is:—

"So oft, within their dusk brown host, proceed
    This ant and that, till muzzle muzzle meet;
    Spying their way, or how affairs succeed."

As for the birds his pages are full of references to them and all of his bird similies are couched in terms that show how sympathetically observant he was of their habits and ways. He knows their different methods of flying in groups and singly, he has observed them on their nests and knows their wonderful maternal anxiety for their young, and describes it with a vividness that would do credit to a naturalist of the modern time who had made his home in the woods. Indeed some of his figures taken from birds constitute examples of the finest passages of poetic description of living nature that have ever been written. The domestic animals, moreover, especially the cat and the dog, come in for their share of this sympathetic observance, and he is able to add greatly to the vividness of the pictures he paints by his references to the well-known habits of these animals. It is no wonder that the tradition has grown up that he was fond of such pets and possessed several of them that were well-known to the early commentators on his poems, and the subject of no little erudition.

Nothing escaped the attention of this acute observer in the world around him, and over and over again one finds surprising bits of observation with regard to natural phenomena usually supposed to be quite out of the range of the interest of medieval students generally, and above all of literary men of this Middle Age. Alexander Von Humboldt calls attention in a well-known passage in his Cosmos to the wonderful description of the River of Light in the Thirtieth Canto of the Paradiso.

"I saw a glory like a stream flow by,
  In brightness rushing and on either shore
Were banks that with spring's wondrous hues might vie.
  And from that river living sparks did soar,
And sank on all sides in the flow'rets' bloom,
  Like precious rubies set in golden ore.
Then, as if drunk with all the rich perfume,
  Back to the wondrous torrent did they roll,
And as one sank another filled its room."

Humboldt explains this with a suggestion that deserves to be remembered.

"It would almost seem as if this picture had its origin in the poet's recollection of that peculiar and rare phosphorescent condition of the ocean in which luminous points appear to rise from the breaking waves, and, spreading themselves over the surface of the waters, convert the liquid plain into a moving sea of sparkling stars."

Probably the best way for a modern to realize how much of interest there may be for him in Dante is to consider the great Italian epic poet in comparison with our greatest of English epic poets, Milton. While any such comparison in the expressive Latin phrase is sure to walk lame, it serves to give an excellent idea of the methods of the two men in the illustration of their ideas. We venture therefore to quote a comparison between these two poets from a distinguished critic who knows both of them well, and whose modern training in English methods of thought, would seem to make him likely to be partial to the more modern poet though as a matter of fact he constantly leans toward the great medieval bard.

"The poetry of Milton differs from that of Dante as the hieroglyphics of Egypt differ from the picture-writing of Mexico. The images which Dante employs speak for themselves; they stand simply for what they are. Those of Milton have a

signification which is often discernible only to the initiated. . . .
However strange, however grotesque, he never shrinks from
describing it. He gives us the shape, the color, the sound,
the smell, the taste; he counts the numbers; he measures the
size. His similes are the illustrations of a traveler. Unlike
those of other poets, and especially of Milton, they are introduced in a plain business-like manner, not for the sake of any
of·the beauty in the objects from which they are drawn; not for
the sake of any ornament they may impart to the poem; but
simply in order to make the meaning of the writer as clear to
the reader as it is to himself."

"Still more striking is the similarity between Dante and
Milton. This may be said to lie rather in the kindred nature of
their subjects, and in the parallel development of their minds,
than in any mere external resemblance. In both the man was
greater than the poet, the souls of both were 'like a star and
dwelt apart.' Both were academically trained in the deepest
studies of their age; the labour which made Dante lean made
Milton blind. The 'Doricke sweetnesse' of the English poet
is not absent from the tender pages of the Vita Nuova. The
middle life of each was spent in active controversy; each lent
his services to the state; each felt the quarrels of his age to be
the 'business of posterity,' and left his warnings to ring in the
ears of a later time. The lives of both were failures. 'On evil
days though fallen, and evil tongues,' they gathered the con-
centrated experience of their lives into one immortal work, the
quintessence of their hopes, their knowledge, and their sufferings. But Dante is something more than this. Milton's voice
is grown faint to us—we have passed into other modes of expression and of thought."

The comparison with Vergil is still more striking and more
favorable to the Italian poet. "Dante's reputation has passed
through many vicissitudes, and much trouble has been spent by
critics in comparing him with other poets of established fame.
Read and commented upon in the Italian universities in the
generation immediately succeeding his death, his name became obscured as the sun of the Renaissance rose higher
towards its meridian. In the Seventeenth Century he was less
read than Petrarch, Tasso, or Ariosto; in the Eighteenth he was

almost universally neglected. His fame is now fully vindicated. Translations and commentaries issue from every press in Europe and America. Dante Societies are formed to investigate the difficulties of his works. He occupies in the lecture-rooms of regenerated Italy a place by the side of those great masters whose humble disciple he avowed himself to be. The Divine Comedy is indeed as true an epic as the Æneid, and Dante is as real a classic as Vergil. His metre is as pliable and flexible to every mood of emotion, his diction as plaintive and as sonorous. Like him he can immortalize by a simple expression, a person, a place, or a phase of nature. Dante is even truer in description than Vergil, whether he paints the snow falling in the Alps, or the homeward flight of birds, or the swelling of an angry torrent. But under this gorgeous pageantry of poetry there lies a unity of conception, a power of philosophic grasp, an earnestness of religion, which to the Roman poet were entirely unknown."

If we would have a very recent opinion as to the position of Dante as a literary man and as a great intellectual force, perhaps no better can be obtained than from some recent expressions of Mr. Michael Rossetti, whose Italian descent, English training, and literary and artistic heredity, seem to place him in an ideal position for writing this generation's ultimate judgment with regard to the great poet of the Thirteenth Century. In his Literature of Italy he said :—

"One has to recur time after time, to that astounding protagonist, phenomenon and hero, Dante Alighieri. If one were to say that Italian literature consists of Dante, it would, no doubt, be an exaggeration, and a gross one, and yet it would contain a certain ultimate nucleus of truth."

"Dante fixed the Italian language, and everyone had to tread in his vestiges. He embodied all the learning and thought of his age and transcended them. He went far ahead of all his predecessors, contemporaries, and successors; he wrote the first remarkable book in Italian prose, La Vita Nuova; and a critical exposition of it in the Convito; in Latin, a linguistic treatise, the De Vulgari Eloquio, which upholds the Vulgare Illustre, or speech of the best cultivated classes, markedly in Tuscany and Bologna, against the common dialects; and a political study, De Monarchia, of the most fundamental quality, which even to us moderns continues to be sane and convincing in its essence, though its direct line of argument has collapsed; and finally, and most important by far, he produced in La Commedia Divina the one poem of modern Europe that counterbalances Shakespeare and challenges antiquity. This is the sole book which makes it a real pity for anyone to be ignorant of Italian. Regarded singly, it is much the most astonishing poem in the world, dwarfing all others by its theme, pulverizing most of them by its majesty and sustainment, unique in the force of its paraded personality and the thunderous reverberation of its judgments on the living and the dead."

ANGEL (RHEIMS)

XX

THE WOMEN OF THE CENTURY.

In generations whose men proved so unending in initiative and so forceful in accomplishment, so commanding in intelligence, so persistent in their purposes, so acute in their searching, so successful in their endeavors, the women of the time could not have been unworthy of them. Some hints of this have been already given, in what has been said about the making of furnishings for the church, especially in the matter of needlework and the handpainting of various forms of ornaments. There are further intimations in the histories of the time, though unfortunately not very definite information, with regard to even more ambitious accomplishments by the women of the period. There are, for instance, traditions that the designs for some of the Cathedrals and certainly for portions of many of them came from women's hands. It is in the ethical sphere, however, that women accomplished great things during the Thirteenth Century. Their influence stood for what was best and highest in the life of the time and their example encouraged not only their own generation, but many people in many subsequent generations "to look up, not down, to look within, not without" for happiness, and to trust that "God's in his heaven and all's well with the world."

There are a number of women of the time whose names the race will not let die. While if the ordinary person were asked to enumerate the great women of the Thirteenth Century it would be rare to find one able properly to place them, as soon as their names are mentioned, it will be recognized that they succeeded in accomplishing work of such significance that the world is not likely to let the reputation of it perish. Some of these names are household words. The bearers of them have been written of at length in quite recent years in English as well as in other languages. Their work was of the kind that ordinarily stands quite apart from the course of history and so dates are usually not attached to it. It is thought of as a portion of the precious heritage of mankind rather than as belonging to any particular period. Three names occur at once. They are St. Clare of Assisi, St. Elizabeth of Hungary, and Queen Blanche of Castile, the mother of St. Louis. To these should be added Queen Berengaria, the sister of Blanche, and the mother of Ferdinand of Castile; Mabel Rich, the London tradesman's wife, the mother of St. Edmund of Canterbury; and Isabella, the famous Countess of Arundel.

The present day interest in St. Francis of Assisi, has brought St. Clare under the lime-light of publicity. There is no doubt at all that her name is well worthy to be mentioned along with his and that she, like him, must be considered one of the strongest and most beautiful characters of all time. She was the daughter of a noble family at Assisi, who, having heard St. Francis preach, became impressed with the idea that she too should have the opportunity to live the simple life that St. Francis pictured. Of course her family opposed her in any such notion. That a daughter of theirs should take up with a wandering preacher, who at that time was looked on not a little askance by the regular religious authorities, and whose rags and poverty made him anything but a proper associate for a young lady of noble birth, could not but seem an impossible idea. Accordingly Clare ran away from home and told Francis that she would never go back and that he must help her to live her life in poverty just as he was doing himself. He sent her to a neighboring convent to be cared for, and also very probably so as to be assured of her vocation.

After a time a special convent home for Clare and some other young women, who had become enamored with the life of poverty and simplicity was established, and to this Clare's sister Agnes came as a postulant. By this time apparently the family had become reconciled to Clare's absence from home, but they would not stand another daughter following such a foolish example. Accordingly Agnes was removed from the convent by force after a scene which caused the greatest excitement in the little town. It was not long, however, before Agnes returned to the convent and within a few years their mother followed them, and became one of the most fervent members

ST. CLARE'S FAREWELL TO THE DEAD ST. FRANCIS (GIOTTO)

of the little community. The peace and happiness that came with this life of absolute poverty soon attracted many other women and Clare was asked to establish houses at a distance. Gradually the order of Poor Clares, the second order of St. Francis, thus came into existence. When it was necessary to draw up constitutions for the order, Clare showed not only the breadth of her intelligence, but the depth of her knowledge of human nature, and her appreciation of what was absolutely necessary in order to keep her order from degeneration. Against the counsels of all the ecclesiastics of her time, including many cardinals and even a Pope, she insisted on the most absolute poverty as the only basis for the preservation of the spirit of her second order of St. Francis. Her character was well manifested in this contest from which she came out victorious.

Her body has been miraculously preserved and may still be seen at Assisi. Anyone who has seen the strongly set lips and full firm chin of the body in the crypt of San Damiano, can easily understand the strength of purpose and of character of this young woman who moulded a generation to her will. The story is told of her, that once when the Saracens invaded Italy and attacked the convent, she mounted the walls with a monstrance containing the Blessed Sacrament in her hands, and the marauders turned away in consternation from the stern brave figure that confronted them, and bothered the nuns no more. After St. Francis' death she, more than anyone else, succeeded in maintaining the spirit of the Franciscan order in the way in which St. Francis would have it go. Long after her death a copy of the original rules was found in the fold of her garments and did much to restore the Franciscan life to its primitive simplicity and purpose, so that even after she was no more on earth, she was still the guardian and promoter of St. Francis' work.

If one wants to know how much of happiness there came to her in life one should read the famous passage which describes her visit to St. Francis, and how she and he with sisters and brothers around them broke bread together, with a sweetness that was beyond human. The passage is to be found in the "Little Flowers of St. Francis of Assisi," which was written within a century after the occurrences described. It recalls nothing so much as the story of the disciples at Emaus and is worthy to be thought of beside the Scripture story. *

What Saint Clare accomplished as her life work was the making of a new vocation for women. There are always a certain number of women who look for peace and quiet rather than the struggle for existence. For these the older monasteries did not supply a place unless they were of the wealthier class as a rule. Among the Poor Clares women of all classes were received. In this way a great practical lesson in equality was

---

*When came the day ordained by Francis, Saint Clare with one companion passed forth from out the convent and with the companions of Saint Francis to bear her company came unto Saint Mary of the Angels, and devoutly saluted the Virgin Mary before her altar, where she had been shorn and veiled; so they conducted her to see the house, until such time as the hour for breaking bread was come. And in the meantime Saint Francis let make ready the table on the bare ground, as he was wont to do. And the hour of breaking bread being come, they set themselves down together, Saint Francis and Saint Clare, and one of the companions of Saint Francis with the companion of Saint Clare, and all the other companions took each his place at the table with all humility. And at the first dish, Saint Francis began to speak of God so sweetly, so sublimely and so wondrously, that the fulness of Divine grace came down on them, and they all were wrapt in God. And as they were thus wrapt, with eyes and hands uplift to heaven, the folk of Assisi and Bettona and the country round about, saw that Saint Mary of the Angels, and all the House, and the wood that was just hard by the house, were burning brightly, and it seemed as it were a great fire that filled the church and the House and the whole wood together: for the which cause the folk of Assisi ran thither in great haste to quench the flames, believing of a truth that the whole place was all on fire. But coming closer up to the House and finding no fire at all, they entered within and found Saint Francis and Saint Clare and all their company in contemplation rapt in God and sitting around that humble board. Whereby of a truth they understood that this had been a heavenly flame and no earthly one at all, which God had let appear miraculously, for to show and signify the fire of love divine wherewith the souls of those holy brothers and holy nuns were all aflame; wherefor they got them gone with great consolation in their hearts and with holy edifying. Then after some long space, Saint Francis and Saint Clare, together with all the others, returning to themselves again and feeling of good comfort from the spiritual food took little heed of the food of the body.

CHURCH (DOBERAN)

SAN DAMIANO (ASSISI)

taught. Women did not have to marry, perhaps unsuitable, often even objectionable men, simply in order to have a mode of life. They could join one of these communities and though in absolute poverty, with many hours each day devoted to meditation and prayer, had time to give to beautiful needlework, to painting and book illumination, and to other feminine occupations; and might thus pass long, happy lives, apart from the bustle of the strenuous time.

Italy at this time, it must be recalled, was a seething cauldron of political and military strife. Wars were waged, and struggles of all kinds engaged in for precedence and power. These women got away from this unfortunate state of affairs. Occasionally in times of pestilence, when they were specially needed, as happened at least once in Saint Clare's life, they took care of the ailing and lent their convent as a hospital. Above all they stood in the eyes of their generation for chosen people who saw things differently from others. They taught the great lesson of not caring too much for the things of this world and of not living one's life in order to get admiration though usually envy comes, nor idle praise for qualities they either do not possess or that are not worthy of notice. They showed people the real value of this life by its reflection upon the other. Many a man turned aside from ambitious schemes that would have injured others, because of the kindly influence of these unselfish women and because of the memory of a sister, or an aunt whose sacrificing life was thus a rebuke to his foolish selfishness. Other women learned something of the vanity of human things by learning to value the character of these Poor Clares and realizing how much of happiness came to them from the accomplishment of their simple duties. Professor Osler said, in his lecture on Science and Immortality, of these self-forgetting ones:—"The serene faith of Socrates with the cup of Hemlock at his lips, the heroic devotion of a St. Francis or a St. Teresa, but more often for each one of us the beautiful life of some good woman whose—

Eyes are homes of silent prayer,

.   .   .   .   .

Whose loves in higher love endure,

do more to keep alive among the Laodiceans a belief in immortality than all the preaching in the land." This is what St. Clare accomplished for her own generation and her influence is still a great living force in the world.

What especially should attract the attention of the modern time is the perfect basis of equality on which the Franciscan and Dominican orders of men and of women were organized. Each community had the opportunity to elect its own superiors. The rules were practically the same for the first (for men) and the second (for women) order of St. Francis, except that while the first order were supposed to live on alms collected by begging from door to door, this menial obligation was not imposed upon the women, who were expected to be supported by alms brought to their convents by the faithful, and by the labor of their own hands. This equality of men and women in the monastic establishments became widespread after the Thirteenth Century and made itself felt in the social order of the time as a factor for feminine uplift. Undoubtedly Saint Clare's work in the foundation of the second order of St. Francis must be held responsible to no small degree for this. Before her death, there were half a dozen scions of royal families in various parts of Europe who had become members of her order, and literally hundreds of the daughters of the nobility, many of them of high rank, had put off their dignity and position in the world, to become poor daughters of Saint Clare. They did so for the peace and the happiness of the vocation, and the opportunity to seek their souls and live their lives in their own quiet way, which her convents afforded them.

After Saint Clare, the best known woman of the Thirteenth Century is undoubtedly Saint Elizabeth of Hungary, of whom the world knows some pretty legends, while the serious historian recognizes that she was the first settlement worker of history. As a child she wandered down from the castle walls in which she lived and saw the poor in their suffering. She felt so much for them that she stripped herself of most of her garments and finally even of her shoes in order to clothe them. When she was taken to task for this, she said that she had suffered whatever inconvenience there was in it only for a few minutes while the poor had suffered all their lives. She became

ST. ELIZABETH'S (MARBURG)

the wife of the Duke of Thuringia, and there were three years of ideal happiness with her husband and her children. When he went away on the Crusade she gave herself up to the care of the poor. When he died, though she was only twenty, and according to tradition one of the handsomest women of her time, she devoted herself still more to her poor and even went to live among them. She tried to teach them, as do the settlement workers of the modern time, something of the true significance of life, to bring them to realize to some degree at least, that so many of the things they so vainly desire are not worth thinking about, but that happiness consists in lopping off one's desires rather than trying vainly, as it must ever be, to satisfy them. It is no wonder that throughout all Germany she came to be called "the dear St. Elizabeth." Literally millions of women since her time have read entranced the story of her beautiful devotion to charity, and have been incited by her example to do more and more for the poor around them. Those who know it only through Kingsley's, "The Saint's Tragedy," though this is disfigured by many failures to understand parts of her career and her environment, can scarcely fail to realize that hers was one of the world's sublimely beautiful characters. All she attempted in the thorny paths of charity was accomplished in such a practical way that the amount of good done was almost incalculable. The simple recital of what she did as it has often been told, is the story of a great individuality that impressed itself deeply upon its generation and left the example of a precious life to act as a leaven for good in the midst of the social fermentations of succeeding generations.

Yet Elizabeth succeeded in accomplishing all this in spite of the fact that she was born the daughter of a king and married the reigning prince of one of the most important ducal houses in Germany. One would expect to find that her life had been long, so many traditions have gathered around her name. She was twenty when her husband died, and she survived him only four years. Literally she had accomplished a long space in a short time and her generation in raising in her honor the charming Gothic Cathedral at Marburg, one of the most beautiful in Germany, was honoring itself nobly as well as her. It is the greatest monument to a woman in all the world.

The next great woman of the century also belonged to a reigning family and is for obvious historical reasons better known, perhaps, than her Saint contemporaries. This was Blanche, daughter of the King of Castile, but intimately related to the English royal family. Married to Louis VIII of France she is known principally as the mother of Louis IX. She ruled France for many years while her boy was a minor and when he came to the age, when he might ordinarily assume the reins of government, he voluntarily permitted his mother to continue her regency for some time longer. France was probably happier under her than under any ruler that the country has ever had with the possible exception of her son Louis. She succeeded in suppressing to a great extent the quarrels so common among the nobility, she strengthened and centralized the power of the crown, she began the correction of abuses in the administration of justice which her son was to complete so well, she organized charity in various ways, and the court was an example to the kingdom of simple dignified life, without any abuse of power, or wealth, or passion. No wonder that when Louis went on the Crusade, he left his mother to reign in his stead confident that all would go well. If one needed a demonstration that women can rule well there is an excellent example in the life of Blanche.

Personally she seems to have had not only an amiable but a deeply intellectual character. She encouraged education and beautiful book-making and the Gothic architecture which was developing in France so wonderfully during her period. Of course she also worshipped her boy Louis, but how much her motherly tenderness was tempered with the most beautiful Christian feeling can be understood from the famous expression attributed to her on good authority, that she "would rather see her boy dead at her feet, than have him commit a mortal offense against his God or his neighbor." One might almost say that it is no wonder that Louis became a saint. As a matter of fact he attributed to his mother whatever of goodness there was in himself. There is a touch of humanity in the picture, however, a trait that shows, that Blanche was a woman, though it is a fault which draws our sympathy to her even more surely than if she were the type of perfection she might have been without it. She did not get on well with her daughter-in-law and one of the trials of Louis' life, as we have said, was to keep the scales evenly balanced between his mother and his wife, both of whom he loved very dearly. After Blanche's life there could be no doubt that a woman, when given the opportunity, can manage men and administer government quite as well as any masculine member of the race, and the Thirteenth Century had given another example of its power to bring out what was best in its fortunate children.

One of the most interesting women of the Thirteenth Century was neither a Saint nor a member of the nobility, but only the wife of a simple London merchant. This was Mabel Rich, the mother of Saint Edmund of Canterbury. Edmund is one of the striking men of a supreme century. He had been a student at Paris, and later a professor at Oxford. Then, he became the treasurer of the Cathedral at Salisbury about the time when, not a little through his influence, that magnificent edifice was receiving the form which was to make it one of the world's great churches for all time. Later he was the Archbishop of Canterbury• and while defending the rights of his church and his people, came under the ban of Henry III, and spent most of the latter years of his life in exile on the continent. Edmund insisted that he owed more to his mother than to any other single factor in life. With her two boys, aged ten and fourteen, Mabel Rich was left to care for the worldly concerns of the household as well as for their education. When they were twelve and sixteen, with many misgivings she sent them off to the University of Paris to get their education. Edmund tells how besides packing their linen very carefully she also packed a hairshirt for each of them, which they were to wear occasionally according to their promise to her, to remind them that they must not look for ease and comfort in life, above all must not yield to sensual pleasures, but must be ready to suffer many little troubles voluntarily, in order that they might be able to resist temptation when severer trials came. Mabel Rich believed in discipline, as a factor in education, and thought that character was formed by habits of fortitude in resisting petty annoyances until, finally, even serious troubles were easy to bear.

Both of her sons proved worthy of her maternal solicitude. Edmund tells how the poor around her home in London blessed her for her charity. All during his life the thought of his mother was uppermost in his mind, and in the immortality that has been given his name, because of the utter forgetfulness of self which characterized his life, his mother has been associated. Unfortunately details are lacking that would show us something of the manner of living of this strong woman of the people, but we know enough to make us realize that she was a fine type of the Christian mother, memory of whose goodness means more not only for her children but for all those who come in contact with her, than all the sermons and pious exhortations that they hear, and often, such is the way of human nature, even than the divine commandments or the personal conscience of those whom she loves.

There were noble women among the gentlewomen of England at this time too, and though space will not let us dwell on them, at least one must be mentioned. This is the famous Isabella, Countess of Arundel, who with a dignity which, Matthew Paris says, was more than that of woman, reproached Henry III (1252), when he sought to browbeat her. She made bold to tell the king, "You govern neither us nor yourself well." On this the king, with a sneer and a grin, said with a loud voice, "Ho, ho, my lady countess, have the noblemen of England granted you a charter and struck a bargain with you to become their spokeswoman because of your eloquence?" She answered, "My liege, the nobles have made no charter, but you and your father have made a charter, and you have sworn to observe it inviolably, and yet many times have you extorted money from your subjects and have not kept your word. Where are the liberties of England, often reduced to writing, so often granted, so often again denied?"*

The question of womanly occupations apart from their household duties will be of great interest to our generation.

A hint of one form of woman's occupation has already been

*Medieval England, English Feudal Society, from the Norman Conquest to the Middle of the Fourteenth Century, by Mary Bateson.

MARRIAGE OF THE BLESSED VIRGIN (GIOTTO, PADUA)

given in discussing the needlework done for the Cathedrals and especially the Cope of Ascoli. It must not be forgotten that this was the age not alone of Cathedrals but also of monasteries and of convents. In all of these convents every effort was made to have whatever was associated with the religious ceremonial as beautiful as possible. Hence it was that needlework rose to a height of accomplishment such as has never been reached since according to the best authorities, and many examples of it have come down to us to confirm such an opinion. This needlework was done not only for religious purposes, however, but also as presents for Kings and Queens and the nobility, and such presents proved to be exemplars of artistic beauty that must have helped to raise the taste of the time. This was essentially woman's work, and in their distant castles the women of the households of the nobility occupied themselves with it to much better effect than their sisters of the modern time with the grievous burden of their so-called social duties.

Miss Bateson* has given a pretty, yet piquant picture of woman at these occupations. She says:—"There are not wanting Thirteenth Century satires to tell the usual story of female levities, and of female devotion to the needle, to German work and pierced work, Saracen work and combed work, cutout work and wool-work, and a multitude of other "works" to which the clue seems to be now wholly lost. Whilst the women are thus engaged, the one who knows most reads to them, the others listen attentively, and do not sleep as they do at mass, 'pur la prise de vanite dont ont grant leesce (joy).' The 'opus anglicum' consisted of chain-stitch in circles, with hollows, made by a heated iron rod, to represent shadows. A cope of this work was made by Rose de Burford at Edward II's order, and sent to Rome. One, known as the Syon cope, passed into the possession of the nuns of Syon, Isleworth, and can be seen at the Victoria and Albert Museum."

Another form of woman's work that came to prominence during the century was the service in hospitals. While the records of the hospitals of the Holy Ghost, which under Innocent Third's fostering care spread so widely throughout Europe in this century, are mainly occupied with the institutions of

* Ibidem.

the Brothers of the Holy Ghost, there were many hospitals
under the care of women, and indeed there was an almost
universally accepted idea, that women patients and obstetrical
cases should be cared for by women rather than men.   It is
easy to make little of the hospitals of this time but any such
thought will be the result of ignorance rather than of any
serious attempt to know what was actually accomplished.
The sisters' hospitals soon usurped the most prominent place
in the life of the time and during succeeding centuries gradually replaced those which had been originally under the control
of men.   It was recognized that nursing was a much more
suitable occupation for the gentler sex and that there were
many less abuses than when men were employed.   The success of these hospitals in gradually eradicating leprosy and in
keeping down the death-rate from St. Anthony's fire, or erysipelas, shows how capable they were of accomplishing great
humanitarian work.

Perhaps the most interesting feature of the story of woman's
position during the Thirteenth Century is that at the Italian
universities at least, co-education was not only admitted in
principle but also in practice, and many women were in attendance at the universities.   In the West of Europe this feature
did not exist.   It is a startling comment on how comparatively
trivial a thing may change the course of history, that the
lamentable Heloise and Abelard incident at the University of
Paris during the Twelfth Century, precluded all subsequent
possibility of the admission of women students to the University of Paris.   Oxford, it will be remembered, was formed by
the withdrawal of students from the University of Paris, and
the same tradition was maintained.   Cambridge was a grand-
daughter of the University of Paris and the French and Spanish
universities must all be considered as standing in the relation
of its direct descendants.   The unfortunate experience at Paris
shaped the policy as to the co-education of the sexes for all
these.   It would have been too much to expect that university
authorities would take the risks which had been so clearly
demonstrated even with regard to a distinguished professor,
and so co-education was excluded.

It is not easy to say what proportion of women there were

in attendance at the university of Bologna during the Thirteenth. Century. Apparently it should not be difficult to take the lists of the matriculates as far as they have been preserved and by a little calculation obtain rather exact figures. Italy, like most of the Latin countries, differs from the Teutonic regions in not being quite so exact in the distribution of names to the different sexes, that the first name inevitably determines whether the individual is male or female. It is not an unusual thing even at the present day for a man to have as a first name in Italy, or France, or Spain, the equivalent of our name Mary. On the other hand, not a few girls are called by men's names and without the feminine termination which is so distinctive among the English speaking peoples. In the olden times this was still more the case. Until very recently at least, if not now, every child born in Venice was given two names at its baptism—Maria and Giovanni—in honor of the two great patron saints of the city and then the parents might add further names if they so desired. A matriculation list of the University of Bologna then, tells very little that is absolute with regard to the sex of the matriculates.

All that we know for sure is that there were women students at the University of Bologna apparently from the beginning of the Thirteenth Century, and that some of them secured the distinction of being made Professors. Of one of these there is a pretty legend told, which seems to illustrate the fact that charming young women of profound intellectual qualities did not lose the characteristic modesty and thoughtfulness for others of their sex, because of their elevation to university professorship. This young woman, Maria di Novella, when only twenty-five became the Professor of mathematics at the University of Bologna. According to tradition she was very pretty and as is usual in life was not unaware of that happy accident. She feared that her good looks might disturb the thoughts of her students during her lessons and accordingly she delivered her lectures from behind a curtain. The story may, of course, be only a myth. One of the best woman educators that I know once said to me, that if the tradition with regard to her beauty were true, then she doubted the rest of the story, but then women are not always the best judges of the actions of other women and especially is this true when there is question of a grave and learned elderly woman passing judgment on a young and handsome professor of mathematics.

The Italians became so much impressed with the advisability of permitting women to study at the universities, that a certain amount of co-education has existed all down the centuries in Italy and not a century has passed since the Thirteenth, which has not chronicled the presence of at least one distinguished woman professor at some Italian university. Indeed it was doubtless the traditional position of tolerance in this matter that made it seem quite natural for women, when the Renaissance period came around, to take their places beside their brothers and their cousins in the schools where the new learning was being taught.

It may be rather difficult for some to understand how with this opening wedge for the higher education of women well placed, the real opportunity for widespread feminine education should only have come in our own time. This last idea, however, which would represent ours as the only generation which has given women adequate opportunities for intellectual development, is one of those self-complacent bits of flattery of ourselves and our own period that is so irritatingly characteristic of recent times. There have been at least three times in the world's history before our own when as many women as wanted them, in the class most interested in educational matters, were given the opportunities for the higher education. As a matter of fact whenever there have been novelties introduced into educational systems, women have demanded and quite naturally—since, "What a good woman wants," said a modern saint, "is the will of God"—have obtained the privilege of sharing the educational opportunities of the time. This was true in Charlemagne's time when the women of the court attended the lectures in the traveling palace school the great Charles founded and fostered. It was true four centuries later, as we have seen, when a great change in educational methods was introduced with the foundation of the universities. It was exemplified again when the "New Learning" came in and the study of the classics took the place of the long hours spent in scholastic disputation, that had previously occupied

MOSAIC (ST. MARK'S, VENICE, 1220)

so much university attention. In our own time it was the introduction of the study of the social sciences particularly, with the consequent appearance of many novelties in the educational curriculum, that once more was the signal for women asking and quite naturally obtaining educational privileges.

Each of the previous experiences in the matter of feminine education has been followed by a considerable period during which there was a distinct incuriousness on the part of women in educational matters. Of course that is only an analogy and though history is worth studying, only because the lessons of the past are the warnings of the future, yet this does not foretell a lessening of feminine interest in educational matters, after a few generations of experience of its vanity to make up to them for the precious special privileges of their nature, the proper enjoyment and exercise of which it is so likely to hamper. It would be interesting to know just why feminine education, after a period of efflorescence during the Thirteenth Century, retrograded during the next century. There have been some ungallant explanations offered, which we mention merely because of their historical interest but without any hint of their having any real significance in the matter.

A distinguished German educational authority has called attention to the fact that a well-known prepared food, for which Bologna is famous, is first heard of about the time that the higher education for women came into vogue at the Italian universities. Towards the end of the same century a special kind of pudding, since bearing the name of its native city, Bologna, which might very well have taken the place of an ordinary dessert, also began to come into prominence. This German writer suggests then, that possibly the serving of meals consisting of these forms of prepared food, which did not require much household drudgery and did not necessitate the bending over the kitchen range or whatever took its place in those days, may have led the men to grumble about the effects of the higher education. After all, he adds, though the women get whatever they want, when they ask for it seriously, if it proves after a time that the men do not want them to have it, then women lose interest and care for it no longer. This, of course, must be taken with the proverbial grain of salt, though it illustrates certain phases of the domestic life of the time as well as affording a possible glimpse into the inner circle of the family life.

The real story of woman's intellectual position in the century is to be found in its literature. How deep was the general culture of the women of the Thirteenth Century, in Italy at least, can be judged from the Sonnets of Dante and his friends to their loved ones at the end of this century. Some of the most beautiful poetry that was ever written was inspired by these women and like the law of hydrostatics, it is one of the rules of the history of poetry, that inspiration never rises higher than its source and that poetry addressed to women is always the best index of the estimation in which they are held, the reflection of the highest qualities of the objects to which it is addressed. Anyone who reads certain of the sonnets of Dante, or of his friends Guido Cavalcanti or Gino da Pistoia or Dante da Maiano, will find ready assurance of the high state of culture and of intellectual refinement that must have existed among the women to whom they were dedicated. This same form of reasoning will apply also with regard to the women of the South of France to whom the Troubadours addressed their poetry; to those of the north of France who were greeted by the Trouvères; and those of the south of Germany for whom the Minnesingers tuned their lyres and invoked the Muses to enable them to sing their praises properly. It would seem sometimes to be forgotten that poetry generally is written much more for women than for men. Everyone realizes that for one man who has read Tennyson's "Idyls of the King" there are probably five women to whom they have been a source of delight. When we think of the Thirteenth Century as not affording opportunities of intellectual culture for its women, we should ask ourselves where then did the Meistersingers and the poets of England, Germany and France who told their romantic tales in verse find an audience, if it was not among the women. The stories selected by the Meistersingers are just those which proved so popular to feminine readers of Tennyson in the Nineteenth Century, and the chosen subjects of interest in the stories show that men and women have not changed much during the intervening centuries. The literature of any period reflects the interest of the women in it and, as interest is itself an index of intellectual development, Thirteenth Century literature must be taken as the vivid reflection of the cultural character of the women of the time, and this is of itself the highest possible tribute to their intelligence and education.

On the other hand the best possible testimony to the estimation of women during the Thirteenth Century, is to be found in the attitude of the men of the generations towards them, as it is clearly to be seen in the literature of the time. In the Holy Graal, the Cid, the Minnesingers and the Meistersingers, woman occupies the higher place in life and it is recognized that she is the highest incentive to good, unfortunately also sometimes to evil, but always the best reward that men can have for their exertions in a great cause. The supreme tribute to woman comes at the end of the century in Dante's apotheosis of her in the Divine Comedy. In this it is a woman who inspires, a woman who leads, a woman who is the reward of man's aspirations, and though the symbolism may be traced to philosophy, the influence of an actual woman in it all is sure beyond all doubt. Nor must it be thought that it was merely in this highest flight of his imagination that this greatest of poets expressed such lofty sentiments with regard to women. Anyone who thinks this does not know Dante's minor poems, which contain to women in the flesh and above all to one of them, the most wonderful tributes that have ever been paid to woman. Take this one of his sonnets for instance.

> So gentle and so fair she seems to be,
>   My Lady, when she others doth salute,
>   That every tongue becomes, all trembling, mute,
> And every eye is half afraid to see;
> She goes her way and hears men's praises free,
>   Clothed in a garb of kindness, meek and low,
>   And seems as if from heaven she came, to show
> Upon the earth a wondrous mystery:
> To one who looks on her she seems so kind,
>   That through the eye a sweetness fills the heart,
>   Which only he can know who doth it try.

And through her face there breatheth from her mind
 A spirit sweet and full of Love's true art,
 Which to the soul saith, as it cometh, "Sigh."

It will be noted that though this contains the highest possible praise of the woman whom he loved, it has not a single reference to any of her physical perfections, or indeed to any of those charms that poets usually sing. We have already called attention to this, that it is not the beauty of her face or her figure that has attracted him, but the charm of her character, which all others must admire—which even women do not envy, it is so beautiful—that constitutes the supreme reason for Dante's admiration. Nor must it be thought that this is a unique example of Dante's attitude in this matter; on the contrary, it is the constant type of his expression of feeling. The succeeding sonnet in his collection is probably quite as beautiful as the first quoted, and yet is couched in similar terms. It will be found in the chapter on Dante the Poet. Need we say more to prove that the women of the century were worthy of the men and of the supreme time in which they lived; that they were the fit intellectual companions of perhaps the greatest generation of men that ever lived?

STONE CARVING (AMIENS)

XXI

CITY HOSPITALS—ORGANIZED CHARITY.

While the Thirteenth Century was engaged in solving the problems of the higher education and of technical education for the masses, and was occupied so successfully, as we have seen, with the questions of the rights of man and the development of law and of liberty, other and more directly social and humanitarian works were not neglected. There had been hospitals in existence from even before the Christian era, but they had been intended rather for the chronic ailments and as the name implies, for the furnishing of hospitality to strangers and others who had for the time no habitation, than for the care of the acutely ill. In the country places there was a larger Christian charity which led people to care even for the stranger, and there was a sense of human duty that was much more binding than in the modern world. The acutely ill were not infrequently taken into the houses of even those who did not know them, and cared for with a solicitude difficult to understand in this colder time. This was not so much typical of the times, however, as of the social conditions, since we have many stories of such events in our colonial days.

In the cities, however, which began more and more to be a feature of life in the Thirteenth Century, though they counted their inhabitants only by a few thousands where ours count them by hundreds of thousands, the need of some other method of caring for such cases made itself distinctly felt. At the end of the Twelfth and the beginning of the Thirteenth centuries this need became demandingly manifest, and the consequence was a movement that proved to be of great and far-reaching practical benevolence. It is to the first Pope of the Thirteenth Century, Innocent III., that we owe the modern city hospital as we have it at the present time, with its main purpose to care for the acutely ill who may have no one to take care of them properly, as well as for those who have been injured or who have been picked up on the street and whose friends are not in a position to care for them.

The deliberateness with which Innocent III. set about the establishment of the mother city hospital of the world, is a striking characteristic of the genius of the man and an excellent illustration of the practical character of the century of which he is so thoroughly representative.

Pope Innocent recognized the necessity for the existence of a city hospital in Rome and by inquiry determined that the model hospital for this purpose existed down at Montpelier in connection with the famous medical school of the university there. Montpelier had succeeded to the heritage of the distinguished reputation in medical matters which had been enjoyed by Salernum, not far from Naples, during the Ninth, Tenth, and Eleventh centuries. The shores of the Mediterranean have always been recognized as possessing a climate especially suitable for invalids and with the diminution of the influence of the Salernitan school, a transfer of its prestige to Montpelier, where the close relationship with Spain had given the medical schools the advantage of intimate contact with the medicine of the Arabs, is not a matter of surprise. At Montpelier the hospital arrangements made by Guy de Montpelier were especially efficient. The hospital of which he had charge was under the care of the members of the order of the Holy Spirit.

Pope Innocent summoned Guy, or Guido as he was known after this, to Rome and founded for him the hospital of the Holy Spirit in the Borgo, not far from St. Peter's, where it still exists. This was the mother and model hospital for the world. Visitors to Rome saw it, and could not fail to admire its great humanitarian work. Bishops from all over the world on their official visits to the head of the Church, admired the policy under which the hospital was conducted, recognized the interest of the Pope in it, and went back to their homes to organize institutions of the same kind. How many of these were established in various parts of Europe is hard to determine. Virchow in his History of the Foundations of the German Hospitals, has a list of over one hundred towns in Germany in which hospitals of the Holy Spirit, or medical institutions modeled on this hospital at Rome were founded.

Many of these towns were comparatively small. Most of them contained at the time less than five thousand inhabitants, so that it can be said without hesitation, that practically every town of any importance, at least in Germany, came under the influence of this great philanthropic hospital movement.

With regard to other countries, it is more difficult to determine the number of places in which such institutions were established. As both France and Italy were, however, much more closely in touch with the Holy See at this time, it would be surprising if they had not been affected as much as Germany by the Pope's enthusiasm in the matter. We do know that in various large cities, as in Florence, Siena, Paris and London, there was a development of existing hospitals and the establishment of new ones, that points to a distinct community of interest in the hospital movement. At Paris, the Hotel Dieu was moved from the Petit Pont, where it had been, to its present situation and received large extensions in size and in usefulness. It was at this time, particularly, that it received donations for endowment purposes that would enable it to be self-supporting. A number of bequests of property, the rent of which was to be paid to the hopsital, were made, and the details of some of these bequests have an interest of their own. Houses were not numbered at this time but were distinguished by various signs, usually figures of different kinds that formed part of their facade. The Hotel Dieu acquired the houses with the image of St. Louis, with the sign of the golden lion of Flanders, with the image of the butterfly, with the group of the three monkeys, with the image of the wolf, with the image of the iron lion, with the cross of gold, with the chimneys, etc. The Hotel Dieu, indeed, seems to have become practically a fully endowed institution during the course of the Thirteenth Century, for there are apparently no records of special revenues voted by the city or the king, though there are such records with regard to other places. For instance the Hospital of St. Louis received the right to collect a special tax on all the salt that came into the city.

In England the hospital movement during the Thirteenth Century is evidently quite as active as in Germany, at least as far as the records go. These refer mainly to London and show that the influence of the work of Innocent III. and his enthusiasm was felt in the English capital. The famous St. Bartholomew's Hospital in London had been a Priory founded at the beginning of the Twelfth Century, which took care of the poor and the ailing, but at the beginning of the Thirteenth Century it became more frankly a hospital in the modern sense of the word. St. Thomas' Hospital, which remains to the present day one of the great medical institutions of London, was founded by Richard, Prior of Bermondsey, in 1213. Bethlehem or Bedlam, which afterwards became a hospital for the insane, was founded about the middle of the Thirteenth Century. The name Bedlam is a corruption of Bethlehem, since adopted into the English language to express a place where fools do congregate. Bridewell and Christ's Hospital, which were the other two of the institutions long known as the five Royal Hospitals of London, also seem either to have been founded, or to have received a great stimulus and reorganization in the Thirteenth Century, but both ceased after some time to be places for the reception of the ailing and became, one of them a prison and the other a school.

The names of some of these institutions became associated with that of Edward VI. about the middle of the Sixteenth Century. For this, however, there was no proper justification, since, at most, all that was accomplished within the reign of the boy king, was the reestablishment of institutions formerly in existence which had been confiscated under the laws of Henry VIII., but the necessity for whose existence had been made very clear, because of the suffering entailed upon the many ailing poor by the fact, that in their absence there was nowhere for them to go to be cared for. As Gairdner points out in his History of the English Church in the Sixteenth Century, "Edward has left a name in connection with charities and education which critical scholars find to be little justified by fact." The supposed foundation of St. Thomas' Hospital was only the reestablishment of this institution, and even when it was granted by him to the citizens of London, this was not, as Gairdner says, "without their paying for it."

•How much all this hospital movement owes to Innocent III. will be best appreciated from Virchow's account of the German

HOLY GHOST HOSPITAL (LÜBECK)

hospitals, the great German scientist not being one of those at all likely to exaggerate, the beneficent influence of the Popes. He says:

"The main cause decisive in influencing and arousing interest of the people of the time in the hospitals of the Holy Ghost was the Papal enthusiasm in the matter. The beginning of their history is connected with the name of that Pope, who made the boldest and farthest-reaching attempt to gather the sum of human interest into the organization of the Catholic Church. The hospitals of the Holy Ghost were one of the many means by which Innocent III. thought to bind humanity to the Holy See. And surely it was one of the most effective. Was it not calculated to create the most profound impression, to see how the mighty Pope who humbled emperors and deposed kings, who was the unrelenting adversary of the Albigenses, turned his eyes sympathetically upon the poor and sick, sought the helpless and the neglected on the streets, and saved the illegitimate children from death in the waters. There is something conciliating and fascinating in the fact that at the very same time at which the Fourth Crusade was inaugurated through his influence, the thought of founding a great organization of an essentially humane character to extend throughout all Christendom, was also taking form in his soul; and that in the same year (1204) in which the new Latin Empire was founded in Constantinople, the newly erected hospital of the Santo Spirito, by the Old Bridge across the Tiber, was blessed and dedicated as the future center of this universal humanitarian organization."

Virchow, of course, considers Innocent's action as due to the entirely interested motive of binding the Catholic world to the Holy See. Others, however, who have studied Innocent's life even more profoundly, have not considered his purpose as due to any such mean motive. Hurter who wrote a history of Pope Innocent III., the researches for which he began as a Protestant with the idea that in the life of this Pope better than anywhere else the pretensions of the papacy could be most effectively exposed, but who was so taken by the character of the man that before he completed his history he had become a Catholic, looks at it in a very different way. Even Virchow himself quotes

Hurter's opinion, though not without taking some exceptions to it. Hurter said with regard to charitable foundations in his history of Pope Innocent III.: "All benevolent institutions which the human race still enjoys, all care for the deserted and needy through every stage of suffering from the first moment of birth to the return of the material part to earth, have had their origin in the church. Some of them directly, some of them indirectly through the sentiments and feelings which she aroused, strengthened and vivified into action. The church supplied for them the model and sometimes even the resources; that these great humanitarian needs were not neglected and their remedies not lacking in any respect is essentially due to her influence upon human character."

With regard to this Virchow says that hospitals had existed among the Arabs and among the Buddhists in the distant East, "nevertheless," he adds, "it may be recognized and admitted, that it was reserved for the Roman Catholic Church and above all for Innocent III., to establish institutions for the care of those suffering from diseases."

A corresponding hospital movement that received considerable attention within the Thirteenth Century was the erection of Leproseries or hospitals for the care of lepers. Leprosy had become quite common in Europe during the Middle Ages, and the contact of the West with the East during the Crusades had brought about a notable increase of the disease. It is not definitely known how much of what was called leprosy at that time really belonged to the specific disease now known as lepra. There is no doubt that many affections which have since come to be considered as quite harmless and non-contagious, were included under the designation leprosy by the populace and even by physicians incapable as yet of making a proper differential diagnosis. Probably severe cases of eczema and other chronic skin diseases, especially when complicated by the results of wrongly directed treatment or of lack of cleansing, were sometimes pronounced to be leprosy. Certain of the severer forms of what is now known as psoriasis—a non-contagious skin disease—running a very slow course and sometimes extremely obstinate to treatment, were almost surely included under the diagnosis of leprosy. Personally I have seen in the General Hospital in Vienna, a patient who had for many months been compelled by the villagers among whom he lived to confine himself to his dwelling, sustained by food that was thrown into him at the window by the neighbors who were fearful of the contagiousness of his skin disease, yet he was suffering from only a very neglected case of psoriasis.

There is no doubt, however, of the existence of actual leprosy in many of the towns of the West from the Twelfth to the Fifteenth centuries, and the erection of these special hospitals proved the best possible prophylactic against the further spread of the disease. Leprosy is contagious, but only mildly so. Years of association with lepers may and usually does bring about the communication of the disease to those around them, especially if they do not exercise rather carefully certain precise precautions as to cleanliness, after personal contact or after the handling of things which have previously been in the leper's possession. As the result of the existence of these houses of segregation, leprosy disappeared during the course of the next three centuries and thus a great hygienic triumph was obtained by sanitary regulation.

This successful hygienic and sanitary work, which brought about practically the complete obliteration of leprosy in the Middle Ages, furnished the first example of the possibility of eradicating a disease that had become a scourge to mankind. That this should have been accomplished by a movement that had its greatest source in the Thirteenth Century, is all the more surprising, since we are usually accustomed to think of the people of those times, as sadly lacking in any interest in sanitary matters. The significance of the success of the segregation movement was lost upon men down almost to our own time. This was, however, because it was considered that most of the epidemic diseases were conveyed by the air. They were thought infectious and due to a climatic condition rather than to contagion, that is conveyed by actual contact with the person having the disease or something that had touched him, which is the view now held. With the beginning of the crusade against tuberculosis in the latter part of the Nineteenth Century, however, the most encouraging factor for those engaged in it, was the history of the success of segregation methods and careful prevention of the spread of the disease which had been pursued against leprosy. In a word the lessons in sanitation and prophylaxis of the Thirteenth Century are only now bearing fruit, because the intervening centuries did not have sufficient knowledge to realize their import and take advantage of them.

Pope Innocent III. was not the only occupant of the papal throne whose name deserves to be remembered with benedictions in connection with the hospital movement of the Thirteenth Century. His successors took up the work of encouragement where he had left it at his death and did much to bring about the successful accomplishment of his intentions in even wider spheres. Honorius III. is distinguished by having made into an order the Antonine Congregation of Vienna, which was especially devoted to the care of patients suffering from the holy fire and from various mutilations. The disease known as the holy fire seems to have been what is called in modern times erysipelas. During the Middle Ages it received various titles such as St. Anthony's fire, St. Francis' fire, and the like, the latter part of the designation evidently being due to the intense redness which characterizes the disease, and which can be compared to nothing better than the erythema consequent upon a rather severe burn. This affection was a great deal commoner in the Middle Ages than in later times, though it must not be forgotten that its disappearance has come mainly in the last twenty-five years.

It is now known to be a contagious disease and indeed, as Oliver Wendell Holmes pointed out over half a century ago, may readily be carried from place to place by the physician in attendance. It does not always manifest itself as erysipelas when thus carried, however, and the merit of Dr. Holmes' work was in pointing out the fact that physicians who attended patients suffering from erysipelas and then waited on obstetrical cases, were especially likely to carry the infection which manifested itself as puerperal fever. A number of cases of this kind were reported and discussed by him, and there is no doubt that his warning served to save many precious lives.

Of course nothing was known of this in the Thirteenth Century, yet the encouragement given to this religious order, which devoted itself practically exclusively to the care in special hospitals of erysipelas, must have had not a little effect in bringing about a limitation of the spread of the disease. In such hospitals patients were not likely to come in contact with many persons and consequently the contagion-radius of the disease was limited. In our own time immediate segregation of cases when discovered has practically eradicated it, so that many a young physician, even though ten years in practise, has never seen a case of it. It was so common in America during the Civil War and for half a century prior thereto, that there were frequent epidemics of it in hospitals and it was generally recognized that the disease was so contagious that when it once gained a foothold in a hospital, nearly every patient suffering from an open wound was likely to be affected by it.

It is interesting then to learn that these people of the Middle Ages attempted to control the disease by erecting special hospitals for it, though unfortunately we are not in a position to know just how much was accomplished by these means. A congregation devoted to the special care of the disease had been organized, as we have said, early in the Thirteenth Century. At the end of this century this was given the full weight of his amplest approval by Pope Boniface VIII., who conferred on it the privilege of having priests among its members. It will be remembered that Pope Boniface VIII. is said to have issued the Bull which forbade the practise of dissection. The decretal in question, however, which was not a Bull, only regulated, as I have shown, the abuse which had sprung up of dismembering bodies and boiling them in order to be able to carry them to a distance for burial, and was in itself an excellent hygienic measure.

Many orders for the care of special needs of humanity were established during the Thirteenth Century. It is from this period that most of the religious habits worn by women originate. These used to be considered rather cumbersome for such a serious work as the nursing and care of the sick, but in recent years quite a different view has been taken. The covering of the head, for instance, and the shearing of the hair must have been of distinct value in preventing communication of certain diseases. There has been a curious assimilation in the last few years, of the dress required to be worn by nurses in operating rooms to that worn by most of the religious communities. The head must be completely covered, and the garments worn are of material that can be washed. It will be recalled that the headdresses of religious, being as a rule of spotless white, must be renewed frequently and therefore must be kept in a condition of what is practically surgical cleanliness. While this was not at all the intention of those who adopted the particular style of headdress worn by religious, yet their choice has proved, in what may well be considered a Providential way, to be an excellent protective for the patients against certain dangers that would inevitably have been present, if their dress had been the ordinary one of the women of their class during these many centuries of hospital nursing by religious women.

The organization of charity is supposed to be a feature of social life that was reserved for these modern times. A subsequent chapter on Democracy, Christian Socialism and National Patriotism, shows how false this notion is from one standpoint; a little additional interpretation will show that the generations which organized the hospitals, took care of the lepers in such a way as to prevent their becoming sources of infection for others, and segregated such severe contagious diseases as erysipelas, not only knew how to organize charitable efforts, but were able to accomplish their purposes in this matter in such a way, that the friction of the charity organization itself absorbed as little as possible of the beneficent energy put into it, and much less than is the case in our own time. Besides the monasteries were really active centers of charity organization of the most practical character. They not only gave to the people when their necessities required it, but they were active employers of labor and in times of scarcity constantly made large sacrifices in order to keep their people employed, and even the community itself went on short rations in order that the suffering in the neighborhood might not be extreme. In times of prosperity there were, no doubt, abuses in monasteries, but no one ever accused them of neglecting the poor during times of famine.

While the Thirteenth Century was so intent upon the relief of the social needs consequent upon illness and injury, it did not neglect other forms of social endeavor. One of the crying

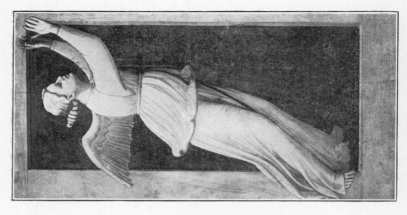

HOPE (GIOTTO)

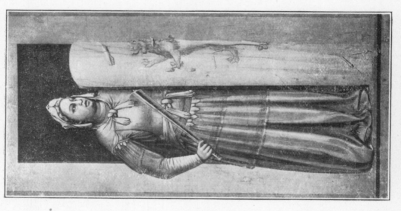

FORTITUDE (GIOTTO)

CHARITY (GIOTTO)

evils of the Thirteenth Century was the fact that mariners and merchants, as well as pilgrims to the Holy Land, were not infrequently captured by corsairs from the northern coast of Africa, and sold into slavery. At times, if there was hope of a very large ransom, news of the condition of these poor victims might find its way to their homes. As a rule, however, they were as much lost to family and friends as if they had actually been swallowed up by the sea, which was usually concluded to have been their fate. The hardships thus endured and the utter helplessness of their conditions made them fitting subjects for special social effort. The institution which was to provide relief for this sad state of affairs had its rise in a typically Thirteenth Century way—what, doubtless, the modern world would be apt to think of as characteristically medieval— but the result achieved was as good an example of practical benevolence as has ever been effected in the most matter-of-fact of centuries.

Shortly after the beginning of the Thirteenth Century two very intelligent men, whose friends honored them very much for the saintliness of their lives—meaning by saintliness not only their piety but their thoughtfulness for others before themselves—had a dream in which they saw poor captives held in slavery and asking for some one out of Christian charity to come and ransom them. One of these men was John of Matha, a distinguished teacher of Theology at the University of Paris. The other was Felix of Valois, more distinguished for his piety than his learning, but by no means an ignorant man. On the same night, though living at a distance from one another, they had this identical dream. Having told it next day to some friends, it happened that after a time it came to their mutual knowledge that the other had had a similar vision. The circumstance seemed so striking to them that they applied to the Pope for an interpretation of it. The Pope, who was Innocent III., the founder of city hospitals, saw in it a magnificent opportunity for the foundation of another great Christian charity.

Accordingly in interpreting it, he directed their thoughts toward the redemption of Christian captives taken by the Saracens. He has as a consequence been regarded as the founder of the order of Trinitarians (A. D. 1198), and did, in

fact, draft its Rule. It was called, from its object, Ordo de
Redemptione Captivorum, (Order for the Redemption of Captives), but its members were more generally known as Trinitarians. They wore a white habit, having a red and blue cross
on the breast. They were well received in France, where they
had originated, were the recipients of large sums of money to
be devoted to the objects of the order, and had large accessions to their number, among whom were many distinguished
by ability and profound learning.

In the year 1200 the first company of ransomed captives arrived from Morocco, and one may easily imagine their joy on
again regaining their freedom and beholding once more their
friends and native land.

The members of this order were sometimes called Mathurins,
from the title of the first church occupied by them in Paris.
They spread rapidly in Southern France, through Spain, Italy,
England, Saxony, and Hungary, and foundations of a similar
kind were also opened for women. Cerfroid, in the diocese
of Meaux, where the first house of the order was opened, became the residence of the General (minister generalis). There
was a fine field for their labors in Spain, where the Moors were
constantly at war with the Christians. The self-sacrificing
spirit of these religious, which led them to incur almost any
dangers in the accomplishment of their purpose, was only
equaled by their zeal in arousing interest for the poor captives.
They became the accredited agents for the ransoming of prisoners, and also for their exchange and even the Mahometans
learned to trust and eventually to reverence them. When they
could not ransom at once they thus succeeded in ameliorating
the conditions in which slave prisoners were kept, and proved
a great source of consolation to them.

Another order, having the same object in view but differing
somewhat in its constitution, was founded in 1218, by Peter of
Nolasco, a distinguished Frenchman, and Raymond of Penna-
fort the famous authority on canon law. In this, too, medieval
supernaturalism evolved the usual practical results. In consequence of a vision, the order was placed under the special
protection of the Blessed Virgin, and called the Order of the
Blessed Virgin of Mercy (Ordo. B. Mariae de Mercede). Its

members bound themselves by vow to give their fortunes and to serve as soldiers in the cause. Their devotion was so ardent that for the accomplishment of their purpose they vowed if necessary to make a sacrifice of their very persons, as Peter actually did in Africa, for the redemption of Christian captives. Hence their members were divided into Knights who wore a white uniform, and Brothers, who took orders and provided for the spiritual wants of the community. Gregory IX., admiring the heroic devotion of these intrepid men, approved the order. Many thousands of captive Christians who would otherwise have dragged out a miserable existence as slaves among the Mahometans of North Africa, were thus rescued and restored to their families and a life of freedom and happiness in Europe. This was a fine practical example of Abolitionism worthy of study and admiration.

THIRTEENTH CENTURY HOSPITAL INTERIOR
(TONERRE)

XXII

GREAT ORIGINS IN LAW.

Perhaps the most surprising phase of Thirteenth Century history is that much of what is most valued and most valuable in our modern laws, especially as they concern the fundamental rights of man, is to be found clearly expressed in the great law-making of the Thirteenth Century. It can scarcely fail to astonish those who look upon the Middle Ages as hopelessly barren in progress, to find that human liberty in its development reached such a pass before the end of the Middle Ages, or that any period so long before the Renaissance and the reformation so-called, could be picked out as representing a distinctive epoch in supremely liberal legislation. After careful study, the surprise is apt to be rather that there should have been comparatively so little advance since that time, seeing how much the generations of this marvelous century were able to accomplish in definitely formulating principles of human rights.

The first great document in the laws of the Thirteenth Century is, of course, Magna Charta, signed in 1215, the foundation of all the liberties of English speaking people ever since. Perhaps the highest possible tribute to the Great Charter is the fact that it has grown in the estimation of intelligent men, rather than lost significance. In quite recent years it has become somewhat the custom to belittle its import and its influence. But it must not be forgotten that over and over again in times of national crises in England, Magna Charta has been confidently appealed to as a fundamental law too sacred to be altered, as a talisman containing some magic spell capable of averting national calamity. Bishop Stubbs said of it, that "the Great Charter was the first supreme act of the nation after it had realized its own identity."

Perhaps in nothing does its supremacy as basic legislation for national purposes so shine forth, as from the fact that it is not a vague statement of great principles, not a mere declaration of human rights, not a documentary rehearsal of fundamental legalities, but a carefully collected series of practical declarations for the solution of the problems that were then disturbing the peace of the kingdom, and leading to charge and countercharge of infringement of right on the part of the king and his subjects. As might have been expected from the men of the Thirteenth Century—from the generations who more than any other in all human history succeeded in uniting the useful with the beautiful in everything from the decoration of their churches and other great architectural structures to the ordinary objects of everyday life—it was of eminently practical character. While it is the custom to talk much of Magna Charta and to praise its wonderful influence there are very few people who have ever actually read its provisions. The classics are said to be books that everyone praises but no one reads, and Magna Charta and the Constitution of the United States are documents that are joined in the same fate. A little consideration of some of the chapters of the Charter will give an excellent idea of its thoroughly straightforward practicalness, though it may serve also to undeceive those who would expect to find in this primal document a lofty statement of abstract human rights, such as the men of the Thirteenth Century were never conscious of, since their thoughts were always in the concrete and their efforts were bent to the solution of the problems lying just before them, and not to the lifting of all the burdens that human nature has to bear.

Before this, of course, there had been some development of legislation to furnish the basis for what was to come in the Thirteenth Century. The famous Constitutions of Clarendon under Henry II. and the Assizes of Clarendon (quite a different matter) and of North Hampton and the Forest under Henry II., gave assurances of rights that had only existed somewhat shadily before. According to the Constitutions of Clarendon sworn men gave their verdict in cases from their own knowledge. This was, of course, quite a different matter from the giving of a verdict from knowledge obtained through witnesses at a trial, but the germ of the jury trial can be seen. It was not, however, until the next reign that the men of England did not merely wait for the free gifts of legal rights but demanded and obtained them. There was a new hitherto undreamt-of spirit abroad in the Thirteenth Century, by which men dared to ask for the rights they considered should be theirs.

The opening chapter of Magna Charta states especially the subjects of the rights that are guaranteed by the document. It is not surprising then to find that the first subject is the Church and that the most extensive guarantees are made that the English Church liberties shall be inviolate. Churchmen had been largely concerned in the movement which secured the signing of Magna Charta, and then after all, as must never be forgotten, the Church at this time was distinctly felt by all to be the spiritual expression of the religious aspirations of the people. Over the concluding sentence of this chapter, "the grant of the unwritten liberties to all freemen of our kingdom," there has been no little discussion. There are some who would consider that it applied to all Englishmen above the condition of villeins or serfs, while there are others who would limit its application practically to those nobly born in the kingdom. Posterity undoubtedly came to translate it in the broader sense, so that, whatever the original intention, the phrase became as a grant eventually to all free Englishmen.

CHAPTER I.: "In the first place we have granted to God, and by this our present charter confirmed for us and our heirs for ever, that the English Church shall be free, and shall have her rights entire, and her liberties inviolate; and we will that it be thus observed; which is apparent from this that the freedom of elections, which is reckoned most important and very essential to the English Church, we of our pure and unconstrained will, did grant, and by our charter confirm and did obtain the ratification of the same from our lord, Pope Innocent III. before the quarrel arose between us and our barons, and this we will observe, and our will is that it be observed in good faith by our heirs for ever. We have also granted to all freemen of our kingdom, for us and for our heirs for ever, all the underwritten liberties, to be had and held by them and their heirs, of us and our heirs for ever."

Perhaps the most interesting feature of Magna Charta is to

be found in the fact, that it did actually in most cases come to be applied ever so much wider than had apparently been the original intention. It was in this sense a vital document as it were, since it had within itself the power of developing so as to suit the varying circumstances for which recourse was had to it. There is no doubt at all of the good faith of the men who appealed to it, nor of their firm persuasion that the document actually intended what they claimed to find in it. Modern criticism has succeeded in stripping from the original expressions many of the added meanings that posterity attached to them, but in so doing has really not lessened the estimation in which Magna Charta must be held.

The position is indeed noteworthily analagous to that of the original deposit of faith and the development of doctrine which has taken place. Higher criticism has done much to show how little of certain modern ideas was apparently contained explicitly in the original formulas of Christian faith, and yet by so doing has not lessened our beliefs, but has rather tended to make us realize the vitality of the original Christian tenets. As everything living in God's creation, they have developed by a principle implanted within them to suit the evolutionary conditions of man's intelligence and the developing problems that they were supposed to offer solutions for. The comparison, of course, like all comparisons, must walk a little lame, since after all Magna Charta is a human document, and yet the very fact that it should have presented itself under so many varying conditions, ever with new significance to succeeding generations of thinking men, is the best evidence of how nearly man's work at its best may approach that of the Creator. It is an exemplification, in a word, of the creative genius of the century, a worthy compeer of the other accomplishments which have proved so enduring and so capable of making their influence felt even upon distant generations.

It is of the very essence of the practicality of Magna Charta that among the early chapters of the important document— Chapter VII.—is one that concerns widows and their property rights immediately after the death of their husbands. Previous chapters had discussed questions of guardianship and inheritance, since it was especially minors who in this rude period were likely to suffer from the injustice of the crown, of their over-lords in the nobility, and even from their guardians. While Magna Charta, then, begins with the principles for the regulation of matters of property as regards children, it proceeds at once to the next class most liable to injustice because of their inability to properly defend themselves by force of arms —the widows.

CHAPTER VII.: "A widow, after the death of her husband, shall forthwith and without difficulty have her marriage portion and inheritance; nor shall she give anything for her dower or for her marriage portion, or for the inheritance which she and her husband held on the day of the death of that husband; and she may remain in the house of her husband for forty days after his death, within which time her dower shall be assigned to her."

CHAPTER VIII.: "Let no widow be compelled to marry, so long as she prefers to live without a husband; provided always that she gives security not to marry without our consent, if she holds of us, or without the consent of the lord of whom she holds, if she holds of another."

The first of these provisions serves to show very well how early in the history of English jurisprudence a thoroughgoing respect for woman's legal rights began to have a place. The beginning Thirteenth Century made an excellent start in their favor. For some reason the movement for justice thus initiated did not continue, but suffered a sad interruption down almost to our own times.

The second of these provisions for widows, embodied in Chapter VIII., sounds a little queer to the modern ear. This protection of widows from compulsion to marry is apt to seem absolutely unnecessary in these modern days. Some of the unmarried are indeed prone to think, perhaps, that widows have more than their due opportunity in this matter without any necessity for protecting them from compulsion. Of course it is to be understood that it was not always so much the charms of the lady herself that must be protected from compulsion, as those of the property which she inherited and the political and martial influence that she might be expected to bring her husband. In these troublous times when disputes with appeals to arms were extremely frequent, it was important to have the regulation, that after the death of a husband there should be no sudden unbalancing of political power because of the compelled marriage of the widow of some powerful noble.

In certain subsequent chapters up to the twelfth there is question mainly of the rights of the Jews, as money-lenders, to collect their debts with interest after the death of the principal to whom it was loaned. For instance, according to Chapter X., the debt shall not bear interest while the heir is under age and if the debt fell to the hands of the crown, nothing but the principal was to be taken. In Chapter XI. if any one died indebted to the Jews his wife should have her dower and pay nothing of that debt. For children under age the same principle held and they had a right to the provision of necessaries in keeping with the condition of their father. This last clause has been perpetuated in the practice of our courts, as some consider even to the extent of an abuse, so that debtors cannot collect from the income of a young man to whom money has been left, if by so doing the income should be impaired to such an extent as to make his method of living unsuitable to the condition in life to which he was born and brought up.

Chapter XII. has been the subject of more discussion perhaps than any other. McKechnie, the most recent commentator on Magna Charta, says of it :*

"This is a famous clause, greatly valued at the time it was framed because of its precise terms and narrow scope (which made evasion difficult), and even more highly valued in after days for exactly opposite reasons. It came indeed to be interpreted in a broad general sense by enthusiasts who, with the fully-developed British constitution before them, read the clause as enunciating the modern doctrine that the Crown can impose no financial burden whatsoever on the people without consent of Parliament."

Readers may judge for themselves from the tenor of the

*Magna Carta, a Commentary on the Great Charter of King John, with an Historical Introduction by William Sharp McKechnie, M.D., LL.B., D.Phil. Glasgow, James Maclehose and Sons, Publishers to the University, 1905.

chapter, how wide a latitude in interpretation it not only permits, but invites.

CHAPTER XII.: "No scutage nor aid shall be imposed in our kingdom, unless by common counsel of our kingdom, except for ransoming our person, for making our eldest son a knight, and for once marrying our eldest daughter; and for these there shall not be levied more than a reasonable aid. In like manner it shall be done concerning aids from the citizens of London."

There is no doubt that it is hard to read in this chapter all that has been found in it by enthusiastic appellants to Magna Charta at many times during the succeeding centuries. As a matter of fact, however, within half a century after it had been promulgated, it was appealed to confidently as one of the reasons why an English Parliament should meet if the King required special levies of money for the purpose of carrying on war. It was during the sixth and seventh decades of the Thirteenth Century that the great principle of English Legislation: "There shall be no taxation without representation"—which six centuries later was to be appealed to by the American Colonies as the justification for their war for independence, gradually came to be considered as a fundamental principle of the relationship between the government and the people. That it had its origin in Magna Charta there seems no doubt, and it is only another example of that unconscious development of a vital principle which, as we know from History, took place so often with regard to chapters of the Great Charter.

Undoubtedly one of the most important chapters of Magna Charta is the very brief one, No. 17, which concerns itself with the holding of a Court of Common Pleas. The whole of the chapter is, "Common Pleas shall not follow our Court but shall be held in some fixed place." This represented a distinct step in advance in the dispensing of justice. It is a little bit hard for us to understand, but all departments of government were originally centered in the king and his household—the court—which attended to royal and national business of every kind. As pointed out by Mr. McKechnie in his Magna Charta, the court united in itself the functions of the modern cabinet of the administrative department—the home office, the foreign office and the admiralty, and of the various legal tribunals. It was the parent of the Court at St. James and the courts at Westminster. Almost needless to say, it is from the fact that the dispensing of justice was a function of royalty, that the places of holding trials are still called courts.

According to this chapter of Magna Charta, thereafter ordinary trials, Common Pleas, did not have to follow the Court, that is the royal household, in its wanderings through various parts of the kingdom, but they were held at an appointed place. In the days of Henry II. the entire machinery of royal justice had to follow the monarch as he passed, sometimes on the mere impulse of the moment, from one of his favorite hunting-seats to another. Crowds thronged after him in hot pursuit, since it was difficult to transact business of moment before the court without being actually present. This entailed almost intolerable delay, extreme annoyance and great expense upon litigants, who brought their pleas for the king's decision. There is an account of the hardships which this system inflicted upon suitors told of one celebrated case. Richard D'Anesty gives a graphic record of his journeyings in search of justice throughout a period of five years, during which he visited in the king's wake most parts of England, Normandy, Aquitaine, and Anjou. Ultimately successful he paid dearly for his legal triumph. He had to borrow at a ruinous rate of interest in order to meet his enormous expenses, mostly for traveling, and was scarcely able to discharge his debts.

All litigation then, that did not directly involve the crown or criminal procedures, could be tried thereafter by a set of judges who sat permanently in some fixed spot, which though not named was probably intended from the beginning to be Westminster. Hence it has been said by distinguished English jurists that Magna Charta gave England a Capital. On the other hand Chapter XXIV. insured justice in criminal cases by reserving these pleas to judges appointed by the crown. This short chapter reads: "No sheriff, constable, coroner, or others of our bailiffs shall hold pleas of our Crown." This last expression did not necessarily mean matters concerned with royal business as might be thought, but had in King John's time come to signify criminal trials of all kinds. It is easy to understand that those accused of crime would look confidently for justice to the representative of the central government, while they dreaded the jurisdiction of the less responsible officials resident in the counties, who had a wide-spread reputation for cruelty and oppression, and for a venality that it was hard to suppress.

It would seem as though these quotations would serve to make even the casual reader appreciate how thoroughly Magna Charta deserves the reputation which it has borne now for nearly seven centuries, of an extremely valuable fundamental document in the history of the liberties of the English speaking people. Some of the subsequent chapters may be quoted without comment because they show with what careful attention to detail the rights of the people were guaranteed by the Chapter, and how many apparently trivial things were considered worthy of mention. We may call attention to the fact that in Chapters forty-one and forty-two there are definite expressions of guarantee for the rights even of aliens, which represent a great advance over the feelings in this respect that had animated the people of a century or so before, and foreshadow the development of that international comity which is only now coming to be the distinguishing mark of our modern civilization.

"A freeman shall not be amerced for a small offence, except in accordance with the degree of the offence; and for a grave offence he shall be amerced in accordance with the gravity of his offence, yet saving always his 'contentment'; and a merchant in the same way, saving his wares; and a villein shall be amerced in the same way, saving his wainage—if they have fallen into our mercy; and none of the aforesaid amercements shall be imposed except by the oath of honest men of the neighborhood.

"If any freeman shall die intestate, his chattels shall be distributed by the hands of the nearest kinsfolk and friends, under the supervision of the church, saving to everyone the debts which the deceased owed to him.

"No constable or other bailiff of ours shall take corn or other provisions from anyone without immediately tendering money therefor, unless he can have postponement thereof by permission of the seller.

"No sheriff or bailiff of ours, or any other person shall take the horses or carts of any freeman for transport duty, against the will of the said freeman.

"All kydells for the future shall be removed altogether from the Thames and Medway, and throughout all England, except upon the sea coast.

"Nothing in the future shall be taken or given for a writ of inquisition of life or limbs, but freely it shall be granted, and never denied.

"No bailiff for the future shall put any man to his 'law' upon his own mere word of mouth, without credible witnesses brought for this purpose.

"No freeman shall be arrested or detained in prison, or deprived of his freehold, or outlawed, or banished, or in any way molested, and we will not set forth against him, nor send against him, unless by the lawful judgment of his peers and by the law of the land.

"To no one will we sell, to no one will we refuse or delay, right or justice.

"All merchants shall have safe and secure exit from England, and entry to England, with the right to tarry there and to move about as well by land as by water, for buying and selling by the ancient and right customs, quit from all evil tolls, except (in time of war) such merchants as are of the land at war with us. And if such are found in our land at the beginning of the war, they shall be detained without injury to their bodies or goods, until information be received by us, or by our chief justiciar, how the merchants of our land found in the land at war with us are treated and if our men are safe there, the others shall be safe in our land.

"It shall be lawful in future for any one (excepting always those imprisoned or outlawed in accordance with the law of the kingdom, and natives of any country at war with us, and merchants, who shall be treated as is above provided) to leave our kingdom, and to return, safe and secure by land and water, except for a short period in time of war, on grounds of public policy—reserving always the allegiance due to us.

"We will appoint as justices, constables, sheriffs or bailiffs only such as know the law of the realm and mean to observe it well.

"We shall have, moreover, the same respite and the same manner in rendering justice concerning the disafforestation or retention of those forests which Henry our father and Richard our brother afforested and concerning the wardship of lands which are of the fief of another (namely, such wardships as we have hitherto had by reason of a fief, which any one held of us by knight's service) and concerning abbeys founded on other fiefs than our own, in which the lord of the fee claims to have right; and when we have returned, or if we desist from our expedition, we will immediately grant full justice to all who complain of such things.

"All fines made with us unjustly and against the law of this land, and all amercements imposed unjusty and against the law of this land, shall be entirely remitted, or else it shall be done concerning them according to the decision of the five and twenty barons of whom mention is made below, in the clause for securing the peace, or according to the judgment of the majority of the same, along with the aforesaid Stephen Archbishop of Canterbury, if he can be present, and such others as he may wish to bring with him for this purpose, and if he cannot be present the business shall nevertheless proceed without him, provided always that if any one or more of the aforesaid five and twenty barons are in a similar suit, they shall be removed as far as concerns this particular judgment, others being substituted in their places after having been selected by the rest of the same five and twenty for this purpose only, and after having been sworn.

"Moreover, all the aforesaid customs and liberties, the observance of which we have granted in our kingdom as far as pertains to us towards our men, shall be observed by all of our kingdom, as well by clergy as by laymen, as far as pertains to them towards their men.

"And, on this head, we have caused to be made out letters patent of Stephen, Archbishop of Canterbury, Henry, Archbishop of Dublin, the bishops aforesaid, and Master Pandulf, as evidence of this clause of security and of the aforesaid concessions."

These last provisions show how closely the Church was bound up with the securing and maintenance of the rights of the English people. The clauses we have quoted just before, need no comment to show how sturdily the spirit of liberty strode abroad even at the beginning of the Thirteenth Century, for Magna Charta was signed in 1215. The rest of the century was to see great advances in liberty and human rights, even beyond the guarantees of the Great Charter.

Magna Charta, glorious as it was, was only the beginning of that basic legislation which was to distinguish the Thirteenth Century in England. About the middle of the century Bracton began his collection of the laws of the land which has since been the great English classic of the Common Law. His work was accomplished while he was the Chief Justiciary during the reign of Henry III. For many years before he had occupied various judicial positions, as Justice Itinerant of the counties of Nottingham and Derby and for seventeen years his name appears as one of the justices of the Aula Regis. This experience put him in an eminently fitting position to be the mouthpiece of English practice and law applications, and his book was at once accepted as an authority. It is a most comprehensive and systematic work in five volumes, bearing the title De Legibus et Consuetudinibus Angliae, and was modeled after the Institutes of Justinian.

It was during the reign of Edward I., the English Justinian as he has been called, that the English Common Law came to its supreme expression, and this monarch has rightly been placed among the great benefactors of mankind for his magnanimous generosity in securing the legal rights of his subjects and framing English liberties for all time. Not a little of Edward's greatness as a law-maker and his readiness to recognize the rights of his subjects, with his consequent willingness to have English law arranged and published, must be attributed to his connection during his earlier years as Prince of Wales with the famous Simon De Montfort. To this man more than to any other the English speaking people owe the development of those constitutional rights, which gradually came to be considered inalienably theirs during the Thirteenth Century. He is undoubtedly one of the very great characters of history and the Thirteenth Century is by so much greater for having been the scene of his labors, during so many years, for the establishment of constitutional limitations to the power of the monarch, and the uplifting of the rights of subjects not only among the nobility, but also among the lower classes.

It was in Edward's time that the English Common Law was fashioned into the shape in which it was to exist for many centuries afterwards. How true this is may perhaps best be judged by the fact that even the laws with regard to real estate have not been changed in essence since that time, though medieval titles to land would seem to be so different to those of the present day. According to the Encyclopedia Britannica the changes which have been made since that time have been mainly due to the action of equity and legislation, the latter sometimes interpreted by the courts in a manner very different from the intention of Parliament. The same authority is responsible for the statement that the reign of Edward I., is notable for three leading real estate statutes which are still law. One of these was with regard to Mortmain, while the important statute known as *Quia Emptores* (the eighteenth of Chapter I. of the Laws of Edward I.) had the practical effect of making the transfer of land thenceforward, more of a commercial and less of a legal transaction. It is to this same period that is owed the writ *Elegit* which introduced the law practice of a creditor's remedy over real estate. How little was accomplished in the matter of law-making in subsequent centuries, may be gathered from the fact that Mr. James Williams who writes the article on real estate in the Encyclopedia Britannica ninth edition, says that from 1290 to the reign of Henry VIII., that is down to the Sixteenth Century, there is no statute of the first importance dealing with real estate.

In a word, then, it may be said that these law-makers of the Thirteenth Century anticipated most of the legal difficulties of the after-time. Their statutory provisions, as in the case of the chapters of Magna Charta, seemed originally only to have a narrow application to certain urgent legal questions of the time, but proved eventually to contain in themselves the essence of legal principles that could be applied in circumstances such as the original law-maker had not even imagined. This is indeed the typical triumph of the century in every line of endeavor, that while apparently it devoted itself only to the narrow problems of its own time, its solutions of them whether in art and architecture or decoration, in literary expression or poetic effectiveness, in educational methods or social uplift, always proved so complete, so thoroughly human in the broadest sense of that word and so consonant with development, that their work did not have to be done over again. No greater praise than this could be bestowed.

SPIRE OF
ST. ELIZABETH'S,
(MARBURG)

XXIII

JUSTICE AND LEGAL DEVELOPMENT.

It must not be thought because we have devoted so much time to the triumphs of English law-making in the Thirteenth Century that, therefore, there is little or nothing to be said about this same admirable feature of the time in other countries. As a matter of fact every nation in Europe saw the foundation of its modern legal system laid, and was responsive witness to the expression of the first principles of popular rights and popular liberties. Montalembert in his Life of St. Elizabeth of Hungary* makes no mention in the Introduction which is really a panegyric of the Thirteenth Century, of the progress of English law-making, and yet considers that he is able to bring together enough evidence to show that legislation had its acme of development just at this time. His paragraph on the subject will serve as the best possible preface to the scant treatment of continental law-making and enforcement of justice in this period, that our limited space will allow. He says:

"Legislation never, perhaps, had a more illustrious period. On the one hand, the Popes, supreme authorities in matters of law as well as of faith, gave to canon law the fullest development possible to this magnificent security of Christian civilization; sat themselves as judges with exemplary assiduity, published immense collections, and founded numerous schools. On the other hand, that period gave birth to most of the national legislation of the various states of Europe; the great *Mirrors* of Swabia and Saxony, the first laws published in the German language by Frederick II. at the diet of Mentz, and the code given by him to Sicily; in France, the Institutes of St. Louis, together with the *Common Law* of Pierre des Fon-

* Life of St. Elizabeth of Hungary by the Count De Montalembert, translated by Francis Deming Hoyt, New York, Longman's, Green and Company, 1904.

taines, and the *Statutes of Beauvoisis* of Philip of Beaumanoir; and lastly the French version of the *Assizes of Jerusalem,* in which is to be found the most complete résumé now extant of Christian and chivalric law. All these precious monuments of the old Christian organization of the world are preserved in the native languages of the various people, and are distinguished less even by this fact than by their generous and pious spirit, from that pernicious Roman law, the progress of which was destined soon to change all the principles of the former."

Most of Montalembert's paragraph refers to the law-making in France with which he is naturally more familiar. He has supplied ample material for consultation for those who wish to follow out this interesting theme further. Even more significant, however, than the law-making in France, were the new ideas with regard to the enforcement in law that came in during the reign of Louis IX. We have not had to wait until this generation to realize, that as a rule it is not the absence of law so much as the lack of enforcement of such laws as exist, that gives rise to many of the injustices between men. St. Louis made it his business to bring about the enforcement of the laws with proper construction of their terms in such a way as to secure the rights of all. He himself sat under the famous old oak of Versailles as a Court of Appeals, reviewing especially the cases of the poor. It soon came to be known, that it would be a sad occasion for any and every court official who was found to have given judgment against the poor because of partiality or the yielding to unlawful influence. On the other hand, in order to keep the right of appeal from being abused, punishments were meted out to those who made appeals without good reason.

Finding that he was unable to hear so many causes as were appealed to him, Louis chose Stephen Boileau to act as Chief Justice and committed the care of proper legal enforcement with confidence into his hands. Boileau had become famous by having condemned some very near relatives, under circumstances such that relationship might have been expected to weigh down the wrong side of the scales of justice, and in a few years he enhanced his reputation by the utter disregard of all motives in the settlement of suits at law, except those of the strictest justice. How much Louis himself did in order to safeguard the rights of the poor can be judged from the famous incident told by all his biographers, in which he risked the enmity of the most powerful among his barons, in order to secure the punishment of one of them who had put two students to death. This was the first time that the rights of men, as men, were asserted and it constitutes the best possible testimony to the development of law and true liberty in France.

"Three young nobles of the county of Flanders were surprised, together with the abbot of St. Nicholas, in a wood pertaining to Coucy, with bows and arrows. Although they had neither dogs nor hunting implements, they were found guilty of having gone out to hunt and were hanged. The abbot and several women of their families made complaint to the king, and Enguerrard was arrested and taken to the Louvre. The king summoned him before him; he appeared, having with him the King of Navarre, the King of Burgundy, the counts of Bar, Soissons, Brittany, and Blois, the Archbishop of Rheims, Sire John of Thorote, and nearly all the great men in the kingdom. The accused said that he wished to take counsel, and he retired with most of the seigneurs who had accompanied him, leaving the king alone with his household. When he returned, John of Thorote, in his name, said that he would not submit to this inquiry, since his person, his honour, and his heritage were at stake, but that he was ready to do battle, denying that he had hanged the three young men, or ordered them to be hanged. His only opponents were the abbot and the women, who were there to ask for justice. The king answered that in causes in which the poor, the churches, and persons worthy of pity, took part, it was not fitting to decide them in battle; for it was not easy to find anyone to fight for such sorts of people against the barons of the kingdom. He said that his action against the accused was no new thing, and he alleged the example of his predecessor Philip Augustus. He therefore agreed to the request of the complainants, and caused Enguerrard to be arrested by the sergeants and taken to the Louvre. All prayers were useless; St. Louis refused to hear them, rose from his seat, and the barons went away astonished and confused.

"They did not, however, consider that they were beaten. They again came together; the King of Navarre, the Count of Brittany, and with them the Countess of Flanders, who ought rather to have intervened for the victims. It was as if they had conspired against the king's power and honour; for they were not content to implore Coucy's release, but asserted that he could not be kept in prison. The Count of Brittany maintained that the king had no right to institute inquiries against the barons of his kingdom in matters which concerned their persons, their heritage or their honour. The king replied, 'You did not speak thus in former times when the barons in direct dependence upon you came before me with complaints against yourself, and offered to sustain them in battle. You then said that to do battle was not in the way of justice.' The barons put forward a final argument, namely, that according to the customs of the kingdom, the king could only judge the accused and punish him in person after an inquiry to which he had refused to submit. The king was resolute, and declared that neither the rank of the guilty man nor the power of his friends should prevent him from doing full justice. Coucy's life was, however, spared. The fact that he had not been present at the judgment, nor at the execution, prevailed in his favour. By the advice of his counsellors, the king condemned him to pay 1200 livres parisis, which, considering the difference in the purchasing power of money, may be estimated at considerably more than 400,000 pounds, and he sent this sum to St. John of Acre for the defense of Palestine. The wood in which the young men were hanged was confiscated to the abbey of St. Nicholas. The condemned man was also constrained to found three perpetual chapelries for the souls of his victims, and he forfeited jurisdiction over his woods and fish ponds, so that he was forbidden to imprison or execute for any offense which had to do with them. Since Enguerrard's defender, John of Thorote, had in his anger told the barons that the king would do well to hang them all, the king, who had been told of this, sent for him and said, 'How comes it, John, that you have said I should hang my barons? I certainly will not have them hanged, but I will punish them when they do amiss.' John of Thorote denied that he had said this, and offered to justify himself on the oath of twenty or thirty knights. The king would not carry the matter further, and let him go."

One of the best evidences of the development of the spirit of law in Germany during this time is the establishment of the famous Fehmic Courts, or Vehmgerichte, which achieved their highest importance during the Thirteenth Century. As with regard to the universities, there is a tradition that carries the origin of these courts back to the time of Charlemagne. They are much more likely to have been developments out of the relics of the ancient free courts of the old Teutonic Tribe. The first definite knowledge of their existence cannot be traced much earlier than a decade or two before the Thirteenth Century. They had their principal existence in Westphalia. Practically the whole country between the Rhine and the Weser was ruled to a subordinate degree by these Fehmic courts. During the Thirteenth Century they were used only in the most beneficial and liberal spirit, supplying a means of redress at a time when the public administration of justice was almost completely in abeyance. As a matter of fact, before their establishment disregard for authority to the extent of utter lawlessness prevailed in this part of Germany.

The significance of these courts has sometimes been missed. They arose, however, out of the justice loving spirit of the people themselves and were meant to supply legal enforcements when the regularly constituted authorities were unable to secure them. They remind one very much of the vigilance committees, which in our own country, in the cities of the distant West, bravely and with the admirable prudence of the race, have so often supplied the place of regular courts and have brought justice and order out of the chaos of lawlessness. The last place most people would expect their prototypes, however, would be here in the Germany of the Thirteenth Century. How much these Vehmgerichte accomplished during the Thirteenth and Fourteenth centuries it would be difficult to say. They represent an outgrowth of the spirit of the people themselves, that constitutes another striking feature of the practical side of the generations of the Thirteenth Century. They had much more to do with bringing about the development of the modern acute sense of justice among the Teutonic peoples

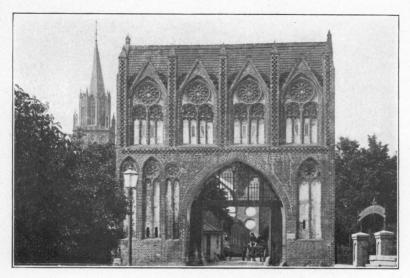

CITY GATE (NEUBRANDENBURG)

RATHAUS (STRALSUND)

than is usually thought. They are the German expression of the same feelings that in England dictated trial by jury, and secured for the English speaking people of all time the precious privileges of even-handed justice and the right to be judged by one's peers.

It was not alone in the western countries of Europe that great advances were made in liberty. The democratic spirit that was abroad made itself felt everywhere and the foundations of rights for the people were laid even in central Europe, in countries which ordinarily are thought of at this time as scarcely more than emerging from barbarism. Hungary may be cited as an example. Andrew II. is usually set down by narrow-minded historians as having been entirely too visionary in his character, and the fact that he led the fifth Crusade, apparently even more fruitless than were most of the others, is supposed to be an additional proof of this. Even Duruy in his History of the Middle Ages says of him, "he organized a state of anarchy by decreeing his Golden Bull, that if the King should violate the privileges of the nobility, they should be permitted to resist him by force and such resistance should not be treated as rebellion." As a matter of fact, his people were thus granted a constitution more liberal even than that of Magna Charta, but containing quite similar provisions in many respects, and the curious historical analogy is heightened when we recall that at the two ends of civilized Europe these constitutions were given in the same decade. One cannot help but wonder whether the Saxon elements which were in both peoples, for many Saxon and Frisian colonists had been induced to settle in certain parts of Transylvania just half a century before, did not have much to do with this extremely interesting development in Hungary, so like the corresponding evolution of the democratic spirit among their western kinsfolk.

In Poland the development in law came a little later but evidently as the result of the same factors that were at work during the Thirteenth Century. Casimir the Great, who was born shortly after the close of the Thirteenth Century, gave wise laws to Poland which have constituted the basis of Polish law ever since. At this time Poland was one of the most important countries in Europe. Casimir, besides giving laws to

his people, also founded a university for them and in every way
encouraged the development of such progress as would make
his subjects intelligently realize their own rights and maintain
them, apparently foreseeing that thus the King would be better able to strengthen himself against the many enemies that
surrounded him in central Europe.

How much the great Popes of the century accomplished for
the foundation and development of law, can only be appreciated
by those who realize the extent of their contributions to the
codification of canon law. It was the arrangement of this in
definite shape that put the civil jurists of the time at work setting their house in order.   Innocent III., who is deservedly
called *Pater Juris,* devoted a great deal of his wonderful energy and genius to the arrangement of canon law.   This
placed for the first time the canon law on an absolutely sure
footing and filled up many gaps that formerly existed.   Gregory IX. commissioned his chaplain, the famous Raymond of
Pennaforte, who had been a professor of canon law in the
University of Bologna, to codify all the decretals since the
time of Gratian.   This work was officially promulgated in 1234,
four years of labor having been devoted to it.   The laws are
in the form of decisions pronounced in cases submitted to the
Pope from all parts of Christendom, including many from the
distant East and not a few from England and Scotland.   Gregory's decretals were published in five books; a supplement under the name of the sixth book was published under Pope
Boniface VIII. in 1298.   In this for the first time abstract
rules of law are laid down extracted from actual judgments.
A compendium of Roman Law was added so as to approximate canon and civil procedure.

This gives the best possible idea of how deeply the popes and
the authorities in canon law of the century were laying the
foundations of canonical practise and procedure for all times.
The origins of modern law are to be found here, and yet not,
as might be anticipated because of the distance in time, in such
a confused or unmanageable fashion that they are not worth
while consulting, but on the contrary with such clarity and dis-
tinctness and with such orderly arrangement, that they have
been the subjects of study on the part of distinguished jur-

ists for most of the centuries ever since, and have never lost
their interest for the great lawyers and canonists, who prefer to know things from the foundation rather than accept
them at second hand.

Some of the commentaries, or glosses as they were called,
on canon law serve to give an excellent idea of the legal ability
as well as the intellectual acumen of the canon lawyers of the
century. The system of teaching was oral, and careful study
was devoted to original authorities in law. Explanatory notes
were added by the professors to their copies of the text. When
later these texts were given out or lent for transcription, the
notes were also copied, usually being written in the margin.
After a time the commentary, however, proved to be, for students at least, as important as the text and so was transcribed
by itself and was called an apparatus, that is a series of mechanical helps, as it were, to the understanding of the text.

Of the names of some of the most distinguished glossatores
the memory has been carefully preserved because they produced so much effect on legal teaching. The gloss written on Gratian by Joannes Teutonicus (John the German),
probably during the first decade of the Thirteenth Century,
was revised and supplemented by Bartholomew of Brescia
about the middle of the Thirteenth Century. Some ten years
later Bernard of Parma wrote a commentary on the decretals
of Gregory. All of these are important fundamental works
in canon law, and they were of very great influence in bringing out the principles of law and showing the basis on which
they were founded. It is almost needless to say that they
aroused additional interest and made the subject much more
easy of approach than it had been. The fact that all of these
magnificent contributions to the science and literatures of law
should have been made during our Thirteenth Century, serves
only to emphasize the fact that everything that men touched
during this period was sure to be illuminated by the practical
genius of the time, and put into a form in which for many centuries it was to be appealed to as a model and an authority in
its own line. How much of legal commentary writing there
was besides these, can be readily understood from the fact that
these represent the activity only of the University of Bologna

which was, it is true, the greatest of universities in its law department, but it must not be forgotten that many other universities throughout Europe also had distinguished professors of law at this time.

All this would seem to be of little interest for the secular law-making of the period, but it must not be forgotten that civil law was closely related to canon law at all times and that the development of canon law always meant a renewed evolution of the principles, and practise, and procedure of the civil law. In such countries as Scotland, indeed, the canon law formed the basis of the civil jurisprudence and its influence was felt even for centuries after the so-called reformation. On the other hand it must not be forgotten that the popes and the ecclesiastics helped to fight the battles of the middle and lower classes against the king and the nobility in practically every country in Europe. A very striking example of this is to be found in the life of that much misunderstood Pope Boniface VIII., the last pope of the century, who had received his legal training at Bologna, and who was one of the great jurists of his time. Circumstances differ so much, however, and obscure realities to such a degree, that at the present time we need the light of sympathetic interpretation to enable us to realize what Boniface accomplished.

He did much to complete in his time that arrangement and codification of canon law which his predecessors during the Thirteenth Century had so efficiently commenced. Like Innocent III. he has been much maligned because of his supposed attempt to make the governments of the time subservient to the Pope and to make the Church in each nation independent of the political government. With regard to the famous Bull Clericis Laicos, "thrice unhappy in name and fortune" as it has been designated, much more can be said in justification than is usually considered to be the case. Indeed the Rev. Dr. Barry, whose "Story of the Papal Monarchy" in the Stories of the Nations series has furnished the latest discussion of this subject, does not hesitate to declare that the Bull far from being subversive of political liberties or expressive of too arrogant a spirit on the part of the Church, was really an expression of a great principle that was to become very prominent in

BONIFACE VIII (GIOTTO)

modern history, and the basis of many of the modern declarations of rights against the claims of tyranny.

He says in part:

"Imprudent, headlong, but in its main contention founded on history, this extraordinary state-paper declared that the laity had always been hostile to the clergy, and were so now as much as ever. But they possessed no jurisdiction over the persons, no claims on the property of the church, though they had dared to exact a tenth, nay, even a half, of its income for secular objects, and time-serving prelates had not resisted. Now, on no title whatsoever from henceforth should such taxes be levied without permission of the Holy See. Every layman, though king or emperor, receiving these moneys fell by that very act under anathema; every churchman paying them was deposed from his office; universities guilty of the like offense were struck with interdict.

"Robert of Winchelsea, Langton's successor as primate, shared Langton's views. He was at this moment in Rome, and had doubtless urged Boniface to come to the rescue of a frightened, down-trodden clergy, whom Edward I. would not otherwise regard. In the Parliament at Bury, this very year, the clerics refused to make a grant. Edward sealed up their barns. The archbishop ordered that in every cathedral the pope's interdiction should be read. Hereupon the chief-justice declared the whole clergy outlawed; they might be robbed or murdered without redress. Naturally, not a few gave way; a fifth, and then a fourth, of their revenue was yielded up. But Archbishop Robert alone, with all the prelates except Lincoln against him, and the Dominicans preaching at Paul's cross on behalf of the king, stood out, lost his lands, and was banished to a country parsonage. War broke out in Flanders. It was the saving of the archbishop. At Westminster Edward relented and apologized. He confirmed the two great charters; he did away with illegal judgments that infringed them. Next year the primate excommunicated those royal officers who had seized goods or persons belonging to the clergy, and all who had violated Magna Charta. The Church came out of this conflict exempt, or, more truly a self-governing estate of the realm. It must be considered as having greatly concurred towards the establishment of that fundamental law invoked long after by the thirteen American Colonies, 'No taxation without representation,' which is the corner stone of British freedom."

We have so often heard it said that there is nothing new under the sun, that finally the expression has come to mean very little, though its startling truth sometimes throws vivid light on historical events. Certainly the last place in the world that one would expect to find if not the origin, for all during the Thirteenth Century this great principle had been gradually asserting itself, at least, a wondrous confirmation of the principle on which our American revolution justified itself, would be in a papal document of the end of the Thirteenth Century. Here, however, is a distinguished scholar, who insists that the Colonists' contention that there must be no taxes levied unless they were allowed representation in some way in the body which determined the mode and the amount of taxation, received its first formal justification in history at the hands of a Roman Pontiff, nearly five centuries before the beginning of the quarrel between the Colonies and the Mother Country. The passage serves to suggest how much of what is modern had its definite though unsuspected origin, in this earlier time.

DECORATION
THIRTEENTH
CENTURY MS.

XXIV

DEMOCRACY, CHRISTIAN SOCIALISM AND NATIONALITY.

Democracy is a word to conjure with but it is usually considered that the thing it represents had its origin in the modern world much later than the period with which we are occupied. The idea that the people should be ready to realize their own rights, to claim their privileges and to ask that they should be allowed to rule themselves, is supposed ordinarily to be a product of the last century or two. Perhaps in this matter more than any other does the Thirteenth Century need interpretation to the modern mind, yet we think that after certain democratic factors and developments in the life of this period are pointed out and their significance made clear, it will become evident that the foundations of our modern democracy were deeply laid in the Thirteenth Century, and that the spirit of what was best in the aspiration of people to be ruled by themselves, for themselves, and of themselves had its birth in this precious seed time of so much that is important for our modern life.

Lest it should be thought that this idea of the development of democracy has been engendered merely in the enthusiastic ardor of special admiration for the author's favorite century, it seems well to call attention to the fact that historians in recent years have very generally emphasized the role that the Thirteenth Century played in the development of freedom. A typical example may be quoted from the History of Anglo-Saxon Freedom by Professor James K. Hosmer,* who does not hesitate to say that "while in England representative government was gradually developing during this century, in Germany the cities were beginning to send deputies to the Imperial Parliament and the Emperor, Frederick II., was allowing a certain amount of representation in the

* Scribners, New York, 1890.

Government of Sicily. In Spain, Alfonso the Wise. of Castile, permitted the cities to send representatives to the Cortez, and in France this same spirit developed to such a degree that a representative parliament met at the beginning of the Fourteenth Century." In none of these countries, however, unfortunately did the spirit of representative government continue to develop as in England and in many of them the privileges obtained in the Thirteenth Century were subsequently lost.

Certain phases of the rise of the democratic spirit have already been discussed, and the reader can only be referred to them now with the definite idea of recognizing in them the democratic tendencies of the time. What we have said about the trade guilds constitutes one extremely important element of the movement which will be further discussed in this chapter. After this comes the guild merchant in its various forms. After all the Hanseatic League was only one manifestation of these guilds. Its widespread influence in awakening in people's minds the realization that they could do for themselves much more, and secure success in their endeavors much better by their own united efforts, than by anything that their accepted political rulers could do or at least would do for them, will be readily appreciated by all who read that chapter.

Hansa must have been a great enlightener for the Teutonic peoples. The History of the league shows over and over again their political rulers rather interfering with than fostering their commercial prosperity. These rulers were always more than a little jealous of the wealth which the citizens of these growing towns in their realm were able to accumulate, and they showed it on more than one occasion. The history of the Hansa towns exhibits the citizens doing everything to dissemble the feelings of disaffection that inevitably came to them as the result of their appreciation of the fact, that they could rule themselves so much better than they were being ruled, and that they could accomplish so much more for themselves by their commercial combination with other cities than had ever been done for them by these hereditary princes, who claimed so much yet gave so little in their turn.

The training in self-government that came with the necessities for defense as well as for the protection of commercial visitors from other cities in the league, who trustfully came to deal with their people, was an education in democracy such as could not fail to bring results. The rise of the free cities in Germany represents the growth of the democratic spirit down to our own time, better than any other single set of manifestations that we have. The international relations of these cities did more, as we have said, to broaden men's minds and make them realize the brotherhood of man in spite of national boundaries than any other factor in human history. Commerce has always been a great leveler and such it proved to be in these early days in Germany, only it must not be thought that these German cities had but faint glimmerings of the great purpose they were engaged in, for seldom has the spirit of popular government risen higher than with them.

How clearly the Teutonic mind had grasped the idea of democracy can be best appreciated perhaps from the attitude of the Swiss in this matter. These hardy mountaineers whose difficult country and rather severe climate separate them effectually from the other nations, soon learned the advisability of ruling themselves for their own benefit. Before the end of the Thirteenth Century they had formed a defensive and offensive union among themselves against the Hapsburgs, and though for a time overborne by the influence of this house after its head ascended the Imperial throne, immediately on Rudolph's death they proceeded to unite themselves still more firmly together. They then formed the famous league of 1291 which represents so important a step in the democracy of modern times. The formal document which constituted this league a federal government deserves to be quoted. It is the first great declaration of independence, and its ideas were to crop out in many another declaration in the after times. It is an original document in the strictest sense of the word. It runs as follows:

"Know all men that we, the people of the valley of Uri, the community of the valley of Schwiz, and the mountaineers of the lower valley, seeing the malice of the times, have solemnly agreed and bound ourselves by oath to aid and defend each other with all our might and main, with our lives and property, both within and without our boundaries each at his own expense, against every enemy whatever who shall attempt to molest us, either singly or collectively. This is our ancient covenant. Whoever hath a lord let him obey him according to his bounden duty. We have decreed that we shall accept no magistrate in our valleys who shall have obtained his office for a price, or who is not a native or resident among us. Every difference among us shall be decided by our wisest men; and whoever shall reject their award shall be compelled by the other confederates. Whoever shall wilfully commit a murder shall suffer death, and he who shall attempt to screen the murderer from justice shall be banished from our valleys. An incendiary shall lose his privileges as a free member of the community, and whoever harbors him shall make good the damage. Whoever robs or molests another shall make full restitution out of the property he possesses among us. Everyone shall acknowledge the authority of a chief magistrate in either of the valleys. If internal quarrels arise, and one of the parties shall refuse fair satisfaction, the confederates shall support the other party. This covenant for our common weal, shall, God willing, endure forever."

In England democracy was fostered in the guilds, which, as we have already seen in connection with the cathedrals, proved the sources of education and intellectual development in nearly every mode of thought and art. The most interesting feature of these guilds was the fact that they were not institutions suggested to the workmen and tradesmen by those above them, but were the outgrowth of the spirit of self help and organization which came over mankind during this century. At the beginning they were scarcely more than simple beneficial associations meant to be aids in times of sickness and trial, and to make the parting of families and especially the death of the head of the family not quite so difficult for the survivors, since affiliated brother workmen remained behind who would care for them. During this century, however, the spirit of democracy, that is the organized effort of the people to take care of themselves, better their conditions, and add to their own happiness, led to the development of the guilds in a fashion that it is rather difficult for generations of the modern time to understand, for our trades' unions do not, as yet at least, present anything that quite resembles their work in our times.

It was because of the effective social work of these guilds that Urbain Gohier, the well-known French socialist and writer on sociological subjects, was able to say not long ago in the North American Review:

"When the workmen of the European Continent demand 'the three eights'—eight hours of work, eight hours of rest and refreshment, physical and mental, and eight hours of sleep— some of them are aware of the fact that this reform already exists in the Anglo-Saxon countries; but all are ignorant of this other fact that, during the Middle Ages, in an immense number of labor corporations and cities, a work-day was often only nine, eight and even seven hours long. Nor have they ever been told that every Saturday, and on the eve of over two dozen holidays, work was stopped everywhere at four o'clock." The Saturday half holiday began it may be said even earlier, namely at the Vesper Hour which according to medieval church customs was some time between two and three p. m. and the same was true on the vigils, as the eves of the important church festivals were called.

The only possible way to give a reasonably good idea of the spirit of the old-time guilds which succeeded in accomplishing such a wonderful social revolution, is to quote some of their rules, which serve to show their intents and purposes at least, even though they may not always have fulfilled their aims. Their rules regard two things particularly—the religious and the social functions of the guild. There was a fine for absence from the special religious services held for the members but also a fine of equal amount for absence from the annual banquet. In this they resemble the rules of the religious orders which were coming to be widely known at the end of the Twelfth and the beginning of the Thirteenth Century, and according to which the members of the religious community were required quite as strictly to be present at daily recreation, that is, at the hour of conversation after meals, as at daily prayer. An interesting phase of the social rules of the guild is that a member was expected to bring his wife with him, or if not his wife then his sweetheart. They were franker in these matters in this simpler age and doubtless the custom encouraged matrimony a little bit more than our modern colder customs.

As giving a fair idea of the ordinances of the pre-Reformation guilds in their original shape the rules of the Guild of St. Luke at Lincoln, may be cited. St. Luke had been chosen as patron because according to tradition he was an artist as well as an evangelist. The patron saint was chosen always so that he might be a model of life as well as a protector in Heaven. Its members were the painters, guilders, stainers, and alabaster men of the city. The first rule provides that on the Sunday next after the feast of St. Luke all the brothers and sisters of the Guild shall, with their officers, go in procession from an appointed place, carrying a great candle, to the Cathedral Church of Lincoln, and there every two of the brethren and sisters shall offer one half-penny or more after their devotion, and then shall offer the great candle before an image of St. Luke within the church. And any who were absent without lawful cause shall forfeit one pound of wax to the sustentation of the said great candle.

On the same Sunday, "for love and amity and good communication to be had for the several weal of the fraternity," the guildmen dined together, every brother paying for himself and his wife, or sweetheart, the sum of four pence. Absentees were fined one pound of wax towards the aforesaid candle.

The third rule provided that four "mornspeeches"—that its business meetings—should be held each year, "for ordering and good rule to be had and made amongst them." Absentees from a mornspeech forfeited one pound of wax to St. Luke's candle. Another rule provided that the decision of ambiguities or doubts about the forfeitures prescribed should be referred to the mayor and four aldermen of the city. Rules 4 to 11, and also 13, regulate the taking of apprentices and the setting up in trade; forbid the employing of strangers; provide for the settlement of disputes and the examination of work not sufficiently done after the sample. Already the tendency to limit the number of workmen that might be employed which was later to prove a stumbling block to artistic progress is to be noted. On the other hand the effort to keep work up to a certain standard, which was to mean so much for artistic accom-

BROKEN ARCH (ST. MARY'S, YORK)

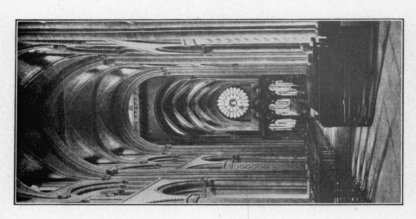

NAVE (DURHAM CATHEDRAL)

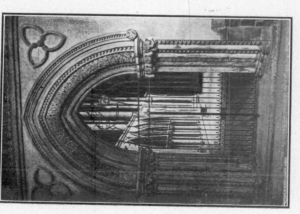

DOORWAY (LINCOLN)

plishment in the next few generations must be noted as a compensatory feature of the Guild regulations.

Rule 12 directs that "when it shall happen any brother or sister of the said fraternity to depart and decease from the world, at his first Mass the gracemen and wardens (skyvens) for the time being shall offer of the goods and chattels of the said fraternity, two pence; and at his eighth day, or thirtieth day, every brother and sister shall give to a poor creature a token made by the dean, for which tokens every brother and sister shall pay the dean a fixed sum of money, and with the money thus raised he shall buy white bread to give to the poor creatures" holding the tokens, the bread to be distributed at the church of the parish in which the deceased lived.

This twelfth rule with regard to the manner of giving charity is particularly striking, because it shows a deliberate effort to avoid certain dangers, the evil possibilities of which our modern organized charity has emphasized. According to this rule of the Guild of St. Luke's at Lincoln, all the members were bound to give a certain amount in charity, for the benefit of a deceased member. This was not, however, by direct alms, but by means of tokens for which they paid a fixed price to the Dean, who redeemed the tokens when they were presented by the deserving poor. This guaranteed that each member would give the fixed sum in charity and at the same time safeguarded the almsgiving from any abuses, since the member of the guild himself would be likely to know something of the poor person and his deservingness, and if not there was always the question of the Dean being informed with regard to the needs of the case. All of this was accomplished, however, without hurting the feelings of the recipients of the charity, since they felt that it was done not for them but for the benefit of a deceased member.

How much the guilds came to influence the life of the people during the next two centuries may be best appreciated from their great increase in number and wealth.

In England, it is computed that at the beginning of the Sixteenth Century there were thirty thousand of these institutions spread over the country. The county of Norfolk alone had nine hundred, of which number the small town of Wy-

mondham had at least eleven still known by names, one—the
Guild of Holy Trinity, Wymondham—being possessed of a
guild-hall of its own, whilst it and the other guilds of the town
are said to have been "well endowed with lands and tene-
ments." In Bury St. Edmunds, Suffolk, there were twenty-
three guilds; Boston, Lincolnshire, had fourteen, of which the
titles and other particulars are known, whilst in London their
number must have been very great. Of the London trade
guilds, Stow, the Elizabethan antiquary, records the names of
sixty of sufficient importance to entitle their representatives to
places at the civic banquets in the reign of Henry VIII. Many
of them are still in existence, having been spared at the time of
the Reformation on the plea that they were trading or secular
associations. Fifteen of the largest of them—including the
merchant tailors, the goldsmiths and the stationers—have at the
present time an annual income of over $50,000 each.

The reasons for their popularity can be readily found in the
many social needs which they cared for. Socialistic cooperation
has, perhaps, never been carried so far as in these medieval institutions which were literally "of the people, by the people,
and for the people." Often their regulation made provisions
for insurance against poverty, fire, and sometimes against burglary. Frequently they provided schoolmasters for the schools.
Their funds they loaned out to needy brethren in small sums
on easy terms, whilst trade and other disputes likely to give rise
to ill-feeling and contention were constantly referred to the
guilds for arbitration. One of the rules of the Guild of our
Lady at Wymondham thus ordains, that for no manner of
cause should any of the brothers or sisters of the fraternity
go to law till the officers of the guild had been informed of the
circumstances and had done their best to settle the dispute and
restore "unity and love betwixt the parties." To assist at the
burial of deceased brethren, and to aid in providing for the
celebration of obits for the repose of their souls, were duties
incumbent on all, defaulters without good excuse being subject to fines and censure.

It must not be thought that these tendencies to true democracy were confined to the trades guilds, however. The historian
of the merchant guilds has demonstrated that they had the

same spirit and this was especially true for the great guild merchant. He says:

"To this category of powerful affinities must be added the Gild Merchant. The latter was from the outset a compact body emphatically characterized by fraternal solidarity of interests, a protective union that naturally engendered a consciousness of strength and a spirit of independence. As the same men generally directed the counsels of both the town and the Gild, there would be a gradual, unconscious extension of the unity of the one to the other, the cohesive force of the Gild making itself felt throughout the whole municipal organism. But the influence of the fraternity was material as well as moral. It constituted a bond of union between the heterogeneous sokes (classes of tenants) of a borough; the townsmen might be exclusively amenable to the courts of different lords, but, if engaged in trade within the town, they were all members of one and the same Gild Merchant. The independent regulation of trade also accustomed the burgesses to self-government, and constituted an important step toward autonomy; the town judiciary was always more dependent upon the crown or mesne lord than was the Gild Merchant."

Because of the supreme interest in everything connected with Shakespeare, the existence of one of the most important guilds in Stratford, has led to the illustration of guilds' works there better than for any English town during this period. The Guild of the Holy Cross was the most important institution of Stratford and enthusiastic Shakespeare scholars have applied themselves to find out every detail of its history as far as it is now available, in order to make clear the conditions—social and religious—that existed in the great dramatist's birthplace. Halliwell, in his Descriptive Calendar of the Records of Stratford on Avon, and Sidney Lee, in his Stratford on Avon in the Time of the Shakespeares, have gathered together much of this information:—"The Guild has lasted, wrote its chief officer in 1309, for many, many years and its beginning was from time whereunto the memory of man reaches not." Bowden, in his volume on the Religion of Shakespeare, has a number of the most important details with regard to Stratford's Guild. The earliest extant documents with regard to it are from the

Reign of Henry III., 1216-1272, and include a deed of gift by one William Sede, of a tenement to the Guild, and an indulgence granted October 7th, 1270, by Giffard, Bishop of Wooster, of forty days to all sincere penitents who after having duly confessed had conferred benefits on the Guild.

By the close of the reign of Edward I., at the beginning of the Fourteenth Century, the Guild was wealthy in houses and lands, and the foundation was laid of its chapel and almshouses which, with the hall of meeting—the "Rode or Reed Hall"—stood where the Guild Hall is at the present day. Edward III. and Richard II., during the Fourteenth Century, confirmed the rights of the Guild and even added to its privileges. Though it was a purely local institution, the fame of its good works had spread so wide during these next centuries that affiliation with it became a distinction, and the nobility were attracted to its ranks. George, Duke of Clarence, brother of Edward, with his wife and children, and the Earl of Warwick, and the Lady Margaret were counted among its members, and merchants of distant towns counted it an honor to belong to it. Later, also, Judge Littleton, one of the famous founders of English law, was on its roll of membership.

The objects of the Guild were many and varied and touched the social life of Stratford at every point. The first object was mutual prayer. The Guild maintained five priests or chaplains who were to say masses daily, hour by hour, from six to ten o'clock for its members, it being expected that some of them would be present at each of the masses. Out of the fees of the Guild one wax candle was to be kept alight every day throughout the year at every mass in the church before the rood, or cross, "so that God and our Blessed Virgin and the Venerated Cross may keep and guard all the brethren and sisters of the Guilds from every ill." The second object was charity, under which was included all the various Works of Mercy. The needs of any brother or sister who had fallen into poverty or been robbed were to be provided for "as long as he bears himself rightly towards the brethren." When a brother died all the brethren were bound to follow the body to the church and to pray for his soul at its burial. The Guild candle and eight smaller ones were to be kept burning by the body from the time of death till the funeral. When a poor man died in the town the brethren and sisters were, for their soul's health, to find four wax candles, a sheet, and a hearse cloth for the corpse. This rule also applied in the event of a stranger's death, if the stranger had not the necessary means for burial. Nor were the efforts of the Guild at Stratford devoted solely to the alleviation of the ills of mankind and the more serious purposes of life. Once a year, in Easter Week, a feast of the members was held in order to foster peace and true brotherly love among them. At this time offerings were made for the poor in order that they too might share in the happiness of the festival time. There was attendance at church before the feasting and a prayer was offered by all the "brethren and sisters that God and our Blessed Virgin and the Venerated Cross in whose honor we have come together will keep us from all ills and sins." This frequent reference to the Cross will be better understood if it is recalled that the Guild at Stratford bore the name of the Guild of the Holy Cross, and the figure of the crucified One was one of its most respected symbols and was always looked upon as a special object of veneration on the part of the members.

The thoroughly progressive spirit of the Guild at Stratford will perhaps be best appreciated by the modern mind from the fact, that to it the town owed the foundation of its famous free school. During the Thirteenth and Fourteenth centuries the study of grammar, and of the various theoretical branches, was not considered the essential part of an education. Gradually, however, there had arisen the feeling that all the children should be taught the ground-work of the vulgar tongue, and that those whose parents wished it should receive education in Latin also; hence the establishment of grammar schools, that at Stratford being founded for the children of the members of the Guild about the middle of the Fifteenth Century. This was only the normal development of the earlier spirit of the Guild which enabled it to meet the growing social needs of the time. It was at this school, as reconstituted under Edward VI., that Shakespeare was educated, and the reestablishment by Edward was only in response to the many complaints which arose because of the absence of the school after its suppression by

Henry VIII. The fact that Shakespeare was educated at an Edward VI. grammar school, has often given occasion for commentators to point out that it was practically the Reformation in England which led to the establishment of free schools. Any such suggestion, however, can be made only in complete ignorance of the preexisting state of affairs in which the people, by organization, succeeded in accomplishing so much for themselves.

As a matter of fact the Guild at Stratford, as in most of the towns in England—for we have taken this as an example only because it is easier to get at the details of its history—was the most important factor in the preservation of social order, in the distribution of charity, in the providing of education, and even the maintenance of the security of the life and property of its inhabitants. When it was dissolved, in 1547, Stratford found itself in a chaotic state and had to petition Edward VI. to reconstitute the Guild as a civil corporation, which he did by charter in 1553.

After this consideration of the guilds and their purpose and success, it is no wonder that we should declare that the wind of the spirit of democracy was blowing in England and carrying away the old landmarks of absolute government. It is to the spirit thus fostered that must be attributed the marvelous progress in representative government, the steps of which we recall.

In 1215, all England united against the odious John Lackland and obliged him to grant the Magna Charta—a declaration of national liberty.

In 1257, the Provisions of Oxford, under Henry III., established, for the moment, the stated recurrence of the great national council of Parliament.

In 1265, under the same Prince, the earl of Leicester admitted to Parliament the knights of the shire and the representatives of the townspeople, who formed later the lower house, or House of Commons, while those personally summoned to attend by the king from the great nobles formed the upper house, or House of Lords.

Beginning with the year 1295, in the reign of Edward I., the attendance of the county and town members became regular, making Parliament really representative of the country.

In 1309, in the reign of Edward II., Parliament revealed its possible strength by putting conditions on its vote for taxes.

There were other factors at work, however, and one of them at least, because of its importance, deserves to be recalled here. In the chapter on Great Beginnings of Modern Commerce we call attention to the fact, that the Crusades were responsible to a great degree for the spirit of enterprise which led to the formation of the Lombard league of cities, and later to the great Hanseatic League, which seems to have taken at least its incentive from the Southern Confederation. In the chapter on Louis IX. we point out that the Crusades, and his connection with them, far from being blots on Louis's career must rather be considered as manifestations of the great heart of the time which was awakening to all needs, and had its religious aspirations stirred so deeply that men were ready to give up everything in order to follow an idea. One thing is certain, the Crusades did more to set ferments at work in the social organization of Europe than would have been possible by any other movement. These ferments brought about two results, one the uplift of the common people, the other the centralization of power in the hands of the kings with the gradual diminution of the influence of the nobility. While fostering the spirit of democracy on the one hand, they gave birth to the spirit of nationality and to all that this has accomplished in modern history.

Storrs, in his life of St. Bernard, recently issued, has given expression to this thought in a very striking fashion. He says:

"It used to be the fashion to regard the Crusades as mere fantastic exhibitions of a temporary turbulent religious fanaticism, aiming at ends wholly visionary, and missing them, wasting the best life of Europe in colossal and bloody undertakings, and leaving effects only of evil for the time which came after. More reasonable views now prevail; and while the impulse in which the vast movement took its rise is recognized as passionate and semi-barbaric, it is seen that many effects followed which were beneficial rather than harmful, which could not perhaps have been at the time in other ways realized. As I have already suggested, properties were to an important extent redistributed in Europe, and the constitutions of states were favorably affected. Lands were sold at low prices by those who were going on the distant expeditions, very probably, as they knew, never to return; and horses and armor, with all martial equipments, were bought at high prices by the Jews, who could not hold land, and the history of whom throughout the Middle Ages is commonly traced in fearful lines of blood and fire, but who increased immeasurably their movable wealth through these transfers of property. Communes bought liberties by large contributions to the needs of their lord; and their liberties, once secured, were naturally confirmed and augmented, as the years went on. The smaller tended to be absorbed in the larger; the larger often to come more strictly under royal control, thus increasing the power of the sovereign— which meant at the time, general laws, instead of local, a less minutely oppressive administration, the furtherance of the movement toward national unity. It is a noticeable fact that Italy took but a comparatively small part in the Crusades; and the long postponement of organic union between different parts of the magnificent peninsula is not without relation to this. The influence which operated elsewhere in Europe to efface distinction of custom and language in separate communities, to override and extinguish local animosities, to make scattered peoples conscious of kinship, did not operate there; and the persistent severance of sections from each other, favored, of course, by the run of the rivers and the vast separating walls of the Apenines, was the natural consequence of the want of this powerful unifying force.*

As a matter of fact very few people realize how much was accomplished for the spirit of democracy, for liberty, for true progress, as regards the rights of men of all classes, and for the feeling of the brotherhood of man itself, by the Crusades. A practical money-making age may consider them examples of foolish religious fanaticism, but those who have studied them most profoundly and with most sympathy, who are deeply interested in the social amelioration which they brought about, and, above all, those who look at them in the higher poetic

* Storrs, "Bernard of Chairvaux," New York (Scribners), 1897 pp. 544-45.

spirit of what they did to lift man above the sordid cares of everyday life, see them in a far different way. Charles Kingsley sang in the poem of The Saints Tragedy:

> "Tell us how our stout crusading fathers
> Fought and bled for God and not for gold."

But quite apart from the poetry of them, from the practical side much can be said which even the most matter of fact of men will appreciate. Here, for instance, are a series of paragraphs from the history of the Middle Ages by George Washington Greene, which he confesses to have taken chiefly from the French,* which will make clear something of the place these great expeditions should be considered as holding in the history of democracy and of liberty:

"Christendom had not spent in vain its treasures and its blood in the holy wars. Its immense sacrifices were repaid by immense results, and the evils which these great expeditions necessarily brought with them were more than compensated for by the advantages which they procured for the whole of Europe.

"The Crusades saved Europe from the Mussulman invasion and this was their immediate good. Their influence was felt, too, in a manner less direct, but not less useful. The Crusades had been preached by a religion of equality in a society divided by odious distinctions. All had taken part in them, the weak as well as the strong, the serf and the baron, man and woman, and it was by them that the equality of man and woman, which Christianity taught, was made a social fact. St. Louis declared that he could do nothing without the consent of his queen, his wife. It was from this period that we must date that influence of woman which gave rise to chivalric courtesy, the first step towards refinement of manners and civilization. The poor, too, were the adopted children of the Christian chivalry of the Crusades. The celebrated orders of Palestine were instituted for the protection of poor pilgrims. The Knights of the hospitals called the poor their masters. Surely no lesson was more needed by these proud barons of the Middle Ages than that of charity and humility.

* New York, Appleton, 1867.

"These ideas were the first to shake the stern despotism of feudality, by opposing to it the generous principles of chivalry which sprang all armed from the Crusades. Bound to the military orders by a solemn vow—and in the interests of all Christendom—the knight felt himself free from feudal dependence, and raised above national limits, as the immediate warrior and servant of the united Christendom and of God. Chivalry founded not upon territorial influence, but upon personal distinction, necessarily weakened nobility by rendering it accessible to all, and diminishing the interval which separated the different classes of society. Every warrior who had distinguished himself by his valor could kneel before the king to be dubbed a knight, and rise up the equal, the superior even, of powerful vassals. The poorest knight could sit at the king's table while the noble son of a duke or prince was excluded, unless he had won the golden spurs of knighthood. Another way by which the Crusades contributed to the decay of feudalism was by favoring the enfranchisement of serfs, even without the consent of their masters. Whoever took the cross became free, just as every slave becomes free on touching the soil of England or France.

"The communities whose development is to be referred to the period of the Crusades, multiplied rapidly; the nobility gladly granting charters and privileges in exchange for men and money. With the communities the royal power grew, and that of the aristocracy decreased. The royal domain was enlarged, by the escheating of a great number of fiefs which had been left vacant by the death of their lords. The kings protected the communities, favored their enfranchisement, and employed them usefully against insubordinate vassals. The extension of the royal power favored the organization of the nation, by establishing a principle of unity, for till then, and with that multitude of masters, the nation had been little else than an agglomeration of provinces, strangers to one another, and destitute of any common bond or common interest. The great vassals, themselves, often united under the royal banner, became accustomed during these distant expeditions to submission and discipline, and learned to recognize a legitimate authority; and if they lost by this submission a part of their personal power, they gained in compensation the honorable distinctions of chivalry.

"But it was not the national feeling alone which was fostered by the Crusades. Relations of fraternity, till then wholly unknown, grew up between different nations, and softened the deep-rooted antipathy of races. The knights, whom a common object united in common dangers, became brothers in arms and formally formed permanent ties of friendship. That barbarous law which gave the feudal lord a right to call every man his serf who settled in his domains was softened. Stranger and enemy seemed to be synonymous, and 'the Crusaders,' say the chroniclers of the times, 'although divided by language, seemed to form only one people, by their love for God and their neighbor.' And without coloring the picture too warmly, and making all due allowance for the exaggerations which were so natural to the first recorders of such a movement, we may say that human society was founded and united and Europe began to pass from the painful period of organization, to one of fuller and more rapid development."

Here in reality modern democracy had its rise, striking its roots deep into the disintegrating soil of the old feudalism whence it was never to be plucked, and though at times it languished it was to remain ever alive until its luxuriant growth in recent times.

ANIMALS FROM BESTIARIUM, THIRTEENTH CENTURY MS.

XXV

GREAT EXPLORERS AND THE FOUNDATION OF
GEOGRAPHY.

Geography is usually considered to be quite a modern subject. The idea that great contributions were made to it in the Thirteenth Century would ordinarily not be entertained. America was discovered at the end of the Fifteenth Century. Knowledge of the East was obtained during the Sixteenth Century. Africa was explored in the Nineteenth and a detailed knowledge of Asia came to us in such recent years that the books are still among the novelties. of publication. Our knowledge of Persia, of Northern India, of Thibet, and of the interior of China are all triumphs of Nineteenth Century enterprise and exploration. As a matter of fact, however, all portions of the East were explored, the Capital and the dominions of Jenghis Khan described, Lhasa was entered and the greater part of China thoroughly explored by travelers of the Thirteenth Century, whose books still remain as convincing evidence of the great work that they accomplished. This chapter of Thirteenth Century accomplishment is, indeed, one of the most interesting and surprising in the whole story of the time.

It is usually considered that the teaching, supposed to have been more or less generally accepted, that the Antipodes did not exist, prevented any significant development of geography until comparatively modern times. While the question of the existence of antipodes was discussed in the schools of the Middle Ages, and especially of the Thirteenth Century when men's minds were occupied with practically all of the important problems even of physical science, and while many intelligent men accepted the idea that there could not be inhabitants on the other side of the world because of physical difficulties which supposedly made it impossible, it would be a mistake to think that this idea was universally accepted. We have already called attention to the fact in the chapter on "What was Taught at the

Universities," that Albertus Magnus, for instance, ridiculed the notion that men could not live with their heads down, as was urged against the doctrine of the existence of antipodes, by suggesting very simply that for those on the other side of the earth what we call down was really not down but up. This expresses, of course, the very heart of the solution of the supposed difficulty.

As a matter of fact it seems clear that many of the great travelers and explorers of the later Middle Ages harbored the notion that the earth was round. As we shall note a little later in mentioning Sir John Mandeville's work, the writer, whoever he was who took that pseudonym, believed thoroughly in the rotundity of the earth and did not hesitate to use some striking expressions—which have been often quoted—that he had heard of travelers who by traveling continually to the eastward had come back eventually to the point from which they started. While in the schools, then, the existence of antipodes may have been under discussion, there was a practical acceptance of their existence among those who were better informed with regard to countries and peoples and all the other topics which form the proper subject matter of geography.

It must be realized, moreover, that though the existence of the Antipodes is an important matter in geography, at this early period it was a mere theory, not a condition antecedent to progress. It was really a side issue as compared with many other questions relating to the earth's surface and its inhabitants with which the medieval mind was occupied. To consider that no knowledge of geography could be obtained until there was a definite acceptance of the right view of the earth's surface, would be to obliterate much precious knowledge. The argument as to the existence of antipodes, as it was carried on, was entirely outside of geography properly so-called. It never influenced in the slightest degree the men who were consciously and unconsciously laying deep and broad the foundations of modern geography. To consider such a matter as vital to the development of as many sided a subject as geography, illustrates very typically the narrowness of view of so many modern scholars, who apparently can see the value of nothing which does not entirely accord with modern knowledge. The really interesting historian of knowledge, however, is he who can point out the beginnings of what we now know, in unexpected quarters in the medieval mind.

As the story of these travels and explorations is really a glorious chapter in the history of the encouragement of things intellectual, as well as an interesting phase of an important origin whose foundations were laid broad and deep in the Thirteenth Century, it must be told here in some detail. Our century was the great leader in exploration and geography as in so many other matters in which its true place is often unrecognized.

The people of the time are usually considered to have had such few facilities for travel that they did not often go far from home, and that what was known about distant countries, therefore, was very little and mainly legendary. Nothing could be more false than any such impression as this. The Crusades during the previous century had given the people not only a deep interest in distant lands, but the curiosity to go and see for themselves. Pilgrimages to the Holy Land were frequent, ecclesiastics often traveled at least as far as Italy, and in general the tide of travel in proportion to the number of population must have been not very much less in amount than in our own day. After the establishment of the religious orders, missionary expeditions to the East became very common and during the Thirteenth Century, as we shall see, the Franciscans particularly, established themselves in many parts of the Near East, but also of the Far East, especially in China. Many of those wrote accounts of their travels, and so the literature of travel and exploration during the Thirteenth Century is one of the most interesting chapters of the literature of these times, while the wonderfully deep foundations that were laid for the science of geography, are worthy to be set beside the great origins in other sciences and in the arts, for which the century is so noteworthy.

To most people it will come as a distinct surprise to learn that the travelers and explorers of the Thirteenth Century— merchants, ambassadors, and missionaries—succeeded in solving many of the geographical problems that have been of deepest interest to the generations of the last half of last century.

The eastern part of Asia particularly was traveled over and very thoroughly described by them. Even the northern part of India, however, was not neglected in spite of the difficulties that were encountered, and Thibet was explored and Lhasa entered by travelers of the Thirteenth Century. Of China as much was written as had been learned by succeeding generations down practically to our own time. This may sound like a series of fairy-tales instead of serious science, but it is the travelers and explorers of the modern time who have thought it worth while to comment on the writings of these old-time wanderers of the Thirteenth Century, and who have pointed out the significance of their work. These men described not only the countries through which they passed, but also the characters of the people, their habits and customs, their forms of speech, with many marvelous hints as regards the relationship of the different languages, and even something about the religious practises of these countries and their attitude toward the great truths of Christianity when they were presented to them.

Undoubtedly one of the greatest travelers and explorers of all times was Marco Polo, whose book was for so long considered to be mainly made up of imaginary descriptions of things and places never seen, but which the development of modern geographical science by travels and expeditions has proved to be one of the most valuable contributions to this department of knowledge that has ever been made. It took many centuries for Marco Polo to come to his own in this respect but the Nineteenth and Twentieth centuries have almost more than made up for the neglect of their predecessors. Marco Polo suffered the same fate as did Herodotus of whom Voltaire sneered "father of history, say, rather, father of lies." So long as succeeding generations had no knowledge themselves of the things of which both these great writers had written, they were distrusted and even treated contemptuously. Just as soon, however, as definite knowledge began to come it was seen how wonderfully accurate both of them were in their descriptions of things they had actually seen, though they admitted certain over-wonderful stories on the authority of others. Herodotus has now come to be acknowledged as one of the greatest of historians. In his lives of celebrated travelers, James Augustus St. John states the change of mind with regard to Marco Polo rather forcibly:

"When the travels of Marco Polo first appeared, they were generally regarded as fiction; and as this absurd belief had so far gained ground, that when he lay upon his death bed, his friends and nearest relatives, coming to take their eternal adieu, conjured him as he valued the salvation of his soul, to retract whatever he had advanced in his book, or at least many such passages as every person looked upon as untrue; but the traveler whose conscience was untouched upon that score, declared solemnly, in that awful moment, that far from being guilty of exaggeration, he had not described one-half of the wonderful things which he had beheld. Such was the reception which the discoveries of this extraordinary man experienced when first promulgated. By degrees, however, as enterprise lifted more and more the veil from Central and Eastern Asia the relations of our traveler rose in the estimation of geographers; and now that the world—though containing many unknown tracts—has been more successfully explored, we begin to perceive that Marco Polo, like Herodotus, was a man of the most rigid veracity, whose testimony presumptuous ignorance alone can call in question."

There is many a fable that clings around the name of Marco Polo, but this distinguished traveler needs no fictitious adornments of his tale to make him one of the greatest explorers of all time. It is sometimes said that he helped to introduce many important inventions into Europe and one even finds his name connected with the mariner's compass and with gunpowder. There are probably no good grounds for thinking that Europe owes any knowledge of either of these great inventions to the Venetian traveler. With regard to printing there is more doubt and Polo's passage with regard to movable blocks for printing paper money as used in China may have proved suggestive.

There is no need, however, of surmises in order to increase his fame for the simple story of his travels is quite sufficient for his reputation for all time. As has been well said most of the modern travelers and explorers have only been developing what Polo indicated at least in outline, and they have been scarcely more than describing with more precision of detail what he first touched upon and brought to general notice. When it is remembered that he visited such cities in Eastern Turkestan as Kashgar, Yarkand, and Khotan, which have been the subject of much curiosity only satisfied in quite recent years, that he had visited Thibet, or at least had traveled along its frontier, that to him the medieval world owed some definite knowledge of the Christian kingdom of Abyssinia and all that it was to know of China for centuries almost, his merits will be readily appreciated. As a matter of fact there was scarcely an interesting country of the East of which Marco Polo did not have something to relate from his personal experiences. He told of Burmah, of Siam, of Cochin China, of Japan, of Java, of Sumatra, and of other islands of the great Archipelago, of Ceylon, and of India, and all of these not in the fabulous dreamland spirit of one who has not been in contact with the East but in very definite and precise fashion. Nor was this all. He had heard and could tell much, though his geographical lore was legendary and rather dim, of the Coast of Zanzibar, of the vast and distant Madagascar, and in the remotely opposite direction of Siberia, of the shores of the Arctic Ocean, and of the curious customs of the inhabitants of these distant countries.

How wonderfully acute and yet how thoroughly practical some of Polo's observations were can be best appreciated by some quotations from his description of products and industries as he saw them on his travels. We are apt to think of the use of petroleum as dating from much later than the Thirteenth Century, but Marco Polo had not only seen it in the Near East on his travels, but evidently had learned much of the great rock-oil deposits at Baku which constitute the basis for the important Russian petroleum industry in modern times. He says:

"On the north (of Armenia) is found a fountain from which a liquor like oil flows, which, though unprofitable for the seasoning of meat, is good for burning and for anointing camels afflicted with the mange. This oil flows constantly and copiously, so that camels are laden with it."

He is quite as definite in the information acquired with regard to the use of coal. He knew and states very confidently that there were immense deposits of coal in China, deposits which are so extensive that distinguished geologists and mineralogists who have learned of them in modern times have predicted that eventually the world's great manufacturing industries would be transferred to China. We are apt to think that this mineral wealth is not exploited by the Chinese, yet even in Marco Polo's time, as one commentator has remarked, the rich and poor of that land had learned the value of the black stone.

"Through the whole Province of Cathay," says Polo, "certain black stones are dug from the mountains, which, put into the fire, burn like wood, and being kindled, preserve fire a long time, and if they be kindled in the evening they keep fire all the night."

Another important mineral product which even more than petroleum or coal is supposed to be essentially modern in its employment is asbestos. Polo had not only seen this but had realized exactly what it was, had found out its origin and had recognized its value. Curiously enough he attempts to explain the origin of a peculiar usage of the word salamander (the salamander having been supposed to be an animal which was not injured by fire) by reference to the incombustibility of asbestos. The whole passage as it appears in The Romance of Travel and Exploration deserves to be quoted. While discoursing about Dsungaria, Polo says:

"And you must know that in the mountain there is a substance from which Salamander is made. The real truth is that the Salamander is no beast as they allege in our part of the world, but is a substance found in the earth. Everybody can be aware that it can be no animal's nature to live in fire seeing that every animal is composed of all the four elements. Now I, Marco Polo, had a Turkish acquaintance who related that he had lived three years in that region on behalf of the Great Khan, in order to procure these salamanders for him. He said that the way they got them was by digging in that mountain till they found a certain vein. The substance of this vein was taken and crushed, and when so treated it divides, as it were, into fibres of wool, which they set forth to dry. When dry these fibres were pounded in a copper mortar and then washed so as to remove all the earth and to leave only the fibres, like

fibres of wool. These were then spun and made into napkins."
Needless to say this is an excellent description of asbestos.

It is not surprising, then, that the Twentieth Century so interested in travel and exploration should be ready to lay its
tributes at the feet of Marco Polo, and that one of the important book announcements of recent years should be that of the
publication of an annotated edition of Marco Polo from the
hands of a modern explorer, who considered that there was no
better way of putting definitely before the public in its true historical aspect the evolution of modern geographical knowledge
with regard to Eastern countries.

It can scarcely fail to be surprising to the modern mind that
Polo should practically have been forced into print. He had
none of the itch of the modern traveler for publicity. The
story of his travels he had often told and because of the wondrous tales he could unfold and the large numbers he found it
frequently so necessary to use in order to give proper ideas of
some of his wanderings, had acquired the nickname of Marco
Millioni. He had never thought, however, of committing his
story to writing or perhaps he feared the drudgery of such literary labor. After his return from his travels, however, he
bravely accepted a patriot's duty of fighting for his native country on board one of her galleys and was captured by the Geno-
ese in a famous sea-fight in the Adriatic in 1298. He was taken
prisoner and remained in captivity in Genoa for nearly a year.

It was during this time that one Rusticiano, a writer by profession, was attracted to him and tempted him to tell him the
complete story of his travels in order that they might be put
into connected form. Rusticiano was a Pisan who had been a
compiler of French romances and accordingly Polo's story was
first told in French prose. It is not surprising that Rusticiano
should have chosen French since he naturally wished his story
of Polo's travels to be read by as many people as possible and
realized that it would be of quite as much interest to ordinary
folk as to the literary circles of Europe. How interesting the
story is only those who have read it even with the knowledge
acquired by all the other explorers since his time, can properly
appreciate. It lacks entirely the egotistic quality that usually
characterizes an explorer's account of his travels, and, indeed,

there can scarcely fail to be something of disappointment because of this fact. No doubt a touch more of personal adventure would have added to the interest of the book. It was not a characteristic of the Thirteenth Century, however, to insist on the merely personal and consequently the world has lost a treat it might otherwise have had. There is no question, however, or the greatness of Polo's work as a traveler, nor of the glory that was shed by it on the Thirteenth Century. Like nearly everything else that was done in this marvelous century he represents the acme of successful endeavor in his special line down even to our own time.

It has sometimes been said that Marco Polo's work greatly influenced Columbus and encouraged him in his attempt to seek India by sailing around the globe. Of this, however, there is considerable doubt. We have learned in recent times, that a very definite tradition with regard to the possibility of finding land by sailing straight westward over the Atlantic existed long before Columbus' time.* Polo's indirect influence on Columbus by his creation of an interest in geographical matters generally is much clearer. There can be no doubt of how much his work succeeded in drawing men's minds to geographical questions during the Fourteenth and Fifteenth centuries.

After Marco Polo, undoubtedly, the most enterprising explorer and interesting writer on Travel in the Thirteenth Century was John of Carpini, the author of a wonderful series of descriptions of things seen in Northern Asia. Like so many other travelers and explorers at this time John was a Franciscan Friar, and seems to have been one of the early companions and disciples of St. Francis of Assisi, whom he joined when he was only a young man himself. Before going on his missionary and ambassadorial expedition he had been one of the most prominent men in the order. He had much to do with its

* My learned friend, Father DeRoo, of Portland, Ore., who has written two very interesting volumes on the History of America before Columbus, does not hesitate to say that Columbus may even have met in his travels and spoken with sailors who had touched on some portions of the American Continent, and that, of course, the traditions with regard to Greenland were very clear.

propagation among the Northern nations of Europe, and occupied successively the offices of custos or prior in Saxony and of Provincial in Germany. He seems afterwards to have been sent as an organizer into Spain and to have gone even as far as the Barbary coast.

It is not surprising, then, that when, in 1245, Pope Innocent IV. (sometime after the Mongol invasion of Eastern Europe and the disastrous battle of Legamites which threatened to place European civilization and Christianity in the power of the Tartars) resolved to send a mission to the Tartar monarch, John of Carpini was selected for the dangerous and important mission.

At this time Friar John was more than sixty years of age, but such was the confidence in his ability and in his executive power that everything on the embassy was committed to his discretion. He started from Lyons on Easter Day, 1245. He sought the counsel first of his old friend Wenceslaus, King of Bohemia, and from that country took with him another friar, a Pole, to act as his interpreter. The first stage in his journey was to Kiev, and from here, having crossed the Dnieper and the Don to the Volga, he traveled to the camp of Batu, at this time the senior living member of Jenghis Khan's family. Batu after exchanging presents allowed them to proceed to the court of the supreme Khan in Mongolia. As Col. Yule says, the stout-hearted old man rode on horseback something like three thousand miles in the next hundred days. The bodies of himself and companion had to be tightly bandaged to enable them to stand the excessive fatigue of this enormous ride, which led them across the Ural Mountains and River past the northern part of the Caspian, across the Jaxartes, whose name they could not find out, along the Dzungarian Lakes till they reached the Imperial Camp, called the Yellow Pavilion, near the Orkhon River. There had been an interregnum in the empire which was terminated by a formal election while the Friars were at the Yellow Pavilion, where they had the opportunity to see between three and four thousand envoys and deputies from all parts of Asia and Eastern Europe, who brought with them tributes and presents for the ruler to be elected.

It was not for three months after this, in November, that the Emperor dismissed them with a letter to the Pope written in Latin, Arabic, and Mongolian, but containing only a brief imperious assertion that the Khan of the Tartars was the scourge of God for Christianity, and that he must fulfil his mission. Then sad at heart, the ambassadors began their homeward journey in the midst of the winter. Their sufferings can be better imagined than described, but Friar John who does not dwell on them much tells enough of them to make their realization comparatively easy. They reached Kiev seven months later, in June, and were welcomed there by the Slavonic Christians as though arisen from the dead. From thence they continued their journey to Lyons where they delivered the Khan's letter to the Pope.

Friar John embodied the information that he had obtained in this journey in a book that has been called Liber Tartarorum (the Book of the Tartars or according to another manuscript, History of the Mongols whom we call Tartars). Col. Yule notes that like most of the other medieval monks' itineraries, it shows an entire absence of that characteristic traveler's egotism with which we have become abundantly familiar in more recent years, and contains very little personal narrative. We know that John was a stout man and this in addition to his age when he went on the mission, cannot but make us realize the thoroughly unselfish spirit with which he followed the call of Holy Obedience, to undertake a work that seemed sure to prove fatal and that would inevitably bring in its train suffering of the severest kind. Of the critical historical value of his work a good idea can be obtained from the fact, that half a century ago an educated Mongol, Galsang Gombeyev, in the Historical and Philological Bulletin of the Imperial Academy of St. Petersburg, reviewed the book and bore testimony to the great accuracy of its statements, to the care with which its details had been verified, and the evident personal character of all its observations.

Friar John's book attracted the attention of compilers of information with regard to distant countries very soon after it was issued, and an abridgment of it is to be found in the Encyclopedia of Vincent of Beauvais, which was written shortly after the middle of the Thirteenth Century. At the end of the Sixteenth Century Hakluyt published portions of the original work, as did Borgeron at the beginning of the Seventeenth Century. The Geographical Society of Paris published a fine edition of the work about the middle of the Nineteenth Century, and at the same time a brief narrative taken down from the lips of John's companion, Friar Benedict the Pole, which is somewhat more personal in its character and fully substantiates all that Friar John had written.

As can readily be understood the curiosity of his contemporaries was deeply aroused and Friar John had to tell his story many times after his return. Hence the necessity he found himself under of committing it to paper, so as to save himself from the bother of telling it all over again, and in order that his brother Franciscans throughout the world might have the opportunity to read it.

Col. Yule says "The book must have been prepared immediately after the return of the traveler, for the Friar Salimbene, who met him in France in the very year of his return (1247) gives us these interesting particulars: 'He was a clever and conversable man, well lettered, a great discourser, and full of diversity of experience. He wrote a big book about the Tartars (sic), and about other marvels that he had seen and whenever he felt weary of telling about the Tartars, he would cause this book of his to be read, as I have often heard and seen. (Chron. Fr. Salembene Parmensis in Monum. Histor. ad Provinceam Placent: Pertinentia, Parma 1857).'"

Another important traveler of the Thirteenth Century whose work has been the theme of praise and extensive annotation in modern times was William of Rubruk, usually known under the name of Rubruquis, a Franciscan friar, thought, as the result of recent investigations, probably to owe his cognomen to his birth in the little town of Rubruk in Brabant, who was the author of a remarkable narrative of Asiatic travel during the Thirteenth Century, and whose death seems to have taken place about 1298. The name Rubruquis has been commonly used to designate him because it is found in the Latin original of his work, which was printed by Hayluyt in his collection of Voyages at the end of the

Sixteenth Century. Friar William was sent partly as an ambassador and partly as an explorer by Louis IX. of France into Tartary. At that time the descendants of Jenghis Khan ruled over an immense Empire in the Orient and King Louis was deeply interested in introducing Christianity into the East and if possible making their rulers Christians. About the middle of the Thirteenth Century a rumor spread throughout Europe that one of the nephews of the great Khan had embraced Christianity. St. Louis thought this a favorable opportunity for getting in touch with the Eastern Potentate and so he dispatched at least two missions into Tartary at the head of the second of which was William of Rubruk.

His accounts of his travels proved most interesting reading to his own and to many subsequent generations, perhaps to none more than our own. The Encyclopedia Britannica (ninth edition) says that the narrative of his journey is everywhere full of life and interest, and some details of his travels will show the reasons for this. Rubruk and his party landed on the Crimean Coast at Sudak or Soldaia, a port which formed the chief seat of communication between the Mediterranean countries and what is now Southern Russia. The Friar succeeded in making his way from here to the Great Khan's Court which was then held not far from Karakorum. This journey was one of several thousand miles. The route taken has been worked out by laborious study and the key to it is the description given of the country intervening between the basin of the Talas and Lake Ala-Kul. This enables the whole geography of the region, including the passage of the River Ili, the plain south of the Bal Cash, and the Ala-Kul itself, to be identified beyond all reasonable doubt.

The return journey was made during the summertime, and the route lay much farther to the north. The travelers traversed the Jabkan Valley and passed north of the River Bal Cash, following a rather direct course which led them to the mouth of the Volga. From here they traveled south past Derbend and Shamakii to the Uraxes, and on through Iconium to the coast of Cilicia, and finally to the port of Ayas, where they embarked for Cyprus. All during his travels Friar William made observations on men and cities, and rivers and mountains, and

PRINCIPAL DOOR OF BAPTISTERY (PISA, DIOTISALVI)

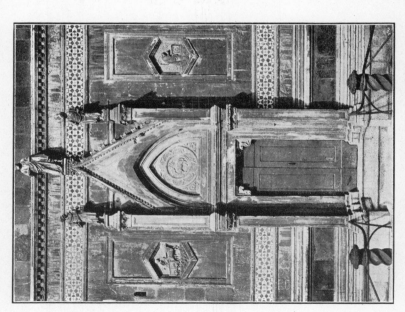

DOORWAY OF GIOTTO'S TOWER

languages and customs, implements and utensils, and most of
these modern criticism has accepted as representing the actual
state of things as they would appear to a medieval sightseer.
Occasionally during the period intervening between his time
and our own, scholars who thought that they knew better, have
been conceited enough to believe themselves in a position to
point out glaring errors in Rubruquis' accounts of what he saw.
Subsequent investigation and discovery have, as a rule, proved
the accuracy of the earlier observations rather than the modern scholar's corrections. An excellent example of this is
quoted in the Encyclopedia Britannica article on Rubruquis
already referred to.

The writer says: "This sagacious and honest observer is de-
nounced as an ignorant and untruthful blunderer by Isaac
Jacob Schmidt (a man no doubt of useful learning, of a kind
rare in his day but narrow and long-headed and in natura¹ acumen and candour far inferior to the Thirteenth Century friar
whom he maligns), simply because the evidence of the latter
as to the Turkish dialect of the Uigurs traversed a pet heresy
long since exploded which Schmidt entertained, namely, that
the Uigurs were by race and language Tibetan."

Some of the descriptions of the towns through which the
travelers passed are interesting because of comparisons with
towns of corresponding size in Europe. Karakorum, for instance, was described as a small city about the same size as the
town of St. Denis near Paris. In Karakorum the ambassador missionary maintained a public disputation with certain
pagan priests in the presence of three of the secretaries of the
Khan. The religion of these umpires is rather interesting from
its diversity: the first was a Christian, the second a Mohamme-
dan, and the third a Buddhist. A very interesting feature of
the disputation was the fact that the Khan ordered under pain
of death that none of the disputants should slander, traduce, or
abuse his adversaries, or endeavor by rumor or insinuations
to excite popular indignation against them. This would seem
to indicate that the great Tartar Khan who is usually considered to have been a cruel, ignorant despot, whose one quality
that gave him supremacy was military valor, was really a large,
liberal-minded man. His idea seems to have been to discover

the truth of these different religions and adopt that one which
was adjudged to have the best groundwork of reason for it.
It is easy to understand, however, that such a disputation
argued through interpreters wholly ignorant of the subject
and without any proper understanding of the nice distinctions
of words or any practise in conveying their proper significance,
could come to no serious conclusion. The arguments, therefore, fell flat and a decision was not rendered.

Friar William's work was not unappreciated by his contemporaries and even its scientific value was thoroughly realized.
It is not surprising, of course, that his great contemporary in
the Franciscan order, Roger Bacon, should have come to the
knowledge of his Brother Minorite's book and should have
made frequent and copious quotations from it in the geographical section of his Opus Majus, which was written some time
during the seventh decade of the Thirteenth Century. Bacon
says that Brother William traversed the Oriental and Northern
regions and the places adjacent to them, and wrote accounts
of them for the illustrious King of France who sent him on
the expedition to Tartary. He adds: "I have read his book
diligently and have compared it with similar accounts." Roger
Bacon recognized by a sort of scientific intuition of his own, certain passages which have proved to be the best in recent times.
The description, for instance, of the Caspian was the best down
to this time, and Friar William corrects the error made by
Isidore, and which had generally been accepted before this, that
the Caspian Sea was a gulf. Rubruk, as quoted by Roger
Bacon, states very explicitly that it nowhere touches the ocean
but is surrounded on all sides by land. For those who do not
think that the foundations of scientific geography were laid until recent times, a little consultation of Roger Bacon's Opus
Majus would undoubtedly be a revelation.

It is probably with regard to language that one might reasonably expect to find least that would be of interest to modern
scholars in Friar William's book. As might easily have been
gathered from previous references, however, it is here that
the most frequent surprises as to the acuity of this medieval
traveler await the modern reader. Scientific philology is so
much a product of the last century, that it is difficult to under-

stand how this old-time missionary was able to reach so many almost intuitive recognitions of the origin and relationships of the languages of the people among whom he traveled. He came in contact with the group of nations occupying what is now known as the Near East, whose languages, as is well known, have constituted a series of the most difficult problems with which philology had to deal until its thorough establishment on scientific lines enabled it to separate them properly. It is all the more surprising then, to find that Friar William should have so much in his book that even the modern philologist will read with attention and unstinted admiration.

With regard to this Colonel Yule, whose personal experience makes him a valuable guide in such matters, has written a paragraph which contains so much compressed information that we venture to quote it entire. It furnishes the grounds for the claim (which might seem overstrained if it were not that its author was himself one of the greatest of modern explorers) that William was an acute and most intelligent observer, keen in the acquisition of knowledge; and the author in fact of one of the best narratives of travel in existence. Col. Yule says:

"Of his interest and acumen in matters of language we may cite examples. The language of the Pascatir (or Bashkirds) and of the Hungarians is the same, as, he had learned from Dominicans who had been among them. The language of the Ruthenians, Poles, Bohemians, and Slavonians is one, and is the same with that of the Wandals or Wends. In the town of Equinus (immediately beyond the Ili, perhaps Aspara) the people were Mohammedans speaking Persian, though so far remote from Persia. The Yugurs (or Uigurs) of the country about the Cailac had formed a language and character of their own, and in that language and character the Nestorians of that tract used to perform their office and write their books. The Yugurs are those among whom are found the fountain and root of the Turkish and Comanian tongue. Their character has been adopted by the Moghals. In using it they begin writing from the top and write downwards, whilst line follows line from left to right. The Nestorians say their service, and have their holy book in Syriac, but know nothing of the lan-

guage, just as some of our Monks sing the mass without knowing Latin.   The Tibet people write as we do, and their letters
have a strong resemblance to ours.   The Tangut people write
from right to left like the Arabs, and their lines advance upwards."

There were other matters besides language and religion on
which Friar William made observations, and though his book
is eminently human giving us a very interesting view of his own
personality and of his difficulties with his dragoman, which
many a modern Eastern traveler will sympathize with, and a
picture that includes the detail that he was a very heavy man,
valde ponderosus, which makes his travel on horseback for some
10,000 miles all the more wonderful; it also contains a mass of
particulars, marvelously true—or so near the truth as to be almost more interesting—as to Asiatic nature, ethnography,
manners, morals, commercial customs, and nearly everything
else relating to the life of the peoples among whom he traveled.
A typical example of this is to be found in the following suggestive paragraph:

"The current money of Cathay is of cotton paper, a palm
in length and breath, and on this they print lines like those of
Mangu Khan's seal: 'imprimunt lineas sicut est sigillum
Mangu' "—a remarkable expression.   "They write with a
painter's pencil and combine in one character several letters,
forming one expression: 'faciunt in una figura plures literas
comprehendentes unam dictionem' "—a still more remarkable
utterance, showing an approximate apprehension of the nature
of Chinese writing.

There are other distinguished travelers whose inspiration
came to them during the Thirteenth Century though their works
were published in the early part of the next century.   Some
of these we know mainly through their adaptation and incorpor-
ation into his work without due recognition, by that first great
writer of spurious travels Sir John Mandeville.   Mandeville's
work was probably written some time during the early part of
the second half of the Fourteenth Century, but he used materials gathered from travelers of the end of the Thirteenth and
the beginning of the next (his own) century. Sir Henry Yule
has pointed out, that by far the greater part of the supposed

more distant travels of Sir John Mandeville were appropriated from the narrative of Friar Odoric, a monk, who became a member of the Franciscan order about the end of the Thirteenth Century, and whose travels as a missionary in the East gave him the opportunities to collect a precious fund of information which is contained in Odoric's famous story of his voyages. Of Odoric himself we shall have something to say presently.

In the meantime it seems well worth while calling to attention, that the accepted narrative of Sir John Mandeville as it is called, and which may have been written by a physician of the name of John of Burgoigne under an assumed name, contains a number of interesting anticipations of facts that were supposed to enter into the domain of human knowledge much later in the intellectual development of the race. In certain passages, and especially in one which is familiar from its being cited by Dr. Johnson in the preface to his dictionary, Mandeville, to use the name under which the story is best known, shows that he had a correct idea of the form of the earth and of position in latitude as it could be ascertained by observation of the Pole Star. He knew also, as we noted at the beginning of this article, that there are antipodes, and if ships were sent on voyages of discovery they might sail around the world. As Col. Yule has pointed out, Mandeville tells a curious story which he had heard in his youth of how "a worthy man did travel ever eastward until he came to his own country again."

Odoric of whom we have already spoken must be considered as the next great missionary traveler of this age. He took Franciscan vows when scarcely a boy and was encouraged to travel in the East by the example of his Holy Father St. Francis, and also by the interest and missionary zeal to convert the East which had been aroused by Marco Polo's travels. His long journeys will be more readily understood, however, if we realize, as is stated in the article on him in the Encyclopedia Britannica, an authority that will surely be unsuspected of too great partiality for the work of Catholic missionaries, that "There had risen also during the latter half of the Thirteenth Century an energetic missionary action, extending all over the East on the part of both the new orders of Preaching and Minorite (or Dominican and Franciscan) Friars which had caused members of these orders, of the last especially, to become established in Persia and what is now Southern Russia, in Tartary and in China."

In the course of his travels in the East Odoric visited Malabar touching at Pandarini (twenty miles north of Calicut), at Craganore and at Quilon, preceding thence, apparently, to Ceylon and to the Shrine of St. Thomas at Mailapur near Madras.

Even more interesting than his travels in India, however, are those in China. He sailed from the Hindustan Peninsula in a Chinese junk to Sumatra, visiting various ports on the northern coast of that island and telling something about the inhabitants and the customs of the country. According to Sir Henry Yule he then visited Java and it would seem also the coast of Borneo, finally reaching Kanton, at that time known to Western Asiatics as Chin Kalan or Great China. From there he went to the great ports of Fuhkeen and Schwan Chow, where he found two houses of his order, thence he proceeded to Fuchau from which place he struck across the mountains into Chekaeng and then visited Hang Chow at that time renowned under the name of Cansay. Modern authorities in exploration have suggested that this might be King Sae, the Chinese name for Royal Residence, which was then one of the greatest cities of the world. Thence Odoric passed northward by Nanking, and, crossing the great Kiang, embarked on the Grand Canal and traveled to Cambaluc or Pekin, where he remained for three years and where it is thought that he was attached to one of the churches founded by Archbishop John of Monte Corvino, who was at this time in extreme old age.

The most surprising part of Odoric's travels were still to come. When the fever for traveling came upon him again he turned almost directly westward to the Great Wall and through Shenshua. From here the adventurous traveler (we are still practically quoting Sir Henry Yule) entered Thibet and appears to have visited Lhasa. Considering how much of interest has been aroused by recent attempts to enter Lhasa and the surprising adventures that men have gone through in the effort, the success of this medieval monk in such an expedition would seem incredible, if it were not substantiated by documents that place the matter beyond all doubt even in the minds of the most distinguished modern authorities in geography and exploration. How Odoric returned home is not definitely known, though certain fragmentary notices seem to indicate that he passed through Khorasan and probably Tabriz to Europe.

It only remains to complete the interest of Odoric's wondrous tale to add that during a large portion of these years' long journeys his companion was Friar James, an Irishman who had been attracted to Italy in order to become a Franciscan. As appears from a record in the public books of the town of Udine in Italy, where the monastery of which both he and Odoric were members was situated, a present of two marks was made by the municipal authorities to the Irish friar shortly after Odoric's death. The reason for the gift was stated to be, that Friar James had been for the love of God and of Odoric (a typical Celtic expression and characteristic) a companion of the blessed Odoric in his wanderings. Unfortunately Odoric died within two years after his return though not until the story of his travels had been taken down in homely Latin by Friar William of Bologna. Shortly after his death Odoric became an object of reverence on the part of his brother friars and of devotion on the part of the people, who recognized the wonderful apostolic spirit that he had displayed in his long wanderings, and the patience and good-will with which he had borne sufferings and hardships for the sake of winning the souls of those outside the Church.

Sir Henry Yule summed up his opinion of Odoric in the following striking passage which bears forcible testimony also to the healthy curiosity of the times with regard to all these original sources of information which were recognized as valuable because first hand:

"The numerous MSS. of Odoric's narrative that have come down to our time (upwards of forty are known), and chiefly from the Fourteenth Century, show how speedily and widely it acquired popularity. It does not deserve the charge of general mendacity brought up against it by some, though the language of other writers who have spoken of the traveler as a man of learning is still more injudicious. Like most of the medieval travelers, he is indiscriminating in accepting strange tales; but while some of these are the habitual stories of the age, many particulars which he recited attest the genuine character of the narrative, and some of those which Tiraboschi and others have condemned as mendacious interpolations are the very seals of truth."

Besides Odoric there is another monkish traveler from whom Mandeville has borrowed much, though without giving him any credit. This is the well-known Praemonstratensian Monk Hayton, who is said to have been a member of a princely Armenian family and who just at the beginning of the Fourteenth Century dictated a work on the affairs of the Orient and especially the history of the nearer East in his own time, of which, from the place of his nativity and bringing up, he had abundant information, while he found all round him in France, where he was living at the time, the greatest thirst for knowledge with regard to this part of the world. His book seems to have been dictated originally in French at Poictiers, and to have attracted great attention because of its subject, many copies of it being made as well as translations into other languages within a few years after its original appearance.

The story of Odoric is a forcible reminder of how much the missionaries accomplished for geography, ethnology, and ethnography in the Thirteenth Century, as they did in succeeding centuries. If what the missionaries have added to these sciences were to have been lost, there would have been enormous gaps in the knowledge with which modern scholars began their scientific labors in philology. It may be a surprise to most people, moreover, to be thus forcibly reminded of the wonderful evangelizing spirit which characterized the later middle age. Needless to say these graduates of the Thirteenth Century universities who wandered in distant eastern lands, brought with them their European culture for the uplifting of the Orientals, and brought back to Europe many ideas that were to be fruitful sources of suggestions not only for geographical, ethnological, philological, and other departments of learning, but also in manufactures and in arts.

We mentioned the fact that Odoric in his travels eventually reached Cambaluc, or Pekin, where he found Archbishop John of Monte Corvino still alive though at an advanced age, and was probably attached for the three years of his stay to one of the churches that had been founded by this marvelous old Friar, who had been made Archbishop because of the wonderful power of organization and administration displayed during his earlier career as a missionary. The story of this grand old man of the early Franciscan missions is another one of the romances of Thirteenth Century travels and exploration which well deserves to be studied in detail. Unfortunately the old Archbishop was too much occupied with his work as a missionary and an ecclesiastic to return to Europe in order to tell of it, or to write any lengthy account of his experiences. Like many another great man of the Thirteenth Century he was a doer and not a writer, and, but for the casual mention of him by others, the records of his deeds would only be found in certain ecclesiastical records, and his work would now be known to the Master alone, for whom it was so unselfishly done.

It will be noted that most of these traveling missionaries were Franciscans but it must not be thought that it was only the Franciscans who sent out such missionaries. The Dominicans (established at the beginning of the Thirteenth Century) also did wonderful missionary work and quite as faithfully as even their Franciscan brothers. Undoubtedly the Franciscans surpassed them in the extent of their labors, but then the Dominicans were founded with the idea of preaching and uplifting the people of Europe rather than of spreading the good news of the Gospel outside the bounds of Christianity as it then existed. From the very earliest traditions of their order the Franciscans had their eyes attracted towards the East. The story that St. Francis himself went to the Holy Land at the beginning of the Thirteenth Century in order to convert Saladin, the Eastern monarch whose name has been made famous by the stories of the Crusade in which Richard Coeur de Lion took part, has been doubted, but it seems to be founded on too good contemporary authority to be considered as entirely apocryphal. St. Francis' heart went out to those in darkness who knew nothing of the Christ whom he had learned to love so ardently, and it was a supreme desire of his life that the good tidings of Christianity should be spread by his followers all over the world. While they did this great work they accomplished unwittingly great things in all the series of sciences now included under the term geography, and gathered precious information as to the races of men, their relations to one another and to the part of the earth in which they live. The scientific progress thus made will always redound largely to their credit in the story of the intellectual development of modern Europe. Most of their work was far ahead of the times and was not to be properly appreciated until quite recent generations, but this must only emphasize our sympathy for those obscure, patient but fruitful workers in a great field of human knowledge. As to what should be thought of those who ignorant of their work proclaim that the Church did not tolerate geography it is hard to say. Our geographical knowledge comes mainly from travelers whose wish it is to gain commercial opportunities for themselves or their compatriots; that of the Middle Ages was gained by men who wished anxiously to spread the light of Christianity throughout the world. The geographical societies of these earlier days were the religious orders who sent out the explorers and travelers, furnished them on their return with an enthusiastic audience to hear their stories, and then helped to disseminate their books all over the then civilized world.

There is probably no better refutation of the expression so often heard from those who know nothing about it, with regard to the supposed laziness of the Monks of the Middle Ages, than this chapter of the story of their exploration and missionary labors during the Thirteenth Century. It is usually supposed that if a Monk was fat he could not possibly have accomplished any serious work in life. Some of these men were *valde ponderosi,* very weighty, yet they did not hesitate to take on themselves these long journeys to the East. Their lives are the best illustration of the expression of Montalembert:

"Let us then banish into the world of fiction that affirmation so long repeated by foolish credulity which made monasteries an asylum for indolence and incapacity, for misanthropy and pusillanimity, for feeble and melancholic temperaments, and for men who were no longer fit to serve society in the world. It was not the sick souls, but on the contrary the most vigorous and healthful the human race has ever produced who presented themselves in crowds to fill them."

XXVI

GREAT BEGINNINGS OF MODERN COMMERCE.

For our present eminently commercial age nothing of all the accomplishment of the Thirteenth Century will probably possess livelier interest than the fact that, in spite of what must have seemed insuperable difficulties to a less enterprising generation, the men of that time succeeded in making such business combinations and municipal affiliations, besides arranging various trade facilities among distant, different peoples, that not only was commerce rendered possible and even easy, but some of the most modern developments of the facilitation of international intercourse were anticipated. The story of the rise of this combination of many men of different nations, of many cities whose inhabitants were of different races and of different languages, of commercial enterprise that carried men comparatively much farther than they now go or trade expeditions, though we have thought that our age had exhausted the possibilities of progress in this matter, cannot fail to have an interest for everyone whose attention has been attracted to the people of this time and must be taken as a symbol of the all-pervading initiative of the generations, which allowed no obstacle to hinder their progress and thought no difficulty too great to be surmounted.

In beginning the history of the great commercial league which in the Thirteenth Century first opened men's minds to the possibilities of peace and commerce among the nations and alas! that it should be said, did more perhaps than any other agent except Christianity to awaken in different races the sense of the brotherhood of man, the English historian of the Hanseatic League, Miss Zimmern in the Stories of the Nations, said:

"There is scarcely a more remarkable chapter in history than that which deals with the trading alliance or association known as the Hanseatic League. The league has long since passed away having served its time and fulfilled its purpose. The needs and circumstances of mankind have changed, and new methods and new instruments have been devised for carrying on the commerce of the world. Yet, if the league has disappeared, the beneficial results of its action survive to Europe though they have become so completely a part of our daily life that we accept them as matters of course, and do not stop to inquire into their origin." This last declaration may seem surprising for comparatively few know anything about this medieval commercial league, yet the effects claimed for it are only what we have seen to be true with regard to most of the important institutions of the period—they were the origins of what is best in our modern life.

Like many of the great movements of the Thirteenth Century the origin of the Hanseatic League is clouded somewhat by the obscurity of the times and the lack of definite historical documents.* There is no doubt, however, that just before the middle of the century it was in flourishing existence, and that by the end of the century it had reached that acme of its power and influence which it was to maintain for several centuries in spite of the jealousy of the nobility, of certain towns that did not have the same privileges, and even of the authorities of the various countries who resented more and more as time went on the growing freedom and independence of these wealthy cities. The impetus for the formation of the League seems to have been given during the Crusades. Like so many other of the important movements of the time commerce was greatly influenced by these expeditions, and the commercial spirit not only aroused but shown the possibility of accom-

---

* Perhaps no better idea of the obscurity of the origin of the Hansa confederation can be given, than is to be derived from the fact that even the derivation of the word Hansa is not very clear. Bishop Ulfilas in his old Gothic translation of the Scriptures used the word "hansa" to designate the mob of soldiers and servants of the High Priest who came to take Christ prisoner in the Garden. Later on the word Hansa was used to mean a tax or a contribution. This term was originally employed to designate the sum of money which each of the cities was compelled to pay on becoming a member of the league, and it is thought to be from this that the terms Hansa and Hanseatic League were eventually derived.

PALAZZO ZABARELLA (PADUA)

PALAZZO DEI CONSOLI (GUBBIO)

plishing hitherto impossible results in the matter of transportation and exchange. The returning crusaders brought back with them many precious Eastern objects whose possession was a source of envy to others and whose value was rated so high as to make even distant travel for them well worth while. The returning crusaders also knew how cheaply objects considered very precious in the West might be purchased in the East, and they told the stories of their own acquisition of them to willing listeners, who were stimulated to try their fortunes in expeditions that promised such rich rewards.

Besides the crusaders on their return through Italy had observed what was accomplished by the League of the Lombard cities which had been in existence in a more or less imperfect way for more than a century, and at the end of the Twelfth and the beginning of the Thirteenth Century had begun to provide an example of the strength there is in union, and of the power for good there is in properly regulated combinations of commercial interests with due regard for civic rights and privileges. This League of the Lombard cities was encouraged by the popes especially by Innocent III. and his successors who are usually said to have given it their approbation for their own purposes, though this is to look at but one side of the case. The German Emperors endeavored to assert their rights over Italian territory and in so doing came into collision with the popes not only in temporal matters but also in spiritual things. As we have noted in the short sketch of the popes of the century, Innocent III. was the first great Italian patriot and original advocate of Italy for the Italians. He constantly opposed the influence of the German Emperor in Italian politics, mainly, of course, because this interfered with the power of the Church, but to a very great degree also because it proved a source of manifold political evil for the Italian cities.

The Germans then, who in the train of the Emperor went down into Italy saw the working of this League of Lombard cities, talked about it on their return, and were naturally tempted to essay what might be accomplished by the same means on German territory. These two elements, the incentive of the crusades and the stimulus of the example of the

Italians, must be considered as at the basis of Hansa, though these were only seeds, and it was the nurture and fostering care of the German mind which ever since the days of Tacitus had been noted as the freest in Europe, that gave the League its wonderful development.

It is difficult to tell how many towns belonged to the Hanseatic League during the Thirteenth Century but at the end of this period, Hansa, as it came to be called, was, as we have said, in its most flourishing condition and we know something definite of its numbers a little more than half a century later. In 1367 deputies from all the towns met in the large council chamber of the famous town hall at Cologne to discuss certain injustices that had been committed against the members of the League, or as the document set forth "against the free German merchants," in order to determine some way of preventing further injuries and inflict due punishment. Altogether the deputies of 77 towns were present and declared most solemnly "that because of the wrongs and the injuries done by the King of Denmark to the common German merchant the cities would be his enemies and help one another faithfully." The distant and smaller cities were not expected to send troops or even naval forces but promised to give contributions in money. Such cities as did not take part in this movement were to be considered as having forfeited their membership and would no longer be permitted to trade with the members of Hansa.

Lest it should be thought that the cities were incapable of enforcing any such boycott with effect, the story of the town of Lübeck must be recalled. Lübeck on one occasion refused to join with the other Hansa towns in a boycott of certain places in Flanders which had refused to observe the regulations as to trading. One of these was to the effect that such vessels as were lost on a coast did not become the property of the people of the neighborhood, though they had a right to a due share for salvage, but a fair proportion must be returned to the citizens of the town that suffered the loss. Lübeck was at the moment one of the most powerful commercial cities in Germany, and her citizens seemed to think that they could violate the Hansa regulation with impunity. For 30 years, however, the Hansa boycott was maintained and so little trading was done in the city that according to one old writer "the people starved, the markets were deserted, grass grew in the street and the inhabitants left in large numbers." Such a lesson as this was enough to make the Hanseatic decrees be observed with scrupulous care and shows the perfection of the organization.

The outcome of the war with Denmark demonstrates the power of the league. The King of Denmark is said to have scorned their declaration of war, and making an untranslatable pun on the word "Hansa" called the members of the League "geese who cackled much but need not be feared." The fleet of the League, however, succeeded in shutting off all the commerce of the coast of Denmark and though there was a truce each winter the war was renewed vigorously, and with summer many of the Danish cities were ransacked and plundered. At the end of the second year Denmark was exhausted and the people so weary of war that they pleaded for peace, and Valdemar had to accept the terms which the "geese" were willing to offer him. This triumph of the common people over a reigning monarch is one of the most striking passages in medieval history. It comes about a half century after the close of the Thirteenth, and is evidently the direct result of the great practical forces that were set in movement during that wonderful period, when the mighty heart of humanity was everywhere bestirring men to deeds of high purpose and far-reaching significance.

As a matter of fact, Hansa became, very early in its career, one of the firmest authorities in the midst of these troubled times and meted out unfailingly the sternest justice against those who infringed its rights if they were outsiders, or broke the rules of the League if they were its members. It was ever ready to send its ships against offenders and while it soon came to be feared, this fear was mingled with respect, and its regulations were seldom infringed. It is a most interesting reflection, that as its English Historian says, "never once in the whole course of its history did it draw the sword aggressively or against its own members." While it was ever on the look-out to increase its power by adding new cities to the League, cities were not forced to join and when it meted out punishments to its members this was not by the levying of war but by fines, the refusal to pay these being followed by the "declaration of boycott," which soon brought the offender to terms. War was only declared in all cases as a last resort, and the ships of the League were constantly spoken of and designated in all documents as "peace ships," and even the forts which the League built for the protection of its towns, or as places where its members might be sure of protection, were described as "Peace Burgs."

Unfortunately, the lessons of peace that were thus taught by commerce were not to bear fruit abundantly for many centuries after the Thirteenth. It is practically only in our own time that they have been renewed, and the last generation or two, has rather plumed itself over the fact that trade was doing so much to prevent war. Evidently this is no guarantee of the perpetuation of such an improvement in national or international morals, for the influence of Hansa for peace came to be lost entirely, after a few centuries. The cities themselves, however, that belonged to the League gradually became more and more free, and more independent of their rulers. It was thus, in fact, that the free cities of Germany had their origin, and in them much more of modern liberty was born than has ever been appreciated, except by those whose studies have brought them close to these marvelous medieval manifestations of the old spirit of Teutonic freedom.

The names of most of the cities that were members of the Hansa League are well known, though it is not easy to understand in the decrepitude that has come over many of them, how they could have been of so much importance as has been claimed for them in the Middle Ages. All the cities of the North Sea and the Baltic Sea were united together, and while we think of these as German, many of them really belonged to Slav people at this time, so that the membership of a number of Russian cities is not surprising. While the Rhenish cities were important factors in the League, Cologne indeed being one of the most important, Bremen and Hamburg and both the Frankforts, and Rostock, and Lübeck and Stralsund, and Tangermunde and Warnemunde, were important members. Novgorod was founded by Hansa for the purpose of trading with the Orientals, and the Volga, the Dnieper, the Dwina, and the Oder were extensively used for the purpose of transporting goods here and there in central Europe. One of their most famous towns, Winetha in German, Julin in Danish, disappeared beneath the waters of the Baltic Sea and gave rise to many legends of its reappearance. It is hard to realize that it was so important that it was called the Venice of the North, and was seriously compared with its great southern rival.

A good idea of the intimate relations of the Hansa towns to England and the English people can be obtained from the article on the subject written by Richard Lodge for the Ninth Edition of the Encyclopedia Britannica. A single paragraph of this compresses much of the external and internal history of the "Rise and Development of Hansa." It was rather to be expected that the commercial relations between England and the various cities situated along the North Sea, as well as the Baltic and up the Rhine, would be active and would have to be submitted to careful regulation. Unless the modern mind is actually brought directly in touch, however, with the complex yet very practical state of affairs, which actually existed, it will utterly fail to appreciate how thoroughly progressive and enterprising were these medieval peoples. Enterprise and practicalness we are apt to think of as the exclusive possession of much more modern generations. Least of all would we be apt to consider them as likely to be found in the Thirteenth Century, yet here they are, and the commercial arrangements which were made are as absolute premonitions of our modern thought as were the literature and architecture, the painting, even the teachings of science at the same period.

"The members of this League (Hanseatic) came to England mostly from Cologne, the first German town which obtained great importance both at home and abroad. Its citizens possessed at an early date a guild-hall of their own (in London), and all Germans who wished to trade with England had to join their guild. This soon included merchants from Dortmund, Soest and Munster, in Westphalia; from Utrecht, Stavern and Groningen, in the Netherlands, and from Bremen and Hamburg on the North Sea. But, when at the beginning of the Thirteenth Century, the rapidly rising town of Lübeck wished to be admitted into the guild, every effort was made to keep her out. The intervention of Frederick II. was powerless to overcome the dread felt by Cologne towards a possible rival to its supremacy. But this obstacle to the extension of the League was soon overcome. In 1260 a charter of Henry III. assured protection to all German merchants. A few years later Hamburg and Lübeck also were allowed to form their own guilds. The Hansa of Cologne, which had long been the only guild, now sinks to the position of a branch Hansa, and has to endure others with equal privileges. Over all the branch Hansas rises the "Hansa Alamanniae," first mentioned in 1282.

This article gives additional information with regard to the many and varied influences at work at the end of the Thirteenth Century. It furnishes in brief, moreover, an excellent picture of the activity of mind and power of organization so frequently displayed during this period in every branch of life. This is after all the highest quality of man. The development of associations of various kinds, especially such as are helpfully purposive, are the outcome of that social quality in man's mind which is the surest index of his rational quality. Succeeding centuries lost for some almost unaccountable reason much of this faculty of organization and the result was a lamentable retrogression from the advances made by older generations, so that it was only in quite recent years that anything like this old international comity was reestablished.

The extent and very natural development of this community of interests must ever attract attention. It is the first time in our modern history that it occurs and men of some seven different races and tongues were at last drawn into it. In this it represents the greatest advance of history, for it led to assimilation of laws and of liberties, with some of the best features of each nation's old-time customs preserved in the new codes. Its extension even to Novgorod, in what is now the heart of Russia is a surprising demonstration of successful enterprise and spread of influence almost incredible. The settling of the trade disputes of this distant Russian City in the courts of a North Sea town, is an evidence of advance in commercial relations emphasized by the writer in the Britannica, that deserves to be well weighed as a manifestation of what is often thought

RATHHAUS LÜBECK

to be the exclusively modern recognition of the rights of commerce and the claims of justice over even national feelings.

"The league between Lübeck and Hamburg was not the only, and possibly not the first, league among the German towns. But it gradually absorbed all others. Besides the influence of foreign commercial interests there were other motives which compelled the towns to union. The chief of these were the protection of commercial routes both by sea and land, and the vindication of town independence as opposed to claims of the landed aristocracy. The first to join the League were the Wendish towns to the East, Wismar, Rostock, Stralsund, etc., which had always been intimately connected with Lübeck, and were united by a common system of laws known as the 'Lübisches Recht' (Lübeck Laws). The Saxon and Westphalian towns had long possessed a league among themselves; they also joined themselves to Lübeck. Lübeck now became the most important town in Germany. It had already surpassed Cologne both in London and Bruges. It soon gained a similar victory over Wisby. At a great convention in which twenty-four towns from Cologne to Revel took part, it was decided that appeals from Novgorod which had hitherto been decided at Wisby should henceforth be brought to Lübeck."

After much travail and vexation of spirit, after much diplomacy and political and parliamentary discussion, after much striving on the part of the men in all nations, who have the great cause of universal peace for mankind at heart, we have reached a position where at least commercial difficulties can be referred to a sort of international court for adjudication. The standing of this court is not very clear as yet. Special arrangements at least are required, if not special treaties in many cases, even for the reference of such merely commercial difficulties as debt-collecting to it. In the last quarter of the Nineteeenth Century special tribunals had to be erected for the settlement of such difficulties between nations. In the Twentieth Century the outlook is more hopeful and the actual accomplishment is indeed encouraging. In the Thirteenth Century with the absence of the telegraph and the cable, with the slowness of sailing vessels and the distance of towns emphasizing all the difficulties of the situation, the Hanseatic League succeeded in obtaining an international tribunal, whose judgments with regard to commercial difficulties were final and were accepted by men of many different races and habits and customs, and to which causes were referred without any of the immense machinery apparently required at the present time.

This is the real triumph of the commercial development of the Thirteenth Century. While it may be astonishing to many modern people to learn how much was accomplished in this utterly unexpected quarter, it will not be a surprise to those who realize the thoroughly practical character of the century and the perfectly matter of fact way in which it went about settling all the difficulties that presented themselves; and how often they succeeded in reaching a very practical if not always ideal solution. The sad feature of the case is to think that most of this coming together of nations was lost by the gradual development of national feeling, much of benefit as there may have been in that for the human race, and by the drawing of the language lines between nations more closely than they had been before, for the next three centuries saw the development of modern tongues into the form which they have held ever since.

Hansa did more than almost any other institution in northern Europe to establish the reign of Law. If it had accomplished no other purpose, this would make it eminently worthy of the study of those who are interested in sociology and social evolution. Before the time of Hansa the merchant by sea or land was liable to all sorts of impositions, arbitrary taxes, injustices, and even the loss of life as well of his goods. As Hansa gained in power however, these abuses disappeared. Perhaps the most noteworthy improvement came with regard to navigation. There is a story told of a famous rock in Brittany on which many ships were wrecked during the Middle Ages. Even as late as the Thirteenth Century sometimes false lights were displayed on this rock with the idea of tempting vessels to their destruction on it. Everything that was thrown ashore in the neighborhood was considered to be the property of the people who gathered it, except that a certain portion of its value had to be paid to the Lord of the Manor. This worthy representative of the upper classes is said to have pointed out the rock to some visiting nobleman friends one day, and declared that it was more precious to him than the most precious stone in the diadem of any ruling monarch in Europe. This represents the state of feeling with regard to such subjects when Hansa started in to correct the abuses.

It may be looked upon as a serious disgrace to the Thirteenth Century that such a low state of ethical feeling should have existed, but it is the amelioration of conditions which obliterated such false sentiments that constitutes the triumph of the period. On the other hand we must not with smug self-complacency think that our generation is so much better than those of the past. It is easy to be pharisaical while we forget that many a fortune in modern times suffers shipwreck on the coasts of business and investment, because the false lights of advertising intended to deceive, are displayed very prominently, for those who are only anxious as were the mariners of the olden times to make their fortunes. Doubtless too the proprietors of many of the papers which display such advertisements, and it is nonsense to say that they are unconscious of the harm they do, are quite as proud of the magnificent revenue that their advertising columns bring to them as was the Breton noble of the Thirteenth Century. Man has not changed much in the interval.

Lest it should be thought that even the present-day initiation into secret societies of various kinds is the invention of modern times, it seems well to give some of the details of the tests through which those seeking to be members of the Hanseatic League were subjected, by those who were already initiated. It may possibly seem that some of these customs were too barbarous to mention in the same breath with the present-day initiations, but if it is recalled that at least once a year some serious accident is reported as the result of the thoughtless fooling of "frat" students at our universities, this opinion may be withdrawn. Miss Helen Zimmern in her story of the Hansa Towns already quoted several times, has a paragraph or two of descriptions of these that we shall quote. It may be well to remember that these tests were not entirely without a serious significance for the members of the Hansa. Much was expected of those who belonged to the Hansa Guild. A number of precious trade secrets were entrusted them, and they alone knew the methods and mysteries of Hansa. In order that these might not by any possibility be betrayed, the members of Hansa who lived in foreign countries were forbidden to marry while abroad and were bound under the severest penalties to live a life of celibacy. They were not supposed to be absent from the houses assigned to them during the night, and their factories so called, or common-places of residence, were guarded by night watchman and fierce dogs in order to secure the keeping of these rules.

Besides torture was a very common thing in those times and a man who belonged to a country that happened to be at war for the moment, might very easily be subjected to torture for some reason or another with the idea of securing important information from him. If the members of Hansa wanted to be reasonably assured that new members would not give up their secrets without a brave struggle, they had no better way than by these tests, for which there was therefore some excuse. As to the brutality of the tests perhaps Miss Zimmern in maidenly way has said too much. We commend her paragraphs to the modern committees of reception of college secret societies, because here as elsewhere this generation may get points from the Thirteenth Century.

"We cannot sully our pages by detailing the thirteen different games or modes of martyrdom that were in use at Bergen. Our more civilized age could not tolerate the recital. In those days they attracted a crowd of eager spectators who applauded the more vociferously the more cruel and barbarous the tortures. The most popular were those practices known as the smoke, water and flogging games; mad, cruel pranks calculated to cause a freshman to lose health and reason. Truly Dantesque hell tortures were these initiations into Hansa mysteries. Merely to indicate their nature we will mention that for the smoke game the victim was pulled up the big chimney of the Schutting while there burned beneath him the most filthy materials, sending up a most nauseous stench and choking wreaths of smoke. While in this position he was asked a number of questions, to which he was forced, under yet more terrible penalties, to reply. If

CITY GATE (NEUBRANDENBURG)

MINSTER (CHORIN, GERMANY)

he survived his torture he was taken out into the yard and plied under the pump with six tons of water." (Even the "Water Cure" is not new).

There was a variety about the tests at different times and places that show no lack of invention on the part of the members of Hansa. With regard to other water tests Miss Zimmern has furnished some interesting details:

"The 'water' game that took place at Whitsuntide consisted in first treating the probationer to food, and then taking him out to sea in a boat. Here he was stripped thrown into the ocean, ducked three times, made to swallow much sea-water, and thereafter mercilessly flogged by all the inmates of the boats. The third chief game was no less dangerous to life and limb. It took place a few days after, and was a rude perversion of the May games. The victims had first to go out into the woods to gather the branches with which later they were to be birched. Returned to the factory, rough horse play pranks were practised upon them. Then followed an ample dinner, which was succeeded by mock combats, and ended in the victims being led into the so-called Paradise, where twenty-four disguised men whipped them till they drew blood, while outside this black hole another party made hellish music with pipes, drums and triangles to deafen the screams of the tortured. The 'game' was considered ended when the shrieks of the victims were sufficiently loud to overcome the pandemonic music." Some of the extreme physical cruelties of the initiations our modern fraternities have eliminated, but the whole story has a much more familiar air than we might have expected.

Probably the most interesting feature of the history of the Hanseatic League is the fact that this great combination for purposes of trade and commerce proved a source of liberty for the citizens of the various towns, and enabled them to improve their political status better than any other single means at this precious time of development of legal and social rights. This is all the more interesting because great commercial combinations with similar purposes in modern times have usually proved fruitful rather of opposite results. A few persons have been very much benefited by them, or at least have made much money by them, which is quite another thing, though money is

supposed to represent power and influence, but the great mass
of the people have been deprived of opportunities to rise and
have had taken from them many chances for the exercise of initiative that existed before.

There is a curious effect of Hansa upon the political fortunes
of the people of the cities that were members of the League
which deserves to be carefully studied. As with regard to so
many other improvements that have come in the history of the
race, it was not a question so much of the recognition of great
principles as of money and revenues that proved the origin of
amelioration of civic conditions. These commercial cities accumulated wealth. Money was necessary for their rulers for
the maintenance of their power and above all for the waging
of war. In return for moneys given for such purposes the cities
claimed for the inhabitants and were granted many privileges.
These became perpetuated and as time went on were added
to as new opportunities for the collection of additional revenues occurred, until finally an important set of fundamental
rights with documentary confirmation were in the hands of the
city authorities. One would like to think that this state of affairs
developed as the result of the recognition on the part of the
ruling sovereign, of the benefits that were conferred on his
realm by having in it, or associated with it, an important trading city whose enterprising citizens gave occupation to many
hands. This was very rarely the case, however, but as was true
of the legal rights obtained by England's citizens during the
Thirteenth Century, it was largely a question of the coordination of taxation and legislative representation and the consequent attainment of privileges.

The most important effect on the life of Europe and the
growth of civilization that the Hanseatic League exerted, was
its success in showing that people of many different nations
and races, living under very different circumstances, might still
be united under similar laws that would enable them to accomplish certain objects which they had in view. Germans, Slavs
and English learned to live in one another's towns and while
observing the customs of these various places maintained the
privileges of their homes. The mutual influence of these people
on one another, many of them being the most practical and en-

terprising individuals of the time, could scarcely fail to produce noteworthy effects in broadening the minds of those with whom they came in contact. It is to this period that we must trace the beginnings of international law. Hansa showed the world how much commercial relations were facilitated by uniform laws and by just treatment of even the citizens of foreign countries. It is to commerce that we owe the first recognition of the rights of the people of other countries even in time of war. If the Hanseatic League had done nothing else but this, it must be considered as an important factor in the development of our modern civilization and an element of influence great as any other in this wonderful century.

HINGE (CATHEDRAL, SCHLESTADT)

APPENDIX.

SO-CALLED HISTORY.

RULERS.

EMPERORS OF GERMANY.

Otho IV............1198-1218
Frederick II.........1212-1250
Conrad IV..........1250-1254
William of Holland..1254-1256
Richard Earl of Cornwall
               1257-1273
Rudolph of Hapsburg.1273-1291
Adolph of Nassau.....1292-1298
Albert of Austria....1298-1308

KINGS OF SCOTLAND.

William 1175-1214
Alexander II.........1214-1249
Alexander III.......1249-1286
Margaret 1286-1292
John Balliol.........1292-1296
Interregnum 1296-1306

KINGS OF CASTILE AND LEON.

Alfonso IX..........1188-1214
Henry I..............1214-1217
St. Ferdinand III....1217-1252
Alfonso X...........1252-1284
Sancho IV...........1284-1295
Ferdinand IV.......1295-1312

KINGS OF ENGLAND.

John Lackland........1199-1216
Henry III............1216-1272
Edward I............1272-1307

KINGS OF FRANCE.

Philip II.............1180-1223
Louis VIII...........1223-1226
Louis IX.............1226-1270
Philip III............1270-1285
Louis IV.............1314-1316

KINGS OF ARAGON.

Pedro II.............1196-1213
James I., the Conqueror
               1215-1276
Pedro III...........1276-1285
Alfonso III..........1285-1291
James II.............1291-1327

KINGS OF NAPLES.

Conrad 1250-1254
Conradin 1254-1258
Manfred 1258-1266
Charles of Anjou.....1266-1285
Charles 1285-1309

EVENTS.

1202.—Fourth great crusade under Boniface, marquis of Montferrat.

1204.—The English stripped of Normandy, etc., by Philip Augustus of France.

1206.—Jenghis-Khan: foundation of the great empire of the Moguls.

1212.—Battle of Ubeda: defeat and fall of Almohads of Africa.

1213.—John Lackland acknowledges himself vassal of the pope.

1213.—Battle of Bouvines won by Philip Augustus.

1215. — Magna Charta. The palatinate of the Rhine goes to the house of Wittelsbach.

1217.—Crusade of Andrew II., King of Hungary.

1218.—Extinction of the dukes of Zarringuia: Switzerland becomes an immediate province of the empire.

1222.—Charter or decree of Andrew II., basis of the Hungarian constitution.

1226.—Renewal of the League of Lombardy to oppose the Emperor Frederick II.

1227.—Battle of Bornhoeved in Holstein: Waldemar II., K'ng of Denmark, loses his conquests on the southern coast of the Baltic.

1228.—Crusade of the Emperor Frederick II.

1230. — The Teutonic order establishes itself in Prussia. Conquest of the Balearic islands by the King of Aragon.

1235.—Formation of the Duchy of Brunswick in favor of the house of the Guelphs.

1236.—Conquest of the Kingdoms of Cordova, Murcia and Seville by the Castilians.

1237.—Conquest of Russia by Baton-Khan: origin of the Mogul or Tartar horde of Kaptschak.

1241.—Invasion of Poland, Silesia, and Hungary by the Moguls.

1248.—Crusade of St. Louis, King of France.

1250.—Beginning of the great interregnum in Germany.

1254.—Accessions of the emperors of different houses in Germany. End of the dominion of the Agubites in Egypt and Syria; beginning of the empire of the Mamelukes.

1256.—Enfranchisement of the serfs at Bologna in Italy.

1261.—Michel Paleologus, emperor of Nice, takes Constantinople; end of the empire of the Latins.

1265.—Accession of the house of Anjou to the throne of the Two Sicilies.

1266.—Admission of the Commons to the Parliament of England.

1268.—Corradino decapitated at Naples; extinction of the house of Hohenstaufen. Suabia and Franconia become immediate provinces of the empire.

1271.—The county of Toulouse passes to the King of France, and the Venaissin to the Pope.

1273.—Accession of the Emperor Rudolph of Hapsburg to the throne of the empire: first election by the seven electors.

1282.—Conquest of Wales by the King of England.

1282.—The Sicilian Vespers, the kingdom of Sicily passes to the King of Aragon. The Emperor Rudolph gives to his sons the duchies of Austria; foundation of the house of Hapsburg.

1283.—The Teutonic order completes the conquest of Prussia.

1289.—Extinction of the male line of the old race of Scotch kings. Contest of Baliol and Bruce.

1290.—Decline of the republic of Piza. Aggrandizement of that of Genoa.

1291.—Taking of Ptolemais and Tyre by the Mamelukes. End of the crusades.

1294.—Decline of the Mogul empire at the death of Kublaï-Khan.

1298.—Introduction of an hereditary aristocracy at Venice.

1300.—Foundation of the modern Turkish empire by Ottoman I. First Jubilee proclaimed by Pope Boniface VIII.

APPENDIX II.

TWENTY-SIX CHAPTERS THAT MIGHT HAVE BEEN.

I. AMERICA IN THE THIRTEENTH CENTURY.

To most people it would seem quite out of the question that a chapter on America in the Thirteenth Century might have been written. One of the most surprising chapters for most readers in the previous edition was that on Great Explorers and the Foundation of Geography, for it was a revelation to learn that Thirteenth Century travelers had anticipated all of our discoveries in the Far and in the Near East seven centuries ago. Certain documents have turned up, however, which make it very clear that with the same motives as those which urged Eastern travelers, Europeans went just as far towards the West at this time. Documents found in the Vatican Archives in 1903 and exhibited at St. Louis in 1904, have set at rest finally and absolutely the long disputed question of the discovery of America by the Norsemen, and in connection with these the story of America in the Thirteenth Century might well have been told. There is a letter from Pope Innocent III., dated February 13, 1206, addressed to the Archbishop of Norway, who held jurisdiction over Greenland, which shows not only the presence of the Norsemen on the American Continent at this time, but also that they had been here for a considerable period, and that there were a number of churches and pastors and large flocks in whom the Roman See had a lively interest. There are Americana from three other Popes of the Thirteenth Century.   John XXI. wrote, in 1276, Nicholas III. two letters, one dated January 31, 1279, and another June 9, 1279, and Martin III. wrote 1282. We have inserted on the opposite page a reproduction of a portion of the first Papal document extant relating to America, the letter of Pope Innocent III., taken from " The Norse Discovery of America" (The Norraena Society, N. Y., 1908). The word *Grenelandie*, underscored, indicates the subject. The writing as an example of the chirography of the century is of interest.

II. A REPRESENTATIVE UPPER HOUSE.

In most historical attempts at government by the people it has been recognized that legislation is better balanced if there are two chambers in the law-making body, one directly elected by the people, the other indirectly chosen and representing important vested interests that are likely to make its members conservative. The initiative for legislation comes, as a rule, from the direct representatives of the people, while the upper chamber represses radical law-making or

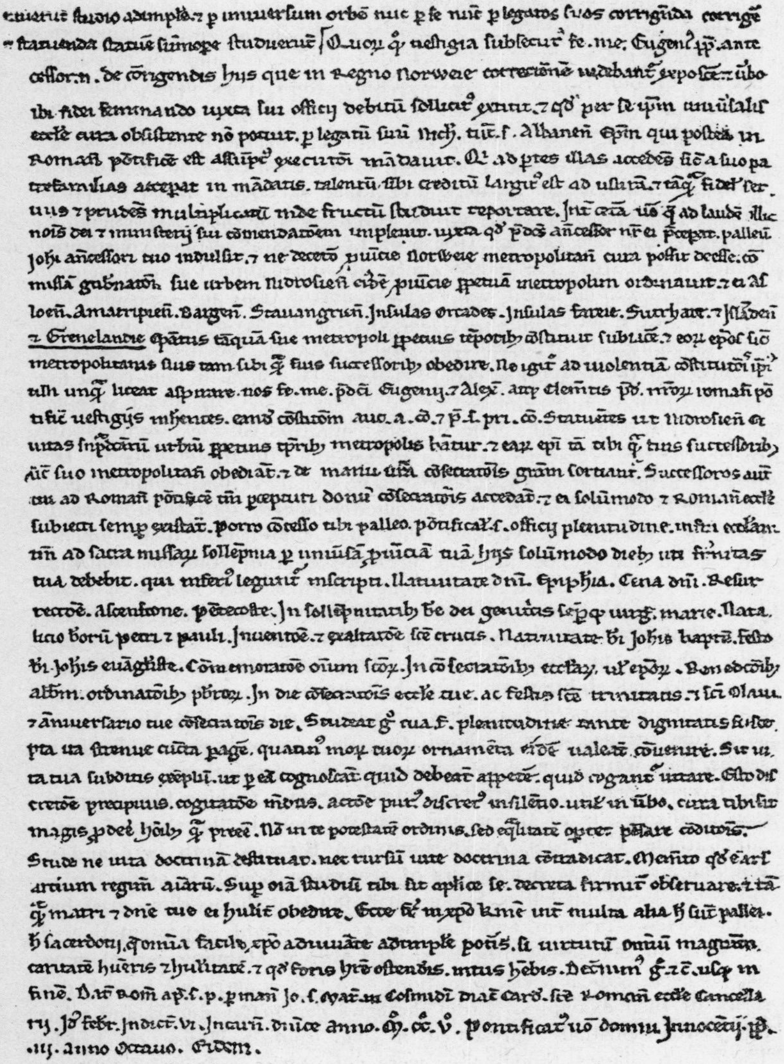

PART OF LETTER OF POPE INNOCENT III. MENTIONING GREENLAND.

sudden changes in legislative policy, yet does not hamper too much the progress of democracy. During the last few years a crisis in English politics has led to a very general demand for a modification of the status of the House of Lords, while almost similar conditions have led to the beginning at least of a similar demand for the modification of our Senate in this country. Both these upper chambers have come to represent vested interests to too great a degree. The House of Lords has been the subject of special deprecation. The remark is sometimes made that it is unfortunate that England is weighted down by this political incubus, the House of Lords, which is spoken of as a heritage from the Middle Ages. The general impression, of course, is that the English House of Lords, as at present constituted, comes down from the oldest times of constitutional government in England. Nothing could well be more untrue than any such idea.

The old upper chamber of England, the medieval House of Lords, was an eminently representative body. Out of the 625 or more of members of the English House of Lords at the present time about five hundred and fifty hold their seats by heredity. Only about seventy-five are in some sense elective. At least one-half of these elected peers, however, must be chosen from the hereditary nobility of Ireland and Scotland. Nearly nineteen-twentieths of the membership of the House of Lords, as at present constituted, owe their place in national legislation entirely to heredity. Until the reformation so-called this was not so. More than one-half of the English House of Lords, a good working majority, consisted of the Lords spiritual. Besides the Bishops and Archbishops there were the Abbots and Priors of monasteries, and the masters of religious orders. These men as a rule had come up from the people. They had risen to their positions by intellectual abilities and by administrative capacity. The abbots and other superiors of religious orders had been chosen by their monks as a rule because, having shown that they knew how to rule themselves, they were deemed most fitting to rule over others.

Even in our day, when the Church occupies nothing like the position in the hearts of the masses that she held in the ages of faith, our Catholic Cardinals, Archbishops and Bishops, both here and in England, are chosen as members of arbitration boards to settle strikes and other social difficulties, because it is felt that the working class has full confidence in them, and that they are thoroughly representative of the spirit of democracy. In England Cardinal Manning served more than once in critical social conditions. In this country we have had a series of such examples. From these we can better understand what the Lords spiritual represented in the English House of Lords. There were abuses, though they were not nearly so frequent as were thought, by which unworthy men sometimes reached such positions, for men abuse even the best things, but in general these clerical members of the House of Lords were the chosen intellectual and moral products of the kingdom. Since they were without families they had less temptation to serve personal interests and, besides, they had received a life-long training in unselfishness, and the best might be expected of them. For an ideal second chamber I know none that can compare with this old English House of Lords of the Middle Ages. How much it was responsible for the foundation of the liberties of which the English-speaking people are deservedly so proud, and which have been treated in some detail in the chapter on Origins in Law, would be interesting to trace.

III. THE PARISH, AND TRAINING IN CITIZENSHIP.

Mr. Toulmin Smith, in his book on "The Parish," and Dom Gasquet, in his volume on "The Parish Before the Reformation," have shown what a magnificent institution for popular self-government was the English medieval parish, and how much this contributed to the solution of important social problems and to the creation of a true democratic spirit. Mr. Toulmin Smith calls particular attention to the fact that when local self-government gets out of the hands of the people of a neighborhood personal civic energy goes to sleep. The feeling of mutual responsibility of the men of the place is lost, to the great detriment of their larger citizenship in municipality and nation. In the parish, however, forming a separate community, of which the members had rights and duties, the primal solid basis for government, the parish authorities took charge of the highways, the roads, the paths, the health, the police, the constabulary, and the fires of their neighborhood. They kept, besides, a registry of births and deaths and marriages. When these essentially local concerns are controlled in large bodies the liability to abuse at once becomes easy and political corruption sets in. He mentions, besides many parochial institutions, a parochial friendly society for loans on security, parish gilds for insurance, and many other phases of that thoroughly organized mutual aid so characteristic of the Middle Ages.

These parishes became completely organized, so as to be thoroughly democratic and representative of all the possibilities of local self-government under King Edward at the end of the Thirteenth and the beginning of the Fourteenth Century. Rev. Augustus Jessopp, in "After the Great Pillage," tells the story of how the parishes were broken up as a consequence of the confiscation of their endowment during the so-called reformation. The quotation from him may be found in Appendix III. in the section on "How it all stopped."

Toulmin Smith is not so emphatic, but he is scarcely less explicit than Jessopp. "The attempts of ecclesiastical authority to encroach on the civil authorities of the parish have been more successful since the reformation." As a matter of fact, at that time all government became centralized, and complete contradiction though it may seem to be of what is sometimes declared the place of the reformation in the history of human liberty, the genuine democratic institutions of England were to a great extent impaired by the reform, and an autocracy, which later developed into an autocratic aristocracy, largely took its place. Out of that England has gradually lifted itself during the Nineteenth Century. Even now, however, as pointed out in the preceding chapter that might have been, the House of Lords is not at all what it was in the Thirteenth and Fourteenth Centuries when the majority of its members were Lords spiritual, men who had come up from the masses as a rule.

IV.   THE CHANCE TO RISE.

We are very prone to think that even though there may have been excellent opportunities for the higher education in the Thirteenth Century and, in many ways, an ideal education of the masses, still there was one great social drawback in those times, the lack of opportunity for men of humble birth to rise to higher stations. Nothing, however, is less true. There probably never was a time when even members of the poorest families might rise more readily or rapidly to the highest positions in the land. The sons of village merchants and village artisans, nay, the sons and grandsons of farmers bound to the soil, could by educational success become clergymen in various ranks, and by attaining a bishopric or the position of abbot or prior of a monastery, reach a seat in the House of Lords. Most of the Lord High Chancellors of England during the Middle Ages—and some of them are famous for their genius as canon and civil lawyers, for their diplomatic abilities and their breadth of view and capacity as administrators—were the sons of humble parents.

Take the single example of Stratford, the details of whose inhabitants' lives, because of the greatness of one of them, have attracted more attention than those of any other town of corresponding size in England. At the beginning of the Fourteenth Century it is only what we would call a village, and it probably did not have 3,000 inhabitants, if, indeed, the number was not less than 2,000. In his book, "Shakespeare the Boy," Mr. Rolfe calls attention to certain conditions that interest us in the old village. He tells us of what happened as a result of the development of liberty in the Thirteenth Century:

"Villeinage gradually disappeared in the reign of Edward VII. (13-27-1337), and those who had been subject to it became free tenants, paying definite rents for house and land. Three natives of the town, who, after the fashion of the time, took their surnames from the place of their birth, rose to high positions in the Church, one becoming Archbishop of Canterbury, and the others respectively Bishops of London and Chichester. John of Stratford and Robert of Stratford were brothers, and Ralph of Stratford was their nephew. John and Robert were both for a time Chancellors of England, and there is no other instance of two brothers attaining that high office in succession."

To many people the fact that the avenue to rise was through the Clergy more than in any other way will be disappointing. One advantage, however, that the old people would insist that they had from their system was that these men, having no direct descendants, were less likely to pursue selfish aims and more likely to try to secure the benefit of the Community than are those who, in our time, rise through the legal profession. The Lord High Chancellors of recent time have all been lawyers. Would not most of the world confess that the advantage was with the medieval peoples?

President Woodrow Wilson of Princeton realized sympathetically this great element of saving democracy in the Middle Ages, and has paid worthy tribute to it. He said: " The only reason why government did not suffer dry rot in the Middle Ages under the aristocratic systems which then prevailed was that the men who were efficient instruments of government were drawn from the church—from that great church, that body which we now distinguish from other church bodies as the Roman Catholic Church. The Roman Catholic Church then, as now, was a great democracy. There was no peasant so humble that he might not become a priest, and no priest so obscure that he might not become Pope of Christendom, and every chancellery in Europe was ruled by those learned, trained and accomplished men—the priesthood of that great and then dominant church; and so, what kept government alive in the Middle Ages was this constant rise of the sap from the bottom, from the rank and file of the great body of the people through the open channels of the Roman Catholic priesthood."

V. INSURANCE.

Insurance is usually supposed to be a modern idea representing one of those developments of the capitalization of mutual risks of life, property, and the like that have come as a consequence of modern progress. The insurance system of the Middle Ages, the organization of which came in the Thirteenth Century, is therefore extremely interesting. It was accomplished, as was every form of co-operation and co-ordination of effort, through special gilds or through the trade or merchant gilds. Among the objects of the gilds enumerated by Toulmin Smith is insurance against loss by fire. This was paid through the particular gild to which the merchant belonged, or in the case of the artisan through a special gild which he joined for the purpose. Provision was made, however, for much more than insurance by fire. Our fire insurance companies are probably several centuries old, so also are our insurance arrangements against shipwreck. Other features of insurance, however, are much more recent. Practically all of these were in active existence during the Middle Ages, though they disappeared with the so-called reformation, and then did not come into existence again for several centuries and, indeed, not until our own time.

The old gilds, for instance, provided insurance against loss from flood, a feature of insurance that has not, so far as I know, developed in our time, against loss by robbery (our burglary insurance is quite recent), against loss by the fall of a house, by imprisonment, and then also insurance against the loss of cattle and farm products. All the features of life insurance also were in existence. The partial disability clauses of life or accident insurance policies are recent developments. In the old days there is insurance against the loss of sight, against the loss of a limb, or any other form of crippling. The deaf and dumb might be insured so as to secure an income for them, and corresponding relief for leprosy might be obtained; so that, if one were set apart from the community by the law requiring segregation of lepers, there might be provision for food and lodging, even though productive work had become impossible. In a word, the insurance system of the Middle Ages was thoroughly developed. It was not capitalistic. The charges were only enough to maintain the system, and not such as to provide large percentage returns on invested stock and on bonds, and the accumulation of huge surpluses that almost inevitably lead to gross abuses. What is best in our modern system of insurance is an imitation of the older methods. Certain of the trade insurance companies which assume a portion of the risk on mills, factories and the like, are typical examples. They know the conditions, enforce proper precautions, keep an absolute check on suspicious losses, accumulate only a moderate surplus and present very few opportunities for insurance abuses. The same thing is true for the fraternal societies that conduct life insurance. When properly managed they represent the lowest possible cost and the best efficiency with least opportunities for fraud and without any temptations to interfere with legislation and any allurements for legislators to spend their time making strike and graft bills instead of doing legislative work.

VI. OLD AGE PENSIONS.

This generation has occupied itself much with the question of old age pensions. Probably most people feel that this is the first time in the world's history that such arrangements have been made. The movement is supposed to represent a recent development of humanitarian purpose, and to be a feature of recent philanthropic evolution. It is rather interesting, in the light of that idea, to see how well they accomplish this same purpose in the Thirteenth and Fourteenth Centuries. In our time it has been a government affair, with all the possibilities of abuse that there are in a huge pension system, and surely no country knows it better than we do here in America. The old countries, Germany and France, have established a contributing system of pension. This was the model of their system of caring for the old and the disabled in the Middle Ages. Toulmin Smith cites a rule of one of the gilds which gives us exactly the status of the old age disability pension question. After a workman had been seven years a member, the gild assured him a livelihood in case of disability from any cause.

When we recall that employer as well as employee as a rule belonged to the gild and this was a real mutual organization in which there was a sharing of the various risks of life, we see how eminently well adapted to avoid abuses this old system was. Where the pensioners appeal to a government pension system, abuses are almost inevitable. There is the constant temptation to exploit the system on the part of the pensioners, because they have the feeling that if they do not, others will. Then the investigation of each particular case is difficult, and favoritism and graft of various kinds inevitably finds its way in. Where the pension is paid by a small body of fellow workmen, the investigation is easy, the temptation to exploit does not readily find place, and while abuses are to some extent inevitable, these are small in amount, and not likely to be frequent. Friends and neighbors know conditions, and men are not pauperized by the system, and if, after an injury that seemed at first so disabling as to be permanent, the pensioner should improve enough to be able to get back to work, or, at least, to do something to support himself, the system is elastic enough so that he is not likely to be tempted to continue to live on others rather than on his own efforts.

VII. THE WAYS AND MEANS OF CHARITY—ORGANIZED CHARITY.

Most of us would be apt to think that our modern methods of obtaining funds for charitable purposes represented definite developments, and that at least special features of our collections for charity were our own invention. In recent years the value of being able to reach a great many people even for small amounts has been particularly recognized. "Tag day" is one manifestation of that. Everyone in a neighborhood is asked to contribute a small amount for a particular charitable purpose, and the whole collection usually runs up to a snug sum. Practices very similar to this were quite common in the Thirteenth Century. As in our time, it was the women who collected the money. A rope, for instance, was stretched across a marketplace, where traffic was busy, and everyone who passed was required to pay a toll for charity. Occasionally the rope was stretched across a bridge and the tolls were collected on a particular day each year. Other forms of charitable accumulation resembled ours in many respects. Entertainments of various kinds were given for charity, and special collections were made during the exhibition of mystery plays partly to pay the expenses of the representation, and the surplus to go to the charities of the particular gild.

Most of the charity, however, was organized. Indeed, it is the organization of charity during the Thirteenth Century that represents the best feature of its fraternalism. The needy were cared for by the gilds themselves. There were practically no poorhouses, and if a man was willing to work and had already shown this willingness, there were definite bureaus that would help him at least to feed his family while he was out of work. This system, however, was flexible enough to provide also for the ne'er-do-wells, the tramps, the beggars, but they were given not money, but tokens which enabled them to obtain the necessaries of life without being able to abuse charity. The committees of the gilds consulted in various ways among themselves and with the church wardens so as to be sure that, while all the needy were receiving help, no one was abusing charity by drawing help from a number of different quarters. Of course, they did not have the problem of large city life that we have, and so their comparatively simple organization of charity sufficed for all the needs of the time, and at the same time anticipated our methods.

VIII. SCIENTIFIC UNIVERSITIES.

In the first edition of this book I called attention to the fact, that science, even in our sense of physical science, was, in spite of impressions to the contrary, a favorite subject for students and teachers in the early universities. What might have been insisted on, however, is that these old universities were scientific universities resembling our own so closely in their devotion to science as to differ from them only in certain unimportant aspects. Because the universities for three centuries before the Nineteenth had been occupied mainly with classical studies, we are prone to think that these were the main subjects of university teaching for all the centuries before. Nothing could well be less true. The undergraduate studies consisted of the seven liberal arts so-called, though these were largely studied from the scientific standpoint. The quotation from Prof. Huxley (Appendix III., Education) makes this very clear. What we would now call the graduate studies consisted of metaphysics, in which considerable physics were studied, astronomy, medicine, above all, mathematics, and then the ethical sciences, under which were studied what we now call ethics, politics and economics. The picture of these medieval universities as I have given them in my lecture on Medieval Scientific Universities, in "Education, How Old the New," makes this very clear. The interests and studies were very like those of our own time, only the names for them being different. Nature-study was a favorite subject, and, as I have pointed out in "The Popes and Science," Dante must be considered as a great nature student, for he was able to draw the most exquisite figures from details of knowledge of living things with which few poets are familiar. The books of the professors of the Thirteenth Century which have been preserved, those of Albertus Magnus, Roger Bacon, Aquinas, Duns Scotus and others, make it very clear that scientific teaching was the main occupation of the university faculties, while the preservation of these huge tomes by the diligent copying of disciples shows how deeply interested were their pupils in the science of the time.

IX. MEDICAL TEACHING AND PROFESSIONAL STANDARDS.

At all times in the history of education, the standards of scientific education, and the institutions of learning, can be best judged from the condition of the medical schools. When the medical sciences are taken seriously, when thorough preparation is demanded before their study may be taken up, when four or five years of attention to theoretic and practical medicine are required for graduation, and when the professors are writing textbooks that are to attract attention for generations afterwards, then, there is always a thoroughly scientific temper in the university itself. Medicine is likely to suffer, first, whenever there is neglect of science. The studies of the German historians, Puschmann, Pagel, Neuberger, and Sudhoff in recent years, have made it very clear that the medical schools of the universities of the Thirteenth Century were maintaining high standards. The republication of old texts, especially in France, has called attention to the magnificent publications of their professors, while a review of their laws and regulations confirms the idea of the good work that was being done. Gurlt, in his history of surgery, "Geschichte der Chirurgie" (Berlin, 1898), has reviewed the textbooks of Roger and Roland and the Four Masters, of William of Salicet and Lanfranc and of many others, in a way to make it very clear that these men were excellent teachers.

When we discover that three years of preparatory university work was required before the study of medicine could be begun, and four years of medical studies were required, with a subsequent year of practice under a physician's direction, before a license for independent practice could be issued, then the scientific character of the medical schools and therefore of the universities to which they were attached is placed beyond all doubt. These are the terms of the law issued by the Emperor Frederick II. for the Two Sicilies. That, in substance, it applied to other countries we learn from the fact that the charters of medical schools granted by the Popes at this time require proper university preliminary studies, and four or five years at medicine before the degree of Doctor could be given. We know besides that in the cities only those who were graduates of properly recognized medical schools were allowed to practice medicine, so that there was every encouragement for the maintenance of professional standards. Indeed, strange as it may seem to our generation, the standards of the Thirteenth Century in medical education were much higher than our own, and their medical schools were doing fine work.

X. MAGNETISM.

For proper understanding of the Thirteenth Century scholars, it is especially important to appreciate their thoroughly scientific temper of mind, their powers of observation, and their successful attainments in science. I know no more compendious way of reaching the knowledge of these qualities in the medieval mind, than a study of the letter of Peregrinus, which we would in our time call a monograph on magnetism. Brother Potamian, in his chapter in "Makers of Electricity" (Fordham University Press, N. Y., 1909) on Peregrinus and Columbus, sums up the very interesting contributions of this medieval student of magnetism to the subject. The list of chapters alone in Peregrinus' monograph (Epistola) makes it very clear how deep were his interests and how thoroughly practical his investigations.

THE DOUBLE PIVOTED NEEDLE OF PEREGRINUS.

They are:—" Part I., Chapter 1, purpose of this work; 2, qualifications of the experimenter; 3, characteristics of a good lodestone; 4, how to distinguish the poles of a lodestone; 5, how to tell which pole is north and which is south; 6, how one lodestone attracts another; 7, how iron touched by a lodestone turns toward the poles of the world; 8, how a lodestone attracts iron; 9, why the north pole of one lodestone attracts the south pole of another, and vice versa; 10, an inquiry into the natural virtue of the lodestone.

"Part II., Chapter 1, construction of an instrument for measuring the azimuth of the sun, the moon or any star then in the horizon; 2, construction of a better instrument for the same purpose; 3, the art of making a wheel of perpetual motion."

In order to illustrate what Peregrinus accomplished it has seemed worth while to reproduce here the sketches which illustrate his epistle. We have the double pivoted needle and the first pivoted compass.

In the light of certain recent events a passage from the "New Naval History or Complete Review of the British Marine" (London, 1757) is of special interest. It illustrates perhaps the new confidence that came to men in sailing to long distances as the result of the realization of the practical value of the magnetic needle during the Thirteenth Century.

"In the year 1360 it is recorded that a friar of Oxford called Nicholas de Linna (of Lynn), being a good astronomer, went in company with others to the most northern island, and thence traveled alone,

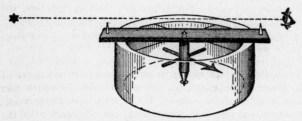

FIRST PIVOTED COMPASS (PEREGRINUS, 1269).

and that he went to the North Pole, by means of his skill in magic, or the black art; but this magic or black art may probably have been nothing more than a knowledge of the magnetic needle or compass, found out about sixty years before, though not in common use until many years after."

XI. BIOLOGICAL THEORIES, EVOLUTION, RECAPITULATION.

Of course only those who are quite unfamiliar with the history of philosophic thought are apt to think that the theory of evolution is modern. Serious students of biology are familiar with the long history of the theory, and especially its anticipations by the Greeks. Very few know, however, that certain phases of evolutionary theory attracted not a little attention from the scholastic philosophers. It would not be difficult to find expressions in Roger Bacon and Albertus Magnus, that would serve to show that they thought not only of the possibility of some very intimate relation of species but of developmental connections. The great teacher of the time, St. Thomas Aquinas, has some striking expressions in the matter, which deserve to be quoted, because he is the most important representative of the philosophy and science of the century and the one whose works most influenced succeeding generations. In the lecture on Medieval Scientific Universities, published in "Education, How Old the New" (Fordham University Press, N. Y., 1910), I called particular attention to this phase of St. Thomas' teaching. Two quotations will serve to make it clear here.

Prof. Osborne, in "From the Greeks to Darwin," quotes Aquinas' commentary on St. Augustine's opinion with regard to the origin of things as they are. Augustine declared that the Creator had simply brought into life the seeds of things, and given these the power to develop. Aquinas, expounding Augustine, says:

" As to production of plants, Augustine holds a different view, . . . for some say that on the third day plants were actually produced, each in his kind—a view favored by the superficial reading of Scripture. But Augustine says that the earth is then said to have brought forth grass and trees *causaliter;* that is, it then received power to produce them." (Quoting Genesis ii: 4) : " For in those first days, . . . God made creation primarily or *causaliter,* and then rested from His work."

Like expressions might be quoted from him, and other writers of the Thirteenth Century might well be cited in confirmation of the fact that while these great teachers of the Middle Ages thoroughly recognize the necessity for creation to begin with and the placing by the Creator of some power in living things that enables them to develop, they were by no means bound to the thought that all living species were due to special creations. They even did not hesitate to teach the possibility of the lower order of living beings at least coming into existence by spontaneous generation, and would probably have found no difficulty in accepting a theory of descent with the limitations that most scientific men of our generation are prone to demand for it.

Lest it should be thought that this is a mere accidental agreement with modern thought, due much more to a certain looseness of terms than to actual similarity of view, it seems well to point out how close St. Thomas came to that thought in modern biology, which is probably considered to be one of our distinct modern contributions to the theory of evolution, though, in recent years, serious doubts have been thrown on it. It is expressed by the formula of Herbert Spencer, " Ontogeny recapitulates phylogeny." According to this, the completed being repeats in the course of its development the history of the race, that is to say, the varying phases of fœtal development from the single cell in which it originates up to the perfect being of the special type as it is born into the world, retrace the history by which from the single cell being the creature in question has gradually developed.

It is very curious to find that St. Thomas Aquinas, in his teaching with regard to the origin and development of the human being, says, almost exactly, what the most ardent supporters of this so-called fundamental biogenetic law proclaimed during the latter half of the Nineteenth Century, thinking they were expressing an absolutely new thought. He says that " the higher a form is in the scale of being and the farther it is removed from mere material form, the more intermediate forms must be passed through before the finally perfect form is reached. Therefore, in the generation of animal and man— these having the most perfect forms—there occur many intermediate forms in generations, and consequently destruction, because the generation of one being is the destruction of another." St. Thomas draws the ultimate conclusions from this doctrine without hesitation. He proclaims that the human material is first animated by a vegetative soul or principle of life, and then by an animal soul, and only ultimately when the matter has been properly prepared for it by a rational soul. He said: "The vegetative soul, therefore, which is first in embryo, while it lives the life of a plant, is destroyed, and there succeeds a more perfect soul, which is at once nutrient and sentient, and for that time the embryo lives the life of an animal: upon the destruction of this there succeeds the rational soul, infused from without."

XII. THE POPE OF THE CENTURY.

The absence of a chapter on the Pope of the Century has always seemed a lacuna in the previous editions of this book. Pope Innocent III., whose pontificate began just before the century opened, and occupied the first fifteen years of it, well deserves a place beside Francis the Saint, Thomas the Scholar, Dante the Poet, and Louis the Monarch of this great century. More than any other single individual he was responsible for the great development of the intellectual life that took place, but at the same time his wonderfully broad influence enabled him to initiate many of the movements that meant most for human uplift and for the alleviation of suffering in this period. It was in Councils of the Church summoned by him that the important legislation was passed requiring the development of schools, the foundation of colleges in every diocese and of universities in important metropolitan sees. What he accomplished for hospitals has been well told by Virchow, from whom I quote a magnanimous tribute in the chapter on the Foundation of City Hospitals. The legislation of Innocent III. did much to encourage, and yet to regulate properly the religious orders of this time engaged in charitable work. Besides doing so much for charity, he was a stern upholder of morals. As more than one king of the time realized while Innocent was Pope, there could be no trifling with marriage vows.

On the other hand, while Innocent was so stern as to the enforcement of marriage laws, his wonderfully judicious character and his care for the weak and the innocent can be particularly noted in his treatment of the children in these cases. While he compelled recalcitrant kings to take back the wives they would repudiate, and put away other women who had won their affections, he did not hesitate to make due provision as far as possible for the illegitimate children. Pirie Gordon, in his recent life of Pope Innocent III., notes that he invariably legitimated the offspring of these illegal unions of kings, and even declared them capable of succession. He would not visit the guilt of the parent on the innocent offspring.

Innocent did more to encourage the idea of international arbitration than anyone up to his time. During his period more than once he was the arbitrator to whom rival national claims that might have led to war were referred. Probably his greatest claim on our admiration in the modern time is his attitude toward the Jews. In this he is centuries ahead of his time and, indeed, the policy that he laid down is far ahead of what is accorded to them by many of the nations even at the present time, and it must not be forgotten that it is only during the past hundred years that the Jew has come to have any real privileges comparable to those accorded to other men. At a time when the Jew had no real rights in law, Innocent insisted on according them all the rights of men. His famous edict in this regard is well known. "Let no Christian by violence compel them to come dissenting or unwilling to Baptism. Further let no Christian venture maliciously to harm their persons without a judgment of the civil power, to carry off their property or change their good customs which they have had hitherto in that district which they inhabit." When, in addition to all this, it is recalled that he was a distinguished scholar and graduate of the University of Paris, looked up to as one of the intellectual geniuses of the time, the author of a treatise " On the Contempt of the World " at a time when the kings of the earth were obeying him, known for his personal piety and for his thorough regulation of his own household, something of the greatness of the man will be appreciated. No wonder that historians who have taken up the special study of his career have always been won over to deep personal admiration of him, and though many of them began prejudiced in his regard, practically all of them were converted to be his sincere admirers.

XIII. INTERNATIONAL ARBITRATION.

During the Peace Conference in New York in 1908 I was on the programme with Mr. William T. Stead of London, the editor of the English *Review of Reviews,* who was very much interested in the volume on the Thirteenth Century, and who suggested that one chapter in the book should have been devoted to the consideration of what was accomplished for peace and for International Arbitration during this century. There is no doubt that there developed, as the result of many Papal decrees, a greater tendency than has existed ever before or since, to refer quarrels between nations that would ordinarily end in war to decision by some selected umpire. Usually the Pope, as the head of the Christian Church, to which all the nations of the civilized world belonged, was selected as the arbitrator. This international arbitration, strengthened by the decrees of Pope Innocent III., Pope Honorius III. and Pope Alexander III., developed in a way that is well worth while studying, and that has deservedly been the subject of careful investigation since the present peace movement began. Certainly the outlook for the securing of peace by international arbitration was better at this time than it has been at any time since. What a striking example, for instance, is the choice of King Louis of France as the umpire in the dispute between the Barons and the King of England, which might have led to war. Louis' position with regard to the Empire and the Papacy was to a great extent that of a pacificator, and his influence for peace was felt everywhere throughout Europe. The spirit of the century was all for arbitration and the adjudication of intranational as well as international difficulties by peaceful means.

XIV. BIBLE REVISION.

Most people will be quite sure that at least the question of Bible revision with critical study of text and comparative investigation of sources was reserved for our time. The two orders of friars founded in the early part of the Thirteenth Century, however, devoted themselves to the task of supplying to the people a thoroughly reliable edition of the Scriptures. The first systematic revision was made by the Dominicans about 1236. After twenty years this revision was set aside as containing too many errors, and another Dominican correction replaced it. Then came that great scholar, Hugh of St. Cher, known later as the Cardinal of Santa Sabina, the author of the first great Biblical Concordance. His Bible studies did much to clarify obscurities in the text. Sometime about 1240 he organized a commission of friars for the revision of what was known as the Paris Exemplar, the Bible text that was most in favor at that time. The aim of Hugh of St. Cher was to establish the old Vulgate of St. Jerome, the text which received this name during this century, but with such revision as would make this version correspond as nearly as possible to the Hebrew and the Greek.

This activity on the part of the Dominicans was rivaled by the Franciscans. We might not expect to find the great scientist, Roger Bacon, as a Biblical scholar and reviser, but such he was, working with Willermus de Mara, to whom, according to Father Denifle, late the Librarian of the Vatican Library, must be attributed the title given him by Roger Bacon of Sapientissimus Vir. The Dominicans under the leadership of Hugh of St. Cher with high ideals had hoped to achieve a perfect primitive text. The version made by de Mara, however, with the approval and advice of Bacon, was only meant to bring out St. Jerome's text as perfectly as possible. These two revisions made in the Thirteenth Century are typical of all the efforts that men have made since in that same direction. Contrary to usual present day impressions, they are characterized by critical scholarship, and probably represent as great a contribution to Biblical lore as was made by any other century.

XV. FICTION OF THE CENTURY.

Ordinarily it would be presumed that life was taken entirely too seriously during the Thirteenth Century for the generation to pay much attention to fiction. In a certain sense this is true. In the sense, however, that they had no stories worthy of the great literature in other departments it would be quite untrue. There is a naïveté about their story telling that rather amuses our sophisticated age, yet all the elements of our modern fiction are to be found in the stories that were popular during the century, and arranged with a dramatic effect that must have given them a wide appeal.

The most important contribution to the fiction of the century is to be found in the collection known as the *Cento Novelle Antiche* or " Hundred Ancient Tales," which contains the earliest prose fiction extant in Italian. Many of these come from a period anterior to Dante, and it is probable from what Manni, the learned editor of the *Novelliero,* says, that they were written out in the Thirteenth Century and collected in the early part of the Fourteenth Century. They did not all originate in Italy, and, indeed, Manni considers that most of them derived their origin from Provence. They represent the interest of the century in fiction and in anecdotal literature.

As for the longer fiction, the pure love story of the modern time, we have one typical example of it in that curious relic of the Middle Ages, " Aucassin and Nocolette." The manuscript which preserved this for us comes from the Thirteenth Century. Perhaps, as M. Paris suggests, the tale itself is from the preceding century. At least it was the interest of the Thirteenth Century in it that saved it for us. For those who think that the love romance in any of its features is novel, though we call it by that name, or that there has been any development of human nature which enables the writer of love stories to appeal to other and deeper, or purer and loftier feelings in his loved ones now than in the past, all that is needed, as it seems to me, is a casual reading of this pretty old song-story.

Perhaps the most interesting feature of this oldest specimen of modern fiction is the number of precious bits of psychologic analysis or, at least, what is called that in the recent time, which occur in the course of it. For instance, when Aucassin is grieving because he cannot find Nicolette he wanders through the forest on horseback, and is torn by trees and brambles, but " he feels it not at all." On the other hand, when he finds Nicolette, though he is suffering from a dislocated shoulder, he no longer feels any pain in it, because of his joy at the meeting, and Nicolette (first aid to the injured) is able to replace the dislocated part without difficulty (the trained nurse in fiction) because he is so happy as not to notice the pain (psychotherapy). The herdsman whom he meets wonders that Aucassin, with plenty of money and victuals, should grieve so much over the loss of Nicolette, while he has so much more cause to grieve over the loss of an ox, which means starvation to him. Toward the end of the story we have the scene in which Nicolette, stolen from home when very young, and utterly unable to remember anything about her childhood, has brought back to her memory by the view of the city of Carthage forgotten events of her childhood (subconscious memory). These represent naïvely enough, it is true, the study of the mind under varying conditions that has in recent years been given the rather ambitious name of psychology in fiction.

XVI. GREAT ORATORS.

Without a chapter on the great orators of the period an account of the Thirteenth Century is quite incomplete. Great as were the other forms of literature, epic, lyric and religious poetry and the prose writing, it is probable that the oratory of the time surpassed them all. When we recall that the Cid, the Arthur Legends, the Nibelungen, the Meistersingers, and the Minnesingers, Reynard the Fox, the Romance of the Rose, the Troubadours, and even Dante are included in the other term of the comparison thus made, it may seem extravagant, but what we know of the effect of the orators of the time fully justifies it. Just before the Thirteenth Century, great religious orators swayed the hearts and minds of people, to the organization of the Crusades. At the beginning of the Thirteenth Century the mendicant orders were organized, and their important duties were preaching and teaching. The Dominicans were of course the Order of Preachers, and we have traditions of their sway over the minds of the people of the time which make it very clear that their power was equal to that exerted in any other department of human expression. There are traditions particularly of the oratory of the Dominicans among the German races, which serve to show how even a phlegmatic people can be stirred to the very depths of their being by the eloquent spoken word. In France the traditions are almost as explicit in this matter, and there are remains of religious orations that fully confirm the reputation of the orators of the time.

Rhetoric and oratory was studied very assiduously. Cicero was the favorite reading of the great preachers of the time, and we find the court preachers of St. Louis, Étienne de Bourbon, Elinand, Guillaume de Perrault and others appealing to his precepts as the infallible guide to oratory. Quintilian was not neglected, however, and Symmachus and Sidonius Apollinaris were also faithfully studied. If we turn to the speeches that are incorporated in the epics, as, for instance, the Cid, or in some of the historians, as Villehardouin, we have definite evidence of the thorough command of the writers of the time over the forms of oratory. M. Paullin Paris, the authority in our time on the literature of the Thirteenth Century, quotes a passage from Villehardouin in which Canon de Bethune speaks in the name of the French chiefs of the Fourth Crusade to the Emperors Isaac and Alexis Comnenus. M. Paris does not hesitate to declare that the passage is equal to many of the same kind that have been much admired in the classic authors. It has the force, the finish and the compression of Thucydides.

XVII. GREAT BEGINNINGS IN ENGLISH LITERATURE.

Only the fact that this work was getting beyond the number of printed pages determined for it in the first edition prevented the insertion of a chapter especially devoted to the great beginnings of English literature in the Thirteenth Century. The most important contributions to Early English were made at this period. The Ormulum and Layamon's Brut, both written probably during the first decade of the Thirteenth Century, have become familiar to all students of Old English. Mr. Gollancz goes so far as to say that "The Ormulum is perhaps the most valuable document we possess for the history of English sound. Orm was a purist in o thography as well as in vocabulary, and may fittingly be described as the first of English phoneticians."

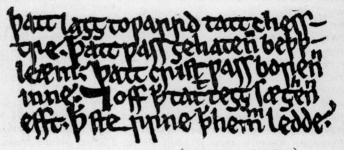

MANUSCRIPT OF ORMULUM (THIRTEENTH CENTURY)

Of Layamon, Garnett said in his "English Literature" (Garnett and Gosse): "It would have sufficed for the fame of Layamon had he been no more than the first minstrel to celebrate Arthur in English song, but his own pretensions as a poet are by no means inconsiderate. He is everywhere vigorous and graphic, and improved upon his predecessor, Wace, alike by his additions and expansions, and by his more spiritual handling of the subjects common to both." Even more important in the history of language than these is *The Ancren Riwle* (The Anchorites' Rule). This was probably written by Richard Poore, Bishop of Salisbury, for three Cistercian nuns. Its place in English literature may be judged from a quotation or two with regard to it. Mr. Kington-Oliphant says: "*The Ancren Riwle* is the forerunner of a wondrous change in our speech. More than anything else written outside the Danelagh, that piece has influenced our standard

English." Garnett says: "*The Ancren Riwle* is a work of great literary merit and, in spite of its linguistic innovations, most of which have established themselves, well deserves to be described as 'one of the most perfect models of simple eloquent prose in our language.'"

The religious poetry of the time is not behind the great prose of *The Ancren Riwle,* and one of them, the *Luve Ron* (Love Song) of Thomas de Hales, is very akin to the spirit of that work, and has been well described as "a contemplative lyric of the simplest, noblest mold." Garnett says: "The reflections are such as are common to all who have in all ages pleaded for the higher life under whatsoever form, and deplored the frailty and transitoriness of man's earthly estate. Two stanzas on the latter theme as expressed in a modernized version might almost pass for Villon's:—

"Paris and Helen, where are they,
    Fairest in beauty, bright to
        view?
Amadas, Tristrem, Ideine, yea
    Isold, that lived with love so
        true?
And Cæsar, rich in power and
        sway,
    Hector the strong, with might
        to do?
All glided from earth's realm
        away,
    Like shaft that from the bow-
        string flew.

"It is as if they ne'er were here,
    Their wondrous woes have
        been a' told,
That it is sorrow but to hear:
    How anguish killed them
        sevenfold,
And how with dole their lives
        were drear;
    Now is their heat all turned to
        cold.
Thus this world gives false hope,
        false fear;
    A fool, who in her strength is
        bold."

XVIII. GREAT ORIGINS IN MUSIC.

In the chapter on the Great Latin Hymns a few words were said about one phase of the important musical development in the Thirteenth Century, that of plain chant. In that simple mode the musicians of the Thirteenth Century succeeded in reaching a climax of expression of human feeling in such chants as the *Exultet* and the *Lamentation* that has never been surpassed. Something was also said about the origin of part music, but so little that it might easily be thought that in this the century lagged far behind its achievements in other departments. M. Pierre Aubry has recently published (1909) *Cent Motets du XIIIe Siècle* in three volumes. His first volume contains a photographic reproduction of the manuscript of Bamberg from which the hundred musical modes are secured, the second a transcription in modern musical notation of the old music, and the third volume studies and commentaries on the music and the times. If anything were needed to show how utterly ignorant we have been of the interests and artistic achievements of the Middle Ages, it is this book of M. Aubry.

Victor Hugo said that music dates from the Sixteenth Century, and it has been quite the custom, even for people who thought they knew something about music, to declare that we had no remains of any music before the Sixteenth Century worth while talking about. Ancient music is probably lost to us forever, but M. Aubry has shown conclusively that we have abundant remains to show us that the musicians of the Thirteenth Century devoted themselves to their art with as great success as their rivals in the other Gothic arts and, indeed, they thought that they had nearly exhausted its possibilities and tried to make a science of it. By their supposedly scientific rules they succeeded in binding music so firmly as to bring about its obscuration in succeeding centuries. This is, however, the old story of what has happened in every art whenever genius succeeds in finding a great mode of expression. A formula is evolved which often binds expression so rigorously as to prevent natural development.

XIX. A CHAPTER ON MANNERS.

Whatever the people of the Middle Ages may have been in morals, their manners are supposed to have been about as lacking in refinement as possible. As for nearly everything else, however, this impression is utterly false, and is due to the assumption that because we are better-mannered than the generations of a century or two ago, therefore we must be almost infinitely in advance, in the same respect, of the people of seven centuries ago. There are ups and downs in manners, however, as there are in education, and the beginnings of the formal setting forth of modern manners are, like everything else modern, to be found in the Thirteenth Century. About the year 1215 Thomasin Zerklaere wrote in German a rather lengthy treatise, *Der Wälsche Gast,* on manners. It contains most of the details of polite conduct that have been accepted in later times. Not long afterwards, John Garland, an Oxford man who had lived in France for many years, wrote a book on manners for English young men. He meant this to be a supplement to Dionysius Cato's treatise, written probably in the Fourth Century in Latin, which was concerned more with morals than manners and had been very popular during the Middle Ages. Garland's book was the first of a series of such treatises on manners which appeared in England at the close of the Middle Ages. Many of them have been recently republished, and are a revelation of the development of manners among our English forefathers. The book is usually alluded to in literature as Liber Faceti, or as Facet; the full title was, "The Book of the Polite Man, Teaching Manners for Men, Especially for Boys, as a Supplement to those which were Omitted by the Most Moral Cato." The "Romance of the Rose" has, of course, many references to manners which show us how courtesy was cultivated in France. In Italy, Dante's teacher, Bruneto Latini, published his "Tesoretto," which treats of manners, and which was soon followed by a number of similar treatises in

Italian. In a word, we must look to the Thirteenth Century for the origin, or at least the definite acceptance, of most of those conventions which make for kindly courtesy among men, and have made possible human society and friendly intercourse in our modern sense of those words.

We are prone to think that refinement in table manners is a matter of distinctly modern times. In "The Babees' Book," which is one of the oldest books of English manners, the date of which in its present form is about the middle of the Fourteenth Century, many of our rules of politeness at table are anticipated. This book is usually looked upon as a compilation from preceding times, and the original of it is supposed to be from the preceding century. A few quotations from it will show how closely it resembles our own instructions to children:

"Thou shalt not laugh nor speak nothing
While thy mouth be full of meat or drink;
Nor sup thou not with great sounding
Neither pottage nor other thing.
At meat cleanse not thy teeth, nor pick
With knife or straw or wand or stick.
While thou holdest meat in mouth, beware
To drink; that is an unhonest chare;
And also physic forbids it quite.
Also eschew, without strife,
To foul the board cloth with thy knife.
Nor blow not on thy drink or meat,
Neither for cold, neither for heat.
Nor bear with meat thy knife to mouth,
Whether thou be set by strong or couth.
Lean not on elbow at thy meat,
Neither for cold nor for heat.
Dip not thy thumb thy drink into;
Thou art uncourteous if thou it do.
In salt-cellar if thou put
Or fish or flesh that men see it,
That is a vice, as men me tells;
And great wonder it would be else."

The directions, "how to behave thyself in talking with any man," in one of these old books, are very minute and specific:—

"If a man demand a question of thee,
In thine answer making be not too hasty;
Weigh well his words, the case understand
Ere an answer to make thou take in hand;
Else may he judge in thee little wit,
To answer to a thing and not hear it.
Suffer his tale whole out to be told,
Then speak thou mayst, and not be controlled;
In audible voice thy words do thou utter,
Not high nor low, but using a measure.
Thy words see that thou pronounce plaine,
And that they spoken be not in vain;
In uttering whereon keep thou an order,
Thy matter thereby thou shalt much forder
Which order if thou do not observe,
From the purpose needs must thou swerve."

XX. TEXTILE WORK OF THE CENTURY.

A special chapter might easily have been written on the making of fine cloths of various kinds, most of which reached their highest perfection in the Thirteenth Century. Velvet, for instance, is mentioned for the first time in England in 1295, but existed earlier on the continent, and cut velvets with elaborate patterns were made in Genoa exactly as we know finished velvet now. Baudekin or Baldichin, a very costly textile of gold and silk largely used in altar coverings and hangings, came to very high perfection in this century also. The canopy for the Blessed Sacrament is, because of its manufacture from this cloth, still called in Italy a *baldichino.* Chaucer in the next century tells how the streets in royal processions were "hanged with cloth of gold and not with serge." Satin also was first manufactured very probably in the Thirteenth Century. It is first mentioned in England about the middle of the Fourteenth Century, when Bishop Grandison made a gift of choice satins to Exeter Cathedral. The word satin, however, is derived from the silks of the Mediterranean, called by the Italians *seta* and by the Spanish *seda,* and the art of making it was brought to perfection during the preceding century.

The art of making textiles ornamented with elaborate designs of animal forms and of floral ornaments reached its highest perfection in the Thirteenth Century. In one of the Chronicles we learn that in 1295 St. Paul's in London owned a hanging "patterned with wheels and two-headed birds." We have accounts of such elaborate textile ornamentation as peacocks, lions, griffins and the like. Almeria in Andalusia was a rich city in the Thirteenth Century, noted for its manufactures of textiles. A historian of the period writes: "Christians of all nations came to its port to buy and sell. Then they traveled to other parts of the interior of the country, where they loaded their vessels with such goods as they wanted. Costly silken robes of the brightest colors are manufactured in Almeria." Marco-Polo says of the Persians that, when he passed through that country (end of the Thirteenth Century), "there are excellent artificers in the city who make wonderful things in gold, silk and embroidery. The women make excellent needlework in silk with all sorts of creatures very admirably wrought therein." He also reports the King of Tartary as wearing on his birthday a most precious garment of gold, and tells of the girdles of gold and silver, with pearls and ornaments of great price on them.

Unfortunately English embroidery fell off very greatly at the time of the Wars of the Roses. These wars constitute the main reason why nearly every form of intellectual accomplishment and artistic achievement went into decadence during the Fourteenth Century, from which they were only just emerging when the so-called reformation, with its confiscation of monastic property, and its destruction of monastic life, came to ruin schools of all kinds, and, above all, those in which the arts and crafts had been taught so successfully. France at the end of the Thirteenth Century saw a similar rise to excellence of textile and embroidery work. In 1299 there is an allusion to one Clément le Brodeur who furnished a magnificent cope for the Count of Artois. In 1316 a beautifully decorated set of hangings was made for the Queen by Gautier de Poulleigny. There are other references to work done in the early part of the Fourteenth Century, which serve to show the height which art had reached in this mode during the Thirteenth Century. In Ireland, while the finer work had its due place, the making of woolens was the specialty, and the dyeing of woolen cloth made the Irish famous and brought many travelers from the continent to learn the secret.

The work done in England in embroidery attracted the attention of the world. English needlework became a proverb. In the body of the book I mentioned the cope of Ascoli, but there were many such beautiful garments. The Syon cope is, in the opinion of Miss Addison, author of "Arts and Crafts in the Middle Ages," the most conspicuous example of the medieval embroiderers' art. It was made by nuns about the middle of the Thirteenth Century, that is, just about the same time as the cope of Ascoli, but in a convent near Coventry. According to Miss Addison "it is solid stitchery on a canvas ground, 'wrought about with divers colors' on green. The design is laid out in a series of interlacing square forms, with rounded and barbed sides and corners. In each of these is a figure or a Scriptural scene. The orphreys, or straight borders, which go down on both fronts of the cope, are decorated with heraldic charges. Much of the embroidery is raised, and wrought in the stitch known as Opus Anglicanum. The effect was produced by pressing a heated metal knob into the work at such points as were to be raised. The real embroidery was executed on a flat surface, and then bossed up by this means until it looked like bas-relief. The stitches in every part run in zig-zags, the vestments, and even the nimbi about the heads, are all executed with the stitches slanting in one direction, from the center of the cope outward, without consideration of the positions of the figures. Each face is worked in circular progression outward from the center, as well. The interlaces are of crimson, and look well on the green ground. The wheeled cherubim is well developed in the design of this famous cope, and is a pleasing decorative bit of archaic ecclesiasticism. In the central design of the Crucifixion, the figure of the Lord is rendered in silver on a gold ground."

XXI. GLASS-MAKING.

A chapter might well have been devoted to Thirteenth Century glass-making quite apart from the stained glass of the cathedral windows. All over Europe some of the most wonderful specimens of colored glass we possess were made in the Thirteenth Century. Recently Mr. Frederick Rolfe has looked up for me Venetian glass, of the three centuries, the Twelfth, the Thirteenth and the Fourteenth. He says Twelfth Century glass is small in form, simple and ignorant in model, excessively rich and brilliant in colors; the artist evidently had no ideal, but the Byzantine of jewels and emeralds.

" Thirteenth Century glass is absolutely different. The specimens are pretty. The work of the Beroviero family is large and splendid in form, exquisite and sometimes elaborate in model, mostly crystal glass reticently studded with tiny colored gem-like knobs. There are also fragments of two windows pieced together, and missing parts filled with the best which modern Murano can do. These show the celebrated Beroviero Ruby glass (secret lost) of marvelous depth and brilliancy in comparison with which the modern work is merely watery. The ancient is just like a decanter of port-wine.
" Fourteenth Century returns to the wriggling ideal and exiguous form of the Twelfth Century, and fails woefully in brilliance of color. It is small and dull and undistinguished. One may find out what war or pest afflicted Murano at this epoch to explain the singular degradation."

This same curious degradation took place in the manufacture of most art objects during the Fourteenth Century. One would feel in Mr. Rolfe's words like looking for some physical cause for it. The decadence is so universal, however, that it seems not unlikely that it follows some little known human law, according to which, after man has reached a certain perfection of expression in an art or craft, there comes, in the striving after originality yet variety, an overbalancing of the judgment, a vitiation of the taste in the very luxuriance of beauty discovered that leads to decay. It is the very contradiction of the supposed progress of mankind through evolution, but it is illustrated in many phases of human history and, above all, the history of art, letters, education and the arts and crafts.

XXII. INVENTIONS.

Most people are sure to think that, at least in the matter of inventions, ours is the only time worth considering. The people of the Thirteenth Century, however, made many wonderful inventions and adaptations of mechanical principles, as well as many ingenious appliances. Their faculty of invention was mainly devoted to work in other departments besides that of mechanics. They were inventors of designs in architecture, in decoration, in furnishings, in textiles, and in the beautiful things of life generally. Their inventiveness in the arts and crafts was especially admirable and, indeed, has been fruitful in our time, since, with the reawakening in this matter, we have gone back to imitate their designs. Good authorities declare these to be endless in number and variety. Such mechanical inventions as were needed for the building of their great cathedrals, their municipal buildings, abbeys, castles, piers, bridges and the like were admirably worked out. Necessity is the mother of invention, and whenever needs asserted themselves, these old generations responded to them, very successfully. There are, however, a number of inventions that would attract attention even in the modern time for their practical usefulness and ingenuity. With the growth of the universities writing became much more common, textbooks were needed, and so paper was invented. With the increase of reading, to replace teaching by hearing, spectacles were invented. Time became more precious, clocks were greatly improved, and we hear of the invention of something like an alarm clock, an apparatus which, after a fixed number of hours, woke the monk of the abbey whose duty it was to arouse the others. Organs for churches were greatly improved, bells were perfected, and everything else in connection with the churches so well fashioned that we still use them in their Thirteenth Century forms. Gunpowder was not invented, but a great many new uses were found for it, and Roger Bacon even suggested, as I have said, that sometime explosives would enable boats to move by sea without sails or oars, or carriages to move on land without horses or men. Roger Bacon even suggested the possibility of airships, described how one might be made, the wings of which would be worked by a windlass, and thought that he could make it. His friend and pupil, Peregrinus, invented the double pivoted compass, and, as the first perpetual-motion faddist, described how he would set about making a magnetic engine that he thought would run forever. When we recall how much they accomplished mechanically in the construction of buildings, it becomes evident that any mechanical problem that these generations wanted solved they succeeded in solving very well. What they have left us as inventions are among the most useful appliances that we have. Without paper and without spectacles, the intellectual world would be in a sad case, indeed. Many of the secrets of their inventions in the arts and crafts have been lost, and, in spite of all our study, we have not succeeded in rediscovering them.

XXIII. INDUSTRY AND TRADE.

We are rather inclined to think that large organizations of industry and trade were reserved for comparatively modern times. To think so, however, is to forget the place occupied by the monasteries and convents in the olden time. We have heard much of the lazy monks, but only from those who know nothing at all about them. Idleness in the monasteries was one of the accusations made by the commission set to furnish evidence to Henry VIII. on which he might suppress the monasteries, but every modern historian has rejected the findings of that commission as false. Many forms of manufacture were carried on in the monasteries and convents. They were the principal bookmakers and bookbinders. To a great extent they were the manufacturers of art fabrics and arts-and-crafts work intended for church use, but also for the decoration of luxurious private apartments. Most of us have known something of all this finer work, but not that they had much to do with cruder industries also. They were millers, cloth-makers, brush- and broom-makers, shoe-makers for themselves and their tenantry; knitting was done in the convents, and all the finer fancy work. A recent meeting of the Institute of Mining Engineers in England brought out some discussion of coal mining in connection with the early history of the coal mines in England. The records of many of the English monasteries show that in early times the monks knew the value of coal, and used it rather freely. They also mined it for others. The monks at Tynemouth are known to have been mining coal on the Manor of Tynemouth in 1269, and shipping it to a distance. At Durham and at Finchale Abbey they were doing this also about the same time. It would require special study to bring out the interesting details, but there is abundant material not alone for a chapter, but for a volume on the industries of the Thirteenth Century, which, like the education and the literature and the culture of the time, we have thought undeveloped, because we knew nothing of them.

The relation of the monasteries to trade, domestic and foreign, is very well brought out in a paragraph of Mr. Ralph Adams Cram's book on "The Ruined Abbeys of Great Britain" (New York, The Churchman Co., 1905), in which he describes the remains at Beaulieu, which show the place of that monastery, not by any means one of the most important in England, in trade. For the benefit of their tenantry others had done even more.

"Some idea of the power of one of these great monasteries may be gained from traces still existing of the center of trade built up by the monks outside their gates. Here, at the head of tide water, in a most out-of-the-way spot, a great stone quay was constructed, to which came ships from foreign lands. Near by was a great market-place, now, as then, called Cheapside, though commerce exists there no longer. At the height of monastic glory the religious houses were actually the chief centers of industry and civilization, and around them grew up the eager villages, many of which now exist, even though their impulse and original inspiration have long since departed. Of course, the possessions of the abbey reached far away from the walls in every direction, including many farms even at a great distance, for the abbeys were then the great landowners, and beneficent landlords they were as well, even in their last days, for we have many records of the cruelty and hardships that came to the tenants the moment the stolen lands came into the hands of lay-men."

XXIV. FAIRS AND MARKETS.

A chapter might well have been devoted to showing the significance of those curious old institutions, the fairs and market days of the

Middle Ages. The country folk flocked into town, bringing with them their produce, and found there gathered from many parts merchants come to exchange and barter. The expense of maintaining a store all the year around was done away with, and profits did not have to be large. Exchanges were direct, and the profits of the middlemen were to a great extent eliminated. It was distinctly to the advantage of the poor, for the expenses of commerce were limited to the greatest possible extent, and every advantage accrued to the customer.

Besides, these market days became days of innocent merriment, amusement and diversion. Wandering purveyors of amusement followed the fairs, and obtained their living from the generosity of the people who were amused. These amusements were conducted out of doors, and with very few of the objectionable features as regards hygiene and morality that are likely to attach themselves to the same things in our day. The amusement was what we would call now vaudeville, singing, dancing, the exhibition of trained animals, acrobatic feats of various kinds, so that we cannot very well say that our people are in advance of their medieval forbears in such matters, since their taste is about the same. Fairs and market days made country life less monotonous by their regular recurrence, and so prevented that emptying of the country into the city which we deprecate in our time. They had economic, social, even moral advantages, that are worth while studying.

XXV. INTENSIVE FARMING.

We hear much of intensive farming in the modern time, and it is supposed to be a distinctly modern invention mothered by the necessity due to great increase of population. One of the most striking features of the story of monasticism in the countries of Europe, however, during the Middle Ages, and especially during the Thirteenth Century, when so many of the greatest abbeys reached a climax of power and influence and beauty of construction, is their successful devotion paid to agriculture. In the modern time we are gradually learning the lesson of growing larger and larger crops on the same area of ground by proper selection of seed, and of developing cattle in such a way as to make them most valuable as a by-product of farming. This is exactly what the old monastic establishments did. At the beginning of the Thirteenth Century many of them were situated in rather barren regions, sometimes, indeed, surrounded by thick forests, but at the end of the century all the great monastic establishments had succeeded in making beautiful luxuriant gardens for themselves, and had taught their numerous tenantry the great lessons of agricultural improvement which made for plenty and happiness.

Many monasteries belonged to the same religious order, and the traditions of these were carried from one to the other by visiting monks or sometimes by the transfer of members of one community to another. The monastic establishments were the great farmers of Europe, and it was their proud boast that their farming lands, instead of being exhausted from year to year, were rather increasing in value. They doubtless had many secrets of farming that were lost and had to be rediscovered in the modern time, just as in the arts and crafts, for their success in farming was as noteworthy. Their knowledge of trees must have been excellent, since they surrounded themselves with fine forests, at times arranged so as to provide shady walks and charming avenues. Their knowledge of simple farming must have been thorough, for the farms of the monasteries were always the most prosperous, and the tenantry were always the happiest. With the traditions that we have especially in English history, this seems almost impossible to credit, but these traditions, manufactured for a purpose, have now been entirely discredited. We have learned in recent years what wonderful scholars, architects, painters, teachers, engineers these monks were, and so it is not surprising to find that they had magnificently developed agricultural knowledge as well as that of every other department in which they were particularly interested.

XXVI. CARTOGRAPHY AND THE TEACHING OF GEOGRAPHY.

In the chapter on Great Explorers and The Foundation of Geography, in the body of the book, much might have been said about maps and map-making, for the Thirteenth Century was a great period in this matter. Lecoy de la Marche among his studies of the Thirteenth Century has included a volume of a collection of the maps of the Thirteenth Century. If the purpose had been to make this a work of erudition rather than of popular information, much might have been said of the cartography of the time even from this work alone (*Receuil de Chartes du XIIIe Siècle,* Paris, 1878). One of the great maps of the Thirteenth Century, that on the Cathedral wall of Hereford, deserves a place here. It was made just at the end of the Thirteenth Century. The idea of its maker was to convey as much information as possible about the earth, and not merely indicate its political divisions and the relative size and position of the different parts. It is to a certain extent at least a résumé of history, of physical geography, and even of geographical biology and anthropology, for it has indications as to the dwelling-place of animals and curious types of men. It contains, besides, references to interesting objects of other kinds. Because of its interest I have reproduced the map itself, and the key to it with explanations published at Hereford.

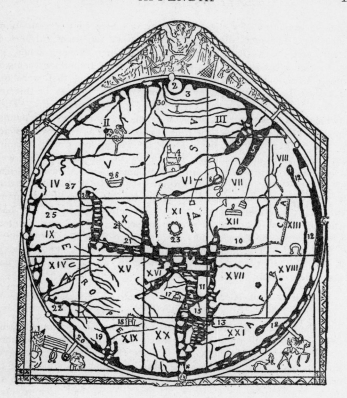

Key to the Photograph of the Ancient Map of the World,

PRESERVED IN HEREFORD CATHEDRAL.

The Map is executed on a single sheet of vellum, 54 in. in breadth, by 63 in. in extreme height. It is fixed on a strong framework of oak. At the top (Fig. 1) is a representation of the Last Judgment. Our Saviour is represented in glory, and below is the Virgin Mary interceding for mankind.

For convenience of reference the Key Map is divided into squares marked by Roman capitals, with the more prominent objects in figures. I.—Commencing with sq. I. the circle marked by Fig. 2 represents the Garden of Eden, with the four rivers, and Adam and Eve eating the forbidden fruit. The remainder of the square, as also in II. and III., is occupied by India. At Fig. 3 is shown the expulsion of Adam and Eve, to the right of which is shown a race of Giants, and to the left the City of Enoch, and still further the Golden Mountains guarded by Dragons. Below these mountains are shown a race of pigmies. In a space bounded by two rivers is placed a crocodile, and immediately below a female warrior. To the left of the latter are a pair of birds called in the Map Alerions. The large river to the left is the Ganges. II.—Shows one of the inhabitants of this part of India, who are said to have but one foot, which is sufficiently large to serve as an umbrella to shelter themselves from the sun. The city in the center is Samarcand. III.—In which is seen an Elephant, to the left a Parrot. A part of the Red Sea is also shown with the Island of Taprobana (Ceylon), on which are shown two Dragons. It also bears an inscription denoting that dragons and elephants are found there. The small Islands shown are Crise, Argire, Ophir, and Frondisia (Aphrodisia). IV.—Contains the Caspian Sea, below which is a figure holding its tail in his hand, and which the author calls the Minotaur. To the left is shown one of the Albani, who are said to see better at night than in the daytime. Below are two warriors in combat with a Griffin (Fig. 27). V.—In the upper part are Bokhara and Thrace, in the latter of which (Fig. 29) is shown the Pelican feeding its young, to the left a singular figure representing the Cicones, and to the right the Camel, in Bactria. Below to the left is the Tiger, and on the right an animal with a human head and the body of a lion, called the Mantichora. Still lower is seen Noah's ark (Fig. 28), in which are shown three human figures, with beasts, birds and serpents. In the lower corner, at Fig. 26, is the Golden Fleece. VI.—The upper parts contain Babylonia, with the City of Babylon (Fig. 4) on the river Euphrates, below which is the city of Damascus, which has on its right an unknown animal called the Marsok. To the right is Lot's wife turned into a pillar of salt (Fig. 8). Decapolis and the River Jordan are near the bottom of the square. Above the River Euphrates is a figure in a frame representing the Patriarch Abraham's residence at Ur of the Chaldees. VII.—The Red Sea (Figs. 5, 5) is the most conspicuous object here. In the fork formed by it is shown the giving of the Tables of The Law on Mount Sinai. Below, and touching the line (Fig. 6) showing the wanderings of the Israelites, is seen the worship of the Golden Calf. The Dead Sea and submerged Cities are shown lower down to the left, and between this and the Red Sea is the Phoenix. At the bottom is a mythical animal with long horns, called the Eale. VIII.—In the upper part is the Monastery of St. Anthony in Ethiopia. The river to the left is the Nile, between this and a great interior lake (Figs. 7, 7) is a figure of Satyr. Beyond the lake, and extending a distance down the Map (Figs. 12, 12, 12), are various singular figures, supposed to represent the races dwelling there. In a circular island to the left (Meroe) is a man riding a crocodile, and at the bottom left-hand corner is a centaur. IX.—The upper part is Scythia, and shows some cannibals, below which (Fig. 25) are two Scythians in combat. Under this again is a man leading a horse with a human skin thrown over it, and to the right of the latter is placed the ostrich. X.—Asia Minor with the Black Sea (Fig. 24). Many cities are shown prominent, among which is Troy (Fig. 21), described as "*Troja civitas bellicosissima.*" Near the bottom to the left is Constantinople. The lynx is shown near the center. XI.—Is nearly filled by the Holy Land. In the center is Jerusalem (Fig. 23), the supposed center of the world, surrounded by a high wall, and above is the Crucifixion. Below Jerusalem to the right is Bethlehem with the manger. Near a circular place to the right, called "*Puteus Juramenti*" (well of the oath), is an unknown bird, called on the Map Avis Cirenus. XII.—Egypt with the Nile. At the upper part (Fig. 9) are Joseph's granaries, i.e., the Pyramids, immediately below which is the Salamander, and to the right of that the Mandrake. Fig. 10 denotes the Delta with its cities. On the other side of the Nile, and partly in sq.

MAP OF THE WORLD (HEREFORD CATHEDRAL)

XIII., is the Rhinoceros, and below it the Unicorn. XIII.—Ethiopia. In the upper left-hand corner is the Sphinx, and near the bottom the Temple of Jupiter Ammon, represented by a singular horse-shoe shaped figure. The camp of Alexander the Great is in the bottom left-hand corner, immediately above which is the boundary line between Asia and Africa. XIV.—At the top of the left is Norway, in which the author has placed the Monkey. The middle is filled by Russia. The small circular islands on the left are the Orkneys, immediately below which is an inscription relating to the Seven Sleepers. Scotland and part of England are shown in the lower part, but the British Isles will be described in sq. XIX. The singular triangular figure in the center of this square cannot be identified. XV.— Germany, with part of Greece, in the upper part to the right. The Danube and its tributaries are seen in the upper part, in the lower is the Rhine. On the bank of the latter the scorpion is placed; Venice is shown on the right. XVI.—Contains Italy and a great part of the Mediterranean Sea (Fig. 14). About the center (Fig. 17) is Rome, which bears the inscription, "Roma caput mundi tenet orbis frena rotundi." In the upper part of the Mediterranean Sea is seen a Mermaid, below (Fig. 11) is the Island of Crete, with its famous labyrinth, to the left of which is the rock Scylla. Below Crete is Sicily (Fig. 15), on which Mount Etna is shown; close to Sicily is the whirlpool Charybdis. XVII.—Part of Africa; in the lower part to the left, on a promontory, is seen Carthage; on the right the Leopard is shown. XVIII.—Also part of Africa. The upper part is Fezzan, below is shown the basilisk, and still lower some Troglodytes or dwellers in caves. XIX.—On the left hand are the British Isles (Figs. 19, 20, 22), on the right France. Great Britain (Figs. 19, 22) is very fully laid down, but of Ireland the author seemed to know but little. In England twenty-six cities and towns are delineated, among which Hereford (H'ford) is conspicuous. Twenty rivers are also seen, but the only mountains shown are the Clee Hills. In Wales, Snowdon is seen, and the towns of Carnarvon, Conway and St. David's. In Ireland four towns, Armagh, Bangor, Dublin and Kildare, with two rivers, the Banne, which, as shown, divides the island in two, and the Shannon. In Scotland there are six towns. In France the City of Paris (Fig. 18) is conspicuous. XX.—The upper part is Provence, the lower Spain. In the Mediterranean Sea are laid down, among others, the Islands of Corsica, Sardinia, Majorca, and Minorca. At the bottom are (Fig. 16) the pillars of Hercules (Gibraltar), which were considered the extreme western limits of the world. XXI.—At the top to the left (Fig. 13) is St. Augustine of Hippo, in his pontifical habit. And at the opposite corner the Lion, below which are the Agriophagi, a one-eyed people who live on the flesh of lions and other beasts. The kingdoms on the shore of the Mediterranean are Algiers, Setif, and Tangier.

APPENDIX III.

CRITICISMS, COMMENTS, DOCUMENTS.

HUMAN PROGRESS.

For most people the impossible would apparently be accomplished if a century so far back as the Thirteenth were to be even seriously thought of as the greatest of centuries. Evolution has come to be accepted so unquestioningly, that of course "we are the heirs of all the ages of the foremost files of time," and must be far ahead of our forbears, especially of the distant past, in everything. When a man talks glibly about great progress in recent times, he usually knows only the history of his own time and not very much about that. Men who have studied other periods seriously hesitate about the claim of progress, and the more anyone knows about any other period, the less does he think of his own as surpassing. There are many exemplifications of this in recent literature. Because this was a cardinal point in many criticisms of the book, it has seemed well to illustrate the position here taken as to the absence of progress in humanity by quotations from recognized authorities. Just as the first edition of this book came from the press, Ambassador Bryce delivered his address at Harvard on "What is Progress?" It appeared in the *Atlantic Monthly* for August, 1907. Mr. Bryce is evidently not at all persuaded that there is human progress in any real sense of the word. Some striking quotations may be made from the address, but to get the full impression of Mr. Bryce's reasons for hesitation about accepting any progress, the whole article needs to be read. For instance, he said:

"It does not seem possible, if we go back to the earliest literature which survives to us from Western Asia and Southeastern Europe, to say that the creative powers of the human mind in such subjects as poetry, philosophy, and historical narrative or portraiture, have either improved or deteriorated. The poetry of the early Hebrews and of the early Greeks has never been surpassed and hardly ever equaled. Neither has the philosophy of Plato and Aristotle, nor the speeches of Demosthenes and Cicero. Geniuses like Dante, Chaucer, and Shakespeare appear without our being able to account for them, and for aught we know another may appear at any moment. It is just as difficult, if we look back five centuries, to assert either progress or decline in painting. Sculpture has never again risen to so high a level as it touched in the fifth century, B. C., nor within the last three centuries, to so high a level as it reached at the end of the fifteenth. But we can found no generalizations upon that fact. Music is the most inscrutable of the arts, and whether there is any progress to be expected other than that which may come from a further improvement in instruments constituting an orchestra, I will not attempt to conjecture, any more than I should dare to raise controversy by inquiring whether Beethoven represents progress from Mozart, Wagner progress from Beethoven.''

Perhaps the most startling evidence on this subject of the absence of evolution in humanity is the opinion of Prof. Flinders Petrie, the distinguished English authority on Egyptology, who has added nearly a millennium to the history of Egypt. His studies have brought him in intimate contact with Egypt from 2,000 to 5,000 B. C. He has found no reason at all for thinking that our generation is farther advanced in any important qualities than men were during this period. In an article on ''The Romance of Early Civilization'' (*The Independent*, Jan. 7, 1909), he said:

''We have now before us a view of the powers of man at the earliest point to which we can trace written history, and what strikes us most is how very little his nature or abilities have changed in seven thousand years; *what he admired we admire; what were his limits in fine handiwork also are ours*. We may have a wider outlook, a greater understanding of things; our interests may have extended in this interval; but so far as human nature and tastes go, man is essentially unchanged in this interval.'' . . . ''This is the practical outcome of extending our view of man three times as far back as we used to look, and it must teach us how little material civilization is likely in the future to change the nature, the weaknesses, or the abilities of our ancestors in ages yet to come.''

Those who think that man has advanced in practical wisdom dur- the 6,000 years of history, forget entirely the lessons of literature. Whenever a great genius has written, he has displayed a knowledge of human nature as great as any to be found at any other time in the world's history. The wisdom of Homer and of Solomon are typical examples. Probably the most striking evidence in this matter is to be found in what is considered to be the oldest book ever written. This is the Instructions of Ptah Hotep to his son. Ptah Hotep was the vizier of King Itosi, of the Fifth Dynasty of Egypt (about 3650 B. C.). There is nothing that a father of the modern time would wish to tell his boy as the result of his own experience that is not to be found in this wise advice of a father, nearly 6,000 years ago. This was written longer before Solomon than Solomon is before us, yet no practical knowledge to be gained from intercourse with men has been added to what this careful father of the long ago has written out for his son.

THE CENTURY OF ORIGINS.

To many readers apparently, it has seemed that the main reason for writing of The Thirteenth as the Greatest of Centuries was the fact that the Church occupied so large a place in the life of that time, and that, therefore, most of what was accomplished must naturally revert to her account. It is not only those who are interested in the old Church, however, who have written enthusiastically about the Thirteenth Century. Since writing this volume, I have found that Mr. Frederick Harrison is almost, if not quite, as ardent in his praise of it as I have been. There are many others, especially among the historians of art and of architecture, who apparently have not been able to say all that they would wish in admiration of this supreme century. Most of these have not been Catholics; and if we place beside Mr. Frederick Harrison, the great Positivist of our generation, Mr. John Morley, the great Rationalist, the chorus of agreement on the subject of the greatness of the Thirteenth Century ought to be considered about complete. Mr. Morley, in his address on Popular Culture, delivered as President of the Midland Institute, England, October, 1876 (Great Essays. Putnam, New York), said:

"It is the present that really interests us; it is the present that we seek to understand and to explain. I do not in the least want to know what happened in the past, except as it enables me to see my way more clearly through what is happening to-day. I want to know what men thought and did in the Thirteenth Century, not out of any dilettante or idle antiquarian's curiosity, but because the Thirteenth Century is at the root of what men think and do in the nineteenth."

EDUCATION.

Many even of the most benevolent readers of the book have been quite sure that it exaggerated the significance of medieval education and, above all, claimed too much for the breadth of culture given by the early universities. Prof. Huxley is perhaps the last man of recent times who would be suspected for a moment of exaggerating the import of medieval education. In his Inaugural Address on Universities Actual and Ideal, delivered as Rector of Aberdeen University, after discussing the subject very thoroughly, he said:

"The scholars of the Medieval Universities seem to have studied grammar, logic and rhetoric; arithmetic and geometry; astronomy, theology and music. Thus their work, however imperfect and faulty, judged by modern lights, it may have been, brought them face to face with all the leading aspects of the many-sided mind of man. For these studies did really contain, at any rate in embryo, sometimes it may be in caricature, what we now call philosophy, mathematical and physical science, and art. *And I doubt if the curriculum of any modern university shows so clear and generous a comprehension of what is meant by culture, as this old Trivium and Quadrivium does.*" (Italics ours.)

The results of this system of education may be judged best perhaps from Dante as an example. In The Popes and Science (Fordham University Press, N. Y., 1908) a chapter is devoted to Dante as the typical university man of the time, above all in his knowledge of science as displayed in his great poem. No poet of the modern time has turned with so much confidence to every phase of science for his figures as this product of medieval universities. Anyone who thinks that the study of science is recent, or that nature study was delayed till our day, need only read Dante to be completely undeceived.

The fact that the scholars and the professors at the universities were almost without exception believers in the possibility of the transmutation of metals in the old days, used to be considered by many educated people as quite sufficient to stamp them as lacking in judgment and as prone to believe all sorts of incredible and even impossible things without justification. Such supercilious condemnation of the point of view of the medieval scholars in this matter, however, has recently received a very serious jolt. Sometime ago, Sir William Ramsey, the greatest of living English chemists, announced at the meeting of the British Association for the Advancement of Science, that he had succeeded in changing copper into lithium. This created a sensation at the time, but represented, after all, a culmination of effort in this direction that had long been expected. More recently, Sir William has reported to the British Chemical Society that he has succeeded in obtaining carbon from four substances not containing this element—bismuth, hydro-fluo-silicic acid, thorium and zirconium. An American professor of chemistry has declared that he would like to remove all traces of silver from a quantity of lead ore, and then, after allowing it to stand for some years, have the opportunity to re-examine it, since he is confident that he would find further traces of silver in it that had developed in the meantime. He is sure that the reason why these two metals always occur together, as do copper and gold, is that they are products of a developmental process, the precious metals being a step farther on in that process than the so-called base metals. It would seem, then, that the medieval scholars were not so silly as they used to appear before we knew enough about the subject to judge them properly. Only their supercilious critics were silly.

It is probably with regard to the exact sciences that most even educated people are quite sure that the Thirteenth Century does not deserve to be thought of as representing great human advance. For them the Middle Ages were drowsily speculative, but never exact in thinking. Of course, such people know nothing of the intense exactness of thought of St. Thomas or Albertus Magnus or Duns Scotus. It would be impossible, moreover, to make them realize, from the writings of these men, how exact human thought actually was in the Thirteenth Century, though the more that modern students devote themselves to scholastic philosophy, the more surely do they appreciate and admire this very quality in the medieval philosophy. For such people, very probably, the only evidence that would have made quite an adequate answer to their objection, would be a chapter on the mathematics of the Thirteenth Century. That might very easily have been made, for Cantor, in his History of Mathematics (Vorlesungen Über Geschichte der Mathematik, Leipzig, 1892), devotes nearly 100 pages of his second volume to the mathematicians of the Thirteenth Century, two of whom, Leonardo of Pisa and Jordanus Nemorarius, did so much in Arithmetic, the Theory of Numbers, Algebra and Geometry, as to make a revolution in mathematics. Cantor says that they accomplished so much, that their contemporaries and successors could scarcely follow them, much less go beyond them. They had great disciples, like John of Sacrobusco (probably John of Holywood, near Dublin), Joannes Campanus and others. Cantor calls attention particularly to the spread of arithmetical knowledge among the masses, which is a well-deserved tribute to the century, for it was a characteristic of the time that the new thoughts and discoveries of scholars were soon made practical and penetrated very widely among the people. Brewer, in the Preface to Roger Bacon's works, quotes some of Bacon's expressions with regard to the value of mathematics. The English Franciscan said: "For without mathematics, nothing worth knowing in philosophy can be attained." And again: "For he who knows not mathematics cannot know any other science; what is more, he cannot discover his own ignorance or find its proper remedy." The term mathematics, as used by Bacon, had a much wider application then than now, and Brewer notes that the Thirteenth Century scientist included therein Geometry, Arithmetic, Astronomy, and Music."

With regard to post-graduate education, the best evidence that, far from any exaggeration of what was accomplished in the Thirteenth Century, there has been a very conservative estimate of it made in the book, may be gathered from the legally erected standards of the medical schools and the legal status of the medical profession. In the Appendix of The Popes and Science, two Bulls are published, issued by Pope John XXII. (*Circa*, 1320), establishing medical schools in Perugia, at that time in the Papal States, and in Cahors, the birthplace of this pope. These bulls were really the formal charters of the medical schools. They require three years of preliminary study at the university and four or five years at medicine before the degree of doctor may be granted, and in addition emphasized that the curricula of the new medical schools must be equal to those of Paris and Bologna. These bulls were issued in the early part of the fourteenth century, and show the height to which the standards of medical education had been raised. There will be found also a law of Frederick II., issued 1241, requiring for all physicians who wished to practice in the Two Sicilies three years of preliminary study—four years at the medical school and a year of practice with a physician before the diploma which constituted a license to practice would be issued. This law is also a pure drug law forbidding the sale of impure drugs under penalty of confiscation of goods, and the preparation of them under penalty of death. Our pure drug law was passed about the time of the issue of the first edition of this book.

Those who ask for the results of this post-graduate training may find them in the story of Guy de Chauliac, the Father of Modern Surgery. His life formed the basis of a lecture before the Johns Hopkins Medical Club that is to be published in the Bulletin of John Hopkins Hospital. It is incorporated in Catholic Churchmen in Science, Second Series (The Dolphin Press, Phila., 1909). We know Chauliac's work not by tradition, but from his great text-book on surgery. This great Papal physician of the fourteenth century operated within the skull, did not hesitate to open the thorax, sewed up wounds of the intestines, and discussed such subjects as hernia, catheterization, the treatment of fractures, and manipulative surgery generally with wonderful technical ability. His book was the most used text-book for the next two centuries, and has won the admiration of everyone who has ever read it.

TECHNICAL EDUCATION OF THE MASSES.

Some of my friends courteously but firmly have insisted with me that I have greatly exaggerated the technical abilities of the village workmen of the Middle Ages. That every town of less than ten thousand inhabitants in England was able to supply such workmen as we can scarcely obtain in our cities of a million inhabitants, and in that scanty population supply them in greater numbers than we can now secure them from our teeming populations, seems to many simply impossible.

What I have been trying to say, however, in the chapters on the Arts and Crafts and on Popular Education, has been much better said by an authority that will scarcely be questioned by my critics. The Rev. Augustus Jessopp, D. D., who has been for twenty years the Rector of Scarning in England, who is an Honorary Fellow of St. John's College and of Worcester College, Oxford, besides being an Honorary Canon in the Cathedral of Norwich, has devoted much time and study to this question of how the cathedrals were built and finished. Twenty years of his life have been spent in the study of the old English parish and of parish life. He has studied the old parish registers, and talks, therefore, not from distant impressions, but from the actual facts as they are recorded. If to his position as an antiquarian authority I add the fact that he is not a member of the Roman Catholic Church, to the credit of which so much of this popular education and accomplishment in the arts and crafts of the century accrues, the value of his evidence is placed entirely above suspicion of partisan partiality. In his chapter on Parish Life in England, in his book "Before the Great Pillage" (Before the Great Pillage with other Miscellanies, by Augustus Jessopp, D. D., London. T. Fisher Unwin, Paternoster Square, 1901), he says:

"The evidence is abundant and positive, and is increasing upon us year by year, that the work done upon the fabrics of our churches, and the other work done in the beautifying of the interior of our churches, such as the woodcarving of our screens, the painting of the lovely figures in the panels of those screens, the embroidery of the banners and vestments, the frescoes on the walls, the engraving of the monumental brasses, the stained glass in the windows, and all that vast aggregate of artistic achievements which existed in immense profusion in our village churches till the sixteenth century stripped them bare—all this was executed by local craftsmen. The evidence for this is accumulating upon us every year, as one antiquary after another succeeds in unearthing fragments of pre-Reformation church-wardens' accounts.

"We have actual contracts for church building and church repairing undertaken by village contractors. We have the cost of a rood screen paid to a village carpenter, of painting executed by local artists. We find the name of an artificer, described as aurifaber, or worker in gold and silver, living in a parish which could never have had five hundred inhabitants; we find the people in another place casting a new bell and making the mould for it themselves; we find the blacksmith of another place forging the iron work for the church door, or we get a payment entered for the carving of the bench ends in a little church five hundred years ago, which bench ends are to be seen in that church at the present moment. And we get fairly bewildered by the astonishing wealth of skill and artistic taste and æsthetic feeling which there must have been in this England of ours, in times which till lately we had assumed to be barbaric times. Bewildered, I say, because we cannot understand how it all came to a dead-stop in a single generation, not knowing that the frightful spoliation of our churches and other parish buildings, and the outrageous plunder of the parish gilds in the reign of Edward the Sixth by the horrible band of robbers that carried on their detestable work, effected such a hideous obliteration, such a clean sweep of the precious treasures that were dispersed in rich profusion over the whole land, that a dull despair of ever replacing what had been ruthlessly pillaged crushed the spirit of the whole nation, and art died out in rural England, and King Whitewash and Queen Ugliness ruled supreme for centuries."

My argument is that a century which produced such artist-artisans everywhere, had technical schools in great profusion, though they may not have been called by any such ambitious name.

HOW IT ALL STOPPED.

To most people it seems impossible to understand how it is that, if artistic evolution proceeded to the perfection which it now seems clear that it actually attained in the thirteenth and fourteenth centuries, we are only just getting back to a proper state of public taste and a right degree of artistic skill in many of these same accomplishments at the present time. That thought has come to many others who, knowing and appreciating medieval progress in art and literature, have tried to work out the reasons for the gap that exists between medieval art and modern artistic endeavor. Some of these explanations, because they serve to make clear why art evolution stopped so abruptly and we are retracing our steps and taking models from the past rather than doing original work that is an advance, must be quoted here. Many people will find in them, I think, the reasons for their misunderstanding of the old times.

Gerhardt Hauptmann, who is very well known, even among English-speaking people, as one of the great living German dramatists, and whose "Sunken Bell" attracted considerable attention in both its German and English versions here in New York, in a recent criticism of a new German book, declared that the reason for the gap between modern and medieval art was the movement now coming to be known as the religious revolt in Germany in the sixteenth century. He said:

"I, as a Protestant, have often had to regret that we purchased our freedom of conscience, our individual liberty, at entirely too high a price. In order to make room for a small, mean little plant of personal life, we destroyed a whole garden of fancy and hewed down a virgin forest of æsthetic ideas. We went even so far in the insanity of our weakness as to throw out of the garden of our souls the fruitful soil that had been accumulating for thousands of years, or else we plowed it under sterile clay.

"We have to-day, then, an intellectual culture that is well protected by a hedge of our personality, but within this hedge we have only delicate dwarf trees and unworthy plants, the poorer progeny of great predecessors. We have telegraph lines, bridges and railroads, but there grow no churches and cathedrals, only sentry boxes and barracks. We need gardeners who will cause the present sterilizing process of the soil to stop, and will enrich the surface by working up into it the rich layers beneath. In my work-room there is ever before me the photograph of Sebaldus' Tomb (model Metropolitan Museum, New York). This rich German symbol rose from the invisible in the most luxuriant developmental period of German art. As a formal product of that art, it is very difficult to appreciate it as it deserves. It seems to me as one of the most wonderful bits of work in the whole field of artistic accomplishment. The soul of all the great medieval period encircles this silver coffin, wrapping it up into a noble unity, and enthrones on the very summit of death, Life as a growing child. Such a work could only have come to its perfection in the protected spaces of the old Mother Church."

Rev. Dr. Jessopp, in his book, already cited, "The Great Pillage," does not hesitate to state in unmistakable terms the reason why all the beauty and happiness went out of English country life some two centuries after the Thirteenth Century, and how it came about that the modern generations have had to begin over again from the beginning, and not where our Catholic forefathers of the medieval period left us, in what used to be the despised Middle Ages. He says:

"When I talk of the great pillage, I mean that horrible and outrageous looting of our churches other than conventual, and the robbing of the people of this country of property in land and movables, which property had actually been inherited by them as members of those organized religious communities known as parishes. It is necessary to emphasize the fact that in the general scramble of the Terror under Henry the Eighth, and of the Anarchy in the days of Edward the Sixth, there was only one class that was permitted to retain any large portion of its endowments. The monasteries were plundered even to their very pots and pans. Almshouses in which old men and women were fed and clothed were robbed to the last pound, the poor alms-folk being turned out into the cold at an hour's warning to beg their bread.

Hospitals for the sick and needy, sometimes magnificently provided with nurses and chaplains, whose very raison d'etre was that they were to look after and care for those who were past caring for themselves—these were stripped of all their belongings, the inmates sent out to hobble into some convenient dry ditch to lie down and die in, or to crawl into some barn or hovel, there to be tended, not without fear of consequences, by some kindly man or woman who could not bear to see a suffering fellow creature drop down and die at their own doorposts.

"We talk with a great deal of indignation of the Tweed ring. The day will come when someone will write the story of two other rings—the ring of the miscreants who robbed the monasteries in the reign of Henry the Eighth was the first; but the ring of the robbers who robbed the poor and helpless in the reign of Edward the Sixth was ten times worse than the first.

"The Universities only just escaped the general confiscation; the friendly societies and benefit clubs and the gilds did not escape. The accumulated wealth of centuries, their houses and lands, their money, their vessels of silver and their vessels of gold, their ancient cups and goblets and salvers, even to their very chairs and tables, were all set down in inventories and catalogues, and all swept into the great robbers' hoard. Last, but not least, the immense treasures in the churches, the joy and boast of every man and woman and child in England, who day by day and week by week assembled to worship in the old houses of God which they and their fathers had built, and whose every vestment and chalice and candlestick and banner, organs and bells, and picture and image and altar and shrine they looked upon as their own and part of their birthright—all these were torn away by the rudest spoilers, carted off, they knew not whither, with jeers and scoffs and ribald shoutings, while none dared raise a hand or let his voice be heard above the whisper of a prayer of bitter grief and agony.

"One class was spared. The clergy of this Church of England of ours managed to retain some of their endowments; but if the boy king had lived another three years, there is good reason for believing that these too would have gone."

Graft prevailed, and the old order disappeared in a slough of selfishness.

COMFORT AND POVERTY.

A number of friendly critics have insisted that *of course* the Thirteenth Century was far behind later times in the comfort of the people. Poverty is supposed to have been almost universal. Doubtless many of the people were then very poor. Personally, I doubt if there was as much poverty, that is, misery due to actual want of necessaries of life, as there is at the present time. Certainly it was not emphasized by having close to it, constantly rendering the pains of poverty poignant by contrast, the luxury of the modern time. They had not the large city, and people in the country do not suffer as much as people in the city. In recent years, investigations of poverty in England have been appalling in the statistics that they have presented. Mr. Robert Hunter, in his book Poverty, has furnished us with some details that make one feel that our generation should be the last to say that the Thirteenth Century was behind in progress, because so many of the people were so poor. Ruskin once said that the ideal of the great nation is one wherein there must be "as many as possible full-breathed, bright-eyed and happy-hearted human creatures." I am sure that, tried by this standard, the Thirteenth Century in Merrie England is ahead of any other generation and, above all, far in advance of our recent generations.

By contrast to what we know of the merrie English men and women of the Thirteenth Century, I would quote Mr. Hunter's paragraphs on the Poverty of the Modern English People. He says:

"A few years ago, England did not know the extent of her own poverty. Economists and writers gave opinions of all kinds. Some said conditions were 'bad,' others said such statements were misleading; and here they were, tilting at each other, backward and forward, in the most ponderous and serious way, until Mr. Booth, a business man, undertook to get at the facts. *No one, even the most radical economist, would have dared to have estimated the povery of London as extending to 30 per cent of the people* (as it proved). The extent of poverty—the number of underfed, underclothed in insanitary houses—was greater than could reasonably have been estimated."

Some of the details of this investigation by Mr. Booth were so startling that some explanation had to be found. They could not deny, in the face of Mr. Booth's facts, but they set up the claim that the conditions in London were exceptional. Then Mr. Rountree made an investigation in York with precisely the same results. More than one in four of the population was in poverty. To quote Mr. Hunter once more:

"As has been said, it was not until Mr. Charles Booth published, in 1891, the results of his exhaustive inquiries that the actual conditions of poverty in London became known. About 1,000,000 people, or about thirty per cent of the entire population of London, were found to be unable to obtain the necessaries for a sound livelihood. They were in a state of poverty, living in conditions, if not of actual misery, at any rate bordering upon it. In many districts, considerably more than half of the population were either in distress or on the verge of distress. When these results were made public, the more conservative economists gave it as their opinion that the conditions in London were, of course, exceptional, and that it would be unsafe to make any generalizations for the whole of England on the basis of Mr. Booth's figures for London. About ten years later, Mr. B. S. Rountree, incited by the work of Mr. Booth, undertook a similar inquiry in his native town, York, a small provincial city, in most ways typical of the smaller towns of England. In a large volume in which the results are published, it is shown that the poverty in York was only slightly less extensive than that of London. In the summary, Mr. Rountree compares the conditions of London with those of York. His comments are as follows: 'The proportions arrived at for the total populations living in poverty in London and York respectively were as under:

London...30.7 per cent
York...27.84 per cent

The proportion of the population living in poverty in York may be re-garded as practically the same as in London, especially when we remember that Mr. Booth's information was gathered in 1887-1892, a period of only average trade prosperity, whilst the York figures were collected in 1899, when trade was unusually prosperous.' ''

He continues: ''We have been accustomed to look upon the poverty in London as exceptional, but when the result of careful inves-tigation shows that the proportion of poverty in London is practically equalled in what may be regarded as a typical provincial town, we are faced by the startling probability that from 25 to 30 per cent of the town populations of the United Kingdom are living in poverty.''

Most of us will be inclined to think that Mr. Rountree must exag-gerate, and what he calls poverty most of us would doubtless be in-clined to think a modest competency a little below respectability. He fixed the standard of twenty-one shillings eight pence ($5.25) a week as a necessary one for a family of ordinary size. He says:

''A family living upon the scale allowed for in this estimate, must never spend a penny on railway fare or omnibus. They must never go into the country unless they walk. They must never purchase a half-penny newspaper or spend a penny to buy a ticket for a popular con-cert. They must write no letters to absent children, for they cannot afford to pay the postage. They must never contribute anything to their church or chapel, nor give any help to a neighbor which costs them money. They cannot save, nor can they join sick club or trade union, because they cannot pay the necessary subscription. The chil-dren must have no pocket money for dolls, marbles or sweets. The father must smoke no tobacco nor drink no beer. The mother must never buy any pretty clothes for herself or for her children, the char-acter for the family wardrobe, as for the family diet, being governed by the regulation, 'Nothing must be bought but that which is absolutely necessary for the maintenance of physical health, and that which is bought must be of the plainest and most economical description.' Should a child fall ill, it must be attended by the family parish doc-tor; should it die, it must be buried by the parish. Finally, the wage-earner must never be absent from his work for a single day.''

More than one in four of the population living below this scale!

Conditions are, if anything, worse on the Continent. In Germany, industry is at the best. Conditions in Berlin have been recently reported in the Daily Consular Reports by a U. S. Government official. Of the somewhat more than two millions of people who live in Berlin, 1,125,000 have an income. Nearly one-half of the incomes, however, are exempt from taxation because they do not amount to the minimum taxable income, though that is only $214—$4 per week. Of the 600,000 who have taxable incomes, nearly 550,000 have less than $700 a year; that is, get about $2 a day or less. Less than sixty thousand out of the total population get more than $2 a day. It is easy to say, but hard to understand, that this is a living wage, because things are cheaper in Germany. Meat is, however, nearly twice as dear; sugar is twice as dear; bread is dearer than it is in this country; coffee is dearer; and only rent is somewhat cheaper.

It is easy to talk about the spread of comfort among the people of our generation and the raising of the standard of living, but if one compares these wages with the price of things as they are now, it is hard to understand on just what basis of fact the claim for betterment in our time, meaning more general comfort and happiness, is made.

People always refuse to believe that conditions are as bad as they really are in these matters. Americans will at once have the feeling, on reading Mr. Hunter and Mr. Rountree's words and the account of the American Consul at Berlin, that this may be true for England and Germany, but that of course it is very different here in America. It is extremely doubtful whether it is very different here in America. In this matter, Mr. Hunter's opinion deserves weight. He has for years devoted himself to gathering information with regard to this subject. He seems to be sure that one in seven of our population is in poverty. Probably the number is higher than this. Here is his opinion:

"How many people in the country are in poverty? Is the number yearly growing larger? Are there each year more and more of the unskilled classes pursuing hopelessly the elusive phantom of self-support and independence? Are they, as in a dream, working faster, only the more swiftly to move backward? Are there each year more and more hungry children and more and more fathers whose utmost effort may not bring into the home as much energy in food as it takes out in industry? These are not fanciful questions, nor are they sentimental ones. I have not the slightest doubt that there are in the United States ten million persons in precisely these conditions of poverty, but I am largely guessing, and there may be as many as fifteen or twenty millions!"

Perhaps Mr. Hunter exaggerates. As a physician, I should be inclined to think not; but certainly his words and, above all, the English statistics will give any one pause who is sure, on general principles, that the great mass of the people are happier now or more comfortable, above all, in mind—the only real happiness—than they were in the Thirteenth Century. After due consideration of this kind, no one will insist on the comparative misery and suffering of the poor in old times. England had less than 3,000,000 in the Thirteenth Century, and probably there was never a time in her history when a greater majority of her people fulfilled Ruskin's and Morris' ideals of happy-hearted human beings. The two-handed worker got at least what the four-footed worker, in Carlyle's words, has always obtained, due food and lodging. England was not "a nation with sleek, well-fed English horses, and hungry, dissatisfied Englishmen."

COMFORT AND HAPPINESS.

There is another side to the question of comparative happiness that may be stated in the words of William Morris, when he says, in "Hopes and Fears for Art," that a Greek or a Roman of the luxurious time (and of course *a fortiori* a medieval of the Thirteenth Century) would stare astonished could he be brought back again and shown the comforts of a well-to-do middle-class house. This expression is often re-echoed, and one is prone to wonder how many of those who use it realize that it is a quotation, and, above all, appreciate the fact that Morris made the statement in order to rebut it. His answer is in certain ways so complete that it deserves to be quoted.

"When you hear of the luxuries of the Ancients, you must remember that they were not like our luxuries, they were rather indulgence in pieces of extravagant folly than what we to-day call luxury—which, perhaps, you would rather call comfort; well, I accept the word, and say that a Greek or a Roman of the luxurious time would stare astonished could he be brought back again and shown the comforts of a well-to-do middle-class house.

"But some, I know, think that the attainment of these very comforts is what makes the difference between civilization and uncivilization—that they are the essence of civilization. Is it so indeed? Farewell my hope then! I had thought that civilization meant the attainment of peace and order and freedom, of good-will between man and man, of the love of truth and the hatred of injustice, and by consequence the attainment of the good life which these things breed, a life free from craven fear, but full of incident; that was what I thought it meant, not more stuffed chairs and more cushions, and more carpets and gas, and more dainty meat and drink—and therewithal more and sharper differences between class and class.

"If that be what it is, I for my part wish I were well out of it and living in a tent in the Persian desert, or a turf hut on the Iceland hillside. But, however it be, and I think my view is the true view, I tell you that art abhors that side of civilization; she cannot breath in the houses that lie under its stuffy slavery.

",Believe me, if we want art to begin at home, as it must, we must clear our houses of troublesome superfluities that are forever in our way, conventional comforts that are no real comforts, and do but make work for servants and doctors. If you want a golden rule that will fit everybody, this is it: 'Have nothing in your houses that you do not know to be useful or believe to be beautiful.'"

COMFORT AND HEALTH.

A comment on William Morris's significant paragraphs may be summed up in some reflections on the scornful expression of a friend who asked, how is it possible to talk of happiness at a time when there were no glass in windows and no heating apparatus except the open fireplace in the great hall of the larger houses, or in the kitchen of the dwelling houses. To this there is the ready answer that, in the modern time, we have gone so far to the opposite extreme as to work serious harm to health. When a city dweller develops tuberculosis, his physician now sends him out to the mountains, asks him to sleep with his window wide open, and requires him to spend just as much of his time as possible in the open air, even with the temperature below zero. In our hospitals, the fad for making patients comfortable by artificial heat is passing, and that of stimulating them by cold, fresh air is gaining ground. We know that, for all the fevers and all the respiratory diseases this brings about a notable reduction in the mortality. Surely, what is good for the ailing must be even better to keep them well from disease. Many a physician now arranges to sleep out of doors all winter. Certainly all the respiratory diseases are rendered much more fatal and modern liability to them greatly increased by our shut-up houses. The medieval people were less comfortable, from a sensual standpoint, but the healthy glow and reaction after cold probably made them enjoy life better than we do in our steam-heated houses. They secured bodily warmth by an active circulation of their blood. We secure it by the circulation of hot water or steam in our houses. Ours may be the better way, but the question is not yet absolutely decided.

A physician friend points to the great reduction in the death-rate in modern times, and insists that this, of course, means definite progress. Even this is not quite so sure as is often thought. We are saving a great many lives that heretofore, in the course of nature, under conditions requiring a more vigorous life, passed out of existence early. It is doubtful, however, whether this is an advantage for the race, since our insane asylums, our hospitals for incurables and our homes of various kinds now have inmates in much greater proportion to the population than ever before in history. These are mainly individuals of lower resistive vitality, who would have been allowed to get out of existence early, save themselves and their friends from useless suffering, and whose presence in life does not add greatly if at all to the possibilities of human accomplishment. Our reduced death-rate is, because of comfort seeking, more than counterbalanced by a reduced birth-rate, so that no advantage is reaped for the race in the end. These reflections, of course, are only meant to suggest how important it is to view such questions from all sides before being sure that they represent definite progress for humanity. Progress is much more elusive than is ordinarily thought, and is never the simple, unmistakable movement of advance it is often thought.

HYGIENE.

The objection that medical friends have had to the claims of The Thirteenth as the Greatest of Centuries is that it failed to pay any attention to hygiene. Here, once more, we have a presumption that is not founded on real knowledge of the time. It is rather easy to show that these generations were anticipating many of our solutions of hygienic problems quite as well as our solutions of other social and intellectual difficulties. In the sketch of Pope John XXI., the physician who became Pope during the second half of the Thirteenth Century, which was published in Ophthalmology, a quarterly review of eye diseases (Jan., 1909), because Pope John wrote a little book on this subject which has many valuable anticipations of modern knowledge, I called attention to the fact that, while a physician and professor of medicine at the medical school of the University of Sienna, this Pope, then known as Peter of Spain, had made some contributions to sanitary science. Later he was oppointed Archiater, that is, Physician in charge of the City of Rome. As pointed out in the sketch of him as enlarged for the volume containing a second series of Catholic Churchmen in Science (The Dolphin Press, Phila., 1909), he seems to have been particularly interested in popular health, for we have a little book, Thesaurus Pauperum—The Treasure of the Poor—which contains many directions for the maintenance of health and the treatment of disease by those who are too poor to secure physicians' advice. The fact that the head of the Bureau of Health in Rome should have been made Pope in the Thirteenth Century, itself speaks volumes for the awakening of the educated classes at least to the value of hygiene and sanitation.

Their attention to hygiene can be best shown by a consideration of the hospitals. Ordinarily it is assumed that the hospitals provided a roof for the sick and the injured, but scarcely more. Most physicians will probably be quite sure that they were rather hot-beds of disease than real blessings to the ailing. That is not what we find when we study them carefully. These generations gave us a precious lesson by eradicating leprosy, which was quite as general as tuberculosis is now, and they made special hospitals for erysipelas, which materially lessened the diffusion of that disease. In rewriting the chapter on The Foundation of City Hospitals for my book, The Popes and Science (Fordham University Press, N. Y., 1908), I incorporated into it a description of the hospital erected at Tanierre, in France, in 1293, by Marguerite of Bourgogne, the sister of St. Louis. Of this hospital Mr. Arthur Dillon, from the standpoint of the modern architect, says:

"It was an admirable hospital in every way, and it is doubtful if we to-day surpass it. It was isolated, the ward was separated from the other buildings; it had the advantage we often lose, of being but one story high, and more space was given to each patient than we now afford.

"The ventilation by the great windows and ventilators in the ceiling was excellent; it was cheerfully lighted, and the arrangement of the gallery shielded the patients from dazzling light and from draughts from the windows, and afforded an easy means of supervision, while the division by the roofless, low partitions isolated the sick and obviated the depression that comes from the sight of others in pain.

"It was, moreover, in great contrast to the cheerless white wards of to-day. The vaulted ceiling was very beautiful; the woodwork was richly carved, and the great windows over the altars were filled with colored glass. Altogether, it was one of the best examples of the best period of Gothic architecture."

In their individual Hygiene there was, of course, much to be desired among the people of the Thirteenth Century, and it has been declared that the history of Europe from the fifth to the fifteenth century might, from the hygienic standpoint, he summed up as a thousand years without a bath. The more we know about this period, however, the less of point do we find in the epigram. Mr. Cram, in the Ruined Abbeys of Great Britain (Pott & Co., N. Y., 1907), has described wonderful arrangements within the monasteries (!) for the conduction of water from long distances for all toilet purposes. There was much more attention to sanitary details than we have been prone to think. Mr. Cram, in describing what was by no means one of the greatest of the English abbeys of the Thirteenth Century, says:

"Here at Beaulieu the water was brought by an underground conduit from an unfailing spring a mile away, and this served for drinking, washing and bathing, the supply of the fish ponds, and for a constant flushing of the elaborate system of drainage. In sanitary matters, the monks were as far in advance of the rest of society as they were in learning and agriculture."

WAGES AND THE CONDITION OF WORKING PEOPLE.

What every reader of the Thirteenth Century seems to be perfectly sure of is that, whatever else there may have been in this precious time, at least the workmen were not well paid and men worked practically for nothing. It is confessed that, of course, working as they did on their cathedrals, they had a right to work for very little if they wished, but at least there has been a decided step upward in evolution in the gradual raising of wages, until at last the workman is beginning to be paid some adequate compensation. There is probably no phase of the life of the Middle Ages with regard to which people are more mistaken than this supposition that the workmen of this early time were paid inadequately. I have already called attention to the fact that the workmen of this period claimed and obtained "the three eights" —eight hours of work, eight hours of sleep and eight hours for recreation and bodily necessities. They obtained the Saturday half-holiday, and also release from work on the vigils of all feast days, and there were nearly forty of these in the year. After the vesper hour, that is, three in Summer and two in Winter, there was no work on the Eves of Holy-days of Obligation. With regard to wages, there is just one way to get at the subject, and that is, to present the legal table of wages enacted by Parliament, placing beside it the legal maximum price of necessities of life, as also determined by Parliamentary enactment.

An Act of Edward III. fixes the wages, without food, as follows. There are many other things mentioned, but the following will be enough for our purpose:

	s.	d.
A woman hay-making, or weeding corn for the day	0	1
A man filling dung-cart	0	3½
A reaper	0	4
Mowing an acre of grass	0	4
Threshing a quarter of wheat	0	4

The price of shoes, cloth and provisions, throughout the time that this law continued in force, was as follows:

	£.	s.	d.
A pair of shoes	0	0	4
Russet broadcloth, the yard	0	1	1
A stall fed ox	1	4	0
A grass fed ox	0	16	0
A fat sheep unshorn	0	1	8
A fat sheep shorn	0	1	2
A fat hog two years old	0	3	4
A fat goose	0	0	2½
Ale, the gallon, by proclamation	0	0	1
Wheat, the quarter	0	3	4
White wine, the gallon	0	0	6
Red wine	0	0	4

An Act of Parliament of the fourteenth century, in fixing the price of meat, names the four sorts of meat—beef, pork, mutton and veal, and sets forth in its preamble the words, "these being the food of the poorer sort." The poor in England do not eat these kinds of meat now, and the investigators of the poverty of the country declare that most of the poor live almost exclusively on bread. The fact of the matter is, that large city populations are likely to harbor many very miserable people, while the rural population of England in the Middle Ages, containing the bulk of the people, were happy-hearted and merry. When we recall this in connection with what I have given in the text with regard to the trades-unions and their care for the people, the foolish notion, founded on a mere assumption and due to that Aristophanic joke, our complacent self-sufficiency, which makes us so ready to believe that our generation *must* be better off than others were, vanishes completely.

It is easy to understand that beef, pork, mutton, veal and even poultry were the food of the poor, when a workman could earn the price of a sheep in less than four days or buy nearly two fat geese for his day's wages. A day laborer will work from forty to fifty days now to earn the price of an ox on the hoof, and it was about the same at the close of the Thirteenth Century. When a fat hog costs less than a dollar, a man's wages, at eight cents a day, are not too low. When a gallon of good ale can be obtained for two cents, no workman is likely to go dry. When a gallon of red wine can be obtained for a day's wages, it is hard to see any difference between a workman of the olden time and the present in this regard. Two yards of cloth made a coat for a gentleman and cost only a little over two shillings. The making of it brought the price of it up to two shilling and six pence. These prices are taken from the Preciosum of Bishop Fleetwood, who took them from the accounts kept by the bursars of convents. Fleetwood's book is accepted very generally as an excellent authority in the history of economics.

Cobbett, in his History of the Protestant Reformation, has made an exhaustive study of just this question of the material and economic condition of the people of England before and since the reformation. He says:

"These things prove, beyond all dispute, that England was, in Catholic times, a real wealthy country; that wealth was generally diffused; that every part of the country abounded in men of solid property; and that, of course, there were always great resources at hand in cases of emergency."......"In short, everything shows that England was then a country abounding in men of real wealth."

Fortesque, the Lord High Chancellor of England under Henry VI., king a century after the Thirteenth, has this to say with regard to the legal and economic conditions in England in his time. Some people may think the picture he gives an exaggeration, but it was written by a great lawyer with the definite idea of giving a picture of the times, and, under ordinary circumstances, we would say that there could be no better authority.

"The King of England cannot alter the laws, or make new ones, without the express consent of the whole kingdom in Parliament assembled. Every inhabitant is at his liberty fully to use and enjoy whatever his farm produceth, the fruits of the earth, the increase of his flock and the like—all the improvements he makes, whether by his own proper industry or of those he retains in his service, are his own, to use and enjoy, without the let, interruption or denial of any. If he be in any wise injured or oppressed, he shall have his amends and satisfactions against the party offending. Hence it is that the inhabitants are rich in gold, silver, and in all the necessaries and conveniences of life. They drink no water unless at certain times, upon a religious score, and by way of doing penance. They are fed in great abundance, with all sorts of flesh and fish, of which they have plenty everywhere; they are clothed throughout in good woollens, their bedding and other furniture in the house are of wool, and that in great store. They are also well provided with all sorts of household goods and necessary implements for husbandry. Every one, according to his rank, hath all things which conduce to make mind and life easy and happy."

INTEREST AND LOANS.

A number of commercial friends have been interested in the wonderful story of business organizations traced in the chapter on Great Beginnings of Modern Commerce. They have all been sure, however, that it is quite idle to talk of great commercial possibilities at a time when ecclesiastical regulations forbade the taking of interest. This would seem to make it quite impossible that great commercial transactions could be carried on, yet somehow these people succeeded in accomplishing them. A number of writers on economics in recent years have suggested that possibly one solution of the danger to government and popular rights from the accumulation of large fortunes might be avoided by a return to the system of prohibition of interest taking. There is much more in that proposition than might possibly be thought by those who are unfamiliar with it from serious consideration. They did succeed in getting on without it in the Thirteenth Century, and at the same time they solved the other problem of providing loans, not alone for business people, but for all those who might need them. We are solving the "loan shark" evil at the present time in nearly the same way that they solved it seven centuries ago. Abbot Gasquet, in his "Parish Life in England Before the Reformation," describes the methods of the early days as follows:

"The parish wardens had their duties towards the poorer members of the district. In more than one instance they were guardians of the common chest, out of which temporary loans could be obtained by needy parishioners, to tide over persons in difficulties. These loans were secured by pledges and the additional security of other parishioners. No interest was charged for the use of the money, and in case the pledge had to be sold, everything over and above the sum lent was returned to the borrower."

THE EIGHTEENTH LOWEST OF CENTURIES.

There is no doubt that the nineteenth century, and especially the latter half of it, saw some very satisfactory progress over immediately preceding times. With the recognition of this fact, that the last century so far surpassed its predecessor there has been a tendency to assume, because evolution occupies men's minds, that the eighteenth must have quite as far surpassed the seventeenth, and the seventeenth the sixteenth, and so on, so that of course we are far ahead in everything of the despised Middle Ages. In recent years, indeed, we have dropped the attitude of blaming the earlier ages, for one of complacent pity that they were not born soon enough, and, therefore, could not enjoy our advantages. Unfortunately for any such conclusion as this, the term of comparison nearest to us, the eighteenth century is without doubt the lowest hundred years in human accomplishment, at least during the past seven centuries.

This is true for every form of human endeavor and every phase of human existence. Prof. Goodyear, of the Brooklyn Institute of Arts and Science, the well-known author of a series of books on art and history, in one of the chapters of his Handbook on Renaissance and Modern Art (New York, The McMillan Co.), in describing the Greek revival of the latter part of the eighteenth century says: "According to our accounts so far throughout this whole book, either of architecture, painting, or sculpture, it will appear that the earlier nineteenth century represents the foot of a hill, whose gradual descent began about 1530." As a matter of fact, in every department of artistic expression the taste of the eighteenth century was almost the worst possible. The monuments that we have from that time, in the shape of churches and municipal buildings, are few, but such as they are, they are the least worthy of imitation, and the art ideas they represent are most to be deprecated of any in the whole history of modern art.

Perhaps the most awful arraignment of the eighteenth and early nineteenth century that was ever made is that of Mr. Cram, in the Ruined Abbeys of Great Britain, from which I have already quoted. He calls attention to the fact that, during this century, some of the most beautiful sculptured work that ever came from the hand of man was torn out of the ruins of St. Mary's Abbey, York, to serve no better purpose than to make lime. His description of the sculpture of the Abbey will give some idea of its beauty and render all the more poignant the loss that was thus inflicted on art. He says:

"Most wonderful of all amongst a horde of smaller statues, a mutilated fragment of a statue of Our Lady and the Holy Child, so consummate in its faultless art that it deserves a place with the master-pieces of sculpture of every age and race. Here in this dim and scanty undercraft is an epitome of the English art of four centuries, precious and beautiful beyond the power of words to describe.

"York Abbey was a national monument, the æsthetic and historic value of which was beyond computation. It is with feelings of horror and unutterable dismay that, as we stand beside the few existing fragments, realizing the irreparable loss they make so clear, we call into mind Henry's sacrilege in the sixteenth century, and his silly palace doomed to instant destruction, and the crass ignorance and stolidity of the eighteenth century with its grants of building material, and the mercenary savagery of the nineteenth century when, from smoking lime kilns rose into the air the vanishing ghosts of the noblest creations that owed their existence to man.

"Nothing is sadder to realize than the failure of appreciation for art of the early nineteenth and the eighteenth century. Men had lost, apparently, all proper realization of the value of artistic effort and achievement. It was an era of travel and commerce and, unfortunately, of industrial development. As a consequence, in many parts of Europe, and especially of England, art remains of inestimable value suffered at the hands of utilitarians who found them of use in their enterprises. We are accustomed to rail against the barbarians and the Turks for their failure to appreciate the remains of Latin and Greek art and for their wanton destruction of them, but what shall we say of modern Englishmen, who quite as ruthlessly destroyed objects of art of equal value at least with Roman and Greek, while the great body of the nation made no complaint, and no protest was heard anywhere in the kingdom."

What is so true of the arts is, as might be reasonably expected, quite as true of other phases of intellectual development. Education, for instance, is at the lowest ebb that it has reached since the foundation of the Universities at the end of the twelfth century. In Germany, there was only one university, that of Göttingen, in which there was a professorship of Greek. When Winckelmann introduced the study of Greek into his school at Seehausen, no school-books for this language were available, and he was obliged to write out texts for his students. What was the case in Germany was also true, to a great degree, of the rest of Europe. Leading French critics ridiculed the Greek authors. Homer was considered a ballad singer and compared to the street singers of Paris. Voltaire thought that the Æneid of Virgil was superior to all that the Greek writers had ever done. No edition of Plato had been published in Europe since the end of the sixteenth century. Other Greek authors were almost as much neglected, and of true scholarship there was very little. When Cardinal Newman, in his Idea of a University, wants to find the lowest possible term of comparison for the intellectual life of the university, he takes the English universities of the middle of the eighteenth century.

With this neglect of education, and above all of the influence that Greek has always had in chastening and perfecting taste, it is not surprising that literature was in every country of Europe at a very low ebb. It was not so feeble as art, but the two are interdependent, much more than is usually thought. Only France has anything to show in literature that has had an enduring influence in the subsequent centuries. When we compare the French literature of the eighteenth with that of the seventeenth century, however, it is easy to see how much of a descent there has been from Corneille, Racine, Molière, Boileau, La Fontaine, Bossuet, Bourdaloue, and Fénelon to Voltaire, Marivaux, Lesage, Diderot, and Bernardin de St. Pierre. This same decadence of literature can be noted even more strikingly in England, in Spain, and in Italy. The seventeenth, especially the first half of it, saw the origin of some of the greatest works of modern literature. The eighteenth century produced practically nothing that was to live and be a vital force in aftertimes.

What is true in art, letters and education is, above all, true in what men did for liberty and for their fellow-men. Hospital organization and the care of the ailing was at its lowest ebb during the eighteenth century. Jacobson, the German historian of the hospitals, says:[1]

"It is a remarkable fact that attention to the well-being of the sick, improvements in hospitals and institutions generally and to details of nursing care, had a period of complete and lasting stagnation after the middle of the seventeenth century, or from the close of the Thirty Years' War. Neither officials nor physicians took any interest in the elevation of nursing or improving the conditions of hospitals. During the first two-thirds of the eighteenth century, nothing was done to bring either construction or nursing to a better state. Solely among the religious orders did nursing remain an interest, and some remnants of technique survive. The result was that, in this period, the general level of nursing fell far below that of earlier periods. The hospitals of cities were like prisons, with bare, undecorated walls and little dark rooms, small windows where no sun could enter, and dismal wards where fifty or one hundred patients were crowded together, deprived of all comforts and even of necessaries. In the municipal and state institutions of this period, the beautiful gardens, roomy halls, and

[1] Beiträge zur Geschichte des Krankencomforts. Deutsche Krankenpflege Zeitung, 1898, in 4 parts.

springs of water of the old cloister hospital of the Middle Ages were not heard of, still less the comforts of their friendly interiors.''

As might be expected, with the hospitals so badly organized, the art of nursing was in a decay that is almost unutterable. Miss Nutting, of Johns Hopkins Hospital, the Superintendent of Nurses, and Miss Dock, the Secretary of the International Council of Nurses, have in their History of Nursing a chapter on the Dark Period of Nursing, in which the decadence of the eighteenth century, in what regards the training of nurses for the intelligent care of the sick, is brought out very clearly. They say: [1]

''It is commonly agreed that the darkest known period in the history of nursing was that from the latter part of the seventeenth up to the middle of the nineteenth century. During the time, the condition of the nursing art, the well-being of the patient, and the status of the nurse, all sank to an indescribable level of degradation.''

Taine, in his History of the Old Regimé of France, has told the awful story of the attitude of the so-called better classes toward the poor. While conditions were at their worst in France, every country in Europe saw something of the same thing. In certain parts of Germany conditions were, if possible, worse. It is no wonder that the French Revolution came at the end of the eighteenth century, and that a series of further revolutions during the nineteenth century were required to win back some of the rights which men had gained for themselves in earlier centuries and then lost, sinking into a state of decadence out of which we are only emerging, though in most countries we have not reached quite the level of human liberty and, above all, of Christian democracy that our forefathers had secured seven centuries ago.

With these considerations in mind, it is easier to understand how men in the later nineteenth century and beginning twentieth century are prone to think of their periods as representing an acme in the course of progress. There is no doubt that we are far above the eighteenth century. That, however, was a deep valley in human accomplishment, indeed, a veritable slough of despond, out of which we climbed; and, looking back, are prone to think how fortunate we are in having ascended so high, though beyond our vision on the other side of the valley the hills rise much higher into the clouds of human aspiration and artistic excellence than anything that we have attained as yet. Indeed, whenever we try to do serious work at the present time, we confessedly go back from four to seven centuries for the models that we must follow. With Renaissance art and Gothic architecture and the literature before the end of the sixteenth century cut out of our purview, we would have nothing to look to for models. This phase of history needs to be recalled by all those who would approach with equanimity the consideration of The Thirteenth as the Greatest of Centuries.

[1] A History of Nursing, by M. Adelaide Nutting and Lavinia L. Dock, in two volumes, illustrated. G. P. Putnam's Sons, New York, 1907.

INDEX.